The Genitive

Case and Grammatical Relations Across Languages (CAGRAL)

For an overview of all books published in this series, please see
http://benjamins.com/catalog/cagral

Volume 5

The Genitive
Edited by Anne Carlier and Jean-Christophe Verstraete

The Genitive

Edited by

Anne Carlier
University of Lille 3, CNRS UMR 8163 STL

Jean-Christophe Verstraete
University of Leuven

John Benjamins Publishing Company
Amsterdam / Philadelphia

The paper used in this publication meets the minimum requirements of the American National Standard for Information Sciences – Permanence of Paper for Printed Library Materials, ANSI z39.48-1984.

Library of Congress Cataloging-in-Publication Data

The genitive / Edited by Anne Carlier and Jean-Christophe Verstraete.

p.   cm. (Case and Grammatical Relations Across Languages ; v. 5)

Includes bibliographical references and index.

1. Grammar, Comparative and general--Possessives. 2. Grammar, Comparative and general--Syntax. 3. Language and languages--Word formation. 4. Case grammar. I. Carlier, Anne, editor of compilation.

P299.P67G46   2013

415'.5--dc23   2013010429

ISBN 978 90 272 2815 4   (Hb ; alk. paper)

ISBN 978 90 272 9105 9   (Eb)

John Benjamins Publishing Co. · P.O. Box 36224 · 1020 ME Amsterdam · The Netherlands

John Benjamins North America · P.O. Box 27519 · Philadelphia PA 19118-0519 · USA

Table of contents

Acknowledgements

This volume is the fifth in the series *Case and Grammatical Relations Across Languages*, initiated by the late Brygida Rudzka-Ostyn and linked with the project 'Case and thematic relations' (IUAP grant no 27). Neither of us was associated with the original project, but when we were asked to step in for this volume, we tried to develop it in the same spirit, combined with our own interests in diachrony and typology.

We would like to express our gratitude to a number of people. First of all, we thank the authors, who contributed and reviewed papers and, in the case of early submitters, had the patience to see them through to publication. All papers considered for the volume were reviewed by one internal and (at least) one external reviewer. We are grateful to the authors, all of whom reviewed papers, and to the following external reviewers: Kersti Börjars, Vladimir Borschev, Michael Daniel, Walter De Mulder, Benjamin Fagard, Alex Grosu, Jukka Havu, Yury Lander, Lutz Marten, Jan Rijkhoff, Anette Rosenbach and An Van linden. At John Benjamins, we would like to thank Anke de Looper, who was always extremely quick and helpful in dealing with any questions we had.

Anne Carlier & Jean-Christophe Verstraete

Genitive case and genitive constructions

An introduction

Anne Carlier and Jean-Christophe Verstraete
University of Lille 3, CNRS UMR 8163 STL and University of Leuven

1. Introduction

A definition of genitives usually starts out from the notion of an inflectional category for nouns, which in its core function labels adnominal relations, prototypically in the domain of possession (see, for instance, Creissels 2006, Lander 2008). The structure in (1) provides an example from Northern Akhvakh, a Northeast Caucasian language spoken in Daghestan and Azerbaijan. The suffix *-ɬi* on the noun for 'girl' marks a dependency relation with the head noun 'dress', in this instance interpreted as a possessive relation of ownership or control.

> (1) Northern Akhvakh (Andic, Northeast Caucasian)
> jašo-ɬi   šišaɬ'è[1]
> girl-GEN dress
> 'the girl's dress'   (Creissels, this volume)

As is well-known from the literature, however, this is really only the prototype of what a 'genitive' can be, or maybe even the linguist's prototype (as noted in Van de Velde's canonical typology approach in this volume). There are a number of ways in which actual genitive forms can differ from this central type. One dimension of variation is semantic. The adnominal relations marked by genitive forms are usually not restricted to possession – even in a broad sense – but can include a range of other relations, up to the point where it becomes difficult to provide any specific semantic description to cover the entire range. An example is provided by the Finnish structure in (2), where the dependency relation marked by the genitive is not one of possession, but could be interpreted as indicating origin.

> (2) Finnish (Finnic, Uralic)
> Lapi-n   mies
> Lapland-GEN man.NOM
> 'a man from Lapland'   (Mahieu, this volume)

A second dimension of variation concerns the way the genitive is marked. In addition to inflectional suffixes, as in Northern Akhvakh and in Finnish, there is a whole range of other types of markers that can cover the same semantic domain. In Swedish, for instance, the genitive marker should be analyzed as a clitic rather than a suffix, given that it can attach to the end of a phrase regardless of the word class of the final item, as illustrated in (3) (Norde, this volume). In Bantu languages, adnominal relations can be expressed by a construction known as the connective construction. In this construction, exemplified in (4), head and dependent noun are linked by a connective relator that agrees with the head noun, but is usually tightly integrated with the dependent noun or noun phrase, and can often be analyzed as a proclitic (Van de Velde, this volume).

(3)   Swedish (Germanic, Indo-European)
       familjen ovanpå=s   ungar
       [family upstairs]=GEN kids
       'the kids of the family (living) upstairs'   (Norde, this volume)

(4)   Kinyamwezi (Bantu, Niger-Congo)
       m̀-zuna w-aa-m̀-kɪíma
       1-younger_sister I-CON-1-woman
       'the younger sister of the woman'
                (Maganga and Schadeberg 1992: 89, cited in Van de Velde, this volume)

Many languages also have other markers or constructions that encroach on the domain covered by genitives, leading to paradigmatic variation with genitives, synchronically or diachronically. In Russian, for instance, genitive constructions for adnominal relations compete with adjectival constructions, with the genitive allowing for more referential individuation in the dependent NP. This is illustrated in (5), with the genitive construction in (5a) and the adjectival construction in (5b). A diachronic equivalent of this situation is found in the development of French, where a construction originating in the Latin preposition *de*, for source or origin relations, gradually took over the domain covered by genitives in Latin. This is illustrated in (6), with the Latin genitive construction exemplified in (6a) and the French prepositional equivalent in (6b).

(5)   Russian (Slavic, Indo-European)
       a. Starš-ij   syn   d'jakon-a   pogib   na front-e.
           eldest-NOM son.NOM deacon-GEN perished on front-LOC
           'Deacon's eldest son was killed at the front.'

       b. D'jakon-ov   syn   priexal v sel-o   k roditel-jam.
           deacon-ADJ.NOM son.NOM came   in village-ACC to parents-DAT
           'Deacon's son came to the village to see his parents.'
                                              (Van Peteghem & Paykin, this volume)

(6) a. Latin (Italic, Indo-European)
     Taur-i   cori-um   protuli-t
     bull-GEN.M.SG hide-ACC.SG bring-PRF.3SG
     'He brought the hide of the bull.'

   b. French (Romance, Indo-European)
     la   maison de   ses   parents
     ART house PREP POSS parents
     'his parents' house'   (Carlier, Goyens & Lamiroy, this volume)

A final type of variation relates to the level on which genitives operate. The same forms that mark the adnominal relations discussed so far, are often also used to mark arguments of verbs, complements of prepositions, adjectives and various other parts of speech, or even adjuncts, as in the floating genitive construction described by Creissels (this volume). An example of an argument-marking genitive is provided by the Russian structure in (7), where the genitive is assigned by the so-called intensional verb 'fear'.

(7) Russian (Slavic, Indo-European)
     Rebënok boitsja vrač-ej.
     child.NOM fears   doctors-GEN
     'A/The child fears doctors.'   (Van Peteghem & Paykin, this volume)

In the rest of this introduction, we will use the parameters sketched here to outline the descriptive and theoretical issues the authors deal with when surveying genitive constructions in this volume. Section 2 is devoted to the semantics of genitives, from synchronic and diachronic perspectives. In Section 3, we discuss the form of genitive markers, including their morphological status, locus of marking and NP ordering, as well as instances of competition between inflectional and non-inflectional types. In Section 4, finally, we briefly survey non-adnominal uses of genitives, and their place in clause structure.

2.   Genitive semantics

As already mentioned, possession is only one of many types of semantic relations that can be marked by genitives, and it is often difficult to find a good semantic characterization to cover all types in a specific language. The authors in this volume deal with this problem from a number of complementary perspectives: from a synchronic perspective, looking for a generalization in specific languages, from a diachronic perspective, charting mechanisms of extension to and from possession, and from a structural perspective, looking at the value of genitives in relation to other cases in the system.

    Possession is a broad notion that goes beyond the concept of ownership, and is often defined in terms of control and a range of parameters like animacy and alienability (see, for instance, Seiler 1983, Baron et al. 2001, McGregor 2009). Some authors in this volume follow Creissels (2006: 143) in defining possessive relations as the "inclusion of an entity (usually called the *possessum*) within the personal ambit of an individual (usually called the *possessor*)". The genitive is not restricted to possession, however, even defined in this broad sense, but covers a much wider range of relations. Some recurrent types identified by the authors in this volume are different types of argument relations, as in (8), spatial relations like location, origin and destination, as in (9), qualifying relations, as in (10), part-whole relations, as in (11), and quantifiers and measure-term relations, as in (12). Some of these cases, may involve dependency reversal, with the genitive-marked noun becoming the semantic head of the NP. In addition, various languages also allow a genitive that merely identifies the referent by its proper name, in relation to a class-marking noun, as illustrated in (13) and (14).

(8)   Finnish (Finnic, Uralic)
       puu-n   tuonti
       tree-GEN import.NOM
       'the import of wood'   (Mahieu, this volume)

(9)   French (Romance, Indo-European)
       un homme de province
       a   man   of province
       'a man with a provincial origin'   (Carlier, Goyens & Lamiroy, this volume)

(10)   Mongo (Bantu, Niger-Congo)
       ntando ĕy=o-lindó
       [9]river IX.CON=3-depth
       'a deep river'   (Hulstaert 1966: 246, cited in Van de Velde, this volume)

(11)   Northern Akhvakh (Andic, Northeast Caucasian)
       mašina-ɬi ĩč̣o
       car-GEN   door
       'the door of the car'   (Creissels, this volume)

(12)   Russian (Slavic, Indo-European)
       stakan   molok-a
       glass.NOM milk-GEN
       'a glass of milk'   (Van Peteghem & Paykin, this volume)

(13)   Mongo (Bantu, Niger-Congo)
       i-bonga   y-ǎ=Mbándáká
       5-town   V-CON=Mbandaka
       'the town of Mbandaka'
                                    (Hulstaert 1966: 250, cited in Van de Velde, this volume)

(14)   Finnish (Finnic, Uralic)
       Virtase-n   perhe
       Virtanen-GEN family.NOM
       'the Virtanen family'   (Mahieu, this volume)

The question is, of course, what all of these semantic relations have in common: is it possible to offer an adequate semantic characterization that covers the different types? From a synchronic perspective, the authors in this volume use a number of ways to organize the range of meanings available in specific languages, for instance by using syntactic and semantic tests (Van Peteghem & Paykin on Russian), by investigating the availability of semantically specialized markers (Van de Velde on connective elements in Bantu and Van Peteghem & Paykin on competing genitive forms in Russian) or by drawing up a typology as the result of diachronic development (Carlier, Goyens & Lamiroy on the successive stages from Latin to Modern French). Some argue, however, that the only way to characterize the semantics of adnominal genitives is as a label for a dependency relation between NPs, with the first NP restricting the second one in some way. Mahieu (this volume) and Van Peteghem & Paykin (this volume) frame this conclusion in terms of the notion of structural case, i.e. the idea that genitives in Finnish and Russian do not mark a particular type of semantic role but merely reflect syntactic dependency. Similarly, Carlier, Goyens & Lamiroy (this volume) show that Modern French *de* lost its spatial meaning in some of its uses and developed into an essentially structural marker indicating a dependency relation without specifying its semantic content.

Another way to shed light on the semantics of genitives is diachronic, by charting the semantic development of the markers and establishing a hierarchy between the different meanings. On the one hand, this can help to identify the core meaning of a genitive marker. Carlier, Goyens & Lamiroy (this volume) argue that when a new grammaticalizing expression replaces an older one, uses representing the core meaning of the old pattern are more resistant to change: for the Latin and Old French data, for instance, this area of resistance is the genitive marking possession. On the other hand, this diachronic perspective also allows one to determine the peripheral or atypical uses of genitives. As pointed out by Hopper (1991: 24), when a source expression develops into a new grammatical role, it often continues to be used in its original context, giving rise to a situation of divergence: the form does not undergo grammaticalization in its original context, but grammaticalizes in its new context. For the French data, Carlier, Goyens & Lamiroy (this volume) show that the *de*-pattern replacing the older inflectional genitive shows atypical behaviour in its original context. *De* + NP cannot be replaced by the corresponding clitic *en* when it has the status of an adjunct, while it can be replaced by *en* when used in adnominal position or as an argument of the verb. The marginal status of adjunct uses is also reflected in the fact that in such instances *de* is often replaced by a more explicit complex preposition. For Finnish, Mahieu (this volume) argues that the so-called dative-genitive, often considered to be on a par with the Finnish genitive, also shows atypical properties that can be traced by to its origin before it became grammaticalized, and is often replaced by locative cases.

A final approach that can provide insight into the semantics of genitives is a paradigmatic perspective, which looks at their relation with other cases in the same language This is, of course, based on the classic Saussurean idea that meaning is a matter of differences:

> Which idea or phonic material a sign contains is less important than what is around it in the other signs. If you add a sign to the language, you reduce the significance of all the others. Conversely, if by some miracle we had chosen at the beginning only two signs, all meanings would be spread over the two signs. (*Cours de Linguistique générale*, p. 160, ed. R. Engler)

In this perspective, the semantics of genitives can be described in terms of their relation to other cases in the same language. If we compare Finnish and Russian, for instance, Finnish has a partitive case while Russian does not have one, which means that the genitive in Russian conveys meanings that are expressed by the partitive in Finnish.

A more general question in paradigmatic terms is the position of genitives with respect to the distinction between the core set of 'grammatical' cases on the one hand, and 'peripheral', 'oblique' or 'semantic' cases on the other hand. For Russian, Van Peteghem & Paykin (this volume) use morphological and distributional arguments to argue that the genitive is close to the nominative and the accusative and should therefore be regarded as a grammatical case. Mahieu (this volume) also proposes this analysis for the genitive in Finnish. For French, Carlier, Goyens & Lamiroy (this volume) show that the adposition *de* evolved from a semantic marker into a strictly grammatical marker. In other languages, by contrast, genitives can be regarded as oblique rather than grammatical cases, for instance when they are close to dative-type cases. This feature, often mentioned as typical for the Balkan Sprachbund (Koptjevskaja-Tamm 2003: 682), is found in Romanian, where datives and genitives are morphologically identical and are grouped together under the label oblique (Giurgea & Dobrovie-Sorin, this volume). In some of the languages in this volume, links between genitives and datives were found in older stages of the language. For Finnish, Mahieu (this volume) mentions that although the genitive case is a strictly grammatical case synchronically, it is historically related to a semantic case, the proto-Uralic lative-dative case. In Old French, the alternation between bare genitives, PPs headed by *de* and PPs headed by *a* (which is the dative marker in French) also points to a link between genitive and dative.

3.   Genitive marking

With respect to marking, the authors in this volume discuss a range of formal parameters in genitive structures, including the morphological status of the genitive marker, the locus of marking, and the order of possessor and possessum NPs. Furthermore, several papers look at synchronic and diachronic relations between inflectional markers and non-inflectional alternatives (like adjectives or PPs) to express relations within the genitive domain.

In addition to the straightforward inflectional affixes found in many languages in this volume, some authors describe morphosyntactically more complex cases. In Modern Swedish, for instance, the genitive marker is no longer an inflectional morpheme as in Old Swedish (15a), but must be analyzed as a clitic that attaches to the right edge of an NP, regardless of the word class of the final element. As argued by Norde (this volume), the clearest evidence for this comes from structures like (15b), where the genitive marker attaches to a postmodifying element in the NP, like a PP or a relative clause. Norde's analysis traces the emergence of this type of construction, including its relation to a number of competing constructions in the history of Swedish. She invokes the argument of processing efficiency to put forward a hypothesis about the diachronic development of structures like (15b).

(15) Swedish (Germanic, Indo-European)
 a. Old Swedish
      alle heþn-a   mann-a   guþa æru diæfla
      all pagan-M.PL.GEN man-M.PL.GEN gods are devils
      'All the gods of pagan men are devils.'   (Norde, this volume)
 b. Modern Swedish
      mann-en på gatan=s   smak
      [man-DEF on street.DEF]=GEN taste
      'the man in the street's taste'   (Norde, this volume)

A second parameter of variation relates to the order of head and dependent in genitive constructions. In Swedish, for instance, Modern Swedish differs from Old Swedish in that constituent order in genitive constructions has become fixed: genitive-marked NPs in Modern Swedish almost exclusively precede their head, as in (15b). In Modern German, by contrast, some types of genitive constructions, predominantly those with proper names, allow both orders. Thus, for instance, the two structures in (16) show that the genitive-marked proper name can both precede and follow its head noun. As argued by Campe (this volume), the choice between the two patterns can be determined by factors like prosodic weight and the type of semantic relation, but the most important factor relates to information structure, specifically which of the NPs is focused and which refers to a more identifiable participant.

(16) German (Germanic, Indo-European)
 a. der Unfalltod   Diana-s
      ART accidental.death Diana-GEN
 b. Diana-s   Unfalltod
      Diana-GEN accidental.death
      'Diana's accidental death'   (Campe, this volume)

A third parameter relates to the locus of marking. Most of the structures described in this volume have the genitive marked on the possessor, either its head or dependents (as in Northern Akhvakh and Latin) or its determiner (as in Romanian). In addition, some languages show indexing of the possessum by means of agreement. This is the case, for instance, in the connective construction in Bantu languages, where the connective marker belongs with the possessor but agrees with the possessum (see example (4) above). Similarly, the genitive particle *al* in Romanian belongs with the possessor but agrees with the possessum, as shown in example (17). The same type of possessum agreement is also found with some possessive pronouns, as discussed below in more detail.

(17) Romanian (Romance, Indo-European)
      prieteni-i buni ai   fete-i
      friends-the good *al*.MPL girl.OBL-the.FSG.OBL
      'the girl's good friends'   (Giurgea & Sorin, this volume)

Many languages also have other markers or constructions that encroach on the domain covered by genitives, leading to paradigmatic variation with genitive constructions, synchronically or diachronically. A first type of competing construction, cross-linguistically very common, is a structure denoting spatial origins, for instance using adpositions meaning 'from'. For the evolution from Latin to French, Carlier, Goyens & Lamiroy (this volume) show that this pattern competes with the preposition-less genitive phrase from Classical Latin onwards, as shown in (18): it extends its distribution in Late Latin, and is nearly generalized at the end of the Old French period. A similar pattern is mentioned by Van Peteghem & Paykin (this volume) for Russian, where prepositional phrases are used instead of genitive phrases for non-contingent relations, as shown in (19). In Romanian, adpositional phrases are used instead of genitive markers for morphological reasons: since genitive case is marked only on determiners (20a), an adpositional phrase is used in the case of bare nouns (20b) or when the determiner has a defective inflection (20c) (Giurgea & Sorin, this volume).

(18) Latin (Italic, Indo-European)
      nemo   multum   /nemo   ex   decem
      nobody.NOM many.GEN.PL nobody.NOM out.from ten
      'none of the many/none of the ten'
                        (Caesar, *Commentarii belli civilis* 3, 97/Cicero, *De legibus* 3, 24)

(19) Russian (Slavic, Indo-European)
      Ja   snova videl devušk-u *(iz)   *poezd-a.*
      I.NOM again saw   girl-ACC *(from) train-GEN
      'I saw the girl from the train again.' (Van Peteghem & Paykin, this volume)

(20) Romanian (Romance, Indo-European)
      a. achiziționare-a cărți-lor /   unor   cărți de către   bibliotecă
          acquisition-the books-the.OBL some.OBL books by towards   library
          'the acquisition of the books/of some books by the library'

      b. achiziționare-a de cărți de către   bibliotecă
          acquisition-the *de* books by towards library
          'the acquisition of books by the library'

    c. achiziționare-a a trei cărți de către bibliotecă
       acquisition-the *a* three books by towards library
       'the acquisition of three books by the library'
                     (Giurgea & Dobrovie-Sorin, this volume)

Some languages, like Russian, have denominal adjectives that compete with genitive markers in the domain of adnominal relations. As illustrated in example (5) above, a genitive construction allows for more referential individuation and syntactic autonomy in the dependent NP than the corresponding adjectival construction, since the genitive-marked NP can convey number marking and can have modifiers or complements. Another type of adjectival construction is found with pronominal possessors, where genitive-marked forms can be in competition with adjectival forms showing agreement with the possessum. As shown by Van Peteghem & Paykin, this is the case in Russian, where the two patterns are not used in the same semantic configurations: for instance, the agreeing possessive form cannot be used in combination with measure terms, as shown in (21a). Moreover, the choice of pattern is also determined by the grammatical features of the possessor: only the genitive-inflected form is available for a non-reflexive third person, as shown in (21b). This is also the case in Romanian, with the additional difference that the agreeing reflexive possessive has lost its original reflexive meaning and can alternate with the genitive-inflected 3rd person pronoun, as shown in (22).

(21) Russian (Slavic, Indo-European)
    a. kusok   men-ja
       piece.NOM me-GEN
       'a piece of me'

    b. Mo-ja/E-go   duš-a   ulybaetsja.
       my-NOM.F/him-GEN soul-NOM.F smiles
       'My/his soul is smiling.'   (Van Peteghem & Paykin, this volume)

(22) Romanian (Romance, Indo-European)
    surori-le sale = surori-le lui/ei
    sisters-the *să*.FPL   sisters-the he.OBL/her.OBL
    'his/her sisters'   (Giurgea & Dobrovie-Sorin, this volume)

4.   Genitives beyond adnominal functions

While markers can be identified as genitives in terms of their adnominal functions, genitive markers are by no means restricted to adnominal modification in most of the languages discussed in this volume. The same forms can also serve to mark arguments of verbs, in finite or non-finite contexts, as well as complements of prepositions, adjectives or numerals, and even adjuncts.

The distribution of genitive marking for verb arguments can be relatively wide, as is the case in Russian and Finnish, or very restricted, as in Northern Akhvakh. Its use can be determined by a range of factors, including morphosyntactic factors like the subordinate status of a clause, or semantic factors like particular classes of verbs or specific configurations of polarity and/or aspect. The former case is illustrated in Finnish, where participial clauses take a genitive subject, as shown in (23). The latter case is illustrated in Russian, where genitive marking is found with a class of intensional verbs, as shown in (7) above, and under negation, usually optionally, as illustrated in (24).

(23)   Finnish (Finnic, Uralic)
Liisa   usko-o   [Peka-n   nukku-neen].
Liisa.NOM believe-3SG Pekka-GEN sleep-PTCP.PST.n
'Liisa believes that Pekka slept.'   (Mahieu, this volume)

(24)   Russian (Slavic, Indo-European)
Saš-a   ne pokupaet knig.
Sasha-NOM NEG buys   books.GEN
'Sasha doesn't buy (any) books.'   (Van Peteghem & Paykin, this volume)

Genitives can be triggered by various other parts of speech, like specific numerals in Russian, or prepositions and adjectives in Finnish or Old Swedish, as illustrated in (25) with the adjective *gamal* 'old' in Old Swedish. Furthermore, genitives can also mark adjuncts, as in the Finnish structure in (26).

(25)   Old Swedish (Germanic, Indo-European)
Fem hundradha ar-a   gamal war noe
Five hundred   year-N.PL.GEN old   was Noah
'Noah was five hundred years old.'   (Norde, this volume)

(26)   Finnish (Finnic, Uralic)
Ole-n opiskel-lut   suome-a   vuode-n.
be-1SG study-PTCP.PST Finnish-PART year-GEN
'I have studied Finnish for a year.'   (Mahieu, this volume)

In addition to straightforward adjuncts like the one in (26), the 'floating genitive' construction described for Northern Akhvakh by Creissels illustrates another clause-level use of genitives. In structures like (27), the genitive-marked element is semantically related to a participant in the clause, as marked by gender agreement. Instead of forming a noun phrase with this participant, however, it serves as an adjunct at clause level, occurring freely at the beginning or the end of the clause. In this sense, Creissels shows that this structure can be analyzed as a type of external possession construction, not the better-known type where the possessor takes up a participant role as beneficiary, but one with the possessor as a framing adjunct.

(27) Northern Akhvakh (Andic, Northeast Caucasian)
      ʁe-ɫi   jaše-ɫi-q̄-e   kʼeha b-ux̄-ari ha-s̄u-be.
      neighborhood-GEN girl-F$_0$-OR$_3$-LOC eye N-fall-PF$_1$ PROX-M[GEN]-N
      'He noticed a young girl from the neighborhood.'
      lit. 'The eye fell on a girl, of him'   (Creissels, this volume)

5.   Papers in this volume

The papers in the first part of this volume provide general surveys of genitive markers
or constructions in specific languages or language families, viz. Finnish, Russian,
Romanian, French and the Bantu languages. The papers in the second part zoom in on
specific constructions within the genitive domain in German, Swedish and Northern
Akhvakh, focusing on semantic, pragmatic and morphosyntactic aspects of these
constructions.

Marc-Antoine Mahieu's paper is devoted to the genitive case and the possessive
construction in Finnish. He argues that there is no strict correlation between genitive
case and possessive meaning, and makes the following three points. (i) The Finnish
genitive is not the possessor case, even in a broad sense. Instead, it is a purely structural case used in an irreducible range of syntactic configurations. (ii) In a few contexts, the -n marker is not a genitive as such but a semantic case with dative sense
which corresponds to a P head in syntactic structure. These uses are likely to be relics
of what the -n case was before it grammaticalized as a genitive. (iii) The Finnish possessive construction appears to be an existential structure starting with a locative
phrase. It is argued that, from a synchronic perspective, it is not a locative inversion
but a transitive sentence with a verb meaning 'have'. The apparent contradiction between morphology and syntax is accounted for by a transformational analysis.

Marleen Van Peteghem & Katia Paykin's paper deals with the genitive case in
Russian, traditionally known as the most complex of the six cases in this language,
both morphologically and syntactically. Their study concentrates on genitive marking
within the NP and the VP. Within the NP, the genitive can be assigned by the noun to
its nominal complement or modifier, or by numerals to an N or an N'. Within the VP,
the authors distinguish between the intensional genitive, assigned by intensional verbs,
the genitive of negation, which appears under negation, and the partitive genitive. The
central question of the study is whether the genitive case in Russian should be analyzed
as a structural case, assigned on purely configurational grounds, or as a lexical case,
sensitive to the lexical properties of the syntactic head. As for Finnish, the authors argue that the Russian genitive is not sensitive to the thematic properties of the head
(although semantic factors do sometimes condition genitive marking). It is therefore
closer to structural cases like the nominative and the accusative, with which it can alternate in certain contexts. This is also apparent in morphology, where the genitive
often has a zero ending in the plural, which elsewhere in the case system is only

available in the nominative and the genitive. From a semantic point of view, the genitive is often related to quantification, indefiniteness, partitivity and decreased referentiality, especially in types authorizing an alternation between the *a*-genitive and the *u*-genitive. The common denominator for all types of genitive studied in Van Peteghem & Paykin's paper is the fact that the nominal in the genitive denotes a property rather than an entity and can be analyzed as an N rather than an NP or a DP.

Ion Giurgea and Carmen Dobrovie-Sorin's study is devoted to the syntax and morphology of the genitival construction in Romanian. The first part of the paper deals with the alternation between bare genitives and genitive phrases introduced by the particle *al*, illustrated in (28a). *Al* agrees with the head noun but is considered to be part of the genitive phrase. It cannot be used immediately following a suffixal definite article on the head noun, as shown in (28b).

(28)   Romanian (Romance, Indo-European)
   a.   aceste reușite   ale   profesoru-lui
        these success.F.PL *al*.F.PL professor-the.OBL
        'these successes of the professor'

   b.   reușit-a   *a   profesoru-lui
        success.[F.SG]-the (*al*.F.SG) professor-the.OBL
        'the professor's success'   (Giurgea & Dobrovie-Sorin, this volume)

The authors hypothesize that *al* is ambiguous between an agreeing case-marker and a [pro-N+D] complex. They argue that the constraints on co-occurrence with the definite suffix can be accounted for by its origin, which goes back to a definite article. The second part of the paper studies the paradigm of pronominal possessors and the alternation between agreeing forms and genitive-inflected forms. The authors claim that agreeing forms – so-called "possessive adjectives" – do not have an adjective-like behavior: their distribution is similar to the genitive, since they combine with *al* and have a person index, like personal pronouns. Next, the authors focus on the alternation between agreeing forms, which exist for the 1st and 2nd person and for the former reflexive 3rd person, and genitive-inflected forms, which are used for the non-reflexive 3rd person. They account for this alternation in terms of a morphological constraint: the possessive cannot simultaneously mark features of the possessor and the possessum. Since non-reflexive 3rd person pronouns mark gender and number of the possessor, they lack an agreeing form, which marks gender, number and case of the possessum.

The paper by Anne Carlier, Michèle Goyens and Béatrice Lamiroy deals with French, a language which progressively lost case inflection in the course of its history. The loss of morphological case inflection in French raises the question whether the category of the genitive is still a relevant notion. The authors argue that it is, by showing that the prepositional phrase *de* + NP, which gradually spread from Latin to Modern French, fundamentally marks dependency of a nominal constituent with respect to another nominal expression, just like the adnominal genitive did in Latin. They show that the preposition *de* underwent a pervasive process of grammaticalization, from a full-fledged preposition introducing adjuncts expressing spatial origin, to a structural marker of arguments of verbal and (especially) nominal heads. This process of grammaticalization occurs in the context of a sharpening contrast between arguments and adjuncts. The authors' analysis of the gradual spread of the new pattern at the expense of the old form can also offer an insight into the mechanisms of linguistic change. On the one hand, uses that form the core meaning of the old form are more resistant to change. On the other hand, the innovative form retains its original features in some of its former uses, hence giving rise to peripheral or atypical uses in the context of the new grammatical function.

Mark Van de Velde's paper, finally, offers a typological study of connective constructions in a sample of Bantu languages. These constructions, illustrated in (29) below, use a relator morpheme (glossed as CON 'connective') that agrees in gender with the head noun, but shows a relatively high degree of morphological bonding with the dependent noun phrase, reflected here in an analysis as a proclitic. Semantically, these constructions are the equivalent of the genitive markers studied in the other papers in that they cover a very similar range of adnominal relations, in the domain of possession and beyond.

(29)   Songye (Bantu, Niger-Congo)
       ba-ntu   b-aá=[ky-ǎbu   kí-pîndi]
       2-people II-CON=VII-their 7-neighbourhood
       'the people of their neighborhood'
                                 (Stappers 1964: 81, cited in Van de Velde, this volume)

Using the framework of canonical typology (Corbett 2007), Van de Velde's study maps out the different ways in which Bantu languages can deviate from the typical connective construction. The variation found in these languages is typologically very interesting, both for the typology of genitives and more generally. In the domain of genitive semantics, for instance, the Bantu data show how connective relators can carve up the range of semantic relations in a specific language, with one relator specializing in possessive relations and another in the non-possessive types. In addition, some Bantu languages show flexibility in the word class of the dependent element in connective constructions, with the typical noun-noun structures shading into adjectival constructions and even relative clause constructions, without any non-arbitrary cut-off point. There is also a range of diachronic processes involving connective constructions, for instance in the development of structures with pronominal dependents to possessive pronouns. As argued by Van de Velde, this connective origin may explain the double agreement pattern found in some Bantu possessive pronouns, with possessum agreement originating in the connector, and possessor agreement in the pronoun. Beyond the domain of genitives, connective constructions show some further typological points of interest, like the occurrence of nominal tense, patterns of dependency reversal, and a number of unusual agreement patterns.

The papers in the second part of the volume focus on semantic, pragmatic and morphosyntactic aspects of specific constructions in the genitive domain, in German, in the history of Swedish, and in Northern Akhvakh. Petra Campe's paper deals with word order variation in German genitive constructions, specifically the position of genitive-marked proper names before or after their head noun, as in (30a–b) below. The analysis is restricted to proper names because this is the only category that allows genuine word order choice: NPs headed by common nouns are a marked option as prenominal genitives, restricted to fixed expressions or archaic styles, as illustrated in (30c).

(30)   German (Germanic, Indo-European)
    a. die   Tibet-Politik China-s
        ART Tibet.policy China-GEN
        'the Tibet policy of China'

    b. China-s   Vorgehen in Tibet
        China-GEN actions   in Tibet
        'China's actions in Tibet'

    c. des   Kaiser-s   neue Kleider
        ART.GEN emperor-GEN new   clothes
        'the emperor's new clothes'   (Campe, this volume)

Campe uses a corpus study to tease out the factors that determine the choice between the two positions. One factor is semantic: if the genitive-marked noun can be construed in an argument relation with the head noun, prenominal genitives tend to favour an agentive interpretation, while postnominal genitives tend to favour a patientive interpretation. A second factor relates to prosodic weight, with genitives for particularly long proper names or combinations of names and titles favouring postnominal position. A third factor relates to principles of information structure. Campe uses a range of corpus counts to measure focus and participant identifiability, showing that the NP in second position in the genitive construction tends to be focused, while the first one tends to refer to an identifiable participant.

Muriel Norde's paper deals with so-called 'group genitives' in Swedish, where the genitive marker attaches to a postmodifying prepositional phrase in the NP. As already mentioned, this type of construction offers the clearest evidence that genitive markers have developed into clitics in modern Swedish, because it shows that they have lost host selectivity. Norde uses both corpus evidence and sociohistorical data to study the emergence of group genitives in relation to a number of competing constructions. In addition to the group genitive construction illustrated in (31d), she investigates two types in which only the nominal head receives genitive marking, with or without PP extraposition, as in (31a–b), and one type in which both genitive and PP receive genitive marking, as in (31c).

(31)   a.   Type 1: [[NP]$_{gen}$ X [PP]] 'the king's son of Denmark'
      b.   Type 2: [[NP]$_{gen}$ [PP] X] 'the king's of Denmark son'

c.   Type 3: [[NP]$_{gen}$ [PP]$_{gen}$ X] 'the king's of Denmark's son'
d.   Type 4: [[[NP] [PP]]$_{gen}$X] 'the king of Denmark's son'

Norde shows that the structure in (31a) is the only type found in Old Swedish, and hence the oldest one. The data from Middle and Early Modern Swedish show competition between the three other types, with several authors in the corpus using more than one type. This type of competition demonstrates that the morphological development involved is gradient, as the genitive in type 2 can still be analyzed as a phrase marker (with host selectivity), while the genitive in type 4 must be analyzed as a clitic (without host selectivity). On the other hand, the competition between the types also shows that there is no hard chronological evidence to chart the development of group genitives in relation to the other types. Given this uncertainty, Norde offers two possible scenarios, one with type 2 in (31b) as a bridge between the oldest type and the group genitive, and another with type 4 in (31d) developing out of the oldest type, and type 2 in (31b) as a later hypercorrection. She uses general principles of processing efficiency to suggest that the second scenario is the more likely one. Structures like (31b) are difficult to process both in terms of possessor-possessum relations (separated by the PP), and in terms of phrase structure (NP and PP separated by the genitive marker), which makes it difficult to conceive how this type of structure could have developed independently.

Denis Creissels' analysis of 'floating genitive' constructions in Northern Akhvakh, finally, illustrates nicely how genitives can take up clause-level functions, in this case as a typologically interesting variant on external possession. In floating genitive constructions, as in (32b) below, the genitive is semantically related to the nominative argument, but it occurs at the beginning or the end of the clause instead of forming a noun phrase with it. In addition, the semantic relation with the nominative argument is reflected in obligatory gender-number agreement, which is optional in the equivalent attributive construction, illustrated in (32a).

(32)   Northern Akhvakh (Andic, Northeast Caucasian)
a.   di   ištuda lãgi   b-uq-ari.
     1SG$_o$[GEN] five   sheep N-get.lost-PF$_1$
     'My five sheep got lost'

b.   ištuda lãgi b-uq-ari   di-be.
     five   sheep N-get.lost-PF$_1$ 1SG$_o$[GEN]-N
     'Five of my sheep got lost'
     lit. 'Five sheep got lost, of me.'   (Creissels, this volume)

Creissels provides semantic evidence to show that floating genitives can be analyzed as frame adjuncts, expressing that the event described in the clause is in "the personal sphere of their referent" (Creissels, this volume). On the one hand, their status as perspectivizers is reflected in the fact that floating genitives are largely restricted to the possessive prototype, i.e. animate possessors in relation to bodyparts, kin or controlled objects, while attributive genitives allow a much broader range of relations. On the other hand, their scope over the event as a whole rather than just the nominative participant is reflected in the fact that they do not show any definiteness effects, again unlike their attributive counterparts that restrict the denotation of the nominative participant. In typological terms, Creissels analyzes floating genitive constructions as a variant on external possession (see, for instance, Payne & Barshi 1999), not the classic type in which a possessor is encoded as a beneficiary, but a frame adjunct "restricting the scope of its predication to the personal sphere of their referent" (Creissels, this volume). Furthermore, he shows that apparent instances of predicative possession in Northern Akhvakh are better analyzed as variants of floating genitive constructions, given that the genitive-marked elements show precisely the same behavior as floating genitives.

References

Baron, Irène, Herslund, Michael and Sørensen, Finn (eds). 2001. *Dimensions of Possession*. Amsterdam/Philadelphia: John Benjamins.

Corbett, Greville. 2007. Canonical typology, suppletion and possible words. *Language* 38, 1, 8–42.

Creissels, Denis. 2006. *Syntaxe générale. Une introduction typologique* (2 vols). Paris: Hermès.

Hopper, Paul. 1991. On some principles of grammaticalization. In *Approaches to Grammaticalization*. Volume 1, Elizabeth Traugott and Bernd Heine (eds), 17–36. Amsterdam/Philadelphia: John Benjamins.

Koptjevskaja-Tamm, Maria, 2003. Possessive noun phrases in the languages of Europe. In *Noun Phrase Structure in the Languages of Europe*, Frans Plank (ed.), 621–722. Berlin: Mouton de Gruyter.

Lander, Yuri. 2008. Varieties of genitive. In *The Oxford Handbook of Case*, Andrej Malchukov and Andrew Spencer (eds), 581–592. Oxford: Oxford University Press.

McGregor, William (ed.). 2009. *The Expression of Possession* (= The Expression of Cognitive Categories 2). Berlin: Mouton de Gruyter.

Payne, Doris and Barshi, Immanuel (eds). 1999. *External Possession*. Amsterdam/Philadelphia: John Benjamins.

Saussure, Ferdinand de. 1968. *Cours de linguistique générale*. Rudolf Engler (ed.). Wiesbaden: Harrassowitz.

Seiler, Hansjakob. 1983. *Possession as an Operational Dimension of Language*. Tübingen: Narr.

Endnotes

1.   Examples will be glossed according to the Leipzig Glossing Rules, available at http://www. eva.mpg.de/lingua/resources/glossing-rules.php.

PART 1

General surveys

The genitive case and the possessive construction in Finnish

Marc-Antoine Mahieu
University Sorbonne Nouvelle – Paris 3 and National Center for Scientific Research, LACITO

In Finnish, the genitive case (marked by -*n*) has a distribution which is both broad and complex, making it one of the primary components of the grammar. Though sometimes assumed to mark the possessor, it is not found in the possessive construction which appears to be an existential sentence beginning with a locative phrase. This paper makes three points: (1) The Finnish genitive is not the possessor case, even in a broad sense; rather, it is a purely structural case appearing in an irreducible range of syntactic configurations. (2) In a few contexts, the -*n* marker is not a genitive as such but rather a semantic case with dative sense which corresponds to a P head in syntactic structure. These uses are likely relics of what the -*n* case was before it became grammaticalized as genitive. (3) The Finnish possessive construction is not a locative inversion, but rather a transitive sentence with a verb meaning 'have'. The apparent contradiction between morphology and syntax can be resolved by using a transformational approach.

1. Introduction[1]

Finnish is the most widely spoken of the languages comprising the Finnic branch of the Uralic family. It has some five million speakers, most of them in Finland. The complexity of its case system has been remarked upon since the 17th century (Korhonen 1987: 92–100); the modern grammatical tradition identifies fifteen different case morphemes in all. Table 1 shows Setälä's (1898: 47–52) analysis of this system. This work is a school grammar which remained the model for codification up to the 1950s.[2] Nowadays, the partitive is usually grouped with the nominative, the accusative, and the genitive on the grounds that these four morphemes share the property of being able to affect the subject and/or the direct object.[3]

At first glance, the Finnish genitive seems to be just what a "genitive" is usually assumed to be. As suggested by the word *omanto*, which is sometimes used to designate

Table 1. The traditional analysis of the Finnish case system

GRAMMATICAL CASES	nominative	Ø	basic form (*nimentö*)
	accusative	0. -*t*, 1. -*n*, 2. Ø	object form (*kohdanto*)
	genitive	-*n*	possession (*omanto*)
GENERAL LOCATIVE CASES	essive	-*na* ~ -*nä*	state (*olento*)
	partitive	-(*t*)*a* ~ -(*t*)*ä*	indefinite quantity (*osanto*)
	translative	-*ksi*	change of state (*tulento*)
INTERNAL LOCATIVE CASES	inessive	-*ssa* ~ -*ssä*	'inside' (*sisäolento*)
	elative	-*sta* ~ -*stä*	'out of' (*sisäeronto*)
	illative	-(*h*)V*n*, -*s*VV*n*	'into' (*sisätulento*)
EXTERNAL LOCATIVE CASES	adessive	-*lla* ~ -*llä*	'on', 'at' (*ulko-olento*)
	ablative	-*lta* ~ -*ltä*	'off' (*ulkoeronto*)
	allative	-*lle*	'onto' (*ulkotulento*)
MARGINAL CASES	abessive	-*tta* ~ -*ttä*	'without' (*vajanto*)
	comitative	-*ine*-	'with' (*seuranto*)
	instructive	-*n*	'by means of' (*keinonto*)

this case in Finnish, it is ostensibly the case that expresses possession. Examples like (1a) or (1b) can be adduced as evidence. At the same time, though, in this language without a verb 'have', the possessive construction uses the adessive and not the genitive. This construction, illustrated by (1c), is generally analyzed as an existential sentence where the adessive has its characteristic locative sense. In this analysis, the literal meaning of (1c) is 'at Pekka is a car'.

(1)   a.   Peka-**n**   auto[4]
　　　　Pekka-**GEN**　car.NOM
　　　　'Pekka's car'

　　b.   Auto　　on　　Peka-**n**.
　　　　car.NOM　be.3SG　Pekka-**GEN**
　　　　'The car is Pekka's.'

　　c.   Peka-**lla**　on　　auto.
　　　　Pekka-**ADE**　be.3SG　car.NOM
　　　　'Pekka has a car.'

This paper will argue against all of the viewpoints expressed thus far. First of all, the broad distribution of the Finnish genitive implies that it cannot be reduced to the "case expressing possession". This is true even in the loose sense assigned to "possession" by linguists, i.e. "inclusion of an entity (usually called the *thing possessed*) within the personal sphere of an individual [or of some cognitively more salient/individuated entity] (usually called the *possessor*)" (Creissels 2006: 143–144). It will be argued here that the

Finnish genitive is in fact a structural case, i.e. the simple manifestation of relationships of syntactic dependency.

Secondly, uses of type (1b) should not be conflated with those of type (1c). In a few more or less fossilized constructions, (1b) among them, the case marked by -*n* is not a true genitive but rather in all probability a vestige of what this case once was, before it became grammaticalized as a genitive morpheme. It will be argued here that -*n* is a semantic case in such uses, rightly called *datiivigenetiivi* ('dative-genitive') in traditional grammar, i.e. the manifestation of a P-category head (or adposition).

Thirdly, contrary to what an analysis based solely on noun and verb morphology would suggest, it can be shown that the Finnish possessive construction cannot be treated as an existential sentence, i.e. an utterance composed of an initial locative phrase, a verb 'be', and a postposed subject. A set of convergent arguments can be used to show, firstly, that the postverbal constituent behaves like a direct object of a 'have'-like head and then, that the initial constituent is not an adpositional phrase but rather a nominal subject, where the adessive becomes something other than a semantic case.

This paper is organized as follows: in Part 2, the structural nature of the Finnish genitive case is demonstrated, and the range of syntactic configurations in which this case can be found is set out. From a typological perspective, the most interesting phenomenon here is without doubt the object genitive and the way it contrasts with other cases. Part 3 discusses the constructions where the morpheme -*n*, though still called genitive, is not a structural case but rather a semantic one with a dative sense. The analysis will include a brief discussion of the origin of the genitive and its cognates in other Uralic languages. Part 4 is devoted entirely to the possessive construction. It will be pointed out that the apparent conclusions drawn from morphology, namely, that this construction is a locative inversion, cannot be reconciled with what can be learned about its structure from a certain number of systematic syntactic manipulations. A transformational analysis is proposed which eliminates the apparent contradiction in the data from a synchronic perspective.

2.   The genitive as a structural case

This section will show that the Finnish genitive is not definable as the case expressing possession, and more broadly speaking, is not a case expressing any semantic operation at all (in this regard, see Jaakola 2004), but rather a structural case. This means that it is merely the surface reflex of a relationship of syntactic dependency, i.e. it is not itself a syntactic category (adpositional head) with a set of semantic properties.

More precisely, I will argue here that the Finnish genitive reflects not just one but a number of different dependency relationships, since it appears in a range of syntactic configurations which cannot be reduced to each other. This means that Vainikka's (1989: 126–183; 1993: 132–140) theory according to which the Finnish genitive can invariably be analyzed as "the structural default case for the specifier position of each of the lexical categories N, A, P and V" must be rejected.

2.1   Preposed NP modifier of a N head

To begin with, the genitive can express a relationship of modification of a nominal head by a preceding NP. This relationship is often assumed to express "possessivization of the noun" on the basis of examples like (1a). It is obvious, however, that an NP in the genitive can take on any one of the many other admissible semantic roles with respect to the nominal head it modifies, e.g. Agent in (2a), Patient in (2b), Theme in (2c), Experiencer in (2d), Beneficiary in (2e), Location in (2f), Source in (2g), or Destination in (2h).

(2) a. Peka-n   lähto
       Pekka-GEN departure.NOM
       'Pekka's departure'

   b. puu-n   tuonti
      tree-GEN import.NOM
      'the import of wood'

   c. musiiki-n   opettaja
      music-GEN teacher.NOM
      'a music teacher'

   d. lapse-n   suru
      child-GEN sorrow.NOM
      'a child's sorrow'

   e. voittaja-n   palkinto
      winner-GEN prize.NOM
      'the winner's prize'

   f. Vietnami-n   sota
      Vietnam-GEN war.NOM
      'the Vietnam War'

   g. Lapi-n   mies
      Lapland-GEN man.NOM
      'a man from Lapland'

   h. Pariisi-n   juna
      Paris-GEN train.NOM
      'the train to Paris'

It is also obvious that the role expressed by an NP in the genitive may be ambiguous out of context or hard to define. In (3a), the genitive NP could be either Patient or Agent; in (3b), either Experiencer or Source; and in (3c), either Theme or Agent or

Possessor. In (4), although the NP has only one possible role, it is not one of major roles exemplified in (2).

(3) a. Peka-**n**   haastattelu
         Pekka-**GEN** interview.NOM
         'the interview Pekka gave, the interview Pekka conducted'

     b. sude-**n**   pelko
         wolf-**GEN** fear.NOM
         'the fear felt by the wolf, the fear caused by the wolf'

     c. ystävä-**n**   kuva
         friend-**GEN** picture.NOM
         'a picture made of a friend, a picture drawn by a friend, a picture owned by a friend'

(4) a. kirja-**n**   kansi
         book-**GEN** cover.NOM
         'a book cover'

     b. päivä-**n**   annos
         day-**GEN** portion.NOM
         'the dish of the day, today's dish'

     c. 5 euro-**n**   paita
         5 euro-**GEN** shirt.NOM
         'a 5-euro shirt'

Given these facts, it can be said that the relationship holding between a genitive NP and the nominal head it modifies is totally unspecified. The only requirement is that the genitive noun phrase restricts the set of possible referents for the head noun to those which may stand in a given relationship to itself, whatever that relationship may be. It is not only impossible to give an *a priori* definition of the semantic role between the genitive NP and the head noun, it is also impossible to say that the genitive NP will invariably take on any given role. Thus, for instance, there are examples like (5), where the NP does no more than identify the entity referred to, in this case by giving its name.

(5) a. Savonlinna-**n**   kaupunki
         Savonlinna-**GEN** city.NOM
         'the city of Savonlinna'

     b. ranska-**n**   kieli
         French-**GEN** language.NOM
         'the French language'

     c. Virtase-**n**   perhe
         Virtanen-**GEN** family.NOM
         'the Virtanen family'

    d.   Virtase-**n**   Pekka
        Virtanen-**GEN** Pekka.NOM
        'Pekka Virtanen' (colloquial)

Of course, it may still be assumed that the genitive case has a semantic value insofar as it restricts the possible referents of the head N. This is not the position that will be defended here. Instead, I will argue that the semantic operation of restriction is a function, not of the genitive marking of the premodifier, but rather of the syntactic relationship of premodification itself, which is defined within a given structural configuration. In other words, the source of the restriction is not the genitive case; the genitive is merely the surface reflex of the dependency relationship that assigns a restrictive function to any preposed NP.

    There is at least one good argument in favor of this assumption, viz. the fact that the dependency relationship and its associated semantic function persist, even when genitive case is not allowed on the restricting NP. This happens when the restricting NP has a possessive suffix, as in the Finnish example (6). This has become the regular situation in Livonian, another Finnic language where the genitive case has practically disappeared.

(6)   tyttö-<u>mme</u>   nimi
      girl.NOM-<u>PX.1PL</u> name.NOM
      '<u>our</u> girl's name'

It now remains to be determined exactly what the structural configuration is for the definition of the dependency relationship reflected by the prenominal genitive. According to Vainikka (1993: 132–133), the prenominal genitive is the case of the nominal specifier. Nelson (1998: 216–217) takes a similar position. This approach ignores important data, however. First of all, the position of the restrictive NP varies with respect to adjectives. When an NP refers to a clearly individuated entity, and takes on a concrete and easily defined semantic role, it precedes the adjective. When, on the other hand, its referent is less individuated, and it has an abstract or less easily defined semantic role, it follows the adjective. This contrast is illustrated in (7).

(7)   a.   fyysiko-**n**   uusi   tutkimuslaitos
         physicist-**GEN** new.NOM research.institute.NOM
         'the physicist's new research institute'

    b.   uusi   fysiika-**n**   tutkimuslaitos
         new.NOM physics-**GEN** research.institute.NOM
         'the new physics research institute'

In addition, the head noun is sometimes preceded by two restrictive NPs. This is illustrated by the examples in (8), taken from Vilkuna (2000: 189–193). In (8b), the head of the second restrictive NP (*ranskan kielen*) is itself modified by an NP in the genitive case. In (8c), the two restrictive NPs are separated by the adjective *uudet*.

(8) a. EU:n   viime vuos-i-**en**   toime-t
     EU-GEN last   year-PL-GEN activity-PL.NOM
     'the last years' activities of the EU, the activities of the EU over the last few years'

    b. Ritu-n   ranska-n   kiele-n   taito
     Ritu-GEN French-GEN language-GEN skill.NOM
     'Ritu's skills in French'

    c. Valio-n   uude-t   litra-n   purki-t
     Valio-GEN new-PL.NOM litre-GEN can-PL.NOM
     'Valio's new one-litre cans'

This implies that the modification relationship reflected by the prenominal genitive needs to be defined in two different structural positions. The restrictive NP may be located either within the head noun's determinative domain, as what Vilkuna (ibid.) would call an "external genitive", or just after the head noun's descriptive domain, as what Vilkuna calls an "internal genitive" (*ulkoinen ~ sisäinen genetiivi*).

Given these facts, it can be assumed that the first position is that of the specifier of a D head (which selects the maximal projection of N) and the second, that of the specifier of the head N. The descriptive domain of N itself consists of any adjectives that may be adjoined to the maximal projection of N. This dual configuration for the assignment of the prenominal genitive is represented in (9).[5]

(9)   [$_{DP}$ NP-GEN [$_{D'}$ D ... [$_{NP}$ NP-GEN [$_{N'}$ N]]]]

2.2   Preposed AP modifier of an A or Adv head

The second dependency relationship expressed by the genitive in Finnish is the modification of an A or Adv head by a preceding AP phrase. Thus, the adjective *kamala*, in the nominative in (10a), takes the genitive in (10b) where it modifies another adjective. The same adjective cannot modify the VP in (10c); the deadjectival adverb, formed with the suffix -*sti*, is required instead. Example (10d) illustrates the case where the adjective in the genitive premodifies an Adv rather than an A head.

(10) a. Ilma   ol-i   kamala.
     weather.NOM be-PRET.3SG terrible.NOM
     'The weather was terrible.'

    b. Ilma   ol-i   kamala-n   kylmä.
     weather.NOM be-PRET.3SG terrible-GEN cold.NOM
     'The weather was terribly cold.'

    c. Minu-a palel-i   kamalasti.
     I-PART feel.cold-PRET.3SG terribly
     'I was terribly cold.'

    d. Eilen   tuul-i   kamala-n   kylmä<u>sti</u>.
        yesterday blow-PRET.3SG terrible-GEN cold<u>ly</u>
        'The wind was terribly cold yesterday.'

It must be stressed that not all classes of adjectives are allowed in the dependency relationship described here. The adjectives used in these constructions are mainly those that express the intensity of the property denoted by the A(dv) head as in (11), or an evaluation of that property as in (12).

(11) a. suhteellise-n kallis
        relative-GEN expensive.NOM
        'relatively expensive'

      b. riittävä-n   luotettava
        sufficient-GEN reliable.NOM
        'sufficiently reliable'

      c. äärettömä-n yksinkertainen
        infinite-GEN simple.NOM
        'infinitely simple'

      d. erityise-n   tarkeä
        particular-GEN important.NOM
        'particularly important'

(12) a. yllättävä-n   suosittu
        surprising-GEN popular.NOM
        'surprisingly popular'

      b. harvinaise-n onnistunut
        rare-GEN   successful.NOM
        'uncommonly successful'

      c. turha-n   kyyninen
        needless-GEN cynical.NOM
        'needlessly cynical'

      d. miellyttävä-n tehokas
        pleasant-GEN efficient.NOM
        'pleasantly efficient'

      e. sairaa-n huolestunut
        ill-GEN worried.NOM
        'pathologically worried' (colloquial)

Adjectives that are not generally allowed to modify another adjective or an adverb include both epistemic and thematic adjectives. In such cases an adverb is required: *selvä<u>sti</u> iloinen* 'clearly happy', *historiallise<u>sti</u> epätarkka* 'historically inaccurate'. Still, exceptions nevertheless exist, like *ilmeisen väärä* 'patently false'. Yet the validity of the main assertion is never in doubt: when an A or Adv head is modified by an adjective, the latter takes the genitive case. Furthermore, in this case, we may follow Vainikka (1993: 131–133) and assume that the AP does so by virtue of being a specifier of the head it modifies:

(13) $[_{A(dv)P}$ AP-**GEN** $[_{A(dv)'}$ A(dv)]]

Two further remarks are required: firstly, there is one very particular set of expressions that can take the genitive in the same syntactic position as the AP in (13), namely swearwords. These are categorially nouns, or they come from nouns. It is otherwise extremely rare for an A or Adv head to be modifiable by an NP in the genitive.[6]

(14) a. helveti-**n** kylmä
           hell-**GEN** cold.**NOM**
           'damn cold'

      b. vitu-**n**   naurettava
           cunt-**GEN** ridiculous.**NOM**
           'bloody ridiculous'

Next, the set of items represented by the Adv head in (13) includes the words *paljon* and *vähän*, which are both quantifying adverbs ('much' and 'little') and quantifying determiners ('a lot of' and 'a bit of').[7] Marginally, we can also find instances of quantifying pronouns/determiners like *moni* 'much' being modified by an AP in the genitive.

(15) a. liia-**n**   paljon (happe-a)
           excessive-**GEN** much oxygen-**PART**
           'far too much (oxygen)'

      b. tavattoma-**n**   vähän (aika-a)
           unusual-**GEN** little time-**PART**
           'unusually little (time)'

      c. kamala-**n**   mone-t   (ihmise-t)
           terrible-**GEN** many-**PL.NOM** person-**PL.NOM**
           'a great many people'

2.3   Preposed NP or AP complement to an A head

A third dependency relationship expressed by the Finnish genitive is the complementization of an A head by a preceding NP or AP. The adjectives involved are all formed with the *-inen* suffix and express a measurable objective property (16), a sensory perception or general impression (17), or a spatiotemporal relationship (18). The adjectives in this last group are complementized only by NPs. (See Hakulinen et al. 2004: 604–606.)

(16) a. tonni-n painoinen
          ton-GEN weight+ADJ.NOM
          'which weighs a ton'

      b. rantee-n   paksuinen
          wrist-GEN thick+ADJ.NOM
          'as thick as a wrist'

      c. minkä   hintainen
          which.GEN price+ADJ.NOM
          'how expensive'

(17) a. etika-n   hajuinen
          vinegar-GEN smell+ADJ.NOM
          'which smells of vinegar'

      b. Ludvig XV:n tyylinen
          Louis.XV-GEN style+ADJ.NOM
          'Louis XV-style'

      c. tyytyväise-n kuuloinen
          happy-GEN   hearing+ADJ.NOM
          'who sounds happy'

(18) a. avioliito-n   ulkopuolinen
          marriage-GEN outside+ADJ.NOM
          'outside of wedlock'

      b. jääkaude-n   jälkeinen
          Ice.Age-GEN after+ADJ.NOM
          'subsequent to the Ice Age'

Note that the complements of adjectives in the comparative (*-mpi*) take the partitive and not the genitive. One thus finds *Pekkaa pitempi* 'bigger than Pekka' but *Pekan pituinen* 'of Pekka's size'. Alternatively, the comparative complement can be postposed and introduced in the nominative by the complementizer *kuin* (*pitempi kuin Pekka*). Note further that some adjectives with a genitive complement can be made into *-sti* adverbs, e.g. *sen mukaisesti* 'in accordance with that'.

   It now remains to be determined what syntactic configuration results in the assignment of genitive case to the adjective complement. In the analysis of Vainikka (1993: 134) the situation described in 2.2 would be assimilated to the present one, and the genitive case would be assigned to the NP or AP complement as specifier of A. This position appears untenable, however. First of all, we are dealing with a true complement subcategorized by the A head rather than just a modifier. It might therefore be expected to stand in a different position. Furthermore, the specifier position is sometimes independently filled, as in *vähän isän näkoinen* 'somewhat like Dad' or *täsmälleen saman kokoinen* 'of exactly the same size'. It must therefore be concluded that the complement of A occupies the sister-of-A position:[8]

(19) $[_{AP} ... [_{A'}$ NP/AP-**GEN** A]]

2.4   Preposed NP complement to a P head

The genitive also expresses the complementization relationship between a P head and a preposed NP. In other words, it is the case governed by postpositions, at least in the "default" situation. By way of comparison, the case governed by prepositions, which are far less numerous in Finnish, is the partitive. Some adpositions can take a preposed NP complement in the genitive or a postposed NP in the partitive, sometimes with a change in meaning, as illustrated in (20).

(20)   a.   maido-n   <u>kanssa</u>   ~   <u>ilman</u>   maito-a
milk-**GEN** with   without milk-**PART**
'with milk'   'without milk'

   b.   yö-n   <u>keskellä</u>   =   <u>keskellä</u>   yö-tä
night-**GEN** in.the.middle   in.the.middle   night-**PART**
'in the middle of the night'

   c.   Suome-n   <u>ympäri</u>   ≠   <u>ympäri</u>   Suome-a
Finland-**GEN** around   all.over   Finland-**PART**
'around Finland'   'all over Finland'

There are a number of facts which complicate this picture. (1) A few postpositions can be shifted to a position before their genitive complement, sometimes with a change in meaning. (2) Several postpositions govern the partitive rather than the genitive. (3) To a greater or lesser extent, prepositions can be shifted to a position following their partitive complement. (4) Many adpositions deriving from the reanalysis of a participle govern a locative case (illative, elative, ablative). An ordered illustration of each of these points is provided in (21) to (24). Exhaustive lists and additional data can be found in Hakulinen et al. (2004: 674–700).

(21)   a.   kaupungi-n <u>läpi</u>   =   <u>läpi</u>   kaupungi-n
town-**GEN**   through   through   town-**GEN**
'through the town'

   b.   pöydä-n <u>alle</u>   ≠   <u>alle</u>   metri-n
table-**GEN** under   less   meter-**GEN**
'under the table'   'less than a meter'

(22)   sinu-a   <u>varten</u> ; joke-a   <u>myöten</u>
you-**PART** for   river-**PART** along
'for you'   'along the river'

(23)   <u>kohti</u>   Turku-a   =   Turku-a   <u>kohti</u>
towards Turku-**PART**   Turku-**PART** towards
'towards Turku'

(24) sää-**hän**   nähden   ; siitä   huolimatta
      weather-ILL considering this.ELA despite
      'considering the weather'' despite this'

It is not straightforward to determine the syntactic position in which the genitive is assigned to the complement of postpositions. According to Vainikka (1993: 135–137), the position is that of specifier of a P head. The partitive in turn should be assigned to the sister-of-P position. There are indeed several arguments which support this point. One is that most postpositions were originally nouns in a locative case with the genitive NP as premodifier (see § 2.1). Sometimes this is evident (*edessä* 'in front of' < *ete-* + *-ssA*), sometimes less so (*kanssa* 'with' < *kansa* + *-ssA* 'in company of'). Furthermore, the constraints on the complement of a P head vary according to whether it is preposed or postposed. For example, a preposed NP cannot contain a postmodifier: *pullon* (*vettä) *sisällä* 'in the (water) bottle'.

In spite of this, it is hard to maintain that postpositions assign the genitive to their specifier, not just because of examples like (21), but also because the specifier position can perfectly well be independently filled: (*lähes*) *kuvan keskellä* '(nearly) in the middle of the photo'; (*osittain*) *rahan vuoksi* '(partly) for money'; (*vähän*) *Pekan takana* '(a little) behind Pekka'; (*ihan*) *talon vieressä* '(right) beside the house'. Given these facts, it seems preferable to assume that the genitive case of the NP comes from its position as sister of the P head:[9]

(25) $[_{PP} ... [_{P'} \text{NP-GEN P}]]$

2.5   NP subject of participial clauses

In Finnish, participial forms (i.e. those verb forms which are neither finite nor infinitive) can be heads of dependent clauses. There is a large array of participial clauses, all of which have a (more usual) finite clause as a functional equivalent. These participial clauses do not always have an overt subject, in particular when the external argument is a non-generic unspecified human agent (in which case the participle appears in the so-called "passive" form), when it is expressed solely by a so-called "possessive" suffix on the participle, or when it is the relativized element in a participial relative clause.

Whenever there is an NP in subject position, however, it takes the genitive case. Clauses that display this phenomenon may be completive or not, and if not, they must be either circumstantial or relative. A few examples follow with comments.[10]

In (26), the bracketed participial clause is the direct object of the verb *uskoo*. If it were finite, it would have to be introduced by a complementizer (*että* 'that'), and have a nominative subject (*Pekka*) with which its tensed verb would agree (*nukkuu* in the present, *nukkui* in the past). Here, however, there is no complementizer, the subject is in the genitive, and the verb has a participial morpheme: either *-vAn*, which expresses the non-anteriority of the process with respect to the finite verb, or *-neen*, which expresses the anteriority of the process with respect to the finite verb. It is interesting to note that both these morphemes contain a vestige of an earlier genitive (< -*vA-n*; <-*nee-n*), which was assigned to the participle as head of the direct object of the finite verb (see § 2.6). This -*n* can no longer be analyzed as a genitive marker, since it does not alternate with the partitive as it otherwise should (Vilkuna 2000: 293).

(26) a. Liisa   usko-o   [Peka-n   nukku-<u>van</u>].
          Liisa.NOM believe-3SG Pekka-GEN sleep-PTCP.PRS.n
          'Liisa believes that Pekka is sleeping/will sleep.'

      b. Liisa   usko-o   [Peka-n   nukku-<u>neen</u>].
          Liisa.NOM believe-3SG Pekka-GEN sleep-PTCP.PST.n
          'Liisa believes that Pekka slept.'

This type of case marking varies in an interesting way in two contexts. In (27a), the finite verb *näyttää* is inaccusative (does not take an external argument), which implies that *Pekka*, the external argument of the participle, must appear in the subject position of the finite verb and take nominative case. (Another option would be to replace the participial proposition by a finite one: *nayttää siltä, että Pekka nukkui huonosti* 'it seems that Pekka slept badly'.) In (27b), on the other hand, it is the participle *olevan* that is inaccusative. It is therefore a part of its complement, the NP *kuolleita*, that appears in the subject position of the participle. Since this NP takes the partitive from the outset, and the partitive is not a structural case, it retains this case as subject of the non-finite verb. Hence, the subject of a participle is exceptionally not in the genitive.[11]

(27) a. Pekka   näyttä-ä   [nukku-<u>neen</u>   huonosti].
          Pekka.NOM seem-3SG   sleep-PTCP.PST.n   badly
          'Pekka seems to have slept badly.'

      b. Usko-n   [kuolle-i-**ta**   ole-<u>van</u>   kymmen-i-ä].
          believe-1SG dead-PL-**PART** be-PTCP.PRS.n ten-PL-PART
          'I believe that dozens of people died.'

In (28), the bracketed participial clause is a circumstantial adjunct. It is not selected but simply modifies the tensed clause. Again, there is no complementizer, the subject *Pekan* is in the genitive, and the verb has a participial morpheme: either -*essA* (known in traditional grammar as the "inessive of the second infinitive"), which expresses the non-anteriority of the process with respect to the finite verb, or -*(t)tUA* ("partitive of the past passive participle"), which expresses anteriority. This construction is strictly equivalent to a finite clause introduced by *kun* 'when' where the subject would take the nominative case.

(28) a. [Peka-n   syöd-essä]   Liisa   läht-i.
          Pekka-GEN eat-PTCP.ssA Liisa.NOM go-PRET.3SG
          'While Pekka was eating, Liisa went away.'

    b. [Peka-n   syö-ty̱ä]   Liisa   läht-i.
        Pekka-GEN eat-PTCP.(t)A Liisa.NOM go-PRET.3SG
        'When Pekka had eaten, Liisa went away.'

The structure in (29), where the participle marked by -mA- ("third infinitive") has the abessive case -ttA, shows that circumstantial clauses are not always used to express temporal relationships. The subject nevertheless remains in the genitive.

(29) Lähd-i-n   [Peka-n   huomaa-m̱a-tta mitään].
      go-PRET-1SG Pekka-GEN notice-PTCP-ABE nothing
      'I went away without Pekka noticing anything.'

Finally, though this is not the only possible analysis, the bracketed participial clause in (30) can be treated as relative. In the corresponding finite clause, which would have to be postposed to the N *auto*, there would be a relative pronoun referring to this N and standing as direct object (*jonka* 'which'), then a nominal subject (*Pekka*) followed by a tensed verb agreeing with the subject (*osti* 'bought'). Here, the participial clause has no relative pronoun; the relativized element, i.e. the internal argument of the participial verb, is not realized. Reference to it is established by the relationship obtaining with the N *auto* which the participial clause premodifies: the head of this clause, i.e. the participle marker -mA-, agrees in case (here inessive) with the N *auto*. The subject is in the genitive.

(30) Istu-i-n   [Peka-n   osta-m̱a-ssa] auto-ssa.
      sit-PRET-1SG Pekka-GEN buy-PTCP-INE car-INE
      'I was sitting in the car which Pekka bought.'

Vainikka's answer (1993: 138–139) to the question which syntactic configuration leads to assignment of the genitive to the subject of all these clauses is: specifier of the V head. This position is hard to maintain. If it were true, one would expect the subject of tensed clauses also to take the genitive. Vainikka accepts this consequence and argues that the situation arises whenever the subject does not agree with the tensed verb. (In case of agreement, it would take the nominative as specifier of Infl, and the genitive should then percolate down to the direct noun object in sister-of-V position, see § 2.6.) In Part 3 of this paper, however, I will show that what Vainikka and many other Finnish grammarians analyze as a genitive subject of a personal verb is actually always an oblique modifier of an impersonal verb.

    If the subject takes the genitive only in participial clauses, it seems natural to argue that the participle itself, i.e., the Ptcp head, assigns the genitive to its specifier. This is consistent with the partially nominal status of participles.

(31) [$_{PtcpP}$ NP-GEN [$_{Ptcp'}$ Ptcp VP]]

2.6   Direct NP object of certain kinds of VP

The Finnish genitive also contrasts with other cases in one last basic dependency relationship. This is the object relationship, i.e. complementization of a V head by an NP. Consider as an initial example:

(32)   Pekka   ost-i   auto-**n**.
        Pekka.NOM buy-PRET.3SG car-**GEN**
        'Pekka bought a car.'

The interpretation of the -*n* on the direct object is a matter of some debate. As Table 1 shows, traditional Finnish grammar, which many scholars follow on this point, takes this to be an accusative rather than a genitive case marker. This is how it is usually glossed, and it is traditionally called *genetiivinkaltainen akkusatiivi* 'genitive-like accusative' or *genetiiviakkusatiivi* 'genitive-accusative'. Another name for it is accusative-1, in contrast to accusative-2 which designates the object's nominative case (see below).

The arguments for this approach are based on historical linguistics. Firstly, some Uralic languages (Nenets, Mari, and Southern Saami) have an accusative case in -*m*. In addition, there is good reason to believe that the rule [-*m* → -*n* / __#] applied during the transition from Proto-Finno-Saamic (or "Pre-Finnic") to Proto-Finnic. Hence, it can be concluded that the object suffix -*n* comes from a Proto-Uralic accusative *-*m*, and thus remains an accusative.

This conclusion is rejected here. First of all, the identity of -*n* on the direct object needs to be determined synchronically, and must therefore be decided on the basis of synchronic arguments. But there is no synchronic formal reason to distinguish object -*n* from a genitive. On the contrary, there are positive reasons for identifying this -*n* with the genitive marker. Kiparsky (2001: 320–321) gives the following example: since human pronouns are the only NPs to have an undeniably accusative form (-*t*), it might be expected that adjectives modifying these pronouns (as *parka* 'poor' in *minä parka* 'poor me') would agree with them in the same (accusative) case, as they do with other cases. This does not in fact happen. (One finds, for example, *minulla paralla* in the adessive, but **minut paran* is ill-formed, showing that -*n* is not an accusative on a par with -*t*). Finally, it is far from evident that object -*n* comes from an accusative *-*m*. Briefly stated (see Mahieu 2007: 163–174 for details), if this were true, Proto-Finnic would have had syntactic transitivity and purely verbal predication. The fact is, however, that today's finite forms derive from earlier verbonominal predicates which are known to assign the genitive to their internal argument as a matter of course (cf. the object of verbal nouns in Celtic). For all these reasons, -*n* on the object should be treated as a genitive.

As already mentioned, the genitive is not the only case that can affect the direct object. There are several conditions to be met which keep it from marking more than one object in five on average (Hakulinen et al. 2004: 1182). The two most frequent cases are the partitive and the nominative, while the accusative is much rarer still.

Which of these cases is chosen can be seen as the result of a hierarchy of constraints which can be stated as follows. Firstly, any one of the following four conditions will suffice for the object to appear in the partitive: (1) the sentence is in the negative; (2) the VP denotes a process without a "telos", i.e. without an end goal; (3) the process denoted by the VP is viewed as "imperfective", i.e. as in the process of coming about; (4) the object denotes an indeterminate quantity of something.[12] Each of these criteria is illustrated in (33). In (33a), the VP is within the scope of negation which, in Finnish, is an inflectional head agreeing with the subject. In (33b), the VP is intrinsically atelic. In (33c), the verb is telic but viewed as not having reached its telos. In (33d), the object is a quantitatively indeterminate mass noun.

(33) a. Pekka   ei   näh-nyt   hän-**tä**.
          Pekka.NOM NEG.3SG   see-PRET he-**PART**
          'Pekka did not see him.'

      b. Pekka   soitta-a   pasuuna-a.
          Pekka.NOM play-3SG   trombone-**PART**
          'Pekka plays/is playing the trombone.'

      c. Pekka   rakens-i   venet-tä.
          Pekka.NOM build-PRET.3SG boat-**PART**
          'Pekka was building a/the boat.'

      d. Pekka   osta-a   piimä-ä.
          Pekka.NOM buy-3SG   sour.mik-**PART**
          'Pekka buys/will buy some sour milk.'

Secondly, whenever none of the conditions for assigning the partitive is met, it suffices that the object should be in the plural for it to take the so-called "nominative plural" morpheme -*t*. The analysis of this morpheme is not without difficulties of its own. It is open to question whether it truly has the plural number feature and the nominative case feature, and whether it is not rather an allomorphic variant of the plural (-*i*-) before nominative case (∅), or even something quite different, e.g. a "specific plural" marker, as Renault (1991: 42–49) suggests.

(34) a. Pekka   tapaa   Virtase-t.
          Pekka.NOM meet.3SG   Virtanen-**PL.NOM**
          'Pekka meets/will meet the Virtanens.'

      b. Pekka   rakens-i   hylly-t.
          Pekka.NOM build-PRET-3SG shelf-**PL.NOM**
          'Pekka built the shelves.'

Thirdly, if the partitive is not required and there is no plural marker, it will suffice that the object be a human pronoun for it to take accusative -*t*. In all, only seven Finnish lexemes can take this case: the six (intrinsically human) personal pronouns and the human interrogative pronoun *kuka* 'who?'.

(35) a. Kene-t   Pekka   tapas-i?
         who-ACC Pekka.NOM meet-PRET.3SG
         'Who Pekka did meet?'

    b. Pekka   löys-i   minu-t.
       Pekka.NOM find-PRET.3SG me-ACC
       'Pekka found me.'

    c. Tuo   heidä-t   tänne!
       bring.IMP.2SG they-ACC here
       'Bring them here!'

Fourthly, if the partitive is not required and the object is a singular noun, it will suffice that there be no nominative subject in the sentence for the object itself to take the nominative. This situation occurs in first and second person imperatives, in so-called "passive" sentences where the verb inflection is exempted from specifying a subject, the latter being interpreted as a non-generic human agent (Mahieu 2012), and in infinitive clauses complementing an impersonal verb. Thus, the object is unquestionably in the nominative in (36), rather than in a special form of the accusative, as traditional grammar would have it (Kiparsky 2001: 319–320).

(36) a. Vie   (sinä)   koira   ulos!
         take.IMP.2SG you.NOM dog.NOM out
         '(You,) take the dog out!'

    b. Nyt vie-dä-än   koira   ulos.
       now take-PASS-one   dog.NOM out
       'Now we will take the dog out.'

    c. Täyty-y   vie-dä   koira   ulos.
       have.to-3SG take-INF dog.NOM out
       'The dog has to be taken out.'

Fifthly and finally, if none of the conditions for assigning the partitive is met, the object is a singular noun, and the sentence contains or can contain a nominative subject, the object takes the genitive case. This is what happens in (32) and again in (37) below. The phrase "can contain" is essential to the rule, as subject pronouns are only expressed for emphasis in the first and second persons. The only sentences in which the object takes the genitive even when there can be no subject in the nominative are "generic" sentences, an example of which appears in (38).

(37) a. Pekka   on   löytä-nyt   avaime-n.
         Pekka.NOM be.3SG find-PTCP.PST key-GEN
         'Pekka has found the key.'

    b. Hän   soitta-a tämä-n   sonaati-n.
       he.NOM play-3SG this-GEN sonata-GEN
       'He will play this sonata.'

    c. (Me)   makso-i-mme koko lasku-n.
         (we.NOM) pay-PRET-1PL all   bill-GEN
         'We paid the whole bill.'

(38) Sieltä   saa   helposti malaria-n.[13]
      from.here get.3SG easily   malaria-GEN
      'One easily catches malaria here.'

To conclude this overview of the main data, it should be noted that in an infinitive clause which complements or modifies a noun, the object will not usually appear in the genitive. If it cannot be assigned either the partitive or the accusative, it takes the nominative. Apparent exceptions can be explained (Ikola 1964: 66–80).

On the other hand, in infinitive clauses which complement a finite verb or are separated from a finite verb only by other non-finite clauses, the object takes the genitive whenever the finite verb has a nominative subject. An example of this kind of "long-distance" dependency (Mahieu 2008) is given in (39).

(39) a. (Minä) yritä-n muista-a   teh-dä harjoitukse-n.
         (I.NOM) try-1SG remember-INF do-INF exercise-GEN
         'I will try to remember to do the exercise.'

      b. Yritä   nyt muista-a   teh-dä harjoitus!
         try.IMP.2SG now remember-INF do-INF exercise.NOM
         'Now try to remember to do the exercise!'

From a typological perspective, the case marking system for verb arguments in Finnish is quite unusual. Once the partitive and plural forms, whose use depends on semantic factors, are set aside, the system can be called "antiergative", a term used by Comrie (1975). The distribution of the genitive forms a mirror image of the ergative case-marking system as found in syntactically accusative languages: the object is only marked when there is an unmarked subject. It may be added that this "antiergativity" is contravened by the human pronouns which follow an accusative marking type.[14]

(40) a. ACCUSATIVE SYNTAX, ACCUSATIVE CASE-MARKING
         S (nominative)   V
         S (nominative)   V   O (**accusative**)
                         V   O (**accusative**)

      b. ACCUSATIVE SYNTAX, ERGATIVE CASE-MARKING
         S (absolutive)   V
         S (**ergative**)   V   O (absolutive)
                         V   O (absolutive)

      c. ACCUSATIVE SYNTAX, ANTIERGATIVE CASE-MARKING
         S (absolutive)   V
         S (absolutive)   V   O (**antiergative**)
                         V   O (absolutive)

Comrie (1975, 1977: 7) provides a purely functionalist interpretation of antiergativity: the distribution of -*n* can be explained simply by a need to distinguish subject and object when both are present in a sentence. This explanation leaves something to be desired. It cannot explain why one marking type occurs rather than another; it cannot explain the existence of split distributions; it cannot explain why one morpheme rather than another is chosen to mark a given relationship; and finally, it does not take into account the fact that subject and object can be distinguished in various other ways, even in a language with loose word order like Finnish.

More complex explanatory hypotheses have since been proposed (see particularly Milsark 1985; Taraldsen 1986; Vainikka 1989, 1993; Maling 1993; Reime 1993; Toivainen 1993; Nelson 1998; Mahieu 2007), but they cannot be discussed here.

There is at least one point that can easily be defended: the genitive is assigned to the object for syntactic reasons; it has no more meaning content than the nominative with which it alternates automatically. Furthermore, the syntactic configuration for its assignment cannot be reduced to any single one of the configurations discussed here thus far.

In particular, it is clear that the source of the object genitive is not the same as that of the subject genitive. This was the theory proposed by Vainikka (1989: 151–181), who saw the genitive appearing as specifier of V in both cases, and presumably percolating down to sister-of-V position whenever the subject is raised to agree with an Infl head. If this were true, one would expect that both subject and object could never bear the genitive in the same clause. While this expectation is met in finite clauses, it is contradicted in participial clauses. In (41), both verb arguments in the bracketed completive can be seen to bear genitive marking. (Here again, the object would only be in the nominative if there were no possible nominative subject of the finite verb.) Given these facts, it must be assumed that the genitive is assigned to subject and object in different configurations. With regard to the object, the simplest hypothesis would be to assume that assignment takes place directly in sister-of-V position as shown in (42).

(41) Tiedä-n [Peka-**n**   osta-neen   auto-**n**].
      know-1SG Pekka-**GEN** buy-PTCP.PST.n car-**GEN**
      'I know that Pekka bought a car.'

(42) $[_{VP} ... [_{V'} \text{ V NP-}\textbf{GEN}]]$

2.7   Postposed NP modifier of certain types of VP

Finally, the genitive expresses a somewhat marginal but nonetheless unexpected dependency relationship under conditions which are nearly identical to the ones which lead to the genitive being assigned to objects. The relevant context is the modification of a VP by an NP denoting quantity, often distance, duration, or frequency. The rule is as follows: if the VP is not within the scope of negation, and the sentence has or can have a subject in the nominative, then the quantifying modifier takes the genitive, provided it is not invariable (as *joka päivä* 'every day', which is always nominative). Otherwise, it takes either the partitive or the nominative.

(43) a. Minä   juokse-n   kilometri-**n**.
          I.NOM   run-1SG   kilometre-**GEN**
          'I will run a kilometre.'

      b. E-n   juokse   kilometri-**ä**.
          NEG-1SG   run   kilometre-**PART**
          'I will not run a kilometre.'

      c. Juokse   vielä   kilometri!
          run.IMP.2SG   still   kilometre.NOM
          'Run one more kilometre!'

      d. Nyt   juos-ta-an   kilometri.
          now   run-PASS-one   kilometre.NOM
          'Now we will run one kilometre.'

The only real difference with respect to the object marking system is that the quantifying modifier does not take the partitive if the VP is atelic or the viewpoint is imperfective. For example, one finds *odotin tunnin* 'I was waiting for an hour' with genitive modifier, but *odotin häntä* 'I was waiting for him' where the object must be partitive. These may be compared with *odota tunti!* 'wait for an hour!', where the modifier is in the nominative in the absence of any possible nominative subject.

In view of these data, it might be assumed that the case marking of the modifier takes place within the same syntactic configuration as the marking of the object, with the NP taking the genitive in sister-of-V position. This does not, however, seem to be true. The VP can quite easily have a direct object in addition to the quantifying modifier, as in (44).

(44) a. Ole-n   opiskel-lut   suome-a   vuode-n.
          be-1SG   study-PTCP.PST   Finnish-PART   year-GEN
          'I have studied Finnish for a year.'

      b. Pekka   luk-i   kirja-a   tunni-n.[15]
          Pekka.NOM   read-PRET.3SG   book-PART   hour-GEN
          'Pekka read the book for an hour.'

      c. Ole-n   näh-nyt   häne-t   yhde-n   kerra-n.
          be-1SG   see-PTCP.PST   he-ACC   one-GEN   time-GEN
          'I have seen him once.'

All in all, it would be better to allow that the quantifying modifier does not take the genitive in sister-of-V position but rather as an adjunct following the VP, as represented in (45).

(45) [$_{VP}$ [$_{VP}$ ...[$_{V'}$ V ...] NP-**GEN**]]

This section has made it clear that there is enough evidence for the conclusion that the genitive in Finnish is neither the case of possession nor, more widely speaking, the case of any given semantic operation. It is a structural case standing in a complex system of contrasts with other cases and reflecting an irreducible range of syntactic relationships.

3.   The "dative-genitive" issue

A good number of ordinary Finnish constructions contain an -*n* morpheme which recent grammars (starting with Hakulinen et al. 2004) do not distinguish from the genitive. It can be shown, however, that this morpheme is not a structural case but rather a semantic case with dative sense, corresponding to a P category in syntactic structure. In traditional Finnish grammar, this case, formally identical to the genitive, was called "dative-genitive".

The constructions in which this -*n* appears will now be described, and the main reasons for not treating it as a structural case will be set out. Its relationship to the genitive will then be examined from a historical perspective, with a view to providing a general explanation of the diachronic origin of the genitive case. It will be glossed "DAT.GEN" to distinguish it from the genitive proper.

3.1   The necessive construction

As a general rule, the necessive construction consists of a necessive predicate and its infinitival complement. The "necessive predicate" can be defined as follows: "a single verb like *täytyy, pitää, tarvitsee* 'must, have to, need to', *kannattaa* 'be worthwhile', *sopia* 'be suitable', or a copular construction like *on hyvää/sopiva/turha/pakko* 'be good/suitable/in vain/a necessity'. One [special] type of necessive construction consists of a copula and the [so-called] passive participle of the verb, as in *on tehtävä* 'has to be done'" (Laitinen and Vilkuna 1993: 24). The important point to note here is that a necessive construction can always be preceded by an NP with the -*n* suffix expressing the experiencer of the obligation.

(46)   a.   Peka-**n**   täyty-y   teh-dä työ-tä.
             Pekan-**DAT.GEN** have.to-3SG   do-INF work-PART
             'Pekka has to work.'

       b.   Häne-**n**   on   mahdoton-ta   lähte-ä.
             he-**DAT.GEN**   be.3SG impossible-PART leave-INF
             'It is impossible for him to leave.'

If this NP were the genitive subject of the necessive predicate, it should not for independent reasons be possible to delete it in the third person. Only the first and second person forms are allowed not to have a full subject in independent sentences. Yet it is in fact possible to delete the experiencer, sometimes with insertion of another topic. Thus, (36c) is an example of a necessive sentence without an experiencer expressed. In this case, the reference to the implicit subject of the infinitive is uncontrolled, hence arbitrary. Consequently, it can be affirmed that necessive predicates are impersonal (which explains why they are in the third person by default), and the *-n*-bearing NP is no more than a predicate modifier.

Moreover, if the case of this modifier were really genitive, it would have no stable meaning (see Part 2) and could not alternate with any semantic case. Yet it has in fact dative meaning (the obligation falls <u>to</u> this or that person) and can alternate with the allative *-lle*. Where alternation is allowed, it is furthermore associated with a meaning difference which is too complicated to be discussed here. Good treatments of this subject can be found, for example, in Laitinen and Vilkuna (1993: 33–34) and Hakulinen et al. (2004: 878).

Experiencer *-n* is therefore not a genitive but rather a semantic case with dative sense. This means that, unlike the genitive, it is not the morphological reflex of a syntactic dependency relationship. It is itself the manifestation of a syntactic category connecting the NP to the rest of the sentence. The fact that the semantic cases are derived from former postpositions which have gradually been cliticized on nouns (Korhonen 1996: 195–206, 219–234) gives grounds for assuming that the semantic cases are P heads, and this can be widely confirmed by synchronic analysis.[16] It can therefore be concluded that the experiencer in the necessive construction is the complement of a dative P head, that this P head is realized by the case marker *-n*, and that the PP in which the experiencer is embedded is an adjunct to the necessive VP.

3.2   The permissive construction

The so-called "permissive" construction minimally consists of one of the five permissive verbs and its infinitival complement. These verbs are *antaa* 'let (someone do)' (the primary meaning of this verb being 'give'), *sallia* 'permit', *käskeä* 'order', *suoda* 'grant', and more marginally *luvata* when it means 'authorize, allow' (and not 'promise'). The permissive verb is usually followed by an *-n*-bearing NP which expresses the experiencer of the permission.

(47)   Liisa   anto-i   Peka-n   men-nä.
       Liisa.NOM let-PRET.3SG Pekan-DAT.GEN go-INF
       'Liisa let Pekka go.'

Here again, it is clear that the NP marked by *-n* is neither a subject nor an object in the genitive. If it were, given that a verb in the infinitive never has an overt subject other than one governed by an ECM (Exceptional Case Marking) verb, it ought to alternate in a paradigm of object cases (see § 2.6). Yet *-n* does not in fact vary with context and can be found within the scope of negation (*en antanut Pekan mennä* 'I didn't let

Pekka go'), on human pronouns (*Liisa antoi hänen mennä* 'Liisa let him go'), and in imperatives (*anna Pekan mennä!* 'let Pekka go!').

It should also be impossible to delete the marked NP, and the case marker should have no meaning. Yet it is in fact possible for the experiencer of permissive sentences to be omitted (Hakulinen et al. 2004: 498), and *-n* clearly has basic dative value, just as in necessive sentences (permission is granted <u>to</u> someone or other). It is furthermore well known that permissive sentences derive from the reanalysis of ordinary sentences where the *-n*-bearing NP was the Beneficiary of the verb *antaa* 'give', as in *anna minun syödä ruokaa!* '<u>let me</u> eat some food!' < *anna minun ruokaa syödä!* '<u>give me</u> some food to eat!' (expressed in contemporary Finnish by *anna minulle ruokaa syödäkseni!*). (On this point, see Leino 2003.)

Given these facts, it can reasonably be concluded that the *-n* marking the experiencer in the permissive construction is not a genitive but again the manifestation of a dative P head having the function of joining its complement, the experiencer, to the rest of the sentence. The PP is thus an adjunct to the permissive VP.

3.3   The experiencer construction

In what is called the "experiencer construction" here, a predicate expressing a feeling or sensation is preceded by an NP marked by *-n* designating the experiencer. The predicate is composed of one of the verbs *on* 'is', *tulee* 'comes', or *käy* 'goes', followed by a noun, an adjective, or an adverb denoting what is felt. This construction is less susceptible to manipulation than the preceding ones, but it is even more obvious that the initial NP does not have structural genitive marking.

(48) a. Peka-**n**   ol-i   jano   / kuuma.
          Pekka-**DAT.GEN** be-PRET.3SG thirst.NOM hot.NOM
          'Pekka was thirsty/hot.'

      b. Minu-**n**   tule-e   sääli   / ikävä   hän-tä.
          I-**DAT.GEN**   come-3SG   pity.NOM   sorrow.NOM he-PART
          'I feel sorry for him./I miss him.'

      c. Liisa-**n**   käv-i   hyvin   / hassusti.
          Liisa-**DAT.GEN** go-PRET.3SG well   funnily
          'Things went well for Liisa./Liisa was unlucky.'

First of all, the NP can be deleted, as in *on kuuma* '[the weather] is hot', *häntä käy sääliksi* 'he is a sorry sight to see, in a pitiful state', or *hyvin kävi* 'it went well'. It can thus be treated as a predicate modifier. In addition, it is almost inconceivable that *-n* should be the meaningless reflex of a syntactic dependency relationship here; it is clearly this case which relates the initial NP syntactically and semantically to the predicate. In its absence, the nature of this relationship could not always be inferred as can be seen from the question *mikä sinun on?* 'what's up with you?'. Finally, the experiencer case can often be replaced by a locative case as in *hänelle kävi hassusti* 'she was unlucky'. In short, the experiencer again appears as the complement of a dative P head projecting a PP adjunct to the predicate of feeling.

3.4   The "dative-genitive" predicate

In the construction exemplified by (1b) and repeated below as (49a), the semantic role of the *-n*-bearing NP is not that of experiencer but rather that of possessor. This NP is furthermore part of the predicate whose subject designates the thing possessed.

(49) a. Auto   on   Peka-**n**.
          car.NOM be.3SG Pekka-**DAT.GEN**
          'The car is Pekka's.'

      b. Kene-**n**   auto   on?
          who-**DAT.GEN** car.NOM be.3SG
          'Whose car is it?'

Once again, *-n* cannot be treated as a meaningless case marker. Unlike *Pekan auto* 'Pekka's car' where the case marked by *-n* is assigned for purely structural reasons and independently of the semantic role assumed by the modifier (see § 2.1), here it is the element which establishes the syntactic and semantic relationship between the two NPs. Furthermore, the dative sense is again recognizable (a thing belongs <u>to</u> someone or other).

Given these facts, it can be concluded that the *-n* marker is the realization of a P head taking the possessor as its complement. The PP is itself the complement of the verb *olla* 'be', and the NP expressing the thing possessed is realized as the subject of this verb.[17]

3.5   The loose "dative-genitive"

The four constructions described above are the only ones in the standard language to use the *-n* case marker with dative sense. This use is also found in at least one other construction in dialect which is cited here both because it has been a topic of prior research (see in particular Huumo and Inaba 1997), and because it provides support for the positions taken here.

In this construction, the *-n*-bearing NP has the semantic role of possessor and appears sentence-initially at a distance from the NP expressing the thing possessed. The following examples are taken from Huumo and Inaba (ibid.).

(50) a. Peka-**n**   on   auto   rikki.
          Pekka-**DAT.GEN** be.3SG car.NOM broken
          'Pekka's car is broken.' (dialectal)

b. Minu-**n**   kuol-i   kissa.
I-**DAT.GEN** die-PRET.3SG cat.NOM
'My cat died.' (dialectal)

c. Puhuja-**n**   men-i-vät   paperi-t   sekaisin.
Liisa-**DAT.GEN** go-PRET-3PL paper-PL.NOM mixed
'The speaker' papers got mixed up.' (dialectal)

d. Elmeri-**n**   putos-i   lompakko järve-en.
Elmer-**DAT.GEN** fall-PRET.3SG wallet.NOM lake-ILL
'Elmer's wallet fell into the lake.' (dialectal)

At first glance, this construction might be analysed as resulting from inversion involving the movement of the verb to a position between the head of a complex NP subject and its preposed genitive modifier. (50a) would thus derive from [*Pekan auto*] *on rikki*. Huumo and Inaba (ibid.) provide numerous convincing arguments to show that this analysis is incorrect.

Here are a few of these arguments. First of all, the semantic role of the NP marked by -*n* is restricted to that of possessor in the strict sense of 'owner'. This would be incomprehensible if the NP were really a preposed genitive modifier of a N head. The situation is thus the same as in 3.4: the case marked by -*n* is used to indicate <u>to whom</u> something belongs. Furthermore, the NP marked by -*n* is not always linked to the subject. In *pojan meni tikku sormeen* 'a splinter got stuck in the boy's finger', the possessive relationship is established with the locative complement. Analysis as inversion is thus unsuitable, and the initial constituent is more like an added element. Finally, there is good reason to think that sentences like (50) are related to an earlier possessive construction, still found in Mordvin and Mari, where the case marked by -*n* was clearly semantic with dative sense. The replacement of this case in Finnic by the external locative cases was probably responsible for marginalizing "loose dative-genitive" sentences. Sentences like *Pekalla on auto rikki*, or *minulta kuoli kissa*, are in any case much more common. In short, we may conclude that the case marked by -*n* in (50) constitutes a dative P head with the possessor as its complement.

3.6   The historical background

It may be helpful at this point to look briefly at the links between the structural genitive case described in Part 2 and the semantic dative case presented in this section. The need to distinguish the two synchronically does not of course imply that they cannot have a common origin. There are two positions on this question, the second of which currently prevails.

The first, discussed in Hakulinen (1968: 86), asserts that there is no historical relationship between the two case forms. The structural genitive case is assumed to have existed in Proto-Uralic where it had the same form, *-*n*, as in modern Finnish. It has on occasion been suggested that this Proto-Uralic genitive may itself have come from a very ancient adjectival derivational morpheme which can still be observed in Mari, Mordvin, and Southern Saamic. (Thus in Mari, *lun* is either the genitive of the noun 'bone' or an adjective meaning 'made of bone'.) The "dative-genitive" in turn is thought to derive from a Proto-Uralic *-ń* marking the lative case. This morpheme is also assumed to have played a role in the creation of the two directional cases, the illative (*-hVn* < *-se* + *-ń*) and the allative (*-lle* < *-le* + *-ń*). It must then have merged formally with the genitive in the transition to Proto-Finnic as a result of the process [*-ń* → *-n*]. In Old Finnish, it must have remained productive and continued to contrast with the genitive as dative for a long period (see Hakulinen ibid. for the data). It later lost ground to the two directional cases.

There are at least two problems with this first approach. The notion that the Proto-Uralic lative must have been a palatalized *-ń*, i.e. formally distinct from the hypothetical genitive *-n*, is totally ad hoc. Vestiges of the "lative-dative" exist in all Uralic languages, and invariably allow reconstruction as non-palatal *-n*. Furthermore, the structural genitive case in *-n* is totally absent from some branches of Uralic, in particular ancient branches like Ugric and Permian. This would mean that the structural genitive must have been lost there.

The second approach is much more convincing. It postulates that the two cases are historically related (Itkonen 1968: 202), and that the structural genitive is the outcome of a long process of grammaticalization of the original Proto-Uralic lative (Korhonen 1996: 222–224). This process is likely to have been as follows: Proto-Uralic had no genitive, but it did have a lative case marked by *-n*, still visible in the Finnish illative *-hVn* and the Mari dative *-lan*, etc. This semantic case must have quickly acquired a new dative value which can be observed in many Finno-Ugric languages. It must still have been present in Old Finnish, where *-n* was often used like the modern allative, and has reached modern Finnish in the constructions described in Part 3 of this paper.

At some stage, certainly after the Ugric and Permian branches had split off, the lative-dative must have begun to be applied to possessors, not only in the possessive construction (as today in Mordvin and Mari) but also in adnominal contexts. According to Korhonen (ibid.), "it is possible that the dative (or the lative in the dative function) started to be used also as an adnominal case in the possessive function if the possessivity was emphasized, or if the referent of the possessive attribute was animate, human, definite, or pronominal. Otherwise, the case of the possessive was the nominative. According to this scenario, the [evolution] would have been similar to that in Hungarian, where the dative with suffix *-nak/-nek* has also taken the function of a genitive."

In its adnominal use, the genitive of possession deriving from the lative-dative must ultimately have been desemanticized and become a simple dependency marker, i.e. a structural case. In this form, it now appears in an irreducible range of contexts in Finnish, as has been seen in Part 2. In contrast, the uses presented in this section, which are relics of what the case marked by *-n* originally was before it became grammaticalized, are losing ground to the locative cases, as might be expected. This process has reached its end in the possessive construction, as Finnish uses only the adessive and not the *-n* case (see Part 4).

There are two features that support the likelihood of the second scenario. First of all, as Korhonen (ibid.) points out, the line of development [lative > dative > genitive] is quite natural from a typological perspective. In addition, the thesis that structural cases come from the grammaticalization of semantic ones, and these ultimately from adpositions, has been widely accepted for some time (see for example Lehmann 1985: 304).

4.   The possessive construction

In the Finnish possessive construction, the possessor, i.e. the entity whose personal ambit is said to include the entity designated as the thing possessed, is an NP bearing, not the case marker *-n* as in Mordvin and Mari, but the external static locative case, the adessive. When the possessor is inanimate, the adessive case is often replaced by the corresponding internal case, the inessive. This contrast is illustrated in (51).

(51) a. Peka-**lla**   on   auto.
          Pekka-ADE be.3SG car.NOM
          'Pekka has a car.'

      b. Auto-**ssa** on   uude-t   renkaa-t.
          car-INE   be.3SG new-PL.NOM wheel-PL.NOM
          'The car has new wheels.'

A superficial look at the Finnish possessive construction might lead to the assumption that it is nothing but a locative inversion. Rather than a transitive structure involving a verb 'have', this construction would then have an initial PP, the verb 'be', and a subject NP in the nominative. The realization of the P head, i.e. the case marking the possessor, would retain its locative sense, and the literal meaning of the construction would be 'at So-and-So is this'. In short, the possessive construction would thus be a subtype of existential sentence, and the structure of the sentences in (51) would be exactly the same as that of the ones in (52).

(52) a. Kadu-**lla**   on   auto.
          street-ADE be.3SG car.NOM
          'There is a car in the street.'

      b. Auto-**ssa** on   kaksi   henkilö-ä.
          car-INE   be.3SG two.NOM person-PART
          'There are two people in the car.'

This approach yields contradictory results for several manipulations. Let us look first at the manipulations in question and then try to provide an explanation for this situation.

4.1   Contra inversion

The first manipulation is pronominalizing the thing possessed. When the thing possessed is a noun, the fact that it takes nominative case proves nothing regarding its syntactic function (see § 2.6). On the other hand, the pronominal form is discriminatory as it must be accusative in this context. On this basis, it can be concluded that the postverbal constituent is the direct object of a transitive head.

(53) Peka-**lla**   on   häne-**t**.
      Pekka-ADE be.3SG she-ACC
      'Pekka has her.'

By way of contrast, the inverted subject of an existential sentence can under no circumstances take the accusative. The nominative would be preferred, but the resulting sentence is not fully acceptable since the inverted subject of existential sentences is supposed to be indefinite, as in the example *kadulla on hänet vs.?kadulla on hän '?there is he in the street'.

The second manipulation changes the order of the two constituents with respect to the verb. When applied to an existential sentence, this operation clearly changes the way in which the information is distributed (and the definiteness of the subject in translation), but the sentence has approximately the same meaning content. Thus, *kadulla on auto* 'there is a car in the street' contrasts with the non-existential sentence *auto on kadulla* 'the car is in the street'. If the possessive construction is a kind of existential sentence, it should behave in the same way, i.e. there should be little to distinguish *Pekalla on auto* 'Pekka has a car' from another sentence, *auto on Pekalla*, meaning something like 'the car is Pekka's'. This is not the case, however. Changing the order completely changes the meaning of the sentence, which no longer expresses a possessive relationship:

(54) a.   Auto   on   Peka-**lla**.
           car.NOM be.3SG Pekka-ADE
           'the car is at Pekka's place'

      b.   Kirja   on   minu-**lla**.
           book.NOM be.3SG me-ADE
           'The book is with me.'

At this point, the conclusion can be drawn that not only is the possessive construction syntactically transitive, but furthermore its possessive sense is not just the sum of the meaning of a static locative case ('<u>at</u> So-and-So') and the verb of existence ('<u>is</u> this'). Instead, the possessive interpretation arises from a specific relationship existing between these two constituents in a specific, apparently non-existential syntactic structure.

The third manipulation is more complex but equally telling. It is based on the contrast shown in (55). In (55a), the subject qualifies as antecedent of the possessive suffix on the locative complement. In (55b), a locative inversion, the initial locative complement cannot qualify as antecedent to the same suffix on the inverted subject, and the sentence is therefore ill-formed. The explanation for this contrast is the fact that Binding Principle A is violated in (55b). Given that possessive suffixes are anaphoric, they must be bound, i.e. c-commanded by a coreferent NP, in their binding domain. (55a) respects this principle: the NP subject locally c-commands the anaphoric constituent. (55b), by contrast, violates it: since the NP in the locative case is embedded in a PP, it cannot c-command the anaphoric constituent.

(55) a. Kapteeni$_i$ nouse-e   laiva-a-$\underline{nsa}_i$.
          captain.NOM   go.up-3SG   boat-ILL-$\underline{PX.3SG}$
          'The captain$_i$ gets in his$_i$ boat.'

  b. *Laiva-an$_i$ nouse-e   kapteeni-$\underline{nsa}_i$.
          boat-ILL   go.up-3SG   captain.NOM-$\underline{PX.3SG}$
          ('*In the boat$_i$ gets its$_i$ captain.')

This being established, the manipulation consists of associating an anaphoric constituent with the thing possessed in the possessive construction. If this construction has the same structure as existential sentences, the possessor must also be embedded in a PP and the result should be ill-formed. Yet as observed by Nikanne (1993: 81–83) confirmed by (56), the result is well-formed. This means that the possessor (the NP in the locative case) is not embedded in a PP.

(56) a. Kansalais-i-$\textbf{lla}_i$ on   uusi   pääministeri-$\underline{nsä}_i$.
          citizen-PL-$\textbf{ADE}$ be.3SG   new.NOM   prime.minister.NOM-$\underline{PX.3SG}$
          'The citizens$_i$ have their$_i$ new prime minister.'

  b. Joka kiele-ssä$_i$ on   oma-t   sana-$\underline{nsa}_i$.
          each language-INE be.3SG   own-PL.NOM   word.PL.NOM-$\underline{PX.3PL}$
          'Each language$_i$ has its$_i$ own words.'

We can therefore conclude that in the Finnish possessive construction, not only does the postverbal constituent behave like the object of a non-existential verb, but the preverbal constituent behaves like the subject of the sentence. The problem then is to determine why this subject is in the locative (see in the next section).

The fourth and last manipulation to be discussed here consists of trying to use the possessive construction in sentences which do not have a possessor in the strict sense. If this construction were a locative inversion, this would in all likelihood be impossible. Indeed, when a language without a verb 'have' uses such a strategy, it does so primarly to express a relationship of ownership, not simply of having in one's possession. This is in fact true of the other Uralic languages (Huumo and Inaba 1997: 39–42; Inaba 1998: 167–169). Remarkably, however, the Finnish possessive construction admits all the semantic functions of a verb 'have':

(57) a. Peka-**lla**   on   kirja-ni   mukana-an.
        Pekka-ADE be.3SG book.NOM-PX.1SG with-PX.3SG
        'Pekka has my book with him.'

    b. Peka-**lla**   on   hauska-a   / kiire.
        Pekka-ADE be.3SG funny-PART   hurry.NOM
        'Pekka has fun/is in a hurry.'

    c. Peka-**lla**   on   kova   yskä.
        Pekka-ADE be.3SG hard.NOM cough.NOM
        'Pekka has a bad cough.'

    d. Peka-**lla**   on   tapa-na valehdel-la.
        Pekka-ADE be.3SG habit-ESS lie-INF
        'Pekka is in the habit of lying.'

The overall conclusion is thus that, while the forms used in the Finnish possessive construction have the appearance of a locative inversion, the results of submitting this construction to various manipulations suggest a [SVO] structure where the verbal head has the semantic content of a verb 'have'.

Diachronically speaking, it is likely that the original structure was a locative inversion which has since been reanalyzed. It is a fairly common observation that syntactic relationships, given their immaterial nature, evolve more quickly than morphology, which is naturally conservative. Should it therefore be assumed that morphology is synchronically unmotivated, that surface forms are only the remains of an earlier syntactic organization? Not necessarily: in the final section of this paper, I will propose an analysis of the possessive construction that synchronically resolves the contradictions set out above.

4.2   A transformational analysis

A fairly unsatisfactory way to account for the data synchronically would be to allow for two different homophonous verbs of the form *olla*, each as a separate lexical entry. One would be the verb 'be' and the other, the verb 'have'. The latter would have the inherent property of assigning locative case to its subject. Since this case is neither structural nor semantic, it will need to be assigned some third status, for instance lexical case, which immediately brings to mind the "quirky subjects" of Icelandic.

There is, however, another solution that is both more economical and more elegant. The starting point, taken from a paper by Benveniste (1966: 187–207), is this: the verb 'have' is not original in the languages where it exists. 'Have' must rather be the spell-out of the verb 'be' plus a prepositional component. In other words, languages cannot be divided into those which have and those which do not have a verb 'have'. There are only languages which incorporate a P head into the verb 'be' (like English, French, etc.) and those which do not (Russian, Hindi, etc.).[18] Given this assumption, both situations might wisely be treated as resulting from syntactic transformations of a single initial structure (see Rouveret 1998 for references and a positive appraisal of this approach).

What should this structure look like? First of all, insofar as 'be' is an inherently impersonal verb, it can reasonably be assumed that as V head it selects a single argument in complement position. Moreover, this sole argument must surely be a small clause with a P-category head. The subject of this clause, i.e. the specifier of the PP, must be the NP expressing the thing possessed. The predicative P' constituent will then associate the NP expressing the possessor with the P head. The outcome should be something like (58).

(58)   ... $[_{VP}$ **be** $[_{PP}$ NP$_{possessee}$ $[_{P'}$ **at** NP$_{possessor}]]]$

This structure clearly displays the two possible choices for any language: if P is not incorporated into V, the P' constituent, i.e. P and the possessor it introduces, must move to the beginning of the sentence where it becomes the support for the predication at the end. This is how a possessive construction without a verb 'have' can arise:

(59)   a.   ... $[_{VP}$ **be** $[_{PP}$ NP$_{possessee}$ $[_{P'}$ **at** NP$_{possessor}]]]$

       b. $[_{P'}$ **at** NP$_{possessor}]_i$ $[_{VP}$ **be** $[_{PP}$ NP$_{possessee}$ $t_i]]$

If, on the other hand, Head Movement incorporates P into V and thus generates a transitive verb meaning 'have', the NP complement of P must become the subject of the predication which follows:

(60)   a.   ... $[_{VP}$ **be** $[_{PP}$ NP$_{possessee}$ $[_{P'}$ **at** NP$_{possessor}]]]$

       b. $[NP_{possessor}]_j$ $[_{VP}$ **be-at**$_i$ $[_{PP}$ NP$_{possessee}$ t_i $t_j]]$

How then does this approach help to explain the apparent contradictions in the Finnish data? To answer this question, it suffices to specify to the commonplace that semantic cases must be the manifestation of P heads. As Nikanne (1993: 77–81) has clearly shown, this notion in no way implies that semantic cases must *themselves* be P heads cliticized on a noun. In Finnish, the position of these morphemes in the word and the phenomenon of case agreement immediately falsify this analysis. The hypothesis which best fits the data would be that "the semantic cases are assigned by empty Ps, each of which correspond[s] to exactly one locative case" (ibid.).

Clearly, if this hypothesis is correct, it provides an interesting solution to the problem stated in 4.1. Historically, the Finnish possessive construction must have been a locative inversion generated as in (59). Thus, the derivation for a sentence like *Pekalla on auto* 'Pekka has a car' must have been as in (61) where the P' constituent moves to the beginning of the sentence after the P head has assigned case to the possessor NP.

(61) a.   ... [$_{VP}$ *on* [$_{PP}$ *auto* [$_{P'}$ P *Pekka-*]]]

b.   ... [$_{VP}$ *on* [$_{PP}$ *auto* [$_{P'}$ P *Peka-lla*]]]

c.   ... [$_{VP}$ *on* [$_{PP}$ *auto* [$_{P'}$ P *Peka-lla*]]]

d.   [$_{P'}$ P *Peka-lla*]$_i$ [$_{VP}$ *on* [$_{PP}$ *auto* t$_i$]]

At some point, however, this construction must have been reanalyzed by speakers without any change in the surface form of the utterance, so that a [SVO] sentence was generated as in (60). This is why *Pekalla on auto* 'Pekka has a car' appears today to be the outcome of the syntactic derivation in (62).

(62) a.   ... [$_{VP}$ *on* [$_{PP}$ *auto* [$_{P'}$ P *Pekka-*]]]

b.   ... [$_{VP}$ *on* [$_{PP}$ *auto* [$_{P'}$ P *Peka-lla*]]]

c.   ... [$_{VP}$ *on* [$_{PP}$ *auto* [$_{P'}$ P *Peka-lla*]]]

d.   ... [$_{VP}$ *on*-P$_i$ [$_{PP}$ *auto* [$_{P'}$ t$_i$ *Peka-lla*]]]

e.   [$_{NP}$ *Peka-lla*]$_j$ [$_{VP}$ *on*-P$_i$ [$_{PP}$ *auto* t$_i$ t$_j$]]

Here the P head without phonetic content is incorporated into V after having assigned case to the possessor NP. This operation results in a transitive verb head (which can therefore assign accusative case) with the semantic content of a verb 'have' but no change of form since the P head is empty. Under these circumstances, the complement of P, the possessor NP, must now move to subject position in the sentence whence it can c-command an anaphoric constituent on the NP for the thing possessed. Its case has no meaning; it is merely the effect of the dependency relationship formed with P at an earlier stage of the derivation.

The value of this kind of analysis is its ability to set up a coherent framework incorporating all the morphological, syntactic, and semantic properties of the Finnish possessive construction. No component is left out. The cost lies in the use of theoretical tools, such as transformations and phonetically null categories, which may give the impression of being too ponderous. Still, this approach "saves the phenomena" just as well if not better than any other. The mere logical possibility that it might be correct should prevent some apparently immediate conclusions from being drawn, such as the assumption that case inflection progressively loses its motivation as syntax evolves.

5. Conclusion

Three major points have been put forward in the present paper: (1) the Finnish genitive case cannot be treated as the semantic case of possession, even in a loose sense. It has neither semantic content nor categorial representation; it merely "reflects" certain syntactic dependency relationships among constituents. It is in short a structural case. (2) As a structural case, the Finnish genitive appears in a wide variety of environments which cannot be subsumed under a common denominator. There are nevertheless a few contexts where apparently genitival forms are actually relics of a semantic lative-dative case which has been progressively grammaticalized into the genitive. (3) In the possessive construction, while other Uralic languages still use a semantic case with dative sense, Finnish requires a static (adessive or inessive) locative case. Although this construction is apparently a locative inversion, it can be shown to consist of a [SVO] sentence, and an explanatory hypothesis can be produced which accounts for all the data.

References

Benveniste, Emile. 1966. *Problèmes de linguistique générale* I. Paris: Gallimard.

Brattico, Pauli and Alina Leinonen. 2009. *Case distribution and nominalization.* Syntax 12: 1–31.

Comrie, Bernard. 1975. The antiergative: Finland's answer to Basque. *Chicago Linguistics Society* 11: 112–121.

Comrie, Bernard. 1977. Subjects and direct objects in uralic languages: a functional explanation of case-marking systems. *Etudes Finno-Ougriennes* 12: 5–17.

Creissels, Denis. 2006. *Syntaxe générale, une introduction typologique* I. Paris: Hermès Lavoisier.

Hakulinen, Auli, Maria Vilkuna, Riitta Korhonen, Vesa Koivisto, Tarja Riitta Heinonen and Irja Alho. 2004. *Iso suomen kielioppi.* Helsinki: Suomalaisen Kirjallisuuden Seura.

Hakulinen, Lauri. 1968. *Suomen kielen rakenne ja kehitys.* Helsinki: Otava.

Havu, Jukka and Carita Klippi. 2006. Une langue, une nation: contexte et corpus de codification du finnois moderne. *Histoire Epistémologie Langage* 28(2): 85–123.

Holmberg, Anders. 2010. The null generic subject pronoun in Finnish: a case of incorporation in T. *Parametric variation: null subjects in minimalist theory,* Theresa Biberauer, Anders Holmberg, Ian Roberts and Michelle Sheehan (eds.), 200–230. Cambridge: Cambridge University Press.

Huumo, Tuomas and Nobufumi Inaba. 1997. Irrallinen genetiivi ja omistusrakenteen ongelma. *Virittäjä* 101(1): 27–48.

Inaba, Nobufumi. 1998. Suomalais-ugrilaisten kielten omistusrakenteesta: typologinen ja geneettinen näkökulma. *Kieliopillistumisesta, analogiasta ja typologiasta,* Anneli Pajunen (ed.), 144–181. Helsinki: Suomalaisen Kirjallisuuden Seura.

Ikola, Osmo. 1964. *Lauseopin kysymyksiä. Tutkielma nykysuomen syntaksin alalta.* Helsinki: Suomalaisen Kirjallisuuden Seura.

Itkonen, Terho. 1968. Zur Frühgeschichte der lappischen und finnischen Lokalkasus. *Congressus secundus internationalis fenno-ugristarum. Pars I. Acta linguistica*, Martti Kahla, Alpo Räisänen and Paavo Ravila (eds.), 202–211. Helsinki: Suomalais-Ugrilainen Seura.

Itkonen, Terho. 1985. *Kieliopas*. Helsinki: Kirjayhtymä.

Jaakola, Minna. 2004. *Suomen genetiivi*. Helsinki: SKS.

Kiparsky, Paul. 2001. Structural case in Finnish. Lingua 111: 315–376.

Korhonen, Mikko. 1987. Les grammaires des langues finno-ougriennes: esquisse historique. *Histoire Epistémologie Langage* 9(1): 91–110.

Korhonen, Mikko. 1996. *Typological and historical studies in language by Mikko Korhonen. A memorial volume published on the 60th anniversary of his birth*. Helsinki: Suomalais-Ugrilainen Seura.

Koskinen, Päivi. 1997. Features and categories. Non-finite constructions in Finnish. PhD dissertation, University of Toronto, Department of Linguistics.

Laitinen, Lea and Maria Vilkuna. 1993. Case-marking in necessive construction and split intransitivity. *Case and other categories in Finnish syntax*, Anders Holmberg and Urpo Nikanne (eds.), 23–48. Berlin and New York: Mouton de Gruyter.

Lehmann, Christian. 1985. Grammaticalization. Synchronic variation and diachronic change. *Lingua e stile* 20: 303–318.

Leino, Jaakko. 2003. *Antaa sen muuttua. Suomen kielen permissiivirakenne ja sen kehitys*. Helsinki: Suomalaisen Kirjallisuuden Seura.

Mahieu, Marc-Antoine. 2007. Cas structuraux et dépendances syntaxiques des expressions nominales en finnois. PhD dissertation, University of Paris-7, Department of Linguistics.

Mahieu, Marc-Antoine. 2008. Les cas structuraux finnois: anti-ergativité scindée et dépendances longue distance. *Etudes Finno-Ougriennes* 39: 65–103.

Mahieu, Marc-Antoine. 2012. Sur la genèse de la phrase dite passive en finnois. *Cahiers d'Études Hongroises et Finlandaises* 18: 47–68.

Maling, Joan. 1993. Of nominative and accusative: the hierarchical assignment of grammatical cases in Finnish. *Case and other categories in Finnish syntax*, Anders Holmberg and Urpo Nikanne (eds.), 49–74. Berlin and New York: Mouton de Gruyter.

Manninen, Satu. 2003. *Small phrase layers. A study of Finnish manner adverbials*. Amsterdam and Philadelphia: John Benjamins.

Milsark, Gary. 1985. Case theory and the grammar of Finnish. *Proceedings of New England Linguistics Society* XV, Steve Berman, Jae-Woong Choe and Joyce McDonough (eds.), 319–331. Amherst: Graduate Linguistic Student Association of the University of Massachusetts.

Nelson, Diane. 1998. *Grammatical case assignment in Finnish*. New York: Garland.

Nikanne, Urpo. 1993. On assigning semantic cases in Finnish. *Case and other categories in Finnish syntax*, Anders Holmberg and Urpo. Nikanne (eds.), 75–87. Berlin and New York: Mouton de Gruyter.

Reime, Hannu. 1993. Accusative marking in Finnish. *Case and other categories in Finnish syntax*, Anders Holmberg and Urpo Nikanne (eds.), 89–109. Berlin and New York: Mouton de Gruyter.

Renault, Richard. 1991. Recherches en syntaxe du finnois: les désinences personnelles. PhD dissertation, University of Paris-8, Department of Linguistics.

Rouveret, Alain. 1998. Points de vue sur le verbe "être". *"Être" et "Avoir". Syntaxe, sémantique, typologie*, Alain Rouveret (ed.), 11–65. Paris: Presses Universitaires de Vincennes.

Sauvageot, Aurélien. 1973. *L'élaboration de la langue finnoise*. Paris: Klincksieck.

Setälä, Emil Nestor. 1898. *Suomen kielioppi: äänne- ja sanaoppi. Oppikoulua ja omin päin opiskelua varten*. Helsinki: Otava.

Taraldsen, Tarald. 1986. On the distribution of nominative objects in Finnish. *Features and projections*, Peter Muysken and Henk van Riemsdijk (eds.), 139–162. Dordrecht: Foris.

Toivainen, Jorma. 1993. The nature of the accusative case in Finnish. *Case and other categories in Finnish syntax*, Anders Holmberg and Urpo Nikanne (eds.), 111–128. Berlin and New York: Mouton de Gruyter.

Vainikka, Anne. 1989. *Deriving syntactic representations in Finnish*. Ahmerst: Graduate Linguistic Student Association of the University of Massachusetts.

Vainikka, Anne. 1993. The three structural cases in Finnish. *Case and other categories in Finnish syntax*, Anders Holmberg and Urpo Nikanne (eds.), 129–159. Berlin and New York: Mouton de Gruyter.

Vilkuna, Maria. 2000. *Suomen lauseopin perusteet*. Helsinki: Edita.

Endnotes

1.   Many thanks to Raymond Boyd, Eva Havu, Jukka Havu, Johanna Kuningas, Alain Rouveret, the two editors of this volume and the two anonymous reviewers for extremely helpful discussion and comments.

2.   This paper focusses on official standard Finnish (*yleiskieli*, the "general language" of the Finnish nation). This standard form is based on the written language (*kirjakieli*) as developed and codified during the second half of the 19th century using features characteristic of the range of regional dialects. It differs in a number of ways from the standard spoken language (*yleispuhekieli*). See Sauvageot (1973); Havu and Klippi (2006).

3.   It will be impossible to discuss all the issues raised by Table 1 in this paper, but closer attention will be given to a few points, particularly the status of the accusative. The genitive morpheme -*n* has several allomorphs including -*den*/-*tten* and -*en* on the plural stem. With the essive, partitive, inessive, elative, adessive, ablative, and abessive cases, the choice of one or the other of these allomorphs will depend on the principle of vowel harmony. For the illative, the symbol V stands for the closest preceding vowel. The comitative and the instructive are non-productive cases.

4.   The glossing in this paper follows the Leipzig Glossing Rules, with the following additions: ABE abessive, ADE adessive, DAT.GEN dative-genitive, ELA elative, ILL illative, INE inessive, PART partitive, PRET preterit, PX possessive suffix.

5.   Note that in Finnish a DP can itself be selected by a D head, as in [$_{DP}$ *tämä* [$_{DP}$ *Pekan* [$_{AP}$ *vanha* [$_{NP}$ *auto*]]]] 'this old car of Pekka's'. For further details on the prenominal genitive in Finnish, see Hakulinen et al. (2004: 566–573). For a more developed theoretical discussion of the conditions on genitive case assignment in the Finnish DP, see Brattico and Leinonen (2009).

6.   Another case would be the adjective *pehmeä* 'soft' in *pumpulin pehmeä* 'soft as cotton'. It is nevertheless possible to account for this case by assuming an N-A compound noun; the components are indeed often written as a single word. Regarding the distribution and semantic value of the genitive in compound nouns, see Hakulinen et al. (2004: 387–421).

7.   It is interesting to note that the quantifiers *paljon* and *vähän* themselves come from a reanalysis of two former nouns in the genitive: *paljo(+n)* 'abundance, large amount' and *vähä(+n)* 'small

amount'. It is uncertain whether they were assigned genitive case for use as preposed noun modifiers (see § 2.1) or, as Toivainen (1993: 122–125) argues, as direct objects of verbs (see § 2.6).

8. In some cases, the adjective in *-inen* and its preposed genitive complement are reanalyzed as a compound: *hyvännäköinen* 'lovely' (< 'fine to be seen'), *luonnonmukainen* 'natural' (< 'matching nature'), *samanikäinen* 'of the same age', *tietyntyyppinen* 'of a certain type', etc.

9. See Manninen (2003) for a more detailed theoretical discussion of the conditions for assignment of the genitive in the Finnish PP.

10. There is no room here for even the briefest discussion of the properties of each of the many types of Finnish participial clauses. See Koskinen (1997) for a detailed theoretical approach to this question.

11. An anonymous reviewer rightly notes that the same construction is acceptable with some inergative verbs (*uskon* [*lapsia leikkivän puistossa*] 'I believe there are children playing in the park'), and even more rarely with some transitive verbs. See Itkonen (1985: 64–65).

12. These are the essential facts. There are, however, complications in specific cases. (1) In interronegative sentences with injunctive import, the object may not take the partitive: *eikö oteta lepohetki?* 'let's take a break!' (< 'don't we take a break?'). (2) A small number of atelic verbs (e.g., *omistaa* 'own', *sisältää* 'contain', *nähdä* 'see', *tietää* 'know', *muistaa* 'remember'), often called "quasi-resultatives", do not assign the partitive to their objects: *omistan talon* 'I own a house'. Conversely, some momentarily telic verbs govern the partitive unless they express the attainment of a resulting state: *ammuin lintua* 'I shot at the bird' (vs. *ammuin linnun* 'I shot the bird dead'). (3) Sometimes in dialogue, if it is clear from the context that a (telic) process is to be viewed as perfective, the partitive can be used, and is even more natural, on the object: – *kirjoitin sen kirjeen* 'I wrote that letter'; – *kuinka kauan kirjoitit sitä?* 'how long did it take you to write it?'; – *kirjoitin sitä pari tuntia* 'I wrote it in a couple of hours'. I thank Jukka Havu and one of the anonymous reviewers for calling my attention to the latter point.

13. See Holmberg (2010) for a theoretical discussion of the issues raised by the syntax of generic sentences.

14. In some varieties of Finnish (child language, eastern dialects), this animacy split would seem also to include given names and the nouns designating immediate kin. In Estonian, it affects only the first and second person pronouns (Mahieu 2008: 76–82).

15. In this sentence, the partitive indicates non-attainment of the telos rather than the atelic nature of the VP as in (44a). If the telos had been attained, the object would have been in the genitive, and the modifier would have shifted to the inessive: *Pekka luki kirjan tunnissa* 'Pekka read the (whole) book <u>in</u> an hour'.

16. See Nikanne (1993: 86): "According to the distribution, binding, and predication facts, the locative and other semantic cases seem to form PPs where the NP in the locative cases is embedded by some head. Because we are dealing with PPs, the head is probably a P." It must be stressed that the notion that semantic cases are the manifestation of P heads in no way implies that these cases are themselves Ps cliticized on nouns (see § 4.2).

17. In a transformational approach, the inherently impersonal nature of the verb *olla* 'be' would suggest that the NP expressing the thing possessed is not directly generated as subject of the sentence but rather as subject of the small clause selected by the verb *olla*, i.e. as specifier of the P head. The deep structure of (49a) would then be $[_{VP}$ *on* $[_{PP}$ *auto* $[_{P'}$ P *Pekan*]]].

18. "'Have' is just 'be-at' turned around" (Benveniste 1966: 199).

The Russian genitive within the NP and the VP

Marleen Van Peteghem and Katia Paykin
Universiteit Gent and Université de Lille 3, UMR 8163 STL

This paper deals with the genitive case in Russian as present within the NP and the VP. We argue that although semantic factors sometimes condition genitive marking, the Russian genitive is not sensitive to the thematic properties of the head and is therefore closer to the structural cases, assigned on purely configurational grounds. From a semantic point of view, the genitive is often related to quantification, indefiniteness, partitivity and decreased referentiality. The common denominator for all types of genitive studied in this paper appears to be the fact that the nominal in the genitive denotes a property rather than an entity and can be analyzed as an N rather than an NP or a DP.

Keywords: genitive, Russian, morphology, case, partitive, numerals, negation, intensional, quantification, indefiniteness, structural case

1. Introduction[1]

The genitive case is known as the most complex among the six Russian cases and has given rise to a huge literature. It is the most irregular case from a morphological point of view and it shows up in a wider range of structures than the genitive in languages such as German or Romanian. It appears not only on adnominal NPs, as in these two languages (1a), but also on various other nominal constituents. It can appear within the VP, on the direct object, as in (1b), and on temporal VP adjuncts, as in (1c).

(1) a. nožk-a *stol-a*[2]
   leg-NOM table-GEN[3]
   'a table's leg'

 b. My ždëm *peremen!*[4]
   we wait.for changes.GEN
   'We are waiting for changes!'

 c. Et-o proizošlo *perv-ogo mart-a.*
   this-NOM happened first-GEN March-GEN
   'This happened on the first of March.'

Furthermore, it can mark arguments of adjectives such as *dostoin* 'worth' or *polon* 'full' (2a) and phrasal comparatives in comparative clauses (2b). In the latter case, it alternates with the clausal comparative introduced by *čem*, which is a *wh*-constituent corresponding to the comparative *than* in English.

(2)   a.   Prijut   ét-ot   dostoin *vnimani-ja*. (RNC)
           shelter.NOM   this-NOM   worth   attention-GEN
           'This shelter is worthy of attention.'

      b.   On vstaët   ran'še   *men-ja*/ran'še,   *čem ja*
           he gets.up   earlier   me-GEN/earlier   than I.NOM
           'He gets up earlier than I do.'

Finally, the genitive case can be assigned[5] by numerous prepositions, expressing, for instance, absence (*bez* 'without', *krome* 'except for'), a goal (*dlja* 'for', *do* 'to', *radi* 'for the sake of'), a source (*iz* 'out of', *ot* 'from', *s* 'down from') or location (*u* 'at', *meždu* 'between'). From a formal point of view, these genitive-assigning prepositions can be simple, as the ones mentioned above, double (*iz-za* 'from behind'), adverbial, which means that they can function either as a preposition or an adverb (*bliz* 'near', *vdol'* 'along'), derived from nouns (*po-sredstv-om* = by + means-INS 'by means of') or resulting from lexicalized PPs (*vo vrem-ja* = in time-ACC 'during').

(3)   a.   Et-o   bljud-o   xarakterno   dlja *finsk-oj*   *kuxn-i*. (RNC)
           this-NOM   dish-NOM   characteristic   for   Finnish-GEN   cooking-GEN
           'This dish is characteristic for Finnish cooking.'

      b.   U nix   ne   vyšlo   nič-ego   iz-za   *pogod-y*. (RNC)
           at they.GEN   NEG   came.out   nothing-GEN   from-behind   weather-GEN
           'Nothing came out of it because of the weather.'

      c.   Ja   plelas'   vdol' *ulic-y*   k dom-u. (RNC)
           I.NOM   dragged.myself   along street-GEN   to house-DAT
           'I was dragging myself along the street to my house.'

As the constraints on all these uses are very different, we will not be able to describe all of them within the space available in this paper. Therefore we have chosen to concentrate on genitive marking within the NP and the VP. Our approach will be primarily descriptive and will take into account both syntactic and semantic properties of the genitive marking. We do not adhere to any particular theoretical framework, but, whenever possible, we will make use of various interesting accounts, mostly in generative grammar (Franks 1994, 1995, 2002, Bailyn 1997, 2004, Harves 2002, Kim 2003, Pesetsky 2007 and many others), which, however, we will not be able to discuss in detail.

The central issue of this study will be to determine whether the genitive case in Russian is a structural or lexical (or inherent) case. The genitive case is generally considered to be a lexical case, which means that it is claimed to be sensitive to the lexical properties of the syntactic head, as opposed to the nominative and accusative cases, which receive their case in a purely configurational way, on the basis of the syntactic position of the NP. However, in Russian, the genitive case can appear both on objects (1b) and on subjects (4), typically structural positions.

(4) a. *Otc-a*   ne   byl-o.
         father-GEN NEG was-IMPERS
         'There was no father.'

  b. Vokrug *ljud-ej*   nabežal-o! (Google)
      around people-GEN came.running-IMPERS
      'People came running from all over!'

Therefore, we will claim that it is a structural case in Russian, in that it is not sensitive to the thematic properties of the head. Semantic factors do sometimes condition genitive marking, especially within the VP, but they are of a totally different nature, and are related to decreased referentiality and quantification.

The study is structured as follows. In Section 2, we will describe genitive morphology in Russian, as it appears on the different lexical categories (nouns, adjectives, pronouns and numerals), and we will discuss its relationship to the so-called direct cases (nominative and accusative) and the oblique cases (dative, instrumental, locative). Section 3 will study the genitive within the NP, i.e. the adnominal genitive (1a), assigned to the nominal complement or modifier of the noun, and the genitive assigned by numerals to an N or an N' (5).

(5) pjat' *jazyk-ov*
     five languages-GEN
     'five languages'

Finally, Section 4 will deal with genitive nominals occurring within the VP, distinguishing among the so-called intensional genitive (6a), assigned by intensional verbs, the genitive of negation (6b), which appears under negation, and the so-called partitive genitive (6c).

(6) a. *Et-oj*   *pravd-y*   vlast'   bojalas' očen' sil'no. (RNC)
         this-GEN truth-GEN authority.NOM feared   very   strongly
         'The authority very much feared this truth.'

  b. Boris   ne   čitaet *knig.*
      Boris.NOM NEG reads books.GEN
      'Boris doesn't read books.'

  c. Ja   nalila *molok-a.*
      I.NOM poured milk-GEN
      'I poured (some) milk.'

2.   Genitive morphology

2.1   The marking of the genitive

Unlike true oblique cases (dative, instrumental, locative), which have only one ending in the plural, neutralizing the opposition between the different genders and inflectional classes, the genitive distinguishes gender both in the singular and in the plural. In the singular, most masculine and neuter nouns take the genitive ending -*a*, whereas most feminine nouns take the ending -*y*. In the plural, the most frequent ending for masculine nouns is -*ov*, whereas most feminine and neuter nouns take a zero ending (cf. Table 1).[6]

The presence of the ending -*a* in both nominative and genitive morphology (with a kind of mirror effect) and the possibility of a zero ending, which is only available in the nominative and in the genitive, have led various authors to group these two cases together (cf. Jakobson 1936, 1957, Feldstein 2002). The genitive plural has even been described as providing the root of the noun, thus as a kind of bare noun (N) or a "primeval" case, opposed to the nominative, which provides the DP (cf. Pesetsky 2007). However, nominative and genitive never display genuine syncretism. Real syncretism is found only between the genitive and oblique cases for one declension class, namely singular feminine nouns ending in a soft consonant (e.g. *žizn'* 'life') or in -*ija* (cf. *armija* 'army'), which have the same form for the genitive, the dative and the locative. Furthermore, it is also found with adjectives[8], whose endings are different from the noun endings and which share their genitive plural form with the locative plural and their feminine singular form with all other oblique cases (i.e. dative, instrumental and locative). As for the personal pronouns, the genitive shows systematic syncretism with the accusative and in the plural also with the locative. Table 2 provides a summary of syncretisms between the genitive case and other cases.

Finally, numerals are also subject to declension, with very irregular patterns, certain numerals showing adjectival morphology (*odin* 'one', *dva* 'two'), others nominal one (*pjat'* 'five'). Still others, such as *sorok* 'forty', *sto* 'one hundred', have only two forms: one form for the nominative/accusative, and a form ending in -*a* for all other cases (*sorok – soroka* 'forty', *sto – sta* 'one hundred').

Table 1. Nominative and genitive forms of nouns[7]

	M		F		N	
	NOM	**GEN**	**NOM**	**GEN**	**NOM**	**GEN**
SG	zak<u>o</u>n-ø 'law'	zak<u>o</u>n-*a*	gaz<u>e</u>t-a 'newspaper'	gaz<u>e</u>t-*y*	d<u>e</u>l-o 'affair'	d<u>e</u>l-*a*
PL	zak<u>o</u>n-y	zak<u>o</u>n-*ov*	gaz<u>e</u>t-y	gaz<u>e</u>t-*ø*	d<u>e</u>l-a	d<u>e</u>l-*ø*

Table 2. Syncretism between genitive and oblique cases

	Nouns	Adjectives		Personal pronouns	
	F ending in a soft consonant[9]	PL	F SG		
NOM	žizn' 'life'	krasiv-ye 'beautiful'	krasiv-aja	ja 'I'	my 'we'
ACC	žizn'	krasiv-ye	krasiv-uju	**men-ja**	**n-as**
GEN	**žizn-i**	**krasiv-yx**	**krasiv-oj**	**men-ja**	**n-as**
DAT	**žizn-i**	krasiv-ym	**krasiv-oj**	mn-e	n-am
INS	žizn'-ju	krasiv-ymi	**krasiv-oj**	mn-oj	n-ami
LOC	**žizn-i**	**krasiv-yx**	**krasiv-oj**	mn-e	**n-as**

In other words, it is not possible to detect a systematic regularity in the syncretisms observed here. In the nominal system, the genitive is opposed to the nominative, without any syncretism. Yet for agreeing categories (adjectives, some pronouns), genuine syncretisms do appear, not between the genitive and the nominative, but between the genitive and oblique cases (mostly the locative).

Furthermore, it should be noted that most endings described above are sensitive to a phonological feature, depending on whether the root ends in a non-palatalized (hard) consonant or in a palatalized (soft) consonant. This phonological feature is pervasive in the phonological system of Russian and is not specific to genitive case morphology. For nouns, it is responsible for the alternation -a/-ja[10] in the masculine and neuter singular, -y/-i in the feminine singular, -ov/-ev or -ej in the masculine and neuter plural, -ø/-ej in the feminine plural, and, for adjectives, between -ogo/ -ego in the masculine/neuter singular, -oj/-ej in the feminine singular and -yx/-ix in the plural.

Table 3 summarizes the possible genitive endings of nouns and adjectives.

Finally, as various studies have pointed out, the absence of systematic correlation between gender and inflection class makes it difficult to establish a hierarchy among the features mentioned above (Bailyn and Nevins 2008). For instance, nouns ending in -a always take the "feminine" genitive ending -y regardless of their gender (7), while, for nouns ending in a soft consonant, it is the gender that determines the inflection class: masculine nouns take the ending -ja, whereas feminine nouns take the ending -i (8).

(7)   a. mužčin-a   –   mužčin-y
         man-NOM.M.SG   man-GEN.M.SG
         'man'

      b. ženščin-a   –   ženščin-y
         woman-NOM.F.SG   woman-GEN.F.SG
         'woman'

Table 3. Overall view of the genitive endings

Ending	Gender/ Number	Examples	Syncretism with	Ending found with other cases for other inflection classes
		NOUNS		
-a/-ja	M SG	M zakon – zakon-a 'law'		NOM F SG
	N SG	M ogon' – ogn-ja 'fire'		NOM N PL
		N okn-o – okn-a 'window'		
		N pol-e – pol-ja 'field'		
-y/-i	F SG	F gazet-a – gazet-y 'newspaper'	all nouns:	
	M SG	F noč – noč-i 'night'	NOM F PL	
	ending in -a	M pap-a – pap-y 'dad'	nouns ending in a soft consonant: DAT SG LOC SG	
-ov/-ev	M PL	M zakon-y – zakon-ov 'laws'		
	N PL (rare)	M gero-i – gero-ev 'heros'		
		N kryl'-ja – kryl'-ev 'wings'		
-ø	F PL	F gazet-y – gazet-ø 'newspapers'		NOM M SG
	N PL	N okn-a – okon-ø 'windows'		
		N zdani-ja – zdanij-ø 'buildings'		
-ej	PL with root ending in a soft consonant	M meč-i – meč-ej 'swords' F noč -i– noč-ej 'nights' N pol-ja – pol-ej 'fields'		INS F SG for nouns ending in a soft consonant
		ADJECTIVES		
-ogo/-ego	M SG N SG	M bol'š-oj/N bol'š-oe – M/N bol'š-ogo 'big' M rann-ij/N rann-ee – M/N rann-ego 'early'		
-oj/-ej	F SG	F bol'š-aja – bol'š-oj 'big' F rann-jaja – rann-ej 'early'	DAT SG INS SG LOC SG	(for -oj only) NOM M SG
-yx/-ix	PL	PL bol'š-ie – bol'š-ix 'big'	DAT PL LOC PL	

(8) a. ogon'   –   ogn-ja
         fire.NOM.M.SG   fire-GEN.M.SG
         'fire'

     b. žizn'   –   žizn-i
         life.NOM.F.SG   life-GEN.F.SG
         'life'

2.2　Genitive/accusative syncretism and animacy

A very particular case of syncretism is found with animate nouns. For masculine animate nouns in the singular and for all animate nouns in the plural, the genitive case lends its morphology to the accusative case, whereas for non-animate nouns and feminine animate nouns in the singular a special genitive form is available (9c), (10c). As noted by Pesetsky (2007), the genitive morphology appears not only on nouns, but also on the agreeing modifier.

(9)　My　　videli　a.　nastojašč-ego　　lingvist-a. (Pesetsky 2007)
　　　we.NOM　saw　　real-GEN.M.SG　　linguist-GEN.M.SG
　　　'We saw　　　　a real linguist.'

　　　　　　vs.　　b.　nastojašč-ij　　　pulemët.
　　　　　　　　　　　real-ACC.M.SG　　machine.gun.ACC.M.SG
　　　　　　　　　　　a real machine gun.'

　　　　　　　　　c.　nastojašč-uju　　sobak-u/lamp-u.
　　　　　　　　　　　real-ACC.F.SG　　dog-ACC.F.SG/lamp-ACC.F.SG
　　　　　　　　　　　a real dog/lamp.'

(10)　My　　videli　a.　*nastojašč-ix*　　*lingvist-ov.*
　　　we.NOM　saw　　real-GEN.M.PL　　linguists-GEN.M.PL
　　　'We saw　　　　real linguists.'

　　　　　　　　　b.　*malen'k-ix*　　　*sobak.*
　　　　　　　　　　　small-GEN.F.PL　　dog.GEN.F.PL
　　　　　　　　　　　(some) small dogs.'

　　　　　　vs.　　c.　nastojašč-ie　　　lamp-y/pulemët-y.
　　　　　　　　　　　real-ACC.F/M.PL　　lamps-ACC.F.PL/
　　　　　　　　　　　　　　　　　　　　machine.guns-ACC.M.PL
　　　　　　　　　　　real lamps/machine guns.'

Moreover, even when a masculine noun has a non-ambiguous accusative ending, as in the case of masculine singular nouns ending in *-a*, which take the accusative ending *-u* just like feminine nouns, the agreeing adjective takes the masculine genitive form (cf. Pesetsky 2007).

(11)　My　　videli *malen'k-ogo*　mužčin-u.
　　　we.NOM　saw　　small-GEN.M.SG　man-ACC.M.SG
　　　'We saw a small man.'

Personal pronouns always have the same form for the genitive and the accusative, even when they do not refer to animates. In the plural, they also share their form with the locative.

(12) a. Et-o   dlja *ne-go*[11] očen' važno.
       this-NOM for him-GEN very important
       'This is very important to him.'

    b. Lar-a   našla *e-go*   (syna, pis'mo) v zelën-om škaf-u.
       Lara-NOM found him/it-ACC (son, letter) in green-LOC closet-LOC
       'Lara found him/it (her son, the letter) in the green closet.'

The behavior of the animate nouns shows that "the syncretic accusative, in both singular and plural, serves to signal the subgender of animacy" (Feldstein 2002). Thus, Russian morphology does seem sensitive to animacy, but this sensitivity is not systematic, as it affects only the accusative case and only singular masculine nouns and all plural nouns.

2.3   *U*-genitive vs. *a*-genitive

Finally, it should be noted that a restricted set of masculine nouns have two genitive forms for the singular: a form ending in *-a/-ja* and a form ending in *-u/-ju* (e.g. *čaj*. NOM – *čaj-a*-GENa or *čaj-u*-GENu 'tea'; *saxar*.NOM – *saxar-a*-GENa or *saxar-u*-GENu 'sugar'), which is morphologically identical to the dative form of these nouns. This *u*-form is considered to be a "second genitive" form (Jakobson 1936), because, for nouns lacking the *u*-form, the *a*-genitive functions as a suppletive form. Furthermore, whenever the *u*-form is possible, it is always a variant of an *a*-form, sometimes giving rise to a different interpretation, as shown by the translation of (13b,c).

(13) a. kusok   *saxar-a* / *saxar-u*
       piece.NOM sugar-GENa / sugar-GENu
       'a piece of sugar'

    b. *Les-a*   net.   b'. *Les-u*   net.
       forest-GENa is.not   forest-GENu is.not
       'There is no forest.'   'There is no wood.'

    c. ujti iz   *dom-a*   c'. ujti iz   *dom-u*
       leave from house-GENa   leave from house-GENu
       'leave one's family'   'leave the house for some time'

Many linguists (Jakobson 1936, Neidle 1988, Paus 1994, Franks 1995) have argued that the *u*-form is a partitive case because it appears mostly on mass nouns such as *saxar* 'sugar', *čaj* 'tea', *mëd* 'honey' or *ris* 'rice'. As we shall see below (§ 3.1.1.5 and § 4.3), it is generally used in semantically partitive contexts, in which it can always alternate with the *a*-genitive (Brown and Franks 1995). As shown by Paus (1994) and Fischer (2003), this form is declining in contemporary Russian.

    However, the *u*-morphology is also available for count nouns such as *raz* 'time', *čas* 'hour', *dom* 'house', and can be used without partitive meaning, namely when it is governed by prepositions (13c). Therefore we will not label this form "partitive" here, reserving this label for a particular use of the genitive (§ 4.3).

3.   Genitive case within the NP

Within the NP, two kinds of genitive case can be distinguished:

- the 'adnominal genitive', which marks the nominal complement or modifier of the head noun of the NP. This is the most typical use of the genitive in case languages;
- the 'genitive of quantification', which marks the noun (and its possible modifier) preceded by a numeral or some other quantifying specifier.

3.1   The adnominal genitive

One of the most widely accepted uses of the genitive case cross-linguistically is the adnominal genitive. While 18th and 19th century Russian could use the adnominal genitive for almost any combination of two nouns (Vinogradov and Švedova 1964), in Modern Russian this use is limited. The adnominal genitive has sometimes been replaced by a PP, in which the preposition can govern various cases, or by a nominal in the dative or instrumental. Nevertheless, even in contemporary Russian, the adnominal genitive still covers a large array of semantic relations between the head noun and the genitive noun. This explains why Russian grammars (cf. among others, Vinogradov and Istrina 1960, Švedova et al. 1980) and authors like Knorina (1988) tend to distinguish several sub-types, based exclusively on the lexical meaning of the nouns combined. Rappaport (2000), in his turn, proposes to divide the adnominal genitive into three sub-types in terms of syntactic relations between the head noun and the genitive noun: specifier, complement and adjunct. In what follows, we will try to combine the two approaches and come up with some semantico-syntactic tests regulating a system that takes into account both the meaning of the two nouns and their syntactic relation.

3.1.1   *Formal criteria*
We will first examine predicate agreement and selectional restrictions. These criteria can allow us to determine the semantic nucleus of the complex NP, which, as we will see, can be either the head noun or the genitive noun. Other criteria we will use are based on the competition between the genitive and other kinds of constituents. We will comment on: (i) possessive pronouns, (ii) possessive and denominal adjectives, (iii) various PPs, and (iv) various interrogatives that can be used to question the adnominal genitive.

As the adnominal genitive generally follows the head noun, we will call the first noun N1 and the adnominal genitive N2, without taking into account its constituent type (N, N', NP, DP[12]).

3.1.1.1   *Predicate agreement and selectional restrictions.* The adnominal genitive is assigned to N2 by N1, which is usually considered as the syntactic head as it governs predicate agreement.

(14)   a.   Obsužden-e   *ét-ogo*   *vopros-a*
            discussion-NOM.N.SG this-GEN.M.SG   question-GEN.M.SG
            zanjal-o   nemalo   vrem-eni. (RNC)
            took-N.SG not.little time-GEN
            'The discussion of this question has taken some time.'

       b.   Ulic-u   peregoražival-a   čërn-aja   kuč-a
            street-ACC   partitioned.off-F.SG black-NOM.F.SG heap-NOM.F.SG
            ljud-ej. (RNC)
            people-GEN.PL
            'A huge crowd was blocking the street.'

Most NPs containing an adnominal genitive do not allow predicate agreement with N2 (15a), although some N1, such as *množestvo* 'multitude' or *para* 'couple', allow double agreement and therefore behave as quantitative specifiers (15b).

(15)   a.   V ét-o   vrem-ja   grupp-a   *ljud-ej*
            at this-ACC time-ACC   group-NOM.F.SG   people-GEN.PL
            otošl-a/*otošl-i   ot   skam'-i. (RNC)
            moved.away-F.SG/*PL   from   bench-GEN
            'At this moment, a group of people moved away from the bench.'

       b.   Neožidanno iz-za   derev'-ev vyskočil-o/vyskočil-i
            suddenly   from-behind   trees-GEN sprang.out-N.SG/PL
            množestv-o   *ljud-ej.* (RNC)
            multitude-NOM.N.SG   people-GEN.PL
            'Suddenly, a multitude of people sprang out from behind the trees.'

Generally, N1 functions not only as a syntactic head, but also as a semantic head, sensitive to the selectional restrictions imposed by the verb or another predicate (16).

(16)   Čelovek *serdečn-ogo um-a*   [...] voznenavidel   bomb-y. (RNC)
       man.NOM hearty-GEN intellect-GEN [...] conceived.a.hatred bombs-ACC
       'A/The man of warm-hearted intellect [...] conceived a hatred for bombs.'

However, in some cases, these complex NPs can be ambiguous, allowing both nouns as a semantic head, depending on the context (17).

(17)   a.   Kol-ja   molča   vypil kružk-u   *piv-a.* (RNC)
            Kolja-NOM   silently drank tankard-ACC beer-GEN
            'Kolja silently drained a glass of beer.'

b. Aleksandr   pododvinul ko mn-e   kružk-u   *piv-a*. (RNC)
   Alexander.NOM pushed   to me-DAT tankard-ACC beer-GEN
   'Alexander pushed toward me a glass of beer.'

Although the adnominal genitive can cover a great variety of semantic relations, it cannot link any two unrelated nouns. Unlike the French *de*-construction, for example, which can produce an infinite number of nominal pairs, Russian adnominal genitive is not fit to express contingent relations, as illustrated in (18). These types of relations are usually specified by various prepositions, governing either the genitive or another case.

(18) a. Ja   snova videl devušk-u *(iz)   *poezd-a*.
         I.NOM again saw   girl-ACC *(from) train-GEN

vs. b. J'ai   revu   la fille *du   train*.
        I have seen.again the girl of.the train
        'I saw the girl from the train again.'

3.1.1.2   *Genitive vs. possessive pronouns.* Our second criterion concerns pronouns that can alternate with N2. Russian has both possessive and genitive pronouns. Possessive pronouns behave syntactically and morphologically as adjectives in that they are mostly placed before the noun (although they can follow it) and agree with the noun in number, case and, in the singular, also in gender (cf. *mo-j* 'my-M.SG' – *mo-ja* 'my-F.SG' – *mo-ë* 'my-N.SG' – *mo-ix* 'my-PL'). By contrast, genitive pronouns generally follow the noun and do not agree with it. Variation depends exclusively on the referent (person, number, and in 3SG also the gender of the antecedent) (cf. *men-ja* 'me-GEN', *teb-ja* 'you-GEN.SG', *e-go* 'him-GEN', *e-ë* 'her-GEN', *n-as* 'we-GEN', *v-as* 'you-GEN.PL', *i-x* 'them-GEN'). For the non-reflexive third person, both singular and plural, Russian possesses exclusively genitive pronouns, which can also function as possessive pronouns.

(19) a. Vozmožna li   registraci-ja   *men-ja/e-go*
         possible   whether registration-NOM me-GEN/him-GEN
         po mest-u   rabot-y? (Google)
         on place-LOC work-GEN
         'Is it possible to register me/him according to the place of work?'

    b. *Mo-ja/E-go*   duš-a   ulybaetsja. (Google)
       my-NOM.F/him-GEN soul-NOM.F smiles
       'My/his soul is smiling.'

Given that 1SG and 2SG pronouns have two distinct forms (*mo-j* 'my' vs. *men-ja* 'me-GEN', *tvo-j* 'your' vs. *teb-ja* 'you-GEN'[13], they are a better criterion for the distinction than the ambiguous third person forms. However, these pronouns are necessarily human, and are, therefore, semantically restricted.

3.1.1.3 *Adnominal genitive vs. adjectival forms.* The adnominal genitive can also alternate with a denominal adjective. Three kinds of adjectives can replace the adnominal genitive.

The so-called possessive adjectives, derived mostly from a kin noun by means of the suffixes *-ov/-ev* and *-in*. They have a strictly possessive meaning, always presenting an individual as a possessor.

(20) a. *D'jakon-ov*   syn   priexal v sel-o
         deacon-ADJ.NOM son.NOM came in village-ACC
         k   roditel-jam. (Google)
         to parents-DAT
         'Deacon's son came to the village to see his parents.'

   b. Starš-ij   syn   *d'jakon-a* pogib   na front-e. (Google)
       eldest-NOM son.NOM deacon-GEN perished on front-LOC
       'Deacon's eldest son was killed at the front.'

Denominal adjectives derived with the suffixes *-skij, -ckij, -ij*. In the early 19th century, they could express possession in a strict sense (Vinogradov and Švedova 1964), but nowadays they are particularly used to express a characteristic pertaining to a person or an object (21a). Nevertheless, when the so-called possessive adjective (of type i) is not available, these adjectives can have a possessive reading even in Modern Russian (21b), just like the genitive nouns, which can also give rise to either a type or a possessive reading.

(21) a. Maš-a   ispolnila svo-j   *sosed-sk-ij*
         Masha-NOM fulfilled   her.own-ACC neighbor-ADJ-ACC
         dolg: proinformirovala Kat-ju   o
         duty.ACC informed   Katia-ACC about
         [dvor-ov-yx   novost-jax]. (Google)
         courtyard-ADJ-LOC news-LOC
         'Masha has fulfilled her neighborly duty: she gave Katia the courtyard news.'

   a'. Ja   vypolnil svo-j   dolg   *sosed-a*. (Google)
       I.NOM fulfilled my.own-ACC duty.ACC neighbor-GEN
       'I fulfilled my neighbor-duty.'

   b. *Sosed-sk-aja*   čërn-aja   košk-a   sidela na
       neighbor-ADJ-NOM black-NOM cat-NOM sat   on
       podokonnik-e. (RNC)
       window.sill-LOC
       'A neighbor's/neighbors' black cat was sitting on the window-sill.'

   b'. E-mu   košk-a *sosed-ej*   razodrala glaz. (Google)
       him-DAT cat-NOM neighbors-GEN tore   eye.ACC
       'A neighbors' cat has torn up his eye.'

Finally, denominal adjectives derived through a variety of suffixes, which can be considered as purely qualitative adjectives.

(22) a. Nin-a   odelas' v bel-oe   *šëlk-ov-oe*   plat'-e. (RNC)
Nina-NOM dressed in white-ACC silk-ADJ-ACC dress-ACC
'Nina put on a white silk dress.'

   b. Mat'   čašče   vs-ego nadevala
mother.NOM most.frequently all-GEN put.on
plat'-e   *sero-golub-ogo šëlk-a*. (RNC)
dress-ACC grey-blue-GEN silk-GEN
'My mother most frequently wore her dress of grey-bluish silk.'

When contrasted with all these adjectives, the adnominal genitive shows two specific features.

–   Since N2 can be pluralized, it can distinguish formally and semantically between individual and group possessors, whereas the corresponding adjective cannot mark this distinction. While example (21b) with the adnominal adjective *sosed-skij* 'neighbor' provides no information about the number of neighbors involved, the adnominal genitive construction, as in (21b') allows the number distinction.

–   Another difference between the adjectives and the adnominal genitive is that the genitive can take modifiers or complements, which is impossible for the adjectives.

(23) a. knig-i   *mo-ej starš-ej sestr-y*
books-NOM my-GEN elder-GEN sister-GEN
'my elder sister's books'

   b. *starš-ie   *sestr-in-y*   knig-i
elder-NOM sister-ADJ-NOM books-NOM

vs. b'. *sestr-in-y*   knig-i
sister-ADJ-NOM books-NOM
'my sister's books'

3.1.1.4   *Adnominal genitive vs. various PPs.* Some adnominal genitive nouns can also alternate with PPs headed by various prepositions, the most frequent ones being *ot* 'of, from' and *iz* 'of, out of, from', both governing the genitive case. The most frequent meaning of both is source or origin, the preposition *iz* emphasizing the fact that the origin is located inside the entity (24c). The same preposition *iz* can also be used to denote constitutive parts or material (25).

(24) a. nožk-a *stol-a*   vs. a'. nožk-a *ot   stol-a*
leg-NOM table-GEN   leg-NOM from table-GEN
'a table's leg'   'a leg from a table'

b. dym   *kostr-a*   vs. b'. dym   *ot*   *kostr-a*
smoke.NOM bonfire-GEN   smoke.NOM from bonfire-GEN
'a bonfire's smoke'   'smoke from a bonfire'

c. čelovek   *gorod-a*   vs. c'. čelovek   *iz*   *gorod-a*
person.NOM city-GEN   person.NOM from city-GEN
'an urban person'   'a person from a city'

(25) a. buket   *cvet-ov*   vs. a'. buket   *iz*   *cvet-ov*
bouquet.NOM flowers-GEN   bouquet.NOM out.of flowers-GEN
'a bouquet of flowers'   'a bouquet made of flowers'

b. plat'-e   *dorog-oj*   *šerst-i*
dress-NOM expensive-GEN wool-GEN
'a dress of expensive wool'

vs. b'. plat'-e   *iz*   *dorog-oj*   *šerst-i*
dress-NOM out.of expensive-GEN wool-GEN
'a dress made of expensive wool'

Some adnominal genitive nouns can alternate with a PP introduced by the preposition *s* 'with' + INS, which denotes contents. Unlike complex NPs with an adnominal genitive, which can be ambiguous in terms of their semantic head, NPs with PPs present N1 as their unambiguous semantic nucleus (26).

(26) a. Viktor   podnjal stakan   *molok-a* / *s*   *molok-om.*
Victor.NOM raised   glass.ACC milk-GEN / with milk-INS
'Victor raised a glass of milk/filled with milk.'

b. Viktor   vypil stakan   *molok-a* / **s*   *molok-om.*
Victor.NOM drank glass.ACC milk-GEN / *with milk-INS
'Victor drank a glass of milk/*filled with milk.'

Another preposition that apparently alternates with the adnominal genitive is the preposition *u* 'at, next to', governing the genitive case as well. However, the *u*-PP is primarily used as a verb argument, and denotes the possessor in constructions of inalienable possession (cf. Paykin and Van Peteghem 2003). It is not part of the NP and competes with the adnominal genitive only inside secondary predication contexts.

(27) a. Sosed   *Svet-y*   / *u Svet-y*   – svjaščennik. (Google)
neighbor.NOM Sveta-GEN / at Sveta-GEN   priest.NOM
'Sveta's neighbor is a priest./Sveta has a neighbor who is a priest.'

vs. b. Esli ty   sosed   *Svet-y*   / **u Svet-y,*
if   you.NOM neighbor.NOM Sveta-GEN / *at Sveta-GEN
ty   *mo-j*   drug.
you.NOM my-NOM friend.NOM
'If you are Sveta's neighbor, you are my friend.'

3.1.1.5   *A-genitive vs.* u-*genitive.* Another criterion is based on the morphological distinction between genitive forms ending in -*a* or -*u*. As noted above (§ 2.3), this criterion can only be used for a limited number of masculine nouns with two genitive forms, but it provides a useful test, as both forms can appear only in certain types of adnominal genitive structures.

(28) a.   cvet   *čaj-a*   / **čaj-u*
            color.NOM tea-GENa / *tea-GENu
            'the color of the tea'

vs.   b.   čašk-a   *čaj-a*   / *čaj-u*
            cup-NOM   tea-GENa / tea-GENu
            'a cup of tea'

3.1.1.6   *Interrogatives.* Various interrogative forms can be used to question N2:

–   *kogo* 'of whom', genitive of *kto* 'who', available only for humans; it is invariable and does not agree with N1;
–   *čego* 'of what', invariable genitive form of *čto* 'what', available only for inanimates; just like *kogo*, it does not agree with N1;
–   *čej* 'whose', used only with humans; it agrees in gender and number, but never in case, with the noun it modifies and always conveys a possessive meaning;
–   *kakoj* 'which, what kind of', behaving as a genuine adjective both syntactically and morphologically as it agrees in gender, number and case with N1.

(29) knig-a   *mo-ego brat-a*
       book-NOM my-GEN brother-GEN
       'my brother's book'

vs.   a.   knig-a   k-ogo?
            book-NOM who-GEN
            'a book of whom?'

vs.   b.   *knig-a   č-ego?
            book-NOM what-GEN

vs.   c.   č'-ja   knig-a?
            whose-NOM book-NOM
            'whose book?'

vs.   d.   #kak-aja   knig-a?[14]
            which-NOM book-NOM
            #'which book?'

(30) čelovek   *vysok-ogo rost-a*
       person.NOM high-GEN height-GEN
       'a tall person'

| vs. | a. | *čelovek | k-ogo? |
| | | person.NOM | who-GEN |

| vs. | b. | *čelovek | č-ego? |
| | | person.NOM | what-GEN |

| vs. | c. | *č-ej | čelovek? |
| | | whose-NOM | person.NOM |

vs.	d.	kak-oj	čelovek?
		which-NOM	person.NOM
		'what kind of a person?'	

Furthermore, the N1 of some complex NPs can be questioned by *skol'ko* 'how much/many', which assigns the genitive only in its invariable adverbial form ending in *-o* (see § 3.2.1 below). It typically questions quantity.

(31) a. stakan   *molok-a*   b. skol'k-o   *molok-a?*
          glass.NOM milk-GEN   how.much-ADV milk-GEN
          'a glass of milk'   'how much milk?'

On the basis of all these formal criteria, we will distinguish several types of the adnominal genitive, which can be further subdivided into various subtypes.

3.1.2   *Semantico-syntactic classification of adnominal genitive constructions*
The criterion of substitution by an interrogative allows us to distinguish three main types of the adnominal genitive, which will be examined successively in this section.

i.   The *kakoj*-type, corresponding to genitive adjuncts. The interrogative form *kakoj* concerns N2 (e.g. *čelovek bol'šogo uma* 'a person of great intelligence' – *kakoj čelovek?* 'what kind of a person?').
ii. The *skol'ko*-type: the interrogative *skol'ko* concerns N1 and provides information on quantity (e.g. *stakan moloka* 'a glass of milk' – *skol'ko moloka?* 'how much milk?').
iii. The *kogo/čego*-type, subsuming several categories of the adnominal genitive (possessive, argumental, etc., as in *sobaka dočeri* 'my daughter's dog' – *sobaka kogo?* 'a dog of whom?').

3.1.2.1   *The* kakoj-*type.* In this type of construction, N2 denotes a characteristic of the N1 referent and can be assimilated to an adjunct. N1 functions as the semantic head. In the majority of cases, N2 contains a modifier[15] and can occur as a predicate.

(32) a. čelovek   *krepk-ogo zdorov'-ja*
          person.NOM strong-GEN health-GEN
          'a person of sound health'

b. Čelovek   ét-ot   byl *krepk-ogo zdorov'-ja*
    person.NOM this-NOM was strong-GEN health-GEN
    'This person was of sound health'

This type of adnominal genitive cannot be replaced by a possessive adjective and never alternates with a pronoun (#*moj čelovek* 'my man'; **čelovek men-ja* man.NOM me-GEN). This is due to the fact that the genitive modifier has no possessive meaning.

However, the relationship between N1 and N2 can be transformed into a possessive one. In this case, we obtain a complex NP of the *kogo/čego*-type (§ 3.1.2.3).

(33) a. čelovek   *krepk-ogo zdorov'-ja*
         person.NOM strong-GEN health-GEN
         'a person of sound health'

     b. (krepk-oe)   zdorov'-e   *čelovek-a*
         (strong-NOM) health-NOM person-GEN
         'the (strong) health of a person'

Furthermore, N2 can give rise to a derived qualitative adjective (type (ii) or (iii), see § 3.1.1.3) thus losing its modifier, as in (34a), or keeping it in an adverbial form, as in (34b).

(34) a. devušk-a *redk-oj   krasot-y*
         girl-NOM rare-GEN beauty-GEN
         'a girl of rare beauty'

     a'. *krasiv-aja*   devušk-a
          beautiful-NOM.F.SG girl-NOM.F.SG
          'a beautiful girl'

     b. dokument   *osobenn-oj   važnost-i*
         document.NOM particular-GEN importance-GEN
         'a document of particular importance'

     b'. *osobenn-o   važn-yj*   dokument
          particular-ADV important-NOM document.NOM
          'a particularly important document'

N2 never displays the *u*-morphology. Depending on the semantic relations between N1 and the genitive modifier, the latter allows alternation with a PP governed by the prepositions *s* + INS or *iz* + GEN.

(35) a. čelovek   *gorjač-ego serdc-a*   [characteristic]
         person.NOM hot-GEN   heart-GEN
         'a person of a fervent heart'

a′. čelovek   s   gorjač-im serdc-em
     person.NOM with hot-INS   heart-INS
     'a person with a fervent heart'

b.   stol   krasn-ogo derev-a   [material]
     table.NOM red-GEN   wood-GEN
     'a table of red wood'

b′. stol   iz   krasn-ogo derev-a[16]
     table.NOM out.of   red-GEN   wood-GEN
     'a table made out of red wood'

3.1.2.2 *The* skol'ko-*type.* In adnominal genitive constructions allowing the interrogative *skol'ko*, N1 is interpreted as expressing quantity and, in this interpretation, the semantic nucleus of the NP is N2. This type of construction is the only type of adnominal genitive that allows N2 as a semantic head. However, it can have another interpretation in which the semantic nucleus is N1. In the latter case, the corresponding interrogative form is *kogo/čego*, the quantity interrogative being unavailable. The question no longer concerns N1 but N2.

(36) a.   stakan   molok-a
           glass.NOM milk-GEN
           'a glass of milk'

      a′. skol'k-o   molok-a?   a″. stakan   č-ego?
           how.much-ADV   milk-GEN   glass.NOM what-GEN
           'how much milk?'   'a glass of what?'

      b.   kusok   xleb-a
           piece.NOM bread-GEN
           'a piece of bread'

      b′. skol'k-o   xleb-a?   b″. kusok   č-ego?
           how.much-ADV   bread-GEN   piece.NOM what-GEN
           'how much bread?'   'a piece of what?'

      c.   kuč-a   utok
           heap-NOM   ducks.GEN
           'a bunch of ducks'

      c′. skol'k-o   utok?   c″. kuč-a   k-ogo?
           how.much-ADV   ducks.GEN   heap-NOM   whom-GEN
           'how many ducks?'   'a heap of what?'
           'how many ducks?'   'a heap of what?'

      d.   ozer-o   krov-i
           lake-NOM   blood-GEN
           'a lake of blood'

    d'. skol'k-o   krov-i?   d". ozer-o   č-ego?
       how.much-ADV blood-GEN   lake-NOM what-GEN
       'how much blood?'   '   a lake of what?'

N2 can only be a mass noun or a bare plural. As for N1, it denotes either a container (36a), a measure (36b), a group (36c), or any other entity that can be interpreted as a measure (36d).

Some of these complex NPs allow an alternation with a genitive pronoun (37a), but never with the possessive pronoun (37b), which always has a possessive reading, with the possessive adjective (37c), or any other kind of adjective (37d).

(37) a. kusok   *men-ja*
          piece.NOM me-GEN
          'a piece of me'

      b. #*mo-j*   stakan
          my-NOM glass.NOM
          #'my glass'

      c. **ut-in-aja*   kuč-a
          duck-ADJ-NOM heap-NOM

      d. **moloč-n-yj* stakan
          milk-ADJ-NOM glass.NOM

When the *u*-form is available, the alternation between the *a*-form and the *u*-form is possible.

(38) a. kusok   *saxar-a* / *saxar-u*
          piece.NOM sugar-GENa / sugar-GENu
          'a piece of sugar'

      b. stakan *čaj-a*   / *čaj-u*
          glass.NOM tea-GENa / tea-GENu
          'a cup of tea'

Depending on the semantic relation expressed, N2 can alternate with PPs governed by various prepositions, such as *iz* (for constitutive parts, cf. (39a)), or *s* (for the content, cf. (39b)). However no alternation with *ot* or *u* is available.

(39) a. buket   *cvet-ov*
          bouquet.NOM flowers-GEN
          'a bouquet of flowers'

      a'. buket   *iz*   *cvet-ov*
          bouquet.NOM out.of flowers-GEN
          'a bouquet made of flowers'

b. stakan   *molok-a*
    glass.NOM milk-GEN
    'a glass of milk'

b'. stakan   *s*   *molok-om*
    glass.NOM with milk-INS
    'a glass with milk'

3.1.2.3 *The* kogo/čego-*type.* The *kogo/čego*-type constitutes the most prototypical use of the adnominal genitive cross-linguistically. Although it subsumes several subtypes, it can be characterized by various formal criteria as a class distinct from the previous two. In addition to the possibility of using the interrogative *kogo/čego*, these criteria are the following:

- N1 always functions as a semantic nucleus (vs. *skol'ko*-type).
- The adnominal genitive can alternate with a possessive adjective, when available (vs. both other types).
- Substitution of the adnominal genitive by a possessive pronoun is generally possible (vs. both other types).
- Nouns with *u*-morphology cannot use it in this construction (vs. *skol'ko*-type).

(40) a. knig-a   mam-y   a'. mam-in-a   knig-a
         book-NOM mom-GEN   mom-ADJ-NOM book-NOM
         'a book of my mom's'   'my mom's book'

     a''. e-ë   knig-a
          she-GEN book-NOM
          'her book'

     b. priezd   mam-y   b'. mam-in   priezd
         arrival.NOM mom-GEN   mom-ADJ.NOM arrival.NOM
         'the arrival of my mom's'   'my mom's arrival'

     b''. e-ë   priezd
          she-GEN arrival.NOM
          'her arrival'

     c. registraci-ja   mam-y
         registration-NOM mom-GEN
         'the registration of my mom's'

     c'. mam-in-a   registraci-ja
         mom-ADJ-NOM registration-NOM
         'my mom's registration'

     c''. e-ë   registraci-ja
          she-GEN registration-NOM
          'her registration'

As is well known, this class is highly heterogeneous and various classifications have been proposed, which we cannot all examine here. Traditionally, three main classes are distinguished, based on the semantic relation between N1 and N2: the 'genitivus possessivus' (40a), the 'genitivus subiectivus' (40b) and the 'genitivus obiectivus' (40c). However, this division does not cover the entire array of semantic relations available (part-whole, cause, source, origin, etc.).[17] On the basis of formal characteristics, the most widely adopted classification contrasts the possessive type (40a) with the argument type, including the 'subject type' (40b) and the 'object type' (40c). In Russian, the possessive subtype can be distinguished from the argument subtype by the possibility of replacing the possessive genitive by the *u*-construction, which is not available for the argument genitive as in (41b, c).

(41) a. Sosed   *Svet-y*   – svjaščennik. (Google)
       neighbor.NOM Sveta-GEN   priest.NOM
       'Sveta's neighbor is a priest.'

   a'. Sosed   *u Svet-y*   – svjaščennik. (Google)
       neighbor.NOM at Sveta-GEN   priest.NOM
       'Sveta has a neighbor who is a priest.'

   b. priezd   *mam-y*
      arrival.NOM mom-GEN
      'my mom's arrival'

   b'. *priezd   *u mam-y*
       arrival.NOM at mom-GEN

   c. registraci-ja   *mam-y*
      registration-NOM mom-GEN
      'the registration of my mom's'

   c'. #registraci-ja   *u mam-y*
       registration-NOM at mom-GEN

Moreover, the argument subtype contrasts with the possessive subtype by the nature of the head noun, which denotes an event (*priezd* 'arrival') or its result (*risunok* 'drawing'), and is often directly related to a verb. Therefore, N1 preserves the verbal argument structure and N2 can correspond either to the subject of the verb, as in (40b), or to its object (40c).

However, other formal criteria allow another dividing line between the possessive and the subject subtypes on the one hand and the object subtype on the other. The most important features supporting this distinction are the following:

– The interrogative *čej* can be used only with the possessive and the subjective subtypes.

(42) a. knig-a   *mam-y*   – *č'-ja*   knig-a?
          book-NOM mom-GEN   whose-NOM book-NOM
          'my mom's book'   'whose book?'

      b. priezd   *mam-y*   – *č-ej*   priezd?
          arrival.NOM mom-GEN   whose-NOM arrival.NOM
          'my mom's arrival'   'whose arrival?'

      c. registraci-ja   *mam-y*   – **č'-ja*   registraci-ja
          registration-NOM mom-GEN   whose.NOM registration-NOM
          'my mom's registration'

–   The objective type can alternate with a genitive pronoun of 1SG/PL and 2SG/PL.

(43) a. registraci-ja   *men-ja*
          registration-NOM me-GEN
          'the registration of myself'

      b. *priezd   *men-ja*
          arrival.NOM me-GEN

      c. *knig-a   *men-ja*
          book-NOM   me-GEN

This distinction corresponds to the syntactic division proposed by Rappaport (2000) between specifiers (possessive and subject subtypes) and complements (object subtype), both contrasted with the adjunct type (our *kakoj*-type). However, Rappaport's specifier subtype also includes our *skol'ko*-type, which is clearly distinct. Therefore, Rappaport's syntactic distinction cannot account for the entire range of formal properties that can be observed.[18]

In spite of the differences between the subtypes of the *kogo/čego*-type, they occupy the same syntactic position, as they cannot appear together with the same head noun.[19] Moreover, like in English, the argumental subtype can be ambiguous between a subject and an object reading, although cases of ambiguity are quite rare in Russian and, according to Paducˇeva (1984), are the exception rather than a rule.

(44) a. [subject]
          Ty   vynosiš semej-n-ye   vopros-y   na
          you.NOM submit family-ADJ-ACC questions-ACC on
          obsuždeni-e   *sosed-ej*. (Google)
          discussion-ACC neighbors-GEN
          'You submit family questions to the discussion among neighbors.'

      b. [object]
          Obsuždeni-e   *sosed-ej*   – ét-o   važna-ja
          discussion-NOM neighbors-GEN this-NOM important-NOM

obščestvenn-aja rabot-a. (Google)
public-NOM   work-NOM
'Discussing neighbors is an important public activity.'

When a transitive deverbal noun preserves both arguments, it is the object noun that is genitive-marked, whereas the subject argument gets the instrumental case.

(45) a. *oformleni-e   *det-ej*   *zal-a*
          decoration-NOM children-GEN hall-GEN

     a'. oformleni-e   *det'-mi*   *zal-a*
          decoration-NOM children-INS hall-GEN
          'the decoration of the hall by children'

     b. *ispolneni-e   *pevic-y*   *sonat-y*
          performance-NOM singer-GEN sonata-GEN

     b'. ispolneni-e   *pevic-ej*   *sonat-y*
          performance-NOM singer-INS sonata-GEN
          'the performance of the sonata by the singer'

When the argument is pronominal, it can be expressed by a possessive pronoun, which can correspond either to a subject or an object argument. When combined with an adnominal genitive, it is always interpreted as the subject; when combined with an instrumental, it is interpreted as the object.

(46) a. [subject reading of *ego*]
          e-go   osuždeni-e   *svjaščenn-oj vojn-y* (Google)
          he-GEN censure-NOM holy-GEN   war-GEN
          'his censure of the holy war'

     b. [object reading of *ego*]
          e-go   osuždeni-e   *avtoritet-ami*   nauk-i (Google)
          he-GEN censure-NOM authorities-INS science-GEN
          'his censure by science authorities'

However, for non-ambiguous genitive pronouns (1SG/PL & 2SG/PL) (47a), only the object interpretation is available. To obtain a non-ambiguous subject reading, the instrumental pronoun should be used, which is only possible with nouns derived from transitive verbs.[20]

(47) a. [non-ambiguous object]
          osuždeni-e   *men-ja*
          censure-NOM me-GEN
          'the censure of me'

    b. [non-ambiguous subject]
        osuždeni-e   *mn-oj*
        censure-NOM me-INS
        'the censure by me'

    c. [intransitive verb]
        *priezd   *men-ja* / *priezd   *mn-oj*
        arrival.NOM me-GEN / arrival.NOM me-INS

Nevertheless, according to Rappaport (2000), two adnominal genitives can co-occur when they belong to different above-mentioned types. For instance, the *kakoj*-type can combine with the *kogo/čego*-type or with the possessive/subject subtype. Unlike what has been noted by Rappaport (2000), however, the order of the two genitives is not rigid, but depends on a number of parameters, which we cannot study here. Moreover, Russian tends to avoid this type of structures, preferring to replace the *kakoj*-type by the equivalent adjective.

(48) a. ?uxod   *mo-ego brat-a   neobyčajn-oj   pospešnost-i*
        departure.NOM my-GEN brother-GEN extraordinary-GEN haste-GEN
        'my brother's departure of extraordinary haste'

      b. ??uxod   *neobyčajn-oj   pospešnost-i mo-ego brat-a*
        departure.NOM extraordinary-GEN haste-GEN   my-GEN brother-GEN
        'my brother's departure of extraordinary haste'

      c. *neobyčajno   pospešn-yj* uxod   *mo-ego brat-a*
        extraordinarily hasty-NOM departure.NOM my-GEN brother-GEN
        'my brother's extraordinarily hasty departure'

In conclusion, the adnominal genitive can express various semantic relations to N1, which necessarily result from a match between the lexical meanings of N1 and N2. When no match is possible, like in contingent relations, the genitive case cannot be used. This confirms the structural nature of this case, which is not predisposed to any particular semantic role. It should be noted that complex NPs allowing the interrogative *skol'ko* show important differences with the other two types: their semantic nucleus can be N2, they accept predicate agreement with N2 and allow the *u*-morphology. These characteristics make the *skol'ko*-type comparable to another type of genitive, which will be studied in the next section.

3.2   The genitive of quantification

Within the NP, the genitive also marks nouns following a numeral or certain other quantifying specifiers such as *skol'ko* 'how much/many' or *mnogo* 'much/many'. Following Jakobson (1936), Bošković (2006), among many others, we will call this kind of genitive the "genitive of quantification". Unlike the adnominal genitive of the *kakoj*-type and of the *kogo/čego*-type, the noun bearing the genitive of quantification is not a complement but the semantic nucleus, in that it meets the selectional restrictions of the verb. One can distinguish three subcategories of quantifiers that impose the genitive case on the noun, according to the different morphosyntactic patterns in which they enter.

1. Numerals such as *tysjača* 'thousand', *desjatok* 'about ten', *sotnja* 'about a hundred', which behave like nouns of the *skol'ko*-type, such as *kuča* 'pile' (§ 3.1.2.2). They always function as the syntactic head of the NP and require a genitive plural noun in whatever case they occur.[21] Therefore, we will not comment on them any further here.

    (49) a. Ja   slyšal tut   *tysjač-u*   *skripač-ej.* (RNC)
              I.NOM heard here thousand-ACC.SG violinists-GEN.PL
              'I heard a thousand violinists here.'

          b. Stran-a   raspolagaet *tysjač-ej*   *pravil.* (RNC)
              country-NOM disposes.of thousand-INS.SG rules.GEN.PL
              'A country has a thousand rules.'

2. Non-paucal quantifiers, which have an opposition between an "homogeneous" and "heterogeneous" agreement pattern, terms proposed by Babby (1980) (§ 3.2.1). This subcategory includes (i) the numerals 'five' and higher, (ii) various other quantitative specifiers, such as *mnogo* 'much/many', *skol'ko* 'how much/ many', *neskol'ko* 'some', *stol'ko* 'so much/many', and (iii) collective numerals possible with animate nouns only, such as *dvoe* 'two', *troe* 'three', *četvero* 'four'.

    (50) pjat' / mnogo / dvoe *det-ej*
          five / many / two children-GEN.PL
          'five/many/two children'

3. Paucal quantifiers, i.e. the numerals 2 through 4 and their compounds (21, 22, 31, 32, etc.), which show a number mismatch between the noun and a modifying adjective (§ 3.2.2), in addition to the homogeneous vs. heterogeneous pattern.

It should be noted that certain quantifying specifiers, namely the numeral *odin* 'one', the universal quantifier *vse* 'all' and the distributive *každyj* 'each', do not govern the genitive case. The noun following the specifier always takes the same case as the specifier.

    (51) a. Mog-u   otkryt' v-am   *odin*   *sekret.* (RNC)
              can-1SG open   you-DAT one.ACC secret.ACC
              'I can reveal one/a secret to you.'

          b. Prišl-os'   otkryt' *vs-e*   *okn-a*   i   *dver-i.* (RNC)
              had.to-IMPERS open   all-ACC windows-ACC and doors-ACC
              'We had to open all windows and all doors.'

    c. On   obdumyval *každ-oe*   *slov-o.* (RNC)
       he.NOM thought.over every-ACC word-ACC
       'He was thinking over every word.'

The absence of the genitive with *vse* and *každyj* can be explained by the fact that these specifiers concern the whole class of referents and do not have a partitive effect. Similarly, the French equivalents of these specifiers are not subject to the *en*-pronominalisation, unlike other quantifiers, such as *deux* 'two' or *beaucoup* 'many' (Carlier, Goyens, Lamiroy, this volume).

(52) a. Il a   lu   chaque article.
          he has read each   article.

      a′. *Il en a   lu   chaque/chacun.
          he EN has read each-ADJ/each-PRO
          'He read each article.'

vs. b. Il a   lu   deux/beaucoup d'articles.
          he has read two/many   of articles
          'He read two/many articles.'

      b′. Il en a   lu   deux/beaucoup.
          he EN has read two/beaucoup
          'He read two of them/many of them.'

However, the absence of the genitive with *odin* 'one' is more difficult to explain. In French, the quantitive pronoun *en* does occur with *un* 'one', unlike the specifiers mentioned above. The behavior of *odin* 'one' is therefore not consistent with the distribution of this quantitive pronoun in French.

(53) Il a   lu   un   article. – Il en a   lu   un.
      he has read one/an article   he EN has read one
      'He read one/an article.'   'He read one of them.'

The morphological form of the specifier *odin* 'one', just like the forms of *vse* 'all' and *každyj* 'every', may provide one of the possible explanations for the lack of genitive on the noun. Unlike other numerals such as *pjat'* 'five' or *šest'* 'six', which do not agree in gender and number with the noun and have only two case forms (NOM/ACC *pjat'* vs. *pjati* for the oblique cases), *odin* 'one' behaves as an adjective agreeing in case and gender with the noun. In addition, it can never behave as an adverb, unlike *mnogo* 'much/many' (see § 3.2.1 below and notes 22 and 23). Further investigation on the subject is, however, necessary.

    These data show that the genitive case appears with partitive semantics only. This is also confirmed by the fact that the *u*-morphology can appear on nouns preceded by specifiers compatible with mass nouns, such as *mnogo* 'much/many' or *skol'ko* 'how much/many'.

(54) mnog-o / stol'k-o *saxar-a/saxar-u*
much-ADV / so.much-ADV sugar-GENa/sugar-GENu
'much/so much sugar'

3.2.1 *Non-paucal numbers*

The so-called "non-paucal numbers" require a genitive plural noun and seem to behave like syntactic heads, in that they assign the genitive case to the noun with which they occur, similarly to nouns of the *skol'ko*-type, such as *kuča* 'pile', etc. (§ 3.1.2.2).

(55) Zvezd-a imeet pjat' *luč-ej*. (RNC)
star-NOM has five.ACC rays-GEN
'A star has five rays.'

However, the genitive case can appear on the noun exclusively when the whole NP receives "structural case" (nominative or accusative), but not when it receives lexical case from a verb or a preposition. In the latter case, both the numeral and the noun take the case assigned by a lexical item, as in (56), where the instrumental case is assigned by the verb *obladat'* 'possess'.

(56) a. Ljub-aja sistem-a obladaet *pjat'-ju*
any-NOM system-NOM possesses five-INS
obšč-imi priznak-ami. (RNC)
general-INS indications-INS
'Any system has five general indications.'

b. E-go sočineni-ja obladajut
he-GEN works-NOM possess
mnog-imi xudožestvenn-ymi sredstv-ami. (RNC)
many-INS artistic-INS means-INS
'His works use many artistic means.'

In other words, in structural case positions, the numeral occurs in its uninflected form and the noun in the genitive plural. The NP then shows, in Babby's (1987) terms, a "heterogeneous" morphosyntactic pattern. In lexical case positions, both constituents take the same lexical case and show a "homogeneous" pattern. The importance of the opposition between structural and lexical case is clearly shown by the behavior of specifiers such as *mnogo* 'much/many', *neskol'ko* 'some', *stol'ko* 'so much/so many', which, even in the nominative or the accusative, show an alternation between the adverbial[22] form ending in -*o* and their agreeing form, thus allowing both the heterogeneous and the homogeneous pattern even in the nominative and the accusative.[23] In typical structural case positions, the most frequent pattern is the heterogeneous one, although the homogeneous pattern is possible but rare. When the accusative is not structural, but assigned by a preposition, the homogeneous pattern is much more frequent. A research on Google (March 18, 2009) showed that the VP 'knows many languages', in which 'many languages' receives structural accusative, appears in 94% of the cases with the heterogeneous pattern (*znaet mnog-o jazyk-ov* 'knows many-ADV languages-GEN.PL'), whereas the homogeneous pattern (*znaet mnog-ie jazyk-i* 'knows many-ACC.PL languages-ACC.PL) is restricted to 6% of the uses. However, when the accusative case is assigned by the preposition *na* ('into') and is therefore lexical, as in the PP 'into many languages', we found the homogeneous pattern (*na mnog-ie jazyk-i* 'into many-ACC.PL languages-ACC.PL') in 99% of the examples and the heterogeneous pattern (*na mnog-o jazyk-ov* 'into many-ADV languages-GEN.PL) only in 1%. These results show that neither of the two patterns is specific to the nominative or the accusative case as such, and they confirm the analysis according to which the pattern depends on the structural or lexical character of the case assignment or, as Babby (1987) puts it, "lexical case somehow overrides structural case".

There seems to be a semantic difference between the two patterns as well. The heterogeneous pattern presents the referent of the noun as a closed whole containing a plurality of elements, while the homogeneous pattern provides access to each separate element. Therefore, the heterogeneous pattern cannot be followed by an enumeration, while the homogeneous pattern can be. Moreover, when it is impossible to identify separate entities of the whole, the use of the homogeneous pattern is excluded.

(57) a. Ja   kupila *mnog-o*   *kartin.*
         I.NOM bought many-ADV paintings.GEN.PL
         'I bought many paintings.'

vs. a'. ???Ja   kupila *mnog-ie*   *kartin-y.*
          I.NOM bought many-ACC.PL paintings-ACC.PL

b. Rossi-ja   kupila *mnog-ie*   *evropejsk-ie*
    Russia-NOM bought many-ACC.PL European-ACC.PL
    pravitel'stv-a   (Germani-i,   Greci-i, ...). (RNC)
    governments-ACC.PL Germany-GEN Greece-GEN
    'Russia bought many European governments (that of Germany, Greece, ...).'

vs. b'. *Rossi-ja   kupila *mnog-o*   *evropejsk-ix*
          Russia-NOM bought many-ADV European-GEN.PL
          pravitel'stv   (Germani-i,   Greci-i, ...).
          governments.GEN.PL Germany-GEN Greece-GEN

Many studies have raised the question which of the two constituents is to be considered as the head of the NP. The heterogeneous pattern suggests that the numeral assigns genitive case to the noun and thus acts as the head, an analysis which has been adopted by Babby (1987) and Franks (1995). In the homogeneous pattern, by contrast, the quantifier agrees with the noun and so only the noun can be analyzed as the head. In recent studies, the latter analysis has been adopted even for the heterogeneous pattern, which has given rise to various accounts in the minimalist framework, which we will not discuss here (Franks 1994, 1995, 2002, Rappaport 2002, Bošković 2006).

NPs with non-paucal numbers allow two types of verb agreement. The verb can agree with the noun or appear in the impersonal form.[24] Word order plays an important role in the agreement selection, the impersonal form occurring more frequently with a post-posed subject.

(58) a. *Pjat'* *čelovek* *uže* *za* *ne-go* *progolosoval-i.* (RNC)
five.NOM persons.GEN already for him-GEN voted-PL
'Five people have already voted for him.'

    a'. *Za Morozov-u* *progolosoval-o pjat'* *čelovek.* (RNC)
for Morozova-ACC voted-IMPERS five.NOM persons.GEN
'Five people voted for Morozova.'

    b. *Mnog-o* *ljud-ej* *priezžal-i* *v* *naš-u* *glubink-u.* (RNC)
many-ADV people-GEN came-PL into our-ACC remote.place-ACC
'Many people came to our remote place.'

    b'. *Na ét-i* *vyxodn-ye* *priexal-o* *mnog-o*
on these-ACC days.off-ACC came-IMPERS many-ADV
dačnik-ov. (RNC)
summer.residents-GEN
'Many summer residents came this weekend.'

3.2.2 *Paucal numbers*

Paucal numbers are even more puzzling. Just like the other numerals, they display an homogeneous vs. heterogeneous pattern, but in addition they exhibit the following two differences with non-paucal numbers.[25]

1. The noun occurs in the genitive singular, although verb agreement shows that the whole NP is viewed as plural.[26]

(59) *Dv-a* *čelovek-a* *igral-i* *v šaxmat-y.* (RNC)
two-NOM persons-GEN.SG played-PL in chess-ACC
'Two people were playing chess.'

2. When the noun is modified by an adjective, the NP exhibits a number mismatch because the adjective is used in its plural form, reinforcing the analysis of the whole NP as having a plural feature.

(60) *dv-a* *nov-yx* *pidžak-a*   (Pesetsky 2007)
two-NOM new-GEN.PL coat-GEN.SG
'two new coats'

Moreover, the adjective can appear in the nominative plural, while the noun stays in the genitive singular, thus leading to both a case and a number mismatch within the NP. According to Bailyn and Nevins (2008), the latter phenomenon affects only feminine nouns that have homophonous forms for the genitive singular and the

nominative plural, and not nouns such as *reka* 'river', which display a formal difference, i.e. a stress difference, between the nominative plural (*re̲ki*) and the genitive
singular (*reki̲*). Therefore, they argue that the NP does not exhibit a case mismatch
between the noun and the adjective.

(61) a.   tri   *prost-yx/prost-ye*   *knig-i*   (Bailyn and Nevins)
           three.NOM simple-GEN.PL/NOM.PL book-GEN.SG
           'three simple books'

      b.   dv-e   *širok-ix*   / **širok-ie*   *rek-i*   (Bailyn and Nevins)
           two-NOM   broad-GEN.PL /*broad-NOM.PL river-GEN.SG
           'two broad rivers'

However, examples like (61b), considered impossibile by Bailyn and Nevins (2008),
are in fact attested.

(62) Dv-e   *moščn-ye*   *severn-ye*   *rek-i*
      two-NOM.F powerful-NOM.F.PL northern-NOM.F.PL river-GEN.F.SG
      razdvigajut Ural'-sk-ie   gor-y. (RNC)
      push.apart Ural-ADJ-ACC mountains-ACC
      'Two powerful Northern rivers push apart the Ural mountains.'

Moreover, as noted by Rappaport (2002: 340), in the 19th century, both cases on the
adjective were also possible with masculine and neuter nouns. Even in contemporary
Russian, this phenomenon still occurs.

(63) a.   Vyšli   iz   pečat-i   dv-a   *nov-ye*   *izdani-ja*. (Google)
           came.out from press-GEN two-NOM new-NOM.M.PL edition-GEN.N.SG
           'Two new editions came out from press.'

      b.   Predstavljajutsja dv-a   nov-ye
           are.presented   two-NOM new-NOM.M.PL
           fizičesk-ie   *zakon-a*. (Google)
           physical-NOM.M.PL law-GEN.M.SG
           'Two new laws of physics are presented.'

Therefore such NPs do exhibit a case mismatch in addition to the number mismatch.
    Another difference between paucal and non-paucal numbers is that in informal
contemporary Russian paucal numbers can show the homogeneous pattern even for
animate direct objects (64a), whereas non-paucal numbers cannot (65b). In other
words, the "paucal genitive" is sensitive to the feature of animacy, while the "non-
paucal" is not.

(64) a.   Žurnalist-y   videli *dv-e   žen̆ščin-y* /
           journalists-NOM   saw   two-ACC.F.PL woman-GEN.SG /

> *dv-ux   ženščin.* (Google)
> two-GEN.PL   women.GEN.F.PL
> 'Journalists saw two women.'

a′. Žurnalist-y   videli *dv-e   knigi /*
     journalists-NOM saw   two-ACC.F.PL book-GEN.SG /
     *dv-ux   knig.
     two-GEN.PL   books.GEN.F.PL
     'Journalists saw two books.'

b. Žurnalist-y   videli *pjat'/*pjat-i   ženščin.*
    journalists-NOM saw   five-ACC/*five-GEN women.GEN.PL
    'Journalists saw five women.'

b′. Žurnalist-y   videli *pjat'/*pjat-i   mašin.*
     journalists-NOM saw   five-ACC/*five-GEN cars.GEN.PL
     'Journalists saw five cars.'

This behavior can be explained by the morphology of these numerals. The paucal numbers from 'two' to 'four' have a typical adjectival declension and a real plural morphology, whereas the non-paucal numbers have a typical nominal declension with singular morphology (see § 2.1). It should be noted, however, that the compounds of paucal numbers (21, 22, etc.) are not sensitive to the feature of animacy, probably due to the fact that the first part of the compound cannot take a plural form, has a nominal declension and can be considered as a non-paucal number.

(65) a. Včera   videl *dv-ux   student-ov.* (RNC)
          yesterday saw two-GEN.PL   students-GEN.PL
          'Yesterday, I saw two students.'

      b. Včera   videl *dvadcat' dv-a   student-a.*
          yesterday saw twenty two-ACC.M.PL student-GEN.M.SG
          'Yesterday, I saw twenty-two of our students.'

All these puzzling facts have led some scholars in recent studies to assume the existence of a paucal case for Russian. This case is then spelled out on the head noun as the genitive singular and is regarded as a "number category" distinct from singular and plural (Rappaport 2002, Bailyn and Nevins 2008). One of the arguments mentioned by Rappaport is the existence of special "paucal" forms for four nouns (*rjad* 'row', *čas* 'hour', *šar* 'sphere' and *šag* 'step'), which have the stress on the ending when following lower numerals, while in other contexts their genitive form is stressed on the stem (e.g. *cvet šara* 'the sphere's color' vs. *dva, tri, četyre šara* 'two, three, four spheres'). However, everywhere beyond the nominative and accusative, the distinction for the paucal feature is neutralized. Furthermore, for some nouns, a special genitive form can also be found with non-paucals, e.g. *čelovek* 'person', as opposed to the normal genitive plural form *ljudej*. However, the pattern is more irregular here. With genuine non-paucal numbers only the quantitative form *čelovek*[27] can appear[28], while *mnogo* is compatible with both genitive plural forms, but has a preference for the normal genitive form.

(66) a. pjat' *čelovek*   vs. a'. *pjat' *ljud-ej*
          five   persons.GEN   five   people-GEN
          'five persons'

      b. mnog-o   *čelovek*   vs. b'. mnog-o   *ljud-ej*
          many-ADV persons.GEN   many-ADV people-GEN
          'many persons'   'many people'

On the basis of the way the noun *čelovek* functions, one could be tempted to distinguish a quantitative case for the genitive plural as well, homonymous with the normal genitive in almost all cases. Although this account seems to be ad hoc, no better account is available for the moment.

4. Genitive case within the VP

As noted above, in Russian the genitive case can appear not only within the NP, but also within the VP. The genitive then marks the internal argument of the verb, mostly the direct object, but in certain cases the subject of unaccusative verbs as well. This "non-canonical" genitive (Kagan 2007) can appear in three contexts. Firstly, it can be assigned by certain intensional verbs such as *bojat'sja* 'fear' or *ždat'* 'wait for'. This is the so-called "intensional genitive" (see § 4.1). Secondly, it can appear under sentential negation, a use which is commonly called "the genitive of negation" (see § 4.2). Finally, the genitive can mark semantically partitive internal arguments: this kind of genitive is often labelled "partitive genitive" (see § 4.3).

In all three cases, the genitive case can alternate with the expected structural case, either the accusative or the nominative. As noted by many grammars and authors, the genitive marking was the norm in the 19th century, but in contemporary Russian it is losing ground to the accusative. This alternation gives rise to much variation in native speaker judgments, since this process of language change is still on-going. Therefore, we will describe tendencies rather than strict rules.

As shown by many linguists (Jakobson 1936, Babby 1980, Neidle 1988, among many others), the choice between cases is associated with different semantic interpretations: the genitive typically gives rise to an indefinite or non-specific reading, whereas the accusative can be interpreted either as definite or indefinite specific. Therefore, recent studies describe the genitive case as being close to predicates or property-denoting NPs, as opposed to the accusative or the nominative, which typically denote entities (Kagan 2007, Borschev et al. 2008). However, we will show that this hypothesis cannot account for all uses of the non-canonical genitive.

It should be noted that, in all three kinds of genitive, both the *a*-form and the *u*-form can appear with nouns that have double genitive morphology. As shown by Paus (1994) and by Fischer (2003), this variation differs from one speaker to another. Although one form may be preferred to another in particular contexts, the two forms are not associated with any marked difference in interpretation. Therefore, we will regard them as mere variants.

4.1   The intensional genitive

Although it is less well-studied than the genitive of negation, the intensional genitive is most likely to be described as an instance of lexical genitive case. As noted above, it can be assigned by certain verbs such as *bojat'sja* 'fear', *ždat'* 'wait for' or *xotet'* 'want' to their internal argument.

(67)   a.   Rebënok   boitsja   *vrač-ej.*
             child.NOM fears   doctors-GEN
             'A/The child fears doctors.'

       b.   Knig-a   ždët   *svo-ej   dostojn-oj   ocenk-i*
             book-NOM awaits its-GEN deserved-GEN appraisal-GEN
             v   pečat-i. (RNC)
             in   press-LOC
             'The book awaits its deserved appraisal in press.'

Table 4 contains the most frequent intensional verbs that assign genitive case in Russian, listed according to their meaning.

All these verbs can be described as opaque or intensional in that they do not necessarily entail the existence of the referent of their internal argument.[30] However, only some of these verbs govern exclusively the genitive case (cf. *dičit'sja* 'shun', *dobivat'sja* 'achieve', *dostigat'* 'attain', *žaždat'* 'crave', *lišat'* 'deprive', *lišat'sja* 'lose'). Most of them allow the competition between the genitive and the accusative (cf. *bojat'sja* 'fear', *opasat'sja* 'apprehend' or *xotet'* 'want') or even between the genitive and the instrumental

Table 4. Verbs assigning intensional genitive case[29]

emotion	*bojat'sja* 'fear', *gnušat'sja* 'loathe', *opasat'sja* 'apprehend', *pugat'sja* 'be frightened of', *stesnjat'sja* 'feel shy about', *stydit'sja* 'be ashamed of'
desire	*dobivat'sja* 'achieve', *dostigat'* 'attain', *žaždat'* 'crave', *želat'* 'wish', *prosit'* 'ask for', *trebovat'* 'demand', *xotet'* 'want'
searching or waiting	*dožidat'sja* 'await', *ždat'* 'wait for', *iskat'* 'search', *ožidat'* 'expect'
avoiding or privation	*dičit'sja* 'shun', *izbegat'* 'avoid', *lišat'* 'deprive', *lišat'sja* 'lose', *osteregat'sja* 'beware of', *storonit'sja* 'shun', *čuždat'sja* 'avoid'
other	*deržat'sja* 'hold', *ispolnjat'sja* 'fill with', *kasat'sja* 'touch', *priderživat'sja* 'adhere', *slušat'sja* 'obey', *udostaivat'* 'deign'

(*gnušat'sja* 'loathe', *ispolnjat'sja* 'fill with', *udostaivat'* 'deign'). Moreover, certain verbs such as *bojatsja* 'fear' have a clear preference for the genitive, while others most frequently govern the accusative (*iskat'* 'search') or the instrumental case (*udostaivat'* 'deign').

An additional problem is that not all classical intensional verbs can assign the genitive case in Russian. As noted by Kagan (2007: 159), typically intensional verbs, such as *izobražat'* 'depict', *napominat'* 'remind, resemble', *obeščat'* 'promise', *planirovat'* 'plan', *predvidet'* 'foresee', *predskazyvat'* 'predict', *predstavljat'* 'imagine', or *risovat'* 'draw', do not govern the genitive case in Russian. Even the prototypical intensional verb 'seek' (*iskat'*) has a clear preference for the accusative case.[31]

Furthermore, the alternation between the genitive and the accusative depends not only on the verb, but also on other factors. According to Kagan (2007), the use of the genitive is more frequent with abstract nouns than with concrete nouns, with plural NPs than with singular ones, with common names than proper names. Similarly, Borschev et al. (2008) note that case assignment by intensional verbs is sensitive to the sortal hierarchy presented in (68), but different verbs choose the borderline differently.

(68)   GEN ← abstract > mass > inanimate > 'role' > animate → ACC

In other words, the choice of the genitive is favored by NPs with decreased referentiality. Moreover, as noted by many authors, when both cases are possible, the genitive generally gives rise to an indefinite or non-specific interpretation, whereas the accusative often induces a definite or specific interpretation. Classical examples are given in (69), in which the verb *ždat'* 'wait for' assigns the genitive to the argument when its interpretation is indefinite (69a) and the accusative when it is associated with a definite interpretation.

(69)   a.   On   ždët   otvet-a   na vopros.   (Neidle 1988: 31)
            he.NOM waits.for answer-GEN   to question.ACC
            'He's waiting for an answer to the question.'

       b.   On   ždët   podrug-u.
            he.NOM waits.for girlfriend-ACC
            'He's waiting for his girlfriend.'

Therefore, the intensional genitive is often taken to express absence of existential commitment. However, according to Kagan (2007: 160), who calls it "Irrealis Genitive", it appears only with "weak intensional verbs", which "lack commitment to existence in any particular world", never with "strong intensional verbs" such as *predvidet'* 'foresee' or *predskazyvat'* 'predict', which "induce sets of possible worlds in which their complement is entailed to hold" (Kagan 2007: 159). If this is correct, the distinction between strong and weak intensional verbs, made by Heim (1992) and Farkas (2003), can account for the fact that not all intensional verbs can assign genitive case in Russian.

Nevertheless, in contemporary Russian, the intensional genitive can appear on intrinsically definite animate NPs, containing a possessive pronoun or a demonstrative, and even on proper names, which always presuppose the existence of their referent.

(70) a. Kol-ja　　vs-ju　　žizn'　stydilsja
　　　　Kolja-NOM entire-ACC life.ACC was.ashamed.of
　　　　svo-ej　　*mater-i.* (RNC)
　　　　his.own-GEN mother-GEN
　　　　'His entire life Kolja was ashamed of his mother.'

　　　b. On　　bojalsja *Irin-y,*　kak melk-ij　travojadn-yj
　　　　he.NOM feared　Irina-GEN as　small-NOM herbivorous-NOM
　　　　zver'　　boitsja krupn-ogo. (RNC)
　　　　animal.NOM fears　large-GEN
　　　　'He feared Irina like a small herbivorous animal fears a large one.'

Further research is needed to establish whether examples such as (70) are remnants of lexical case assignment. Still, it is clear that the use of the genitive with intensional verbs becomes more and more sensitive to the above-mentioned factors. This suggests that the intensional genitive can no longer be considered as a lexical case, in that it alternates with a purely structural case, its appearance being dependent on referential factors rather than on thematic ones.

4.2　The genitive of negation

The most studied and most problematic use of the Russian genitive is without any doubt the so-called "genitive of negation", which has given rise to a multitude of studies presenting various points of view, on which we cannot comment here (Restan 1960, Babby 1980, 2001, Apresjan 1985, 1995, Padučeva 1992, 2004, 2005, 2006, Bailyn 1997, Borschev and Partee 1998, 2002a, 2002b, Brown 1999, Pereltsvaig 1999, Partee and Borschev 2002, 2004, Harves 2002, Kim 2003, Kagan 2007, Partee 2007, Borschev et al. 2008, and many others). In what follows, we will concentrate on the least controversial issues.

As is well known, this kind of genitive can appear under negation on the direct object of transitive verbs (71a) and on the subject of certain unaccusative verbs, which then take their impersonal form (see note 24) and do not agree with the genitive subject (71b).

(71) a. Saš-a　　　ne　pokupaet *knig.*
　　　　Sasha-NOM NEG buys　　books.GEN
　　　　'Sasha doesn't buy (any) books.'

　　　b. Zdes' ne　rast-ët　　　*grib-ov.*　　　　　　(Babby 1980)
　　　　here　NEG grows-IMPERS mushrooms-GEN
　　　　'No mushrooms grow here.'

Marginally, the same structure is possible with unergative verbs, such as 'work' or 'sleep', provided that (i) the context supplies the necessary spatial anchoring, and that (ii) the verb takes an existential reading.[32]

(72) V ét-oj   bibliotek-e *det-ej*   nikogda ne   rabotal-o.
     in this-LOC library-LOC children-GEN never NEG worked-IMPERS
     'There have never been any children working in this library.'

With subjects of transitives and with arguments bearing dative or another lexical case in the corresponding affirmative sentence, the genitive of negation is completely unacceptable. In other words, it can only appear on underlying objects, as has been argued in many studies (see among others Bailyn 1997, Harves 2002, Kim 2003).

Another syntactic constraint is that the negation has to be "clausemate" and sentential (Bailyn 1997, Brown 1999, Kim 2003). This implies that it cannot affect an NP occurring in a different clause (73a), and that it is not possible under constituent negation (73b).

(73) a. *Ja   ne   obeščaju [pisat' *stix-ov*]   (Timberlake 1986: 347)
         I.NOM NEG promise [write poems-GEN]

     b. U ne-go   v ruk-ax   ne   *slovar'/*slovar-ja*
         at him-GEN in hands-LOC NEG dictionary.NOM/*dictionary-GEN
         'It isn't a dictionary that he has in his hands (it is something else).'
                                              (Kim 2003: 298)

These notorious facts are no longer subject to discussion. However, the genitive of negation still gives rise to much debate because, unlike other Slavic languages such as Polish, its use in Russian is optional in most of the contexts described here.[33] It is mandatory only in the existential construction without an explicit verb.

(74) Na stol-e   net *stakan-ov/*stakan-y.*
     on table-LOC NEG glasses-GEN/*glasses-NOM
     'There are no glasses on the table.'

Thus, in most cases, the genitive alternates either with the accusative or with the nominative. Examples (71a) and (71b) can be contrasted with (75a) and (75b) respectively.

(75) a. Saš-a   ne   pokupaet *knig-i.*
         Sasha-NOM NEG buys   books-ACC
         'Sasha doesn't buy books.'

     b. Zdes' *grib-y*   ne   rast-ut.
         here mushrooms-NOM NEG grow-AGR
         'Mushrooms do not grow here.'

Various syntactic accounts have linked the alternation between the genitive and the accusative/nominative to the scope of negation, the genitive being assigned to an NP occurring within the scope of negation and the accusative or nominative to an NP that is outside its scope (Bailyn 1997, Brown 1999, Harves 2002, Kim 2003). Nevertheless, the genitive NP can occur before the negated predicate.[34]

(76)   a.   *Problem*   ne   byl-o.
        problems.GEN NEG was-IMPERS
        'There were no problems.'

     b.   *Syr-a*   ja   ne   el.
        cheese-GEN I.NOM NEG ate
        'I didn't eat any cheese.'

This syntactic scope account has been linked to the semantic differences induced by the case alternation. As noted by many authors, the genitive is generally associated with an interpretation of non-existence, whereas the accusative/nominative case presents the referent as existing. Therefore, as in the case of the intensional genitive (see § 4.1), the choice between the two cases has been explained by the referential status of the argument, the genitive giving rise to an indefinite or non-specific interpretation and the accusative to a definite or specific interpretation (see Jakobson 1936, Timberlake 1986, Babby 1980, Neidle 1988). This led authors like Neidle (1988) and Kagan (2007) to argue that the relevant semantic factors are the same as in the case of the intensional genitive and that the genitive of negation basically expresses a lack of existential commitment. This is confirmed by the fact that the genitive of negation is favored by the same lexico-semantic factors, such as abstract nouns, inanimate nouns and plurals (Restan 1960, Kagan 2007). Furthermore, as shown in Paykin and Van Peteghem (2002), the genitive of negation is also sensitive to certain aspectual restrictions. Indeed, it is combined more easily with an imperfective than with a perfective verb. With verbs denoting an event implying a pre-existing object, such as 'to close' or 'to read', the genitive case is incompatible with the perfective form because negation bears not on the event itself, but on its complete achievement. Therefore, the existence of the object cannot be denied and the use of the genitive is impossible.

(77)   a.   Ja   ne   zakryvala *okn-a.*
        I.NOM NEG closed.IPFV window-GEN
        'I did not close any window.'

     b.   *Ja   ne   zakryla   *okn-a.*
        I.NOM NEG closed.PFV window-GEN

Conversely, when the existence of the object results from the event itself (= incremental object), as with verbs of creation such as 'to write', the cooccurrence of the genitive with the perfective aspect is possible because the negation bears on the realization of the event and, consequently, on the existence of the final object.[35]

(78)   a.   Ja   ne   pisala   *pis'm-a.*
        I.NOM NEG wrote.IPFV letter-GEN
        'I did not write any letter.'

     b.   Ja   ves'   večer   pytalas'   pisat'
        I.NOM entire.ACC evening.ACC tried.IPFV to.write.IPFV

> k   teb-e,   no   tak i   ne   napisala   *pis'm-a.*
> to   you-DAT but   so   and   NEG   wrote.PFV   letter-GEN
> 'I tried writing to you the entire evening and yet did not (manage to) write any letter.'

However, the absence of presupposition of existence does not account for all uses of the genitive of negation. As shown in many studies (Borschev and Partee 2002a, 2002b, Kim 2003, Padučeva 2004), it can also be assigned to inherently referential arguments, such as proper names or pronouns, even more frequently than with the intensional genitive.

(79)   a.   Ja   *Maš-i*   včera   ne   videla.
            I.NOM Masha-GEN yesterday NEG saw.IPFV
            'I have seen no Masha yesterday.' [I expected to see her]

vs.   a'.   Ja   *Maš-u*   včera   ne   videla.
            I.NOM Masha-ACC yesterday NEG saw.IPFV
            'I haven't seen Masha yesterday.'

     b.   *Men-ja*   ne   byl-o   v   Moskv-e.
            me-GEN NEG   was-IMPERS in   Moscow-LOC
            'I wasn't in Moscow.'

vs.   b'.   *Ja*   ne   byl   v   Moskv-e.
            I.NOM NEG   was.AGR in   Moscow-LOC
            'I haven't been to Moscow.'

In these examples, the use of the genitive case cannot be claimed to imply the non-existence of the referent, but entails other differences in interpretation. For instance, the translation of (79a) with a genitive object suggests that the genitive case signals the unexpected absence of the referent at a given place. As shown by Paykin and Van Peteghem (2002) and by Borschev and Partee (1998, 2002a,b), the same semantic effect is obtained with the much better-studied genitive subject.[36] In both cases, the global interpretation must involve a subject of consciousness whose expectations regarding the localisation of the referent do not match up to reality.[37] For the genitive object, the semantic effect can be compared to the effect of indefinite negative objects in languages such as English (as in the translation of (79a)) or Dutch (see (80a)), as opposed to sentence negation (see also Padučeva 2006 and Borschev et al. 2008).

(80)   a.   Ik heb daar *geen Masha* gezien.
          I   have there no   Masha   seen
          'I have seen no Masha there.'

vs.   b.   Ik heb *Masha* daar *niet* gezien.
           I   have Masha there not   seen
           'I haven't seen Masha there.'

As for the genitive subject, it is very frequent with the verb *byt'* 'to be', whose behavior is unique, and has therefore given rise to many studies (see among others Pigin 1962,

Ickovič 1974, Babby 1980, Borschev and Partee 1998, 2002a,b, Padučeva 1992, 2004, 2005). When it is used without a spatial adjunct, as in (81), genitive marking is obligatory and has the same effect as with other verbs in negative contexts, i.e. negation bears upon the referent's existence.

(81) a. *Problem*   ne   byl-o.
          problems.GEN NEG was-IMPERS
          'There were no problems.'

     b. *Otc-a*   ne   byl-o.
          father-GEN NEG was-IMPERS
          'There was no father.'

However, when the sentence contains a spatial adjunct, both the nominative and the genitive case may be used, triggering different verb interpretations. Used with a nominative subject, the verb means 'to go somewhere', whereas used with a genitive subject, it means 'to be present' (Padučeva 1992, 2004, 2005).

(82) a. *Otec*   ne   *byl*   v kino.
          father.NOM NEG was.AGR in cinema
          'My father did not go to the cinema.'

     b. *Otc-a*   ne   *byl-o*   v kino.
          father-GEN NEG was-IMPERS in cinema
          'My father was not at the cinema.' [Somebody was looking for him there]

Thus, the use of the nominative necessarily yields the 'go-somewhere' reading of the verb *byt'*, and a special context is needed to make the sentence interpretable.

(83) a. *Men-ja* ne *byl-o*   dom-a.
          me-GEN NEG was-IMPERS home-GEN
          'I was not home.'

     b. *Ja*   ne *byl*   dom-a   uže   dv-a   god-a.
          I.NOM NEG was.AGR home-GEN already two-ACC year-GEN.SG
          'I have not been home for two years already.'

As shown by Kagan (2007) and Borschev et al. (2008), all of these semantic differences associated with the choice between cases pose problems for purely syntactic accounts. However, the fact that the genitive case only alternates with purely structural cases and that it is not sensitive to thematic roles suggests that it behaves as structural rather than lexical case, in spite of the semantic constraints.

4.3 The partitive genitive

The last kind of genitive we will study appears on internal verb arguments containing mass nouns and bare plurals, as illustrated in (84).

(84) a. Ja   kupila *vod-y*   / *jablok.*
         I.NOM bought water-GEN / apples.GEN
         'I bought (some) water/apples.'

     b. Ja   kupila *vod-u*   / *jablok-i.*
         I.NOM bought water-ACC / apples-ACC
         'I bought (the) water/(the) apples.'

This is the so-called "partitive" genitive. As we have seen above, the label "partitive" is also used in a strictly morphological sense, for the *u*-form described in § 2.2. However, we will use this term in its broader syntactico-semantic interpretation.

In most cases, the partitive genitive competes with the accusative, giving rise to different interpretations. The genitive marking of the direct object yields an indefinite interpretation, similar to the absence of a determiner in English and to the partitive article *du*/*de la* or the indefinite plural *des* in French (as in the French translation of (84a), 'J'ai acheté de l'eau/des pommes'). The accusative-marked direct object, in its turn, may give rise to either a definite or an indefinite interpretation, as shown in (84b). Hence, both the accusative and the partitive genitive can be used with an indefinite interpretation.

Still, the genitive case is obligatory with some prefixed verbs insisting on quantity, such as *napit'sja* 'drink, quench one's thirst'.

(85) On   napilsja *vod-y* / **vod-u.*
     he.NOM drank.PFV water-GEN / *water-ACC
     'He quenched his thirst with water.'

In Paykin and Van Peteghem (2002), we have argued that the ungrammaticality of the accusative with such verbs is due to the fact that their prefix entails an exclusively quantitative reading, therefore imposing the use of the genitive case. However, these verbs cannot be considered as assigning lexical genitive case: when their complement takes an explicit quantifier, like *mnogo* 'many' in (86), it cannot appear in the genitive case (see § 3.2.1).[38]

(86) Van-ja   na-kupil   mnog-o/*mnog-ix   knig.
     Vanya-NOM NA-bought.PFV many-ADV/*many-GEN books.GEN
     'Vanya bought (up) many books.'

As noted by Pereltsvaig (2006) and Bailyn (2004), the prefix does not change the case-selection properties from structural accusative to lexical genitive, but only modifies the selectional properties of the verb, which allows exclusively quantified complements.

Conversely, with some verbs such as *doest'* 'to eat up' (87), the genitive case is completely excluded due to the fact that the prefix used (*do-*) yields a holistic meaning, compatible with definite reference only.

(87)   On   doel   *pirog/*pirog-a.*
       he.NOM ate.up.PFV pie.ACC/pie-GEN
       'He ate up the pie.'

However, the opposition between the accusative and the partitive does not coincide with the opposition between definite and indefinite NPs as expressed by articles in such languages as English or French, since the accusative case allows both interpretations. Our hypothesis is that the indefiniteness expressed by both the genitive and the accusative is semantically different, the genitive NP emphasizing quantity, and the accusative NP denoting a class (Paykin and Van Peteghem 2002). Following Neidle (1988), Brown and Franks (1995), we can argue that partitive case is assigned by a null quantifier that is inherent to certain verbs and that can be triggered with others in certain contexts.

One of these triggers is perfective aspect. In Russian, the partitive genitive is much more frequent with perfective than imperfective verbs. According to Klenin (1978), this phenomenon can be viewed as an "unexpected wrinkle" because many studies assimilate partitive case to the imperfective aspect. For instance, Kiparsky (1998) claims that the partitive case in Finnish and the imperfective aspect in Russian both express the unboundedness of the VP. Similarly, in French, the use of a partitive article in the object confers a non-bounded reading to the predicate (Bosveld 2000: 52–54). In Russian, however, aspectual marking is explicitly present on the verb, independently from tense marking, and imperfectivity is always expressed on the verb, independently from the case of the object. Moreover, the imperfective aspect is hardly ever compatible with the partitive case.[39]

(88)   *Ja   pokupaju *xleb-a.*
       I.NOM buy.IPFV bread-GEN

The impossibility of using the partitive genitive in contexts like the one in (88) shows that its function is very different from that of the partitive article in French (cf. *J'achète du pain* 'I am buying some bread'). As the Russian partitive denotes a quantity, it always requires bounding by the process, which is provided by the perfective aspect.

Finally, it should be noted that the partitive genitive appears not only on objects, but also on subjects of unaccusative verbs used in their impersonal form, although partitive genitive subjects are less frequent than negative genitive subjects. The genitive subject in the impersonal construction can alternate with a nominative subject in the personal construction and appears mostly in exclamative contexts insisting on quantity.

(89)   a.   *Sneg-u*   navalil-o! (Google)
            snow-GEN   piled.up-IMPERS
            'There were piles of snow!'

       a'. *Sneg*   navalil. (RNC)
            snow.NOM   piled.up.3SG
            'Snow has piled up.'

b. Srazu   *ljud-ej*   nabežal-o! (Google)
    immediately people-GEN came.running-IMPERS
    'People came running immediately!'

b′. Srazu   *ljud-i*   nabežal-i. (Google)
    immediately people-NOM came.running-PL
    'People came running immediately.'

In conclusion, we can argue that, although the partitive genitive is semantically conditioned and is obligatory with certain verbs, it cannot be considered as a lexical case. It marks internal arguments of verbs denoting a process affecting a certain quantity, but it is not imposed by the thematic structure of the verb.

5. Conclusion

Although incomplete, this survey of the genitive uses allows us to draw some provisional conclusions. The most salient fact is that the different kinds of genitive described can be grouped into two major types, according to the alternation between the *a*-genitive and the *u*-genitive for nouns authorizing this alternation.

1. Two types allow only the *a*-form and never the *u*-form: the adnominal genitive of the *kakoj*-type and of the *čego/kogo*-type.
2. All the other types allow both forms: the adnominal *skol'ko*-type, the genitive of quantification, the intensional genitive, the genitive of negation and the partitive genitive. The latter kinds share yet another property: the genitive has decreased referentiality and is interpreted as indefinite, non-existing, or quantified.

This second major type can be accounted for by the hypothesis of Bailyn (2004), according to which the Russian genitive is the "Case of Q". However, this hypothesis is less convincing for the first major type. The hypothesis defended by Kagan (2007) and Borschev et al. (2008), according to which the genitive nominal denotes a property rather than an entity, seems more appropriate. It accounts not only for the intensional genitive and the genitive of negation, as shown by the authors mentioned above, but also for the two other types of type 2, in which the genitive noun can be analyzed as an N rather than an NP or a DP. Furthermore, it can account even for the adnominal genitives of type 1: the adnominal *kakoj*-type clearly denotes a property and even the adnominal *kogo/čego*-type, although it mostly corresponds to definite DPs in languages with articles, contributes to characterizing the N1, without making the referent of the genitive nominal salient.

Unlike other languages like German or Romanian, in which the genitive is marked on the determiner and is associated with definiteness and specificity, the Russian genitive is thus associated with indefiniteness or rather with absence of reference to entities. This tendency is probably related to the non-existence of articles in Russian. As shown by Pesetsky (2007), the genitive often marks the bare noun, without any determination, although it does not always correspond to bare nouns in languages with articles.

Within the case system of Russian, the genitive is much closer to structural cases (accusative, nominative) than to oblique cases (dative, instrumental, locative). This is shown in the morphology, the genitive often displaying a zero ending in the plural (which confirms its bare noun status), like the nominative masculine singular. Furthermore, it shares its morphology with the accusative for plural animate and masculine singular nouns. From a syntactic point of view, within the VP it appears only in structural case positions (direct object, subject) and, although semantically conditioned, it is never sensitive to the thematic structure of the head. Whenever it is sensitive to thematic roles, it necessarily appears with a preposition expressing the thematic relation. Further research is necessary, however, to decide whether these conclusions can be extended to the types of genitive that we could not study here, i.e. the genitive assigned by prepositions and the comparative genitive.

References

Apresjan, Jurij D. 1985. Sintaksičeskie priznaki leksem. *Russian Linguistics* 9: 289–317.

Apresjan, Jurij D. 1995. Leksikografičeskie portrety (na materiale glagola BYT'). *Izbrannye trudy, t. 2. Integral'noe opisanie jazyka i sistemnaja leksikografija*, 503–537. Moskva: Jazyki Russkoj Kul'tury.

Babby, Leonard H. 1980. *Existential Sentences and Negation in Russian*. Ann Arbor: Karoma Publishers.

Babby, Leonard H. 1987. Case, Prequantifiers, and Discontinuous Agreement in Russian. *Natural Language and Linguistic Theory* 5: 91–138.

Babby, Leonard H. 2001. The Genitive of Negation: a Unified Analysis. *Annual Workshop on Formal Approaches to Slavic Linguistics: The Bloomington Meeting 2000 FASL 9*, Steven Franks; Tracy Holloway King and Michael Yadroff (eds), 39–55. Ann Arbor: Michigan Slavic Publications.

Bailyn, John F. 1997. Genitive of Negation is Obligatory. *Annual Workshop on Formal Approaches to Slavic Linguistics: The Cornell Meeting 1995*, Wayles Browne, Ewa Dornsich, Natasha Kondrashova and Draga Zec (eds), 84–114. Ann Arbor: Michigan Slavic Publications.

Bailyn, John F. 2004. The Case of Q. *Annual Workshop on Formal Approaches to Slavic Linguistics 12*, Olga Arnaudova; Wayles Browne; María-Luisa Rivero and Danijela Stojanovic (eds), 1–35. Ann Arbor: Michigan Slavic Publications.

Bailyn, John F. and Nevins, Andrew. 2008. Russian Genitive Plurals are Impostors. *Inflectional Identity*, Asaf Bachrach and Andrew Nevins (eds), 237–270. Oxford: Oxford University Press.

Borschev, Vladimir and Partee, Barbara H. 1998. Formal and Lexical Semantics and the Genitive in Negated Existential Sentences in Russian. *Formal Approaches to Slavic Linguistics 6: The Connecticut Meeting 1997*, Željko Bošković, Steven Franks and William Snyder (eds), 75–96. Ann Arbor: Michigan Slavic Publications.

Borschev, Vladimir and Partee, Barbara H. 2002a. The Russian Genitive of Negation: Theme-Rheme Structure or Perspective Structure? *Journal of Slavic Linguistics* 10: 105–144.

Borschev, Vladimir and Partee, Barbara H. 2002b. The Russian Genitive of Negation in Existential Sentences: the Role of Theme-Rheme Structure Reconsidered. *Travaux du Cercle Linguistique de Prague (nouvelle série)*, vol. 4, Eva Hajičová, Petr Sgall, Jiri Hana and Tomáš Hoskovec (eds), 185–250. Amsterdam: John Benjamins.

Borschev, Vladimir, Paducheva, Elena V., Partee, Barbara H., Testelets, Yakov G. and Yanovich, Igor. 2008. Russian genitives, non-referentiality, and the property-type hypothesis. *Formal Approaches to Slavic Linguistics: The Stony Brook Meeting 2007 FASL 16*, Andrei Antonenko, John F. Bailyn and Christina Bethin (eds), 48–67. Ann Arbor: Michigan Slavic Publishers.

Bošković, Željko. 2006. Case and Agreement with Genitive of Quantification in Russian. *Agreement Systems*, Cedric Boeckx (ed.), 99–121. Amsterdam/Philadelphia: John Benjamins.

Bosveld, Léonie. 2000. Les syntagmes en *des* et *du*: un couple curieux parmi les indéfinis. *De l'indétermination à la qualification: les indéfinis*, Léonie Bosveld, Marleen Van Peteghem and Danièle Van de Velde (eds), 17–116. Artois Presses Université.

Brown, Sue. 1999. *The Syntax of Negation in Russian: A Minimalist Approach*. Stanford: CSLI.

Brown, Sue and Franks, Steven. 1995. Asymmetries in the Scope of Russian Negation. *Journal of Slavic Linguistics* 3(2): 239–287.

Farkas, Donka F. 2003. Assertion, Belief and Mood Choice. Paper presented at the workshop on Conditional and Unconditional Modality. ESSLLI, Vienna. http://people.ucsc.edu/~farkas/papers/mood.pdf.

Feldstein, Ronald F. 2002. A Binary Feature Approach to Russian Nominal Declension. *The Slavic and East European Language Resource Center*, Issue 2, *Glossos*. http://seelrc.org/glossos/ glossos@seelrc.org.

Fischer, Susann. 2003. Partitive *vs.* Genitive in Russian and Polish: an Empirical Study on Case Alternation in the Object Domain. *Experimental Studies in Linguistics* 1, Susann Fischer, Ruben van de Vijver and Ralf Vogel (eds), *Linguistics in Potsdam* 21: 73–89.

Forbes, Graeme. 2008. Intensional Transitive Verbs. *Stanford Encyclopedia of Philosophy*, Edward Zalta (ed.). http://plato.stanford.edu/entries/intensional-trans-verbs/.

Franks, Steven. 1994. Parametric Properties of Numeral Phrases in Slavic. *Natural Language and Linguistic Theory* 12: 570–649.

Franks, Steven. 1995. *Parameters of Slavic Morphosyntax*. New York: Oxford University Press.

Franks, Steven. 2002. A Jakobsonian Feature Based Analysis of the Slavic Numeric Quantifier Genitive. *Journal of Slavic Linguistics* 10: 141–181.

Harves, Stephanie. 2002. Genitive of Negation and the Syntax of Scope. *Proceedings of ConSOLE IX*, Marjo van Koppen, Erica Thrift, Erik Jan van der Torre and Malte Zimmerman (eds), 96–110. http://www.hum2.leidenuniv.nl/pdf/lucl/sole/console9/console9-harves.pdf.

Heim, Irene. 1992. Presupposition Projection and the Semantics of Attitude Verbs. *Journal of Semantics* 9: 183–221.

Ickovič, Viktor A. 1974. Očerki sintaksičeskoj normy. *Sintaksis i norma*, Galina A. Zolotova (ed.), 43–106. Moscow: Nauka.

Jakobson, Roman. 1936/1962. Beitrag zur allgemeinen Kasuslehre. Gesamtbedeutungen der Russischen Kasus. *Selected Writings*. Vol. 2, 23–71. The Hague/Paris: Mouton.

Jakobson, Roman. 1957. The Relationship between Genitive and Plural in the Declension of Russian Nouns. *Scando-Slavica* 3(1): 181–186.

Kagan, Olga. 2007. Property-Denoting NPs and Non-Canonical Genitive Case. *Semantics and Linguistic Theory (SALT) 17*, Tova Friedman and Masayuki Gibson (eds), 148–165. Ithaca, NY: Cornell University.

Kim, Min-Joo. 2003. The Genitive of Negation in Russian: a Relativized Minimality Account. *Formal Approaches to Slavic Linguistics* 11, Wayles Browne, Ji-Yung Kim, Barbara H. Partee and Robert A. Rothstein (eds), 295–314. Ann Arbor: Michigan Slavic Publications.

Kiparsky, Paul. 1998. Partitive Case and Aspect. *The Projection of Arguments: Lexical and Compositional Factors*, Miriam Butt and Wilhelm Geuder (eds), 265–307. Stanford: CSLI Publications.

Klenin, Emily. 1978. Quantification, Partitivity, and the Genitive of Negation in Russian. *International Review of Slavic Linguistics*, Special Issue 1978, Bernard S. Comrie (ed.), 163–182.

Knorina L.V. 1988. Klassifikacija leksiki i slovarnye definicii. *Nacional'naja specifika jazyka i ee otraženie v normativnom slovare*, Jurij N. Karaulov (ed.), 60–63. Moscow: Nauka.

Neidle, Carol. 1988. *The Role of Case in Russian Syntax*. Dordrecht: Kluwer.

Padučeva, Elena V. 1984. Pritjažatel'noe mestoimenie i problema zaloga otglagol'nogo imeni. *Problemy strukturnoj lingvistiki 1982*, Viktor P. Grigor'ev (ed.), 50–66. Moscow: Nauka.

Padučeva, Elena V. 1992. O semantičeskom podxode k sintaksisu i genitivnom sub'ekte glagola BYT'. *Russian Linguistics* 16: 53–63.

Padučeva, Elena V. 1997. Roditel'nyj sub'ekta v otricatel'nom predloženii: sintaksis ili semantika? *Voprosy Jazykoznanija* 2: 101–116.

Padučeva, Elena V. 2004. The Genitive Subject of the Verb *byt'*. *Studies in Polish Linguistics* 1: 47–59.

Padučeva, Elena V. 2005. Ešče raz o genitive sub'ekta pri otricanii. *Voprosy Jazykoznanija* 5: 84–99.

Padučeva, Elena V. 2006. Genitiv dopolnenija v otricatel'nom predloženii. *Voprosy Jazykoznanija* 6: 21–43.

Partee, Barbara H. 2007. Negation, Intensionality, and Aspect: Interaction with NP Semantics. *Theoretical and crosslinguistic approaches to the semantics of aspect*, Susan Rothstein (ed.), 291–317. Amsterdam: John Benjamins.

Partee, Barbara H. and Borschev, Vladimir. 2002. Genitive of Negation and Scope of Negation in Russian Existential Sentences. *Annual Workshop on Formal Approaches to Slavic Linguistics: the Second Ann Arbor Meeting 2001 (FASL 10)*, Jindrich Toman (ed.), 181–200. Ann Arbor: Michigan Slavic Publications.

Partee, Barbara H. and Borschev, Vladimir. 2004. The Semantics of Russian Genitive of Negation: The Nature and Role of Perspectival Structure. *Proceedings of Semantics and Linguistic Theory (SALT) 14*, Kazuha Watanabe and Robert B. Young (eds), 212–234. Ithaca, NY: CLC Publications.

Paus, Charles. 1994. Social and Pragmatic Conditioning in the Demise of the Russian Partitive Case. *Russian Linguistics* 18(2): 249–266.

Paykin, Katia and Van Peteghem, Marleen. 2002. Definiteness in a Language without Articles: a Case-study of Russian. *Recherches linguistiques de Vincennes* 31: 97–112.

Paykin, Katia and Van Peteghem, Marleen. 2003. External vs. Internal Possessor Structures and Inalienability in Russian. *Russian Linguistics* 27: 329–348.

Pereltsvaig, Asya. 1999. The Genitive of Negation and Aspect in Russian. *McGill Working Papers in Linguistics* 14, Yvan Rose and Jeff Steele (eds), 111–140. Montreal: McGill University.

Pereltsvaig, Asya. 2006. Negative Polarity Items in Russian and the 'Bagel Problem'. *Negation in Slavic*, Adam Przepiorkowski and Sue Brown (eds), 153–178. Bloomington: Slavica Publishers.

Pesetsky, David. 2007. Russian Case Morphology and the Syntactic Categories. http://web.mit. edu/linguistics/people/faculty/pesetsky/Pesetsky_Harvard_morphology_workshop_ handout.pdf.

Peškovskij, Aleksandr M. 1914/1956. *Russkij sintaksis v naučnom osveščenii*, 7th edition. Moscow: Gosučpedgiz.

Pigin, M. I. 1962. Iz istorii otricatel'nyx bezličnyx predložbenij v russkom jazyke. *Lingvističeskij sbornik* 1: 3–45.

Rappaport, Gilbert C. 2000. The Slavic Noun Phrase in Comparative Perspective. *Comparative Slavic Morphology*, George Fowler (ed.). Bloomington: Slavica Publishers.

Rappaport, Gilbert C. 2002. Numeral Phrases in Russian: A Minimalist Approach. *Journal of Slavic Linguistics* 10(1/2): 329–342.

Restan, Per A. 1960. The Objective Case in Negative Clauses in Russian: the Genitive or the Accusative. *Scando-Slavica* 6: 92–112.

Revzin, Isaak I. 1973. Transformacionnoe issledovanie konstrukcij s sub'ektnym i ob'ektnym priimennym dopolneniem. Genitivus subjectivus i Genitivus objectivus. *Problemy grammatičeskogo modelirovanija*, Andrej A. Zaliznjak (ed.), 88–95. Moscow: Nauka.

Schoorlemmer, Maaike. 1998. Complex Event Nominals in Russian: Properties and Readings. *Journal of Slavic Linguistics* 6(2): 205–254.

Spencer, Andrew and Zaretskaya, Marina. 1999. The Essex Database of Russian verbs and their Nominalizations. *Essex Research Reports in Linguistics* 25: 2–34.

Švedova, Natalija Ju. et al. (eds). 1980. *Russkaja grammatika, t. 2. Sintaksis*. Moskva: Nauka.

Timberlake, Alan. 1986. Hierarchies in the Genitive of Negation. *Case in Slavic*, Richard D. Brecht and James S. Levine (eds), 338–360. Columbus, Ohio: Slavica Publishers.

Veyrenc, Jacques. 1972. Existe-t-il un genitif de l'objet? Discussion à partir du russe contemporain. *Bulletin de la Société de linguistique de Paris* 67: 215–238.

Vinogradov, Viktor V. and Istrina, Evgenija S. (eds). 1960. *Grammatika russkogo jazyka, t. 2. Sintaksis I*. Moskva: Akademija Nauk SSSR.

Vinogradov, Viktor V. and Švedova, Natalija Ju. (eds). 1964. *Očerki po istoričeskoj grammatike russkogo literaturnogo jazyka XIX veka. Izmenenija v sisteme slovosočetanij v russkom literaturnom jazyke XIX veka*. Moskva: Nauka.

Endnotes

1.   We would like to express our gratitude to the two anonymous reviewers for their insightful remarks. Needless to say, we are responsible for all remaining imperfections.

2.   Wherever appropriate, we have used attested examples coming from different sources: the Russian National Corpus, texts after 1960 (RNC – http://www.ruscorpora.ru), Internet (Google) and various linguistic studies. We have also included our own examples, all tested with native speakers.

3.   The abbreviations and glossing conventions used follow the Leipzig Glossing Rules. Besides standard abbreviations, we have used the following ones: AGR: agreeing form; GENa: genitive ending in -*a* (indicated only when relevant); GENu: genitive ending in -*u* (indicated only when

relevant); IMPERS: impersonal form (in the present tense: non agreeing third person; in the past: neuter singular form); PRO: pronoun. Our glosses systematically indicate noun cases. Other grammatical information is provided only when necessary for our analysis.

4.   We will single out the relevant form with italics.

5.   We use the term "assign" without any theoretical commitment.

6.   The zero ending appears also with masculine nouns in *-in* (*gospodin* 'gentleman' – *gospod-ø*). There are also some nouns that have two forms for the plural, one ending in *-ov/-ev* or *-ej* and another form with a zero ending, such as *kilogram* 'kilogram' – *kilogramm-ov* or *kilogramm-ø*, *pomidor* 'tomato' – *pomidor-ov* or *pomidor-ø*, *sveč-a* 'candle' – *sveč-ej* or *sveč-ø*. The tendency in Modern Russian is to use the short form.

7.   Stressed vowels are underlined, and genitive endings are marked in italics.

8.   Adjectival determiners, such as demonstratives (*étot* 'this', *tot* 'that') or quantifiers (*ves* 'entire'), have different endings, but show a similar pattern to that of ordinary adjectives.

9.   The same pattern applies to nouns such as *armija* 'army' with a root ending in a soft consonant.

10.   We will not discuss the boundary between the root ending in a soft consonant and the ending, our glosses being based on the Cyrillic orthographic system. Therefore we will consider *-ja* (*-я*) as an ending.

11.   For phonological reasons, Russian 3SG/PL personal pronouns used after prepositions take the initial consonant *n*: *ego – dlja nego* 'him – for him'; *ix – dlja nix* 'them – for them', etc.

12.   Sometimes, the presence of an explicit determiner can orient the analysis either toward the NP type (i) or toward the N type (ii), but in the majority of cases, the exact constituent type is difficult to establish.

    (i)   *stakan étogo vina*   'glass of this wine'

    (ii)   *étot stakan vina*   'this glass of wine'

13.   The reflexive possessive pronoun has also an adjectival form, which can be contrasted with its genitive form, e.g. *svo-j* 'his/her/its/their own' vs. *seb-ja* 'self-GEN'.

14.   The sign # indicates that the sentence is grammatically correct, but does not have an appropriate meaning in the given context.

15.   The modifier is mostly an adjective, but can take various other forms (genitive NP, relative clause, etc.).

    (i)   bilet-y   cvet-a   *svež-ej*   *zelen-i* (RNC)
        bank-notes-NOM   color-GEN   fresh-GEN   greens-GEN
        'bank-notes of the color of fresh greens'

    (ii)   avtomobil-i   to-go   cvet-a,   *kotor-yj*   *zakazyval-i* (RNC)
        cars-NOM   that-GEN   color-GEN   which-ACC   ordered-PL
        'cars of the very color that was ordered'

16.   In Modern Russian, the prepositional construction is preferred in these cases.

17.   These semantic relations can be identified through possible alternations between the adnominal genitive and various PPs:

- PPs with *ot* typically express part-whole relations (*nožka stola* 'a table's leg' – *nožka ot stola* 'a leg from a table'), source (*dym kostra* 'a bonfire's smoke' – *dym ot kostra* 'smoke from a bonfire'), cause (*slëzy vostorga* 'tears of joy' – *slëzy ot vostorga* 'tears from joy'), etc.

- PPs with *iz* denote a source, an origin (*čelovek goroda* 'an urban person' – *čelovek iz goroda* 'a man from a city').

It should be noted that these PPs do not share all formal characteristics of the possessive genitive in a strict sense (they do not accept the interrogative form *čej* 'whose' and they do not always authorise the possessive pronoun, the possessive adjective and the *u*-construction).

18. In addition, against what is argued in Rappaport (2000), NPs like *slëzy vostorga* 'tears of joy' should not be considered as adjuncts, as N2 cannot function as a predicate, the relationship between N1 and N2 cannot be reversed, there is no modifier on N2 and N2 can be replaced by a PP with the preposition *ot* (§ 3.1.2.1).

19. We do not agree with Rappaport (2000), who provides examples combining a subject and a possessive adnominal genitive, which we consider ungrammatical. For a discussion about whether the process noun has one or two adnominal positions, see Veyrenc (1972), Revzin (1973), Rappaport (2000).

20. When the subject argument is pronominal, Russian uses the possessive pronoun rather than the instrumental case of the personal pronoun, although both are possible.

Vaš-e   ispolneni-e/Ispolneni-e   *vam-i*   Glink-i
your-NOM   performance-NOM/performance-NOM you-INS Glinka-GEN
bylo prekrasno.
was wonderful
'Your performance of Glinka was wonderful.'

The description of the various semantic differences between the two structures goes beyond the scope of the present paper. For more details, see Padučeva (1984), Schoorlemmer (1998) and Spencer & Zaretskaya (1999).

21. Analogous facts are also found in other languages, in which certain numerals behave like nouns (e.g. Romanian *o sută* 'one hundred', *o mie* 'one thousand'). Even in English, numerals such as *hundred* and *thousand* are used with a determiner (*a/one hundred, a/one thousand*).

22. *Mnog-o* 'much' is the adverb corresponding to the variable adjective *mnog-ij*. In Russian morphology, the *o*-ending is also typically neuter, because it is found as the neuter ending of past tense verbs and singular predicative adjectives.

(i)   Derev-o   upal-o.
      tree-NOM.N.SG fell-N.SG
      'A/The tree fell.'

(ii) Et-o   derev-o   neobyknovenno krasiv-o
      this-NOM.N.SG tree-NOM.N.SG   singularly   beautiful-NOM.N.SG
      osen'-ju. (RNC)
      fall-INS
      'This tree is singularly beautiful in the fall.'

It is also the ending of impersonal verbs in the past (e.g. *doždil-o* 'it was raining').

23. Not all adverbial specifiers show both forms in the structural cases. *Skol'ko* 'how much/many', *neskol'ko* 'some' and *stol'ko* 'so much/many' have a variable form only in oblique cases. As for *malo* 'few/little' and *dostatočno* 'sufficiently', they can function as quantitative specifiers only in their adverbial form. Although they do have an agreeing form, it functions as a qualitative adjective, meaning respectively 'small' and 'sufficient'. When a quantitative specifier is needed in the oblique case, Russian resorts to the structure [ADJ + *količestvo* 'quantity' + N-GEN.PL].

(i) On   znaet   *mal-o*   *jazyk-ov/*mal-ye*   *jazyk-i.*

he.NOM knows few-ADV languages-GEN/*few-ACC.PL languages-ACC.PL

'He knows few languages.'

(ii) *On   vladeet *mal-ymi*   *jazyk-ami/mal-o*   *jazyk-ov*

he.NOM possesses few-INS.PL languages-INS.PL/few-ADV languages-GEN

(iii) On   vladeet *mal-ym*   *količestv-om*   *jazyk-ov.*

he.NOM possesses little-INS.SG quantity-INS.SG languages-GEN.PL

'He knows few languages.'

24. In Russian, a predicate is impersonal when it occurs in the third person singular without agreement or takes a neuter form in the past tenses, which normally agree in number and gender with the subject.

25. Differences between paucal and non-paucal numbers are also found in other languages, such as Romanian, where the limit between the two kinds of numbers is fixed between 19 (paucal) and 20 (non-paucal). The paucal numbers are immediately followed by the noun, while the non-paucal numbers require the presence of the preposition *de* between the numeral and the noun (*treisprezece cărţi* '13 books' vs. *treizeci de cărţi* thirty DE books, 'thirty books'). However, it is worth noting that, although Romanian has genitive case, it uses the preposition *de* instead of the genitive here.

26. For *pluralia tantum* nouns, such as *brjuki* 'trousers' or *sutki* 'twenty-four hours', the use of paucal numbers is impossible. Numbers 'two' to 'four' are replaced by collective numerals, which are normally used with animate nouns only, e.g. *dvoe brjuk* 'two pairs of trousers'. The paucal compounds are completely excluded.

27. In contemporary Russian, the noun *čelovek* 'person' has lost its morphological plural form *čeloveki*, which has been replaced by a "suppletive" plural *ljudi*. The genitive plural form *čelovek* seems to be a remnant of this obsolete form.

28. A Google search does show the form *pjat' ljudej* 'five people' (around 400 hits).

Pjat' ljud-ej   stal-i   žertv-ami   avtoavari-i.

five   people-GEN became victims-INS car.crash-GEN

'Five people became victims in a car crash.'

29. We mention only the imperfective form. The case assignment is the same for the perfective form(s).

30. As summarized by Forbes (2008), "a verb is intensional if the verb phrase (VP) it forms with its complement is anomalous in at least one of three ways: (i) interchanging expressions in the complement referring to the same entity can change the truth-value of the sentence embedding the VP; (ii) the VP admits of a special "unspecific" reading if it contains a quantifier, or a certain type of quantifier; (iii) the normal existential commitments of names and existential quantifiers in the complement are suspended even when the embedding sentence is negation-free." A typical example is *Max imagined/wanted/needed/looked-for a unicorn*, in which the existence of the referent of the direct object is not presupposed.

31.   The genitive is mostly used with partitive meaning (see § 4.3).

32.   Padučeva (1997), Babby (2001), Kim (2003) and many others have argued that genitive marking of the subject is allowed only if the verb is semantically empty or existential or if it can be interpreted as having an existential meaning as a result of semantic bleaching. In these contexts, the unergative verb can be considered to have an "unaccusative use", since its unique argument is introduced in the complement position.

33.   According to Peškovskij (1914), the Russian grammatical tradition accepted nothing but the genitive for an object occurring in a negative context. Over time, the accusative became more and more common until it eventually started to compete with the genitive (see also Restan 1960).

34.   For a discussion on sentence initial negative subjects, see Borschev & Partee (1998, 2002a,b), who argue against Babby (1980) and his rhematic status of the genitive subject. On the basis of examples like the following, Borschev & Partee claim that the choice of the case depends on the information structure, but not solely on the informative status of the subject. Other constituents of the clause, such as time constituents or locative arguments, should be taken into account as well.

> Ja   iskal   kefir.   *Kefir-a* v   magazin-e ne   byl-o.
> I.NOM   looked.for kefir.ACC kefir-GEN in store-LOC NEG   was-IMPERS
> 'I was looking for kefir. There wasn't any kefir in the store.'
>
> (Borschev & Partee 1998, 2002a,b)

For a syntactic account of sentence initial negative genitive subjects, see Bailyn (1997).

35.   For other lexical restrictions on the genitive of negation, see Borschev et al. (2008).

36.   The genitive object has been less well-studied, which is probably due to the syncretism between accusative and genitive case for masculine animate nouns and for all pronouns.

37.   See Partee & Borschev (2004), who relate the case choice to what they call the "perspectival structure".

38.   However, verbs with the affix *-sja* (cf. *naest'sja* 'eat one's fill' or *napit'sja* 'quench one's thirst'), always assign genitive case and, therefore, cannot be combined with accusative quantifiers.

39.   The partitive genitive can be found, for instance, with imperfective verbs such as *nabirat'sja* 'accumulate', containing the prefix *na–* and the reflexive affix *-sja*, which denote actions with a cumulative effect.

> Mužčin-a nabiraetsja   *um-a*   k   28 god-am. (Google)
> man-NOM   accumulates.IPFV intellect-GEN to 28 years-DAT
> 'A man accumulates his intelligence by 28 years of age.'

Nominal and pronominal possessors in Romanian

Ion Giurgea and Carmen Dobrovie-Sorin
'Iorgu Iordan – Al. Rosetti' Institute of Linguistics of the Romanian
Academy and Institute of LLF/CNRS & Université Paris VII

We describe the syntax and morphology of the genitival construction of
Romanian, and we insist on the syntactic analysis of some peculiar properties
of these constructions: the alternation between genitives introduced by the
agreeing particle *al* and those without *al*, the status of this agreeing particle, the
similarity in distribution between genitives and agreeing possessors, and the
alternation between agreeing and genitival forms in the paradigm of pronominal
possessors. We argue that the absence of *al* after the suffixal definite article is the
result of a PF-deletion rule. We conclude that *al* is probably ambiguous between
an agreeing case-marker and a [pro-N+D] complex, and we show that this
peculiar distribution results from the history of *al* (which goes back to a definite
article). We argue that agreeing possessors – so-called "possessive adjectives"
– are pronouns rather than adjectives, which is particularly clear in Romanian
given their genitival distribution. The alternation between agreeing and genitive-
marked pronominal possessors is shown to obey a morphological constraint,
which disallows pronominal roots in combination with more than one set of
inflectional phi-features. This explains why agreeing forms are only found where
the inherent phi-features of the pronoun are marked on the root, whereas 3rd
person pronouns, which mark the inherent phi-features on the inflectional
morpheme, have genitive forms.

1. Introduction

In this paper, we will present the most important generalizations in the distribution of
genitive DPs in Romanian, and we will discuss in detail some properties that distinguish Romanian from other Romance languages and English and that are not adequate-
ly described by the available syntactic analyses: (i) the alternation between genitives
with and without the genitive particle *al*, and the status of this genitive particle, and
(ii) the alternation between genitive-marked and agreeing pronominal possessors.

Romanian genitive case is marked by special endings only on determiners. These endings are the same as those found in dative marked DPs, hence the cover term 'oblique case'. They mark case together with gender and number, in a bundled morpheme (m.sg. *-ui*, f.sg. *-ei*, pl. *-or*)[1]:

(1) a.   un băiat / (niște) băieți / băiat-ul / băieți-i[2]
          a   boy   (some) boys   boy-the   boys-the

     b.   un-**ui** băiat / un-**or** băieți   / băiatu-l-**ui**   / băieți-l-**or**
          a-OBL boy   / some-OBL boys / boy-the-OBL   / boys-the-OBL

For nouns and adjectives, the oblique case is marked only in the feminine singular, where a form identical to the plural appears if the DP is introduced by a determiner bearing the oblique morpheme:

(2) a.   o   alt-ă   cas-ă
          a.FSG other-FSG house-FSG
          'another house'

     b.   alt-**e**   cas-**e**
          other-FPL house-FPL
          'other houses'

     c.   un-*ei*   alt-**e**   cas-**e**
          a-OBL.FSG other-*e* house-*e*
          'to/of another house'

If the determiner introducing the noun phrase has a defective inflection (cardinals, some quantity words, neuter indefinite pronouns), the genitive is not marked by an ending, but by the preposition *a*. With bare nouns, the preposition *de* 'of' is used. The full paradigm is given below. We illustrate this with a complex event noun (cf. Grimshaw 1990), where we can see clearly that the three types of genitive occupy the same position (here, the complement position):

(3) a.   achiziționare-a **cărți-lor**   / **unor**   cărți de către
          acquisition-the books-the.OBL   some.OBL books of towards
          bibliotecă
          library
          'the acquisition of the books/of some books by the library'

     b.   achiziționare-a **a trei**   cărți de către   bibliotecă
          acquisition-the *a* three books of towards library
          'the acquisition of three books by the library'

     c.   achiziționare-a **de cărți** de către   bibliotecă
          acquisition-the *de* books of towards library
          'the acquisition of books by the library'

The inflectional genitive has a peculiar distribution: it either immediately follows the suffixal definite article, or the so-called 'genitival (or possessive) article' *al*, an item which agrees in gender and number with the head noun (the 'possessee')[3]:

(4) a. prieteni-**i**   fete-i
         friends-the girl.OBL-the.FSG.OBL
         'the girl's friends'

     b. prieteni-**i**   buni **ai**   fete-i
         friends-the good *al*.MPL girl.OBL-the.FSG.OBL
         'the girl's good friends'

     c. un/acest/oricare prieten **al**   fete-i
         a/ this/ any   friend[M] *al*.MSG girl.OBL-the.FSG.OBL
         'a/this/any friend of the girl'

Pronominal possessors have a non-uniform paradigm: 3rd person pronouns are morphologically marked for the Genitive, on a par with DPs headed by nouns, whereas 1st and 2nd person pronouns are not Case-marked but instead use agreeing forms (the so-called 'possessive adjectives'). These agreeing forms have the same distribution as DPs marked by inflectional genitive: they appear immediately after the definite article or after *al*:

(5) a. un/acest/oricare prieten al   meu
         a/this/any   friend[M] *al*.MSG my.MSG
         'a/this/any friend of mine'

     b. prieteni-**i**   mei
         friends[MASC]-the my.MPL
         'my friends'

For the 3rd person singular, in addition to genitive pronouns there is also an agreeing form (*său, sa*), formerly a reflexive.

The distribution of genitive-marked and agreeing personal pronouns (which we will label 'pronominal possessors') differs slightly from the distribution of other genitives (see Section 2.4):

(6) prieteni-i   {mei   / lui   / *naturi-i}   buni
     friends[M]-the my.MPL / he.OBL / nature.OBL-the.OBL good.MPL
     'my/his/*nature's good friends'

The article is organized as follows: in Section 2 we examine the distribution of the genitive article *al* and the alternation between 'bare genitives' (i.e., inflectional genitives not preceded by *al*) and *al*-genitives. In Sub-Section 2.1, we discuss Grosu's (1988, 1994) analysis of the alternation between *al*- and bare genitives (Grosu 1988, 1994) and we show that it faces serious problems in dealing with non-pronominal genitives (i.e. all genitives except personal pronouns). We present a solution that has been proposed independently by Ortmann & Popescu (2000) and Dobrovie-Sorin & Giurgea (2005) (and, in slightly different wording, by Cornilescu (1994)), according to which bare genitives are *al*-genitives in which *al* has been deleted by a rule applying in the morphological component (under linear adjacency with the definite article). In § 2.2 we examine various possible analyses of *al* and we show that a unified account for all of its uses is difficult to achieve. In § 2.3, we briefly present the historical developments which led to the present-day complex situation. In § 2.4 we concentrate on pronominal possessors (genitive-marked and agreeing possessors), and we explain why they behave differently from nominal possessors. In Section 3 we examine the alternation between agreeing and genitive-marked forms in the paradigm of pronominal possessors.

2.   The alternation between bare genitives and *al*-genitives and the status of *al*

2.1   The distribution of bare genitives and *al*-phrases

As already mentioned in the introduction, the 'genitival article' *al* cannot appear immediately after the suffixal definite article. In all other contexts, *al* immediately precedes an inflectional genitive or agreeing possessor:[4]

(7) a. aceste reuşite   *(ale) profesoru-lui
         these successes[F] *al*.FPL professor-the.OBL
         'these successes of the professor'

     b. aceste reuşite   *(ale) mele
         these successes[F] *al*.FPL my.FPL
         'these successes of mine'

(8) a. reuşit-a   (*a)   profesoru-lui
         success[F]-the (*al*.FSG) professor-the.OBL
         'the professor's success'

     b. reuşit-a   (*a)   mea
         success[F]-the (*al*.FSG) my.FSG
         'my success'

Given that the genitival article *al* bears a strong resemblance to the suffixal definite article, as can be seen in (9) below, it has been proposed that *al* contains an instance of the definite article (Grosu 1988, 1994 analyzes *al* as P(reposition)+D; d'Hulst et al. (1997) analyze it as N+D, where *a-* represents a pro-N), and that genitive case is assigned by the definite article under government and adjacency (Grosu 1988).

(9) *al*   Definite article, Nom-Acc. forms
     M.SG   *al*   -(u)l, -le
     F.SG   *a*   -a
     M.PL   *ai*   -i
     F.PL   *ale* -le

The adjacency constraint on the assignment of Genitive Case can be illustrated in examples such as (10), which show that even if the definite article is present, *al* obligatorily appears to mark a genitive that is not adjacent to the N:

(10) a. maşin-a albă a mame-i
car[F]-the white *al*.FSG mother.OBL-the.OBL
'mother's white car'

b. starea economică a Români-ei
situation[F]-the economic *al*.FSG Romania.OBL-the.OBL
'Romania's economic situation'

c. frumoasa carte a Mari-ei
beautiful-the book[F] *al*.FSG Maria.OBL-the.OBL
'Maria's beautiful book'

The adjacency constraint on the assignment of Genitive Case is problematic, however, since other Cases, like Accusative Case, are not subject to any adjacency constraint in Romanian.

The relation between *al* and the definite determiner is obvious for DP-initial *al*-phrases. In this construction, no other determiner is present and the matrix DP has a definite interpretation. Note, however, that this construction, which was more frequent in old Romanian, is nowadays obsolete and restricted to poetry, as shown in (11a), except for *wh*- words, as shown in (11b):

(11) a. ⁇ai ţări-i eroi
al.MPL country.OBL-the.OBL heroes
'the country's heroes'

b. ai căr-ei eroi
al.MPL which-FSG.OBL heroes
'whose heroes'

This construction probably reflects the origin of *al* (as we will show in § 2.3, *al* must have been the strong form of the definite article in an unattested stage of Romanian). The standard language now has *cel* as an independent definite article, a form derived from the distal demonstrative (*acel(a)*).

The definite determiner use is still alive in cases of ellipsis of the possessee: as illustrated in (12), 'free-standing' *al*- phrases may appear in argument positions, interpreted as definite DPs with the possessee elided.

(12) Maşina mea e parcată în faţ-a case-i.
car[F]-the my is parked in face-the house.OBL-the.OBL
A Mariei e după colţ.
al.FSG Maria.OBL-the.OBL is behind corner
'My car is parked in front of the house. Maria's is behind the corner.'

This use supports the analysis of *al* as N+D (*a-* being a pro-N and D the definite article), proposed by d'Hulst et al. (1997). Remember that the idea that *al* contains the definite article is crucial in explaining the alternation between bare genitives and *al*-genitives by the definite article under government and adjacency.

However, the hypothesis that genitive is assigned by the suffixal definite article faces severe problems in the case of non-pronominal possessors. Note that in order to explain (8), we must assume that N has raised to D and that genitive is assigned to the specifier of a projection immediately below D (Cornilescu 1993, 1994 proposes AgrGenP; we can also call it PossP, nP or NP):

(13) $[_D [_N\text{reușită}]-[_D a] [_{NP/PossP} \text{profesorului } t_N]]$

But then, since adjectives are normally postnominal in Romanian, we expect to find the order N+D-Gen-Adj.:

(14) $[_{DP} D [_{NP/PossP} \text{Gen } [N \text{ Adj}]] \rightarrow [_{DP} N+D [_{NP/PossP} \text{Gen } [t_N \text{ Adj}]]]$

However, for non-pronominal genitives, this order is severely restricted, being excluded with classifying adjectives and only marginally allowed with light quality adjectives (i.e., adjectives without complements or modifiers or very long stems) if they are contrastively focused (see (15c)). Only heavy APs are allowed in the post-genitive position (see (15d)):

(15)   a.   *stare-a   Români-ei   economică
             situation-the Romania.OBL-the.OBL economic
             'Romania's economic situation'

       b.   ??mașin-a Mari-ei   albă
             car-the   Maria.OBL-the.OBL white
             'Maria's white car'

       c.   mașina Mari-ei   ALBĂ
             car-the Maria.OBL-the.OBL white
             'Maria's WHITE car'

       d.   parte-a țări-i   [bogată în cereale]
             part-the country.OBL-the.OBL rich   in cereals
             'the part of the country rich in corn'

Note, furthermore, that DP-initial adjectives can carry the suffixal definite article. In this case, if the genitive were assigned by the definite D under adjacency to the Spec of a projection immediately below, we would expect to find the order Adj-Def – N – Gen. But this order is excluded with non-pronominal genitives (see Section 2.4 below for pronominal genitives occupying this position):

(16)   a.   *frumoas-a   Mari-ei   carte
             beautiful-the Maria.OBL-the.OBL book
             'Maria's beautiful book'

b. *prim-a   profesori-lor   reuniune
   first-the professors-the.OBL reunion
   'the professors' first reunion'

The hypothesis that genitive Case is assigned under adjacency by the definite article is also problematic in the light of data regarding coordinated genitives. If genitive were assigned to a Spec immediately below D, it should be assigned to both members of the conjunction, and therefore we expect *al* to be absent in the second conjunct. This expectation is confirmed by examples like (17), where the coordinated DP is the argument of an eventive noun that selects a group (which correspond to "the physicians and journalists met", not to "the physicians met and the journalists also met"):

(17) întâlnire-a   [medici-lor   şi   jurnalişti-lor]
      reunion-the physicians-the.OBL and journalists-the.OBL
      'the physicians and journalists' reunion'

Note that if the definite article does not immediately precede the genitive, coordination under *al* appears:

(18) prima   întâlnire   a   [medici-lor   şi   jurnalişti-lor]
      first-the reunion[F] *al*.FSG physicians-the.OBL and journalists-the.OBL
      'the first reunion of the physicians and the journalists'

However, in examples like (19), where the coordinated DP refers to two possessors of the same apartment, the use of *al* in the second conjunct is obligatory, as indicated in (19a), or at best optional, as in examples such as (19b–c), where the two conjuncts have a similar simple syntactic form, e.g. two proper names:

(19) a. Apartament-ul mame-i   mele   şi   *(al)
          apartment-the mother.OBL-the.OBL my.FSG.OBL and *(*al*.MSG)
          Mari-ei   a   fost vândut
          Maria.OBL-the.OBL has been sold
          'My mother and Maria's apartment has been sold'

      b. apartament-ul Mari-ei   şi   al   Cristine-i
          apartment-the Maria.OBL-the.OBL and *al*.MSG Cristina.OBL-the.OBL
          'Maria and Cristina's apartment'

      c. apartament-ul Mari-ei   şi   Cristine-i
          apartment-the Maria.OBL-the.OBL and Cristina.OBL-the.OBL
          'Maria and Cristina's apartment'

The examples in (17)–(18) show that two genitives may be coordinated under either *al* or a definite article suffixed on a noun, as expected if genitive Case is assigned to the DP that dominates the two coordinated DPs. However, the examples in (19a–c) show that an *al*-genitive can be coordinated with a bare genitive, which is unexpected under the analysis under discussion here. As shown by the singular agreement on the verb,

(19a) involves one possessee, which means that the phrase *al Mariei* is not a free-standing possessive DP coordinated to [*apartamentul mamei mele*]. Instead, it is the two genitives that are coordinated:

(19)   a.   Apartamentul [[mamei mele] şi [al Mariei]]

A characteristic property of coordination structures is that the conjuncts can appear in any order. But then, if we assume that the Spec position below the definite D hosts the two coordinated genitives (the bare genitive and the *al*- phrase), we should be able to find them in any order. This is not what happens: *al* is totally excluded after the definite article.

(20)   *apartament-ul [[al   Mari-ei]   şi   [(al)
        apartment-the *al*.MSG Maria.OBL-the.OBL and *al*.MSG
        mame-i   mele]]
        mother.OBL-the.OBL my.FSG.OBL

A different account for the distribution of genitives was proposed by Dobrovie-Sorin (2000, 2002), based on a comparison with the Hebrew Construct State: in both constructions, the Possessor would occupy a rightward SpecDP position that must be adjacent to the head N. In *al*- genitives, the head noun is *a*-, analyzed as a pro-N, to which the definite article is suffixed (as proposed by d'Hulst et al. 1997). In addition to the fact that adjacency between N and SpecDP is stipulated, this account is problematic because it predicts that bare genitives cannot be followed by NP-internal material, but only by DP-adjuncts. But bare genitives may be followed by complements of the noun (see (21b)), which are NP-internal, so they cannot be attached above SpecDP:

(21)   a.   raportare-a oameni-lor   la   divinitate
            relating-the people-the.OBL to   divinity
            'the way people see their relation with the divinity'

       b.   căsători-a   Ioane-i   cu   Silviu
            marriage-the Ioana.OBL-the.OBL with Silviu
            'Ioana's marriage with Silviu'

The coordination facts illustrated in (19) above are also problematic, because bare genitives and *al*- genitives occupy different syntactic positions according to this account (bare genitives are analyzed as specifiers of DP, and *al*- genitives as DP-adjuncts).

The various problems observed above can be solved if we adopt a PF-based account (Phonological Form) for the alternation between *al*- and bare genitives: according to Ortmann and Popescu (2000) and Dobrovie-Sorin and Giurgea (2005), bare genitives (examples like (8), where Possessors follow a definite article suffixed to the head N) can themselves be analyzed as containing an underlying *al*, which has been deleted by a PF-rule, i.e. a rule that applies at the level of Phonologic Form (PF):

(22) a. reuşit-**a**   a̶   profesoru-lui
       success[F]-the *al*.FSG professor-the.OBL

b. reuşit-**a**   a̶   mea
       success[F]-the *al*.FSG my.FSG

The postulated deletion is phonologically plausible: *al* is made up of an invariable part *a-*, followed by a suffixal morpheme expressing bundled Number-Gender, which is identical to the most frequent forms of the suffixal definite article (*-l, -a, -i, -le*). This implies that the rule deleting *al* is similar to haplology, which deletes one of two adjacent identical elements. Cornilescu (1994) proposed a very similar analysis: she also holds that the functional item *al* (which she analyzes as an expletive determiner) is present in bare genitives. Because its features are the same as those of the definite article, in case of adjacency, they "incorporate, or merge with those of the definite article, so that the genitival article is no longer lexicalized" (Cornilescu 1994: 320).

Note that not only DP-internal constituents, but also parentheticals intervening between the definite article and the genitive require the presence of *al*:

(23) Început-ul,   aşadar/de altfel, *(al) romanu-lui   era   plictisitor
     beginning-the thus/ by the way *al*.MSG novel-the.OBL was boring
     'The beginning, thus/by the way, of the novel was boring.'

This is immediately explained under the hypothesis of *al*-deletion under PF-adjacency: parentheticals disrupt adjacency, so deletion cannot apply. The hypothesis of genitive assignment by D makes the wrong prediction in this case: since parentheticals such as those in (23) are not adnominal/DP-internal constituents, the genitive can be taken to occupy a specifier position immediately below D, so it should be able to receive genitive from D.

The hypothesis that bare genitives are *al*-genitives syntactically (i.e. in the syntactic representation) predicts that bare genitives have the same syntactic distribution as postnominal *al*-genitives (leaving aside the case of adjacency with the definite article, of course). This prediction is confirmed by the data in (24), which show that the constraints on the relative order between adjectives and postnominal bare genitives observed in (15) above also apply to postnominal *al*-genitives:

(24) a. această stare   (*a   Români-ei)   economică
       this   situation[F] (*al*.FSG Romania.OBL-the.OBL) economic
       (a   Români-ei)
       (*al*.FSG Romania.OBL-the.OBL)
       'this economic situation of Romania'

b. o carte   (*a   Mari-ei)   frumoasă (a
       a book[F] (*al*.FSG Maria.OBL-the.OBL) beautiful (*al*.FSG
       Mari-ei)
       Maria.OBL-the.OBL)
       'a nice book of Maria('s)'

    c. o carte   a   Mari-ei   [foarte renumită]
      a book[F] *al*.FSG Maria-the.GEN very   famous
      'a very famous book of Maria('s)'

    d. *o frumoasă a   Mari-ei   carte
      a beautiful *al*.FSG Maria.OBL-the.OBL book[F]
      'a beautiful book of Mary'(s)'

The PF-deletion hypothesis can also account for the data regarding coordinated configurations. Granting that postnominal genitives are underlyingly *al*-genitives, the optionality of *al* in the second conjunct of the example in (19b–c) can be analyzed as being due to the two possible configurations shown in(19'b–c):

(19)' b. apartament-ul [[a̶l̶   Mari-ei]   şi   [al
      apartment-the   *al*.MSG Maria.OBL-the.OBL and   *al*.MSG
      Cristine-i]]
      Cristina.OBL-the.OBL
      'Maria and Cristina's apartment'

    c. apartament-ul [a̶l̶   [Mari-ei   şi   Cristine-i]]
      apartment-the   *al*.MSG Maria.OBL-the.OBL and Cristina.OBL-the.OBL
      'Maria and Cristina's apartment'

In (19'b) each of the two conjuncts is an *al*-genitive: the first one is deleted under adjacency, and the second one survives at PF. In (19'c), on the other hand, *al* takes as a complement a coordinated DP made up of two simple genitives, and is deleted under adjacency.

2.2   The analysis of *al*-phrases

Having concluded that (non-pronominal) bare genitives are disguised *al*-phrases, let us turn now to the analysis of *al* itself.

    We have seen that free-standing genitives (see (12) above, repeated below) support an analysis of *al* as composed of a pro-N element (realized as *a-*) standing for the Possessee, followed by the suffixal definite article carrying the φ-features of the Possessee (*-l, -a, -i, -le*; in the feminine singular, *a-+-a > a*) (Coene 1999, d'Hulst, Coene & Tasmowski 1997, Dobrovie-Sorin (2000, 2002)):

(12) Maşin-a   mea e parcată în faţ-a   case-i.
     car[F]-the my is parked in face-the house.OBL-the.OBL
     A   Mari-ei   e după   colţ.
     al.FSG Maria OBL-the.OBL is behind corner
     'My car is parked in front of the house. Maria's is behind the corner.'

(12)' $[_{DP} [_{N}a] [_{D}a] [_{DPGen} Mariei]]$

For the postnominal use, the analysis of *al* as N+D is difficult, since the Possessee is expressed by an overt N. This problem could be solved by assuming that *al* is a mere D (without any N) (cf. Cornilescu 1994). However, this analysis is also problematic, because no double definiteness effect can be observed in this configuration. Indeed, postnominal *al* genitives can combine with any determiner on the head noun, or with no determiner at all (see 25b):

(25) a. o/fiecare/vreo/nicio carte   a   Ioane-i
          a/every/some/no   book[F] *al*.FSG Ioana.OBL-the.OBL
          'a/each/some/no book of Ioana'(s)'

      b. Ionescu este acum președinte al   Camere-i
          Ionescu is   now   president *al*.MSG Chamber.OBL-the.OBL
          Deputați-lor
          Deputies-the.OBL
          'Ionescu is now president of the Chamber of Deputies.'

In order to solve this problem, Dobrovie-Sorin (2000) proposed that in postnominal position, *al* functions as a relativizer:

(25)′ [$_{DP}$ [$_{DP}$ o carte] [$_{DP}$ [$_{D+N}$ al] [$_{DPGen}$ Ioanei]]]

This hypothesis is problematic, however, for *al*-phrases functioning as complements, which cannot be analyzed as reduced relatives (see also (7))[5]:

(26) a. prim-a reprezentare a   piese-i
          first-the performing *al*.FSG play.OBL-the.OBL
          'the first performance of the play'

      b. acest prieten al   Ioane-i
          this friend *al*.FSG Ioana.OBL-the.OBL
          'this friend of Ioana'

Note that *al*-genitives may appear as complements of complex event nominalizations, whose argument status is well-established:[6]

(27) a. cumpărare-a pripită a   întreprinderi-i   de către
          buying[F]-the rash   *al*.FSG enterprise.OBL-the.OBL   of towards
          stat
          state
          'the reckless buying of the enterprise by the state'

      b. discutare-a   frecventă a   acestor probleme în consiliu
          discussion[F]-the frequent *al*.FSG these.OBL problems in council
          'the frequent discussion of these problems in the council'

      c. prim-a atribuire   a   premiu-lui   de stat unui   străin
          first-the attribution[F] *al*.FSG prize-the.GEN of state a.DAT foreigner
          'the first awarding of the state prize to a foreigner'

Cornilescu (1993) analyzed *al* as an 'expletive determiner', whose only function is to assign genitive case. Grosu (1994) decomposes *al* into the preposition *a-* and a functional item that is somehow related to the definite article *-L*, but that lost its determiner force ("a functional head obtained from the definite article by neutralizing the feature [N]" (Grosu 1994: 165), neutralization which would also explain "de-semanticization, specifically, the loss of definiteness" (ibid.)). According to other authors, *al* is an agreeing case-marker (Giurgea 2008, Giusti 2008). The idea that in adnominal positions *al* is a preposition or case marker brings *al*-genitives close to the prepositional genitives used with nominal projections which cannot inflect for case (see (2): *a* + determiners not inflected for case, *de* + bare nouns). We can say that depending on the type of nominal projection, structural adnominal case is realized by different functional prepositions/case markers (*al, a, de*) (see Cornilescu 1993 for a similar view). *Al* has the peculiarity of agreeing with the head noun and of combining with a DP marked as dative. We suggest that by developing the marker *al*, Romanian restored the distinction between genitive and dative. The existence of genitive markers agreeing with the possessee is also attested in Bantu languages (see Carstens 1991) and Albanian (see Faensen 1975).

We will now try to see whether the analysis of *al* as a genitive marker with agreement features can be extended to the uses which support a determiner status of *al* (the free-standing use and the prenominal use).

If *al* does not contain a pro-N (as in the analysis in (12)′), we should assume that the free-standing use illustrated in (12) relies on the ellipsis of the possessee:

(28)   [$_D$ D [[$_N$Ø] [a Mariei]]   or   [[a Mariei] D [$_N$Ø]]

We still have to explain how the matrix DP comes to be interpreted as definite, in the absence of the definite article. Since prenominal *al*-phrases also mark the DP as definite, Cornilescu (1994) proposed that free-standing *al*-phrases are DP-initial *al*-phrases followed by noun ellipsis.[7] However, prenominal *al*-phrases are no longer in use, except for the relative *al cărui*, while free-standing *al*-phrases are fully grammatical. This suggests that we cannot reduce free-standing *al*-phrases to prenominal *al-* phrases followed by noun ellipsis. Another fact which leads to the same conclusion is that the elided noun phrase cannot contain any overt adnominal material, but only material which can follow a postnominal *al*-phrase (see (29a) vs. c–d). Light adjectives, which, as we have seen, cannot precede genitives (see (15a–b)), cannot follow a free-standing *al*-phrase (see (29a)), but require the insertion of the independent definite article *cel* (see (29b)). If the free-standing *al*-phrase were a prenominal *al*-phrase followed by ellipsis, we would expect any adnominal material to be able to follow it, because prenominal *al*-phrases precede the entire NP-material (they are DP-initial).

(29)   a.   *Maşin-a   veche   a   bunici-i   merge mai
             car[F]-the old   al.FSG grandmother.OBL-the.OBL   runs   more

bine decât a   Ioane-i   nouă
good than *al*.FSG Ioana.OBL-the.OBL new
'Grandmother's old car runs better than Ioana's new one.'

b. Maşina   veche a   bunici-i
    car[F]-the old   *al*.FSG grandmother.OBL-the.OBL
    merge mai bine decât cea noua a   Ioane-i
    runs more good than the new   *al*.FSG Ioana.OBL-the.OBL
    'Grandmother's old car runs better than Ioana's new one.'

c. Vom   discuta mai multe eseuri recent   apărute,
    will.1PL discuss more many essays recently issued
    între care al   lui Liiceanu despre dragoste.
    among which *al*.MSG OBJ Liiceanu about   love
    'We will discuss several recently issued essays, among which Liiceanu's
    one about love.'

d. [discussing movies]:
    L-ai   văzut pe al   Marie-i   de
    3MSG.CL.ACC-have.2SG seen OBJ *al*.MSG Maria.OBL-the.OBL of
    an-ul   trecut?
    year-the passed
    'Have you seen Maria's (movie) from the last year?'

Data like these support the idea that free-standing *al*-genitives represent postnominal
genitives in ellipsis contexts. One may adopt a haplology-like rule as proposed above for
bare genitives: if the D position is adjacent to *al* (no adjective intervenes, like in (29b)),
it can remain empty. The context is almost the same – D$_{def}$ *al* – the only difference being
that D is not cliticized. We can say that the PF-rule deletes D in this context, or that D
is allowed to cliticize on *al*, and one of the two identical φ-morphemes, of *al* and of D,
disappears, by the same haplology rule responsible for *al* deletion after suffixal D:

(30) a. [$_D$ D$_{+def}$ [$_{NP}$ Ø nouă a Ioanei]] → **cea** nouă a Ioanei

      b. [$_D$ **D$_{+def}$** [$_{NP}$ Ø al Mariei de anul trecut]] → **al** Mariei de anul trecut

However, unlike the *al* deletion rule, the PF-phenomenon responsible for free-standing
al-phrases is optional. Thus, the independent article *cel* may appear immediately before *al*, although free-standing *al* seems to be preferred in the spoken language:

(31) Îl   prefer   pe cel al   Livi-ei
      3MSG.CL.AC prefer.1SG OBJ the *al*.MSG Livia.OBL-the.OBL
      'I prefer Livia's.'

Another potential problem for the hypothesis that *al* is a genitive-marker in this context is that prepositional genitives (those marked by *a* or *de*, see Section 1, ex. (3b–c))
do not allow this 'free-standing' use:

(32) a. Al   copiilor   e acolo
      al.MSG children-the.OBL is there
      'The children's is over there'

    b. *A trei   copii   e acolo
      a three children is there

Another analysis which may account for the difference between prenominal and free-standing *al*-phrases is that *al* has a different status in the latter case, representing a determiner which incorporates a grammatical noun ("pro-N" or n), which allows noun ellipsis, and has the property of assigning oblique case to a DP without the mediation of *al*:

(33) $[_{DP} [_{n+D} a] [_{nP} [_{DPGen} Mariei] t_n (_N \emptyset)]]$

If we analyze the suffixation of definite D as PF-lowering, we may also assume that *al* spells-out the complex n+D obtained by lowering of D to a special n *a-*, and that the genitive is in SpecNP:

(34) $[_{DP} D [_n n] [_{NP} [_{DPGen} a Mariei] [_N \emptyset]]]$

Note that like in other cases of DPs without an overt noun, free-standing *al*- phrases may be interpreted either by noun ellipsis ('nominal anaphora') or receive a general interpretation of the descriptive content (+human, in the plural feminine also -animate):

(35) a. Maşin-a Ioane-i   merge mai bine decât a
      car-the Ioana.OBL-the.OBL runs more good than *al*.FSG
      Marie-i
      Maria.OBL-the.OBL
      'Ioana's car runs better than Maria's.'

    a´. $[_{DP} [_{n+D} a] [_{nP} [_{DPGen} Mariei] t_n (_N maşină)]]$

    b. Acum manifestează ai   lui Băsescu
      now   manifest.3PL *al*.MPL OBL Băsescu
      'Now Băsescu's people (i.e., supporters) are manifesting.'

    b´. $[_{DP} [_{n+D} ai] [_{nP} [_{DPGen} lui Băsescu] t_{n (+human)}]]$

The idea that free-standing *al* is distinct from adnominal *al* is supported by the existence of a formal difference between the two: free-standing *al*, especially in the non-elliptical '+human' interpretation, may receive the oblique ending in the plural (yielding *alor*), while otherwise case endings cannot attach to *al*:

(36) a. Le-am   spus alor   mei
      3PL.CL.DAT-have.1SG said the.PL.OBL my.MPL
      'I told it to my family.'

b. Le-am   spus unor   prieteni *alor   / ai
3PL.CL.DAT-have.1SG said a.PL.OBL friends my.PL.OBL   *al*.MPL
mei
my.MPL
'I told it to some friends of mine.'

However, this analysis cannot explain the ban on post-genitive adjectives in (29a).
Possibly, free-standing *al* oscillates between the structures in (30b) (used with post-
genitive modifiers and complements) and (33)–(35) (perhaps specialized for the interpretation without ellipsis).

For the prenominal use in the present-day language, Cornilescu (1994) proposed that the *al*-phrase occupies SpecDP, and in virtue of the presence of a definiteness feature of *al*, it can mark the matrix DP as definite, allowing a null definite article (by a double filled Spec-Head filter applying to the DP level):

(37) $[_{DP} [ai_{+def}$ țări-i] $[_{D'} [_{D} Ø_{+def}] [_{NP}$ eroi]]]
      al.MPL country.OBL-the.OBL heroes

Dobrovie-Sorin and Giurgea (2005) also argued in favor of this analysis, showing that
this type of definiteness marking is independently needed in other cases – superlatives
((38a)) and ordinals (39) . For superlatives, the fact that *cel* forms a constituent with
the DegP is shown, among other tests, by the possibility to appear before a cardinal –
see (38a) –, where APs without *cel* are not allowed – see (38b):

(38) a. $[_{DP} [cei mai   mari] [[_{D} Ø] [doi autori]]]$
          the more great   two authors
          'the two greatest authors'

      b. *marii   doi autori /*acești mari doi autori
          great-the two authors these   great two authors

(39) $[_{DP} [a$ doua] [[_{D} Ø] [problemă]]]$
      al.FSG second   problem(F)
      'the second problem'

A SpecDP position appears appropriate for *wh*-genitives. Recall that present-day
Romanian only allows the *wh*-genitive *al cărui* in prenominal position – always in DP-
initial position, marking the matrix DP as definite (although no D attaches to the head
N). It is clear that the feature responsible for the DP-initial position of *wh*-genitives is
[wh] or [rel]. It is standardly assumed that DPs are cyclic domains – phases, in recent
minimalism (Chomsky 2000, 2001) – so features such as wh or rel inside a DP must be
present in SpecDP in order to be visible for attraction in the clausal periphery. It is
reasonable to assume, therefore, that the DP-initial *wh*-genitive occupies SpecDP:[8]

(40) $[_{DP}$ [ai cărei] $[_{D'}$ $[_D\emptyset_{+def}]$ $[_{NP}$ eroi]]]]

We can thus say that prenominal *wh*-genitives are fully grammatical because the wh-feature allows raising into the DP-periphery, while poetic genitives are no longer in use because there is no feature they can check in the DP-periphery in present-day Romanian.

Prenominal *wh*-genitives also obey a weight condition: the genitive DP is restricted to the determiner head (*cărui/cărei/căror* 'which.GEN' or *cui* 'who.GEN') – it cannot contain an overt NP:

(41) a. [a   cărui]   casă
          al.FSG which.GEN house
          'whose house'

      b. *[a   cărui   om] casă
          al.FSG which.GEN man house

Moreover, these determiners appear in the unaugmented form in prenominal position, although in the absence of an overt noun they normally take the 'augment' *-a* (yielding the augmented endings *-uia, -eia, -ora*), like all determiners marked as oblique:

(42) a. prim-a maşină [a   unui   profesor] / [a   unui-a]   /
          first-the car[F]   *al*.FSG a.OBL professor / *al*.FSG a.OBL-AUGM
          [*a   unui]
          al.FSG a.OBL
          'a professor's/one's first car'

      b. prim-a maşină [a   cărui   profesor] /
          first-the car(F)   *al*.FSG which.OBL professor /
          [a   cărui-a]   /[*a   cărui]
          al.FSG which.OBL-AUGM *al*.FSG which.OBL
          'which professor's/whose first car'

      c. [a   cărui]   (primă) maşină
          al.FSG whose.OBL (first) car[F]
          'whose first car'

      d. [*a   cărui-a]   (primă) maşină
          al.FSG whose.OBL-AUGM (first) car[F]

We conclude that prenominal *wh*-genitives are weak forms, possibly forming a complex X^0 with *al*. In § 2.4, we will see that the same is true for pronominal possessors. Interestingly, pronominal possessors also allow a prenominal position, although in different circumstances (after an adjective bearing the suffixal article). We can conclude that only weak genitives may raise to prenominal positions in present-day Romanian.

Since we adopted an analysis of prenominal genitives in which *al* forms a constituent with the genitive, it is not necessary to say that *al* bears definiteness. The definiteness feature is on the null D. Adopting Cornilescu's (1994) suggestion that Romanian has a doubly-filled Spec-Head filter operating on DPs, we may assume that what allows the definite D to be null is not a feature of *al*, but only the fact that SpecDP is filled. As already explained above, the feature which triggers the raising of the *al*-phrase to SpecDP is the *wh*-feature.

Summing up, the analysis of *al* as a genitive marker with agreement features is difficult to extend to all uses of *al*. For such an extension, the following assumptions would be required: (i) a filled SpecDP allows the definite D to remain null or the presence of a definiteness feature on *al* in SpecDP licenses a null definite D (for the DP-initial use); (ii) when the definite article has no host for suffixation and is adjacent to *al*, it can have a null realization, possibly via cliticization on *al* and haplology (for the free-standing use). The alternative (iii) – which we prefer – is to assume that *al* is ambiguous, representing an N+D complex in the argumental free-standing use. We have also shown that the free-standing use cannot be derived from the prenominal use. The non-uniform analysis of *al* resembles the structural ambiguity of other genitive-markers, like *of* in English, which participates in different structural configurations, e.g. *a son of John, a book of John, a book of John's*, or *de* in French, which has been argued by Milner (1982) to be either a Case-marker (when the head N is governed by a definite article) or a preposition (when the head N is governed by other determiners).

2.3   The history of *al*. From determiner to genitive marker.

The peculiar distribution of *al*, and its special relation with definiteness in particular, are the result of its origin.

In old Romanian (i.e. XVI-XVII centuries), *al* could be found immediately after the definite article:

(43) a. păcate-le ale   tuturor   (Densusianu 1938: §115, p. 703)
          sins-the   *al*.FPL all.OBL
          'everybody's sins'

      b. duh-ul   al   Domnu-lui   nostru   (ibid.)
          spirit-the *al*.MSG Lord-the.OBL our
          'our Lord's spirit'

      c. urdzire-a   a   lumi-ei   (ibid.)
          creation-the *al*.FSG world.OBL-the.OBL
          'the creation of the world'

Genitives without *al* immediately following the definite article were also attested in old Romanian, and prenominal genitives were not so restricted as today:

(44) cuvinte-le evangheli-ei   (Coresi, *Evanghelie cu învăţătură*, 1581)
      words-the gospel.OBL-the.OBL
      'the words of the gospel'

(45) a. cum şi   al   evangheli-ei   cuvânt auzi-văm   (ibid.)
          as also *al*.MSG gospel.OBL-the.OBL word   hear-will.1PL
          'as we will also listen to the word of the gospel'

      b. cine-ş   va   căuta ale   lui   păcate, (...)   (ibid.)
          who-REFL.DAT will examine *al*.FPL he.GEN sins
          'he who will examine his own sins, ...'

These facts suggest that the present-day distribution is the result of the following historical developments: in an unattested stage of Romanian, *al* was a strong form of the
definite determiner, which could appear before genitives either in cases of noun ellipsis, or when the genitive was prenominal (see Giurgea 2012):

(46) a. $[_{DP} [_D$ ale] $[_{NP} [_{DPGen}$ evangheliei] [cuvinte]]]

      b. $[_{DP} [_D$ ale] [evangheliei $[_N Ø]]]$,   or $[_{DP}[_N$ale] $[[_N Ø]$ evangheliei]]

The idea that *al* was once a strong (independent) definite article is supported by various pieces of independent evidence: (i) *al* was still used as a definite article before the
alternative, in old Romanian *al-alt* 'other' (today *cel-ălalt*, composed of *alalt* and the
present-day strong article *cel*); (ii) it has the same origin as the suffixal definite article,
namely Latin *ille* (see Tiktin 1895, Puşcariu in DA 1913, Găzdaru 1929)[9]. In addition
to genitival *al*, other forms that continue this article are ordinal *al* (see note 2) and the
determiner *alde* (=*al+de* 'of'), whose original meaning is "the group of ..." (see Hasdeu
1887, Zafiu 2009)[10].

Since Romanian has double definiteness[11] in all its attested phases, it is likely that
[*al*+Genitive] constituents were also able to appear postnominally, in a double definiteness construction (like *cel*+AP/PP today).

Then, since the independent definite article was not frequent and started to be in
competition with the demonstrative *cel*, at least in the noun ellipsis context,[12] the article *al* in adnominal position was reinterpreted as a genitive marker. The reanalysis of
al was favored by the fact that the genitive was probably the most frequent adnominal
constituent that took *al* with noun ellipsis, in the double definiteness construction and
in prenominal position, because adjectives received the suffixal article in all these cases, a situation that is still preserved in old Romanian (see Densusianu (1938). (In the
present-day language, postnominal adjectives with noun ellipsis and in the double
definiteness construction require the strong article *cel*). As a result of this reinterpreta-
tion, postnominal *al* lost its definiteness. This stage is already reached in the oldest
texts (XVIth century):

(47) să   şază întru un loc   al   lui
      SUBJ sits in   a place *al*.MSG he.OBL
      'He should sit in a place of his.'   (Coresi, *Evanghelie cu învăţătură*, 90)

As a result, the construction in which the genitive immediately followed the definite article became minimally different from the construction with *al* (the two no longer differed in terms of semantic features, since no definiteness feature was associated with *al*). This made it possible for genitives without *al* to be reinterpreted as a reduction of the sequence article + *al*; this reduction became a grammaticalized morphological rule, hence obligatory. Therefore, examples (43) are ungrammatical in present-day Romanian.

A further stage in the development of *al*, which is a consequence of its genitive marker status, is the loss of agreement, with *al* appearing in the invariable form *a*. This stage is attained in various regional varieties – a wide area of Daco-Romanian, and the Romanian dialects south of the Danube (Aromanian, Meglenoromanian, Istroromanian). The oldest texts from the northern Daco-Romanian area already show non-agreeing *a* alongside agreeing *al*. Interestingly, the loss of agreement did not immediately lead to the loss of the capacity of genitive phrases to mark definiteness in ellipsis and in DP-initial position:

(48) a. Svârşescu picioare-le meale ca [a cerbu-lui]
          render.1SG feet-the my like *a* deer-the.OBL
          'I make my feet like the deer's.' (*Psaltirea Hurmuzachi* (c. 1500), 13r, 34)

     b. Aduce-se-vor [a împăratu-lui] feate (ibid., 39r, 15)
          bring-REFL-will.3PL *a* emperor-the.OBL girls
          'The emperor's daughters will be brought.'

(49) a. [ăl feat-a noastră] bărbat ăi doctur[13]
          GEN daughter-the our man is physician
          'Our daughter's husband is a physician.'
                              (Meglenoromanian: Atanasov 2002)

     b. Carne-a di curşută mai nu-i bună di [lu ţerbu]
          meat-the of doe more not-is good than GEN stag-the
          'The doe's meat isn't better than the stag's.'
                              (Meglenoromanian: Capidan 1925)

2.4 The syntax of pronominal possessors

We use the term 'pronominal possessors' for possessor forms of the personal pronouns. The distribution of pronominal possessors, both agreeing and genitive-marked, is at first sight identical to that of genitives in general: they immediately follow *al* or the suffixal definite article:

(50) a. un/acest/oricare prieten al meu / al ei
          a/this/any friend[M] *al*.MSG my.MSG *al*.MSG she.OBL
          'a/this /any friend of mine/of hers'

    b. prieteni-**i**   mei   / ei
         friends[M]-the my.MPL / she.OBL
         'my/her friends'

However, there are two differences between the distribution of pronominal possessors and that of the other genitive-marked DPs. Agreeing pronominal possessors and genitive-marked pronouns pattern alike.[14]

    Unlike what we have seen for non-pronominal genitives in (15)–(16) above, pronominal possessors can follow a prenominal adjective with the suffixal definite article or appear between a noun carrying the article and a classifying or light non-contrastive adjective:

(51) a. prim-a noastră / lor   întâlnire[15]
          first-the our.FSG / they.OBL meeting[F]
          'our/their first meeting'

      b. *prim-a profesori-lor   întâlnire
          first-the professors-the.OBL meeting
          'the professors' first meeting'

(52) a. situați-a   noastră / lor   economică
          situation-the our.FSG / they.OBL economic
          'our/their economic situation'

      b. *situația   României   economică
          situation-the Romania-the.OBL economic

Another difference is that pronominal possessors cannot be coordinated under *al* (*al* must be repeated in the second conjunct):

(53) a. *prim-a reuniune   a   [noastră și   lor]
          first-the assembly[F] *al*.FSG our.FSG and they.OBL

      b. prim-a reuniune a   [profesorilor   și   studenților]
          first-the assembly *al*.FSG professors-the.OBL and students-the.OBL
          'the first assembly of the professors and the students'

      c. *prim-a reuniune a   [noastră și   studenți-lor]
          first-the assembly *al*.FSG our.FSG and students-the.OBL

The special syntactic behavior of pronominal possessors can be explained by assuming that they are 'weak pronouns' (Cardinaletti 1998, Cardinaletti & Starke 1999), i.e. X° constituents that have a morpho-syntactic status intermediate between clitics and free standing pronouns. The ungrammaticality of (53a,c) is due to the impossibility of coordinating weak pronouns (see Cardinaletti & Starke 1999). The weak pronoun status only applies to 'bare' pronominal possessors (i.e. without *al*). The phrase *al* + pronominal possessor does not have the special properties noted above, but behaves like any other *al*-phrase; thus, one can coordinate an *al*-phrase containing an agreeing possessor with another *al*-phrase, which may contain either a pronominal possessor or a genitive DP:

(54) a. această problemă comună a   noastră și   a
          this   problem[F] common *al*.FSG our.FSG and   *al*.FSG
          voastră/ lor
          your.FSG/ they.OBL
          'this common problem of ours and yours/theirs'

      b. această problemă comună a   noastră și
          this   problem[F] common *al*.FSG our.FSG and
          a   francezi-lor
          al.FSG French.PL-the.OBL
          'this common problem of ours and the French'

According to Cardinaletti & Starke (1999), weak pronouns always move to case positions. Assuming that genitive is assigned by a functional nominal head, say Poss, we can explain the order in (51)–(52) by allowing weak forms – and only them – to raise to SpecPoss (as proposed by Giusti 2008 for weak pronominal possessors in Italian and Romanian; Giusti calls this head F):

(55) a. $[_{DP}[_{AP}$ prim-$]$ $[[_{D}$-a$]]$ $[_{FP}$ $t_{primă}$ $[_{PossP}$ noastră $[_{NP}$ întâlnire $t_{noastră}]]]]]$, or

      a′. $[_{DP}[_{AP}$ prim-$]$ $[[_{D}$-a$]]$ $[_{PossP}$ noastră $[_{FP}$ $t_{primă}$ $[_{NP}$ întâlnire $t_{noastră}]]]]]$

      b. $[_{DP}[_{D}[_{N}$situați-$]$ $[_{D}$-a$]]$ $[_{PossP}$ noastră $[_{NP}$ $t_{situație}$ economică $t_{noastră}]]]$

However, this analysis encounters some problems. So far, we have claimed that *al* is always present in syntax. Applying this idea to bare pronominal possessors, we would have to assume that what raises to SpecPoss in (51)–(52)/(55) is *al*+Pronoun. But we never find (overt) *al* in this position. The special pronominal position is always adjacent to the definite article (a position where *al* must be deleted). *Al*+pronoun phrases are excluded in such environments, behaving exactly like non-pronominal possessors:

(56) *o (frumoasă) a   ei   (frumoasă) carte
       a beautiful *al*.FSG she.OBL beautiful   book

(57) ??această situație a   lor   economică
       this   situation *al*.FSG they.OBL economic

Since we have seen that *al*+Pronoun phrases can behave as strong pronouns (see (54)), one may conclude that weak pronominal possessors do not contain *al*. The possibility that a case marker appears on strong DPs but not on weak pronouns is found in the Romance pronominal systems (not only with clitics, but also with weak pronouns, see the Italian dative plural *loro* (weak) vs. *a loro* (strong)). Another fact which suggests that *al* is absent is the difference in case agreement between bare possessors and *al*-possessors. As we have seen in the introduction (ex. (2)), DPs headed by determiners with oblique case display case concord in the feminine singular: feminine singular nouns and adjectives have a distinct form, which is identical to the plural. Now, the property of pronominal possessors that is important for our discussion is that agreeing possessors not introduced by *al* have obligatory case concord, while if *al* is present, case concord is normally absent:

(58) a. prietene-i   noastr-e   / *noastr-ă
          friend.F.OBL-the.OBL our-F.OBL / our-FSG
          'of/to our friend'

      b. acestei   prietene   a   noastr-ă/?a   noastr-e /? a-le
          this.OBL friend.F.OBL *al*.FSG our-FSG/ *al*.FSG our-F.OBL/ *al*-F.OBL
          noastr-e
          our-F.OBL
          'of/to this friend of ours'

However, the idea that bare possessors do not contain *al* and raise in virtue of being weak also encounters a problem. Since genitive assignment is not a property of D, we expect to find raising of weak forms to SpecPoss with any determiner. But this is not possible, as already mentioned: the weak possessor must be adjacent to the definite article. The word order in (56)–(57) remains impossible even if we omit *al*:

(59) *o (frumoasă) ei   (frumoasă) carte
       a beautiful   she.OBL beautiful book

(60) *această situaţie lor   economică
       this   situation they.OBL economic

It thus appears that the licensing of weak pronouns crucially involves the suffixal definite article.[16] If we assimilate placement of weak pronouns to cliticization, we can say that weak pronouns are specified for taking a word inflected for definiteness as their host.

3. Feature uniqueness and the choice between agreeing and non-agreeing possessors

In this section we will concentrate on the alternation between agreeing and genitive-marked forms in the paradigm of pronominal possessors, illustrated below:

(61) a. băieţi-i   me-i   / tă-i   / noştr-i / voştr-i
          boys-the my-MPL / your$_{sg}$-MPL / our-MPL / your$_{pl}$-MPL
          'my/your(sg.)/our/your(pl.) boys'

      b. fetele   me-le   / ta-le   / noastr-e / voastr-e
          girls-the my-FPL / your$_{sg}$-FPL / our-FPL / your$_{pl}$-FPL
          'my/your(sg.)/our/your(pl.) girls'

(62) a. băieţi-i   ei   / lui   / lor
        boys-the she.OBL / he.OBL / they.OBL
        'his/ her/ their boys'

     b. fete-le   ei   / lui   / lor
        girls-the she.OBL / he.OBL / they.OBL
        'his/ her/ their girls'

Before providing an account for this alternation (Sections 3.2.-3.4), we present evidence that agreeing possessors are pronouns rather than adjectives (Section 3.1).

3.1 Agreeing pronominal possessors are referential expressions

We have seen that agreeing and genitive-marked pronominal possessors have the same distribution (see 2.4 above). In this sub-section, we provide further evidence that agreeing possessives do not pattern with adjectives, but rather with pronouns. This will lead us to conclude that agreeing possessors are pronouns and, therefore, that the traditional label 'possessive *adjective*' is inadequate.

The following examples show that pronominal possessors can function as antecedents of reflexive pronouns. This possibility clearly distinguishes agreeing possessors from thematic adjectives:

(63) a. opini-a   noastră despre noi înşine
        opinion[F]-the our.FSG about ourselves
        'our opinion about ourselves'

     b. *opini-a   americană despre ei înşişi
        opinion-the American about   themselves
        '*the American$_i$ opinion about themselves$_i$'

This property is also found in languages where agreeing possessors occupy a different position from genitive DPs – for instance in Romance languages other than Romanian:

(64) a. il nostro   giudizio su   noi stessi   (Italian)
        the our.MSG opinion about ourselves
        'our opinion about ourselves'

     b. *il Americano giudizio su   sè stessi
        the American   opinion about themselves
        '*the American$_i$ opinion about themselves$_i$'

Moreover, agreeing pronominal possessors can receive a secondary predication or an appositive relative, like canonical DPs:[17]

(65) a. o poză   a   mea   blond
        a picture(F) *al*.FSG my.FSG blond.MSG
        'a picture of me when I was blond'

    b. Ce   să   mai spunem de   disput-a   noastră,
       what SUBJ still say.1PL about dispute[F]-the our.FSG.
       care   ne   înțelegeam   înainte atât de bine
       which REFL got-along.1PL before so   well
       'Not to mention the dispute between us, who used to get along so well.'

These facts indicate that agreeing pronominal possessors carry a referential index. This property clearly distinguishes them from adjectives, including thematic adjectives. We can thus safely conclude that agreeing pronominal possessors are pronominal DPs rather than adjectives. The fact that they carry features that agree with the head N (the Possessee) has no consequence for their syntactic properties. In sum, the so-called possessive 'adjectives' are possessive pronouns that have the peculiarity of copying the features of the head N (instead of being marked with Genitive Case).

3.2   Feature uniqueness and the choice between agreeing and non-agreeing possessors

As illustrated in (61)–(62) above, Romanian pronominal possessors choose between agreeing and non-agreeing (i.e. oblique) forms depending on the person: the 1st and 2nd persons have agreeing forms, while the 3rd person has oblique forms.[18]

    For the 3rd person singular there is the option of using agreeing forms that are based on a reflexive root (s-) but are no longer restricted to reflexive use:

(66) a. Băieți-i   săi
        boys-the his/her.MPL
        'his/her boys'

      b. fete-le   sale
        girls-the his/her.FPL
        'his/her girls'

Our account of this non-uniform paradigm is based on the distinction between *inflectional* and *lexical* φ-features: inflectional features are those features that appear on inflectional morphemes, whereas lexical features belong to the root itself (a good example of a lexical φ-feature is gender on nouns in most Indo-European languages). Based on this distinction, we derive the distribution of agreeing and non-agreeing possessor forms among pronouns from a constraint of Feature Uniqueness:

(67) Pronominal roots merge with at most one set of inflectional φ-features.

Feature Uniqueness allows inflectional φ-features to co-occur with lexical φ-features, hence the observable agreeing forms of pronominal possessors, but it prevents a set of inherited/unvalued inflectional features from co-occurring with a set of inherent/valued inflectional features, which explains why certain pronominal possessors cannot agree with the head N° (Possessee).

The traditional notion of 'inheritance' or 'copying' suggests a mechanism by virtue of which features of a given element are transferred to another element that lacked them before that particular mechanism applied. Such a copying mechanism is problematic, since it is crucial for grammatical theory to assume that any relation, and in particular the agreement relation, can occur only if the two elements to be related are somehow eligible for this relation.

In other words, the targets (the controlees or the Goal) of agreement must be marked as eligible for agreement prior to the application of the agreement relation. This 'marking' of targets of agreement can be technically implemented by assuming a distinction between features (or feature attributes) and feature values: Person, Number and Gender are the three universal φ-feature attributes (Harley & Ritter 2002), and 1st/2nd, plural, feminine, etc. are feature values. Both the controller and the controlee/target carry feature attributes. The difference is that at the beginning of the derivation, the feature attributes are valued on the controller and unvalued on the target (Chomsky 2000, 2001). The unvalued formal features thus have the role of marking concord-eligibility of the agreement target.

3.3   The morphosyntactic make-up of pronouns

In this section we will show that 3rd person pronouns have inflectional inherent φ-features, while 1st and 2nd person pronouns have only lexical inherent φ-features.

As shown in Table 1, the strong forms of Romanian 3rd person pronouns can be decomposed into an invariable root *el/l*[19] (with *-l-* deleted in certain contexts)[20] and gender-number-case morphemes, which are also found on determiners like the strong definite article, demonstratives or *alt* 'other'. The strong oblique forms are likewise composed of the same root, and fused gender+number+case morphemes are also found with other determiners (this morpheme is bold-faced in Table 1):

Table 1. The Inflection of Determiners and Strong Pronouns

	Personal pronoun	strong[21] definite article	distal demonstrative	'other'
Direct case (Nom-Acc): m.sg.	el-Ø	cel-Ø	acel-Ø	alt-Ø
f.sg.	e-**a**	ce-**a**	ace-**a**	alt-**ă**
m.pl.	e-**i**	ce-**i**	ace-**i**	alț-**i**
f.pl.	el-**e**	cel-**e**	acel-**e**	alt-**e**
Oblique: m.sg.	l-**ui**	cel-**ui**	acel-**ui**	alt-**ui**
f.sg.	-**ei**	cel-**ei**	acel-**ei**	alt-**ei**
pl.	l-**or**	cel-**or**	acel-**or**	alt-**or**

These paradigms clearly indicate that the Number and Gender features of Romanian 3rd person pronouns are inflectional, in the sense that they have an exponent distinct from the exponent of the root. In line with Distributed Morphology (see Halle & Marantz 1993), we assume that the output of the syntactic derivation contains X^0s carrying abstract labels (D, N, Adj, etc.) and feature-attributes (e.g Gender, Number), which are valued as masculine or feminine, singular or plural, etc.. The vocabulary insertion rules replace these elements with phonological matrices called *exponents*. We assume that inflectional morphemes are merged with other X^0s (either by first merge or by head-to-head movement) and typically form a complex head with their sister.

Turning now to 1st and 2nd Person pronouns, they cannot be decomposed into a root expressing person and an inflectional morpheme expressing number and gender. Indeed, in Romanian, as in most Indo-European languages, 1st and 2nd pronouns do not display any gender opposition, and plural forms are built on roots that are distinct from the corresponding singular forms:

(68) a. *eu,*   *tu,*   *noi,*   *voi*
         'I,   you(sg.), we,   you(pl.)'   *Romanian*
      b. *je,*   *tu,*   *nous,*   *vous,*   *French*
      c. *jag,* *du,*   *vi,*   *ni*   *Swedish*
      d. *ja,*   *ty,*   *my,*   *vy*   *Russian*

In these forms, the Number feature is not inflectional. Our criterion for morphological decomposition is the existence of minimal pairs that have a separable common element (the root), and contrasting elements corresponding to different values of the same feature attribute. The elements shown in Table 1 are of this type. Pronouns of 1st and 2nd person, on the other hand, do not have inflectional number, because the singular versus plural contrast is not ensured by X^0 elements that are distinct from a common root. Of course, the mere presence of an element that seems to encode plurality, e.g., -*i* in the Romanian forms *noi* 'we' and *voi* 'you$_{pl}$' or the -*s* in the French forms *nous* or *vous*, is not sufficient to assume that number is inflectional. The existence of a common root is crucial. In other words, *noi* and *voi* or *nous* and *vous* have lexical rather than inflectional number, because the corresponding singular forms are not obtained by removing the marker -*i* or -*s* (the exponents of the Speaker and the Hearer are not **no(u)* and **vo(u)*) but instead are expressed by a different root (Fr. *je, tu*). Note, moreover, that in Romanian, -*i* in *noi, voi* can be regarded as a case marker, being opposed to the oblique forms *nouă, vouă*. We can thus isolate the roots *no-, vo-* (appearing in the extended forms *nostr-* and *vostr-* in agreeing possessors) which encode person and plurality (the corresponding clitic forms, used for accusative and dative, keep the consonant but have a different vowel: *ne/ni* and *vă*). Since case and number normally have a syncretic exponent in Romanian, we can argue that the -*i* of the direct (nominative-accusative) case *noi, voi* redundantly marks the plural, duplicating a feature already present on the root. In conclusion, it seems reasonable to assume that the plural feature in first and second person pronouns is not inflectional but rather lexical, i.e. encoded in the root itself.

As we have seen in ex.(66), for 3rd person singular possessors there is the option, in addition to the use of the genitive, of using agreeing forms based on a root *să/sa-*:

(69) a. frate-le   său   = frate-le   lui/ei
          brother-the *să*.MSG   brother-the his/her
          'his/her brother'

   b. sor-a   sa   = sor-a   lui/ei
       sister-the *să*.FSG   sister-the his/her
       'his/her sister'

   c. frați-i   săi   = frați-i   lui/ei
       brothers-the *să*.MPL   brothers-the his/her
       'his/her brothers'

   d. surori-le   sale   = surori-le   lui/ei
       sisters-the *să*.FPL   sisters-the his/her
       'his/her sisters'

Like 1st and 2nd pronouns, the forms based on the root *să/sa-* have only lexical inherent features: 3rd person and singular number are marked on the root, and there is no gender opposition. The peculiarity of this root is that it is restricted to the possessor use: although it is historically related to the reflexive (the root *s-* found in *sine, sie, se, (î)și*), it lost its reflexive meaning. Another difference is that the reflexive root has no inherent number specification (e.g. *sine* 3 REFL.ACC corresponds to 'himself', 'herself', 'itself', 'themselves', etc.), while *să/sa-* is restricted to singular possessors (note that a similar development is attested in Italian and French).[22]

3.4   Accounting for the (im)possibility of agreeing pronominal possessors

Given this analysis of pronouns, the (im)possibility of agreeing forms in pronominal paradigms follows from the Feature Uniqueness constraint in (67), which we repeat below:

(67)   Pronominal roots merge with at most one set of inflectional φ-features.

Because Feature Uniqueness only concerns inflectional features, nothing prevents a root that has inherent φ-features from merging with unvalued inflectional φ-features. Thus, 1st and 2nd pronouns may merge with an inflectional morpheme (which we will call *inflectional feature matrix*, IFM) containing unvalued gender and number. In addition, in languages with case concord, this morpheme also contains case, since agreeing possessors also agree in case with the Possessee. In Romanian, case concord is very restricted (see introduction, ex. (2) and ex. (58) above): feminine singular agreeing possessors have an oblique form distinct from the direct case form:

(70) a. fete-i   mele
        daughter.OBL-the.OBL my.FSG.OBL
        'to/of my daughter'

     b. fat-a   mea
        daughter-the.DIR my.FSG.DIR
        'my daughter'

The feature composition of agreeing pronominal possessors in Romanian (listed in (71)) is given in (71)′, where unvalued features are marked with the prefix *u*:[23]

(71) a. me-u   /me-a /me-i /me-le
        my -MSG /-FSG /-MPL /-FPL

     b. tă-u   /ta   /tă-i /ta-le
        your$_{sg}$ -MSG /-FSG /-MPL /-FPL

     c. nostr-u   /noastr-ă /noştr-i /noastr-e
        our -MSG /-FSG   /-MPL   /-FPL

     d. vostr-u   /voastr-ă /voştr-i /voastr-e
        your$_{pl}$ -MSG /-FSG   /-MPL   /-FPL

     e. să-u   /sa /să-i /sa-le
        3rd$_{sg}$ -MSG /FSG /-MPL /-FPL

(71)′ a. me- [$_D$ Person=1, Number=sg] [$_{IFM}$ uNumber, uGender, uCase]

     b. ta- [$_D$ Person=2, Number=sg] [$_{IFM}$ uNumber, uGender, uCase]

     c. no- [$_D$ Person=1, Number=pl] [$_{IFM}$ uNumber, uGender, uCase]

     d. vo- [$_D$ Person=2, Number=pl] [$_{IFM}$ uNumber, uGender, uCase]

     e. să- [$_D$ Person=3, Number=sg] [$_{IFM}$ uNumber, uGender, uCase]

According to these feature matrices, agreeing possessors have lexical Person and Number, which give indications about the referent of the Possessor, and they have unvalued features for Number and Gender, which are assigned a value via agreement with the head N (Possessee).

On the other hand, 3rd person pronouns have valued inflectional gender and number, as shown in Table 1:

(72) a. *el* (Oblique Case *lui*)[$_D$ Person=3] [$_{IFM}$ Number=Sg;Gender=Masc,uCase]

     b. *ea* (Oblique Case *ei*)[$_D$ Person=3] [$_{IFM}$ Number=Sg;Gender=Fem,uCase]

     c. *ei* (Oblique Case *lor*)[$_D$ Person=3] [$_{IFM}$ Number=Pl;Gender=Masc,uCase]

     d. *ele* (Oblique Case *lor*)[$_D$ Person=3] [$_{IFM}$ Number=Pl;Gender=Fem,uCase]

The absence of agreeing forms for these pronouns is predicted under our proposal, because the feature matrices given in (73) are ruled out (as indicated by the # diacritic) by the constraint of Feature Uniqueness in (67):

(73) a. #$[_D$Person=3] $[_{IFM}$Number=Sg,Gender=Masc]

   $[_{IFM}$uNumber,uGender,uCase]

   b. #$[_D$Person=3] $[_{IFM}$Number=Sg,Gender=Fem]

   $[_{IFM}$uNumber,uGender,uCase]

   c. #$[_D$Person=3] $[_{IFM}$ Number=Pl,Gender=Masc]

   $[_{IFM}$ uNumber,uGender,uCase]

   d. #$[_D$Person=3] $[_{IFM}$ Number=Pl,Gender=Fem]

   $[_{IFM}$ uNumber,uGender,uCase]

For the purposes of this paper, IFM is a functional head restricted to X° constituents: in other words, IFM is strictly speaking 'inflectional' (compare the use of 'Infl' in the post-Aspects generative grammar, where Infl designates a functional head that selects a phrasal constituent, VP, vP, AGRP, etc.).[24]

In Romanian and related languages, the maximal set of features contained in the pronouns' IFM is [Gender, Number, Case]. While case is always unvalued, gender and number can be either valued or unvalued. All pronouns have at least one unvalued feature, namely Case: in line with standard generative assumptions, formal licensing of nominals (including pronouns) is accomplished via valuation of unvalued inflectional features. The difference between agreeing and non-agreeing possessors is that at the beginning of the syntactic derivation, the former also have the Gender and Number in their IFM unvalued. Therefore, these pronouns can be licensed by φ- valuation. When these pronouns appear in contexts where valuation by agreement is impossible (i.e. in a non-nominal environment), we assume that an IFM without these features is chosen.

A derivation involving unvalued features comprises the following steps (we exemplify it with the derivation of the form *mei* 'my.MPL'):

i. Merge root with unvalued inflectional features:
    [Root] + $[_{IFM}$ uF] → [[Root] [uF]]
    e.g. $[_D+1^{st}+sg]+[_{IFM}$uGender,uNumber]→[[$_D$+1st+sg] $[_{IFM}$uGender,uNumber]]
ii. Assign a value by Agree:
    [[$_D$+1st+sg] $[_{IFM}$ uGender, uNumber]]→[[$_D$ +1st+sg] $[_{IFM}$ +masc, +pl]]
iii. Spell-out: insert the exponents of the morphemes:
    $[_D$+1st+sg] → *m(e)*-
    $[_{IFM}$ +masc, +pl]] → *-i*
    [[$_D$ +1st+sg] $[_{IFM}$ +masc, +pl]] → *mei*

It is important to note that inflectional features have the same exponent for a given feature value, regardless of whether the feature had been introduced as valued or unvalued at the beginning of the derivation (e.g. the masculine plural exponent *-i* appears in *mei* 'my.MPL', where the feature was introduced as unvalued, but also in *ei* 'they(MASC)', where the feature was introduced as valued). This is the case because valued and un-valued inflectional features can no longer be distinguished at the point of vocabulary insertion (step (iii)), since unvalued features have been previously valued (step (ii)).

Although it is not a universal principle, the constraint of Feature Uniqueness in (67) is not limited to Romanian. In Dobrovie-Sorin and Giurgea (2011) we have shown that Feature Uniqueness holds in an important number of Indo-European languages. On the one hand, as observed in footnote 18, there are languages which behave like Romanian in that they have non-uniform paradigms for pronominal possessors, in which agreeing forms are found for 1st and 2nd persons and Genitive-marked and non-agreeing forms for 3rd person (see, amongst others, Albanian, Latin, Slavic languages, Gothic and Scandinavian languages) On the other hand, some languages have agreeing forms for 3rd person too, like Romanian *său*, but sometimes for both numbers (see French sg. *son*, pl. *leur* or German *sein* 'his,its'/*ihr* 'her,their'). In all of these cases, however, inherent number (and sometimes even gender, see German) is a lexical feature: the forms have only one inflectional mor-pheme, encoding inherited gender and number (and case, in German). Inherent number is either not expressed (Sp. *su(o)* 'his, her, its, their'), or expressed by root alternation (French *son, sa, ses* – singular vs. *leur, leurs* – plural). German, like French, also has a root alternation encoding inherent features, which also comprise gender (the root *sein-* is used for masculine and neuter singular, and the root *ihr-* for feminine and plural). Finally, some languages have a 3rd person agreeing form only for one of the numbers (It. *suo*).

References

Abney, Steven. 1987. *The English noun phrase in its sentential aspect.* PhD Dissertation, MIT.

Atanasov, Petar. 2002. *Meglenoromâna astăzi.* Bucharest: Editura Academiei Române.

Baker, Mark. 2008. *The Syntax of Agreement and Concord.* Cambridge: Cambridge University Press.

Capidan, Theodor. 1925. *Meglenoromânii.* Bucharest: Cultura Națională.

Cardinaletti, Anna. 1998. On the deficient/strong position in possessive systems. *Possessors, Predicates and Movement within Determiner Phrase*, Artemis Alexiadou and Chris Wilder (eds.), 17–53. Amsterdam: John Benjamins.

Cardinaletti, Anna and Michal Starke. 1999. The typology of structural deficiency: A case study of the three classes of pronouns. *Clitics in the Languages of Europe*, Henk van Riemsdijk (ed.), 145–234. Berlin: Mouton de Gruyter.

Carstens, Vicky. 1991. *The morphology and syntax of determiner phrases in Kiswahili.* PhD Dissertation, University of California, Los Angeles.

Chomsky, Noam. 2000. Minimalist inquiries: the framework. *Step by step: Essays on minimalist syntax in honor of Howard Lasnik*, Roger Martin, David Michaels and Juan Uriagereka (eds.), 89–155. Cambridge, MA: MIT Press.

Chomsky, Noam. 2001. Derivation by phase. *Ken Hale: A Life in Language*, Michael Kenstowicz (ed.), 1–52. Cambridge, MA: MIT Press.

Coene, Martine. 1999. *Definite Null Nominals in Romanian and Spanish.* PhD Dissertation, Universiteit Antwerpen.

Cornilescu, Alexandra. 1993. Notes on the Structure of Romanian DP and the Assignment of the Genitive Case. *University of Venice Working Papers in Linguistics* 3.2.

Cornilescu, Alexandra. 1994. Remarks on the Romanian Ordinal Numeral. Towards a Unitary Description of Phrases Headed by AL. *Revue Roumaine de Linguistique*, 39: 303–334

Cornilescu, Alexandra. 1999. Aspect and Nominalizations: The Case of Romanian. *Crossing Boundaries: Advances in the Theory of Central and Eastern European Languages.* I. Kenesei (ed.), 211–238. Amsterdam: John Benjamins.

DAR. *Dicţionarul limbii române.* 1st vol. (A–B) 1913, Sextil Puşcariu (coord.). Bucharest: Librăriile Socec & Comp. şi C. Sfetea.

Densusianu, Ovide. 1938. *Histoire de la langue roumaine,* II. *Le XVIe siècle.* Paris: Ernest Leroux.

Dobrovie-Sorin, Carmen. 2000. (In)definiteness Spread: from Romanian Genitives to Hebrew Construct State Nominals. *Comparative Studies in Romanian Syntax*, Virginia Motapanyane (ed.), 177–226. Oxford: Elsevier.

Dobrovie-Sorin, Carmen. 2002. From DPs to NPs: A Bare Phrase Structure Account of Genitives. *From NP to DP. Volume 2: The expression of possession in noun phrases*, Martine Coene and Yves D'Hulst (eds.). Amsterdam/ Philadelphia: John Benjamins (Linguistik Aktuell/ Linguistics Today).

Dobrovie-Sorin, Carmen and Ion Giurgea. 2005. Romanian Genitives and Determiners. *Bucharest Working Papers in Linguistics*, 7, 1: 89–101.

Dobrovie-Sorin, Carmen, and Ion Giurgea. 2006. The Suffixation of Definite Articles in Balkan languages. *Revue Roumaine de Linguistique*, LI:1, 73–103.

Dobrovie-Sorin, Carmen and Ion Giurgea. 2011. Pronominal Possessors and Feature Uniqueness. *Language* 87, 1: 127–157.

Faensen, Johannes. 1975. Genitiv und Adjektiv im Albanischen. *Zeitschrift für Balkanologie* 11, 2, 40–47.

Găzdaru, Dimitrie. 1929. *Descendenţii demonstrativului latin* ille *în limba română.* Iaşi: Viaţa Românească.

Giurgea, Ion. 2008. Recherches sur la structure interne des pronoms et des expressions nominales sans nom exprimé. PhD Dissertation, University of Paris 7.

Giurgea, Ion. 2009. Elipsa nominală în grupuri cu determinanţi definiţi. *Studii de gramatică. Omagiu Doamnei Profesoare Valeria Guţu Romalo*, Rodica Zafiu, Blanca Croitor and Ana-Maria Mihail (eds.), 85–97. Bucharest: Editura Universităţii din Bucureşti.

Giurgea, Ion. 2010. *Pronoms, déterminants et ellipse nominale. Une approche minimaliste.* Bucharest: Editura Universităţii din Bucureşti.

Giurgea, Ion. 2012. The Origin of the Romanian "Possessive-Genitival Article" *al* and the Development of the Demonstrative System. *Revue Roumaine de Linguistique*, LVII, 1, 35–65.

Giusti, Giuliana. 2008. Agreement and Concord in Nominal Expressions. *The Bantu–Romance Connection: A comparative investigation of verbal agreement, DPs, and information structure*, Cécile De Cat and Katherine Demuth (eds.), 201–237. Amsterdam: John Benjamins.

Grimshaw, Jane. 1990. *Argument Structure.* Cambridge, Mass., MIT Press.

Grosu, Alexander. 1988. On the Distribution of Genitive Phrases in Romanian. *Linguistics* 26: 931–949.

Grosu, Alexander. 1994. *Three Studies in Locality and Case.* London, New York: Routledge.

Halle, Morris and Alec Marantz. 1993. Distributed morphology and the pieces of inflection. *The view from building 20*, Kenneth Hale and Samuel J. Keyser (eds.), 111–176. Cambridge, Mass.: MIT Press.

Harley, Heidi and Elizabeth Ritter. 2002. A feature-geometric analysis of person and number. *Language* 78: 482–526.

Hasdeu, Bogdan Petriceicu. 1887. *Etymologicum Magnum Romaniae*, 1st vol. Bucharest: Socec și Teclu.

d'Hulst, Yves, Martine Coene and Lilianne Tasmowski. 1997. On the Syntax of Romanian Possession Phrases. *Revue roumaine de linguistique*, 42: 149–166.

Miklosich, Franz. 1881. *Beiträge zur Lautlehre der rumunischen Dialekte*, Vienna: Gerold.

Milner, Jean-Claude. 1982. *Ordres et raisons de langue*. Paris: Le Seuil.

Ortmann, Alexander and Alexandra Popescu. 2000. Haplology involving morphologically bound and free elements: evidence from Romanian. *Yearbook of Morphology*, 43–70.

Taraldsen, Knut Tarald. 1990. D-projections in Norwegian. *Grammar in progress: GLOW essays for Henk van Riemsdijk*, Joan Mascaró & Marina Nespor (eds.), 419–431. Dordrecht: Foris.

Tiktin, Hariton. 1895. *Rumänisch-Deutsches Wörterbuch* (1st vol.). Bucharest: Imprimeria Statului.

Zafiu, Rodica. 2009. Utilizări actuale ale lui *alde*. *Dinamica limbii române actuale – aspecte gramaticale și discursive*, Gabriela Pană-Dindelegan (ed.), 163–180. Bucharest: Editura Academiei Române.

Endnotes

1.   For anthroponyms, which in Romanian behave like Ns occupying the D position, there are two ways of encoding the inflectional oblique: feminine nouns whose stem ends in a vowel identical to the suffixal definite article (*-a*) may use the oblique form of the article. All other anthroponyms use a preposed marker *lui* (etymologically the masculine oblique definite article), a strategy that is also available for the first class of anthroponyms.

2.   The Leipzig glossing rules are used for all the examples.

3.   Prepositional genitives (those introduced by *a* and *de*, see (3) above) behave differently: *al* is never used; note also that the dative has a different preposition (*la*):

  (i)   un tată   a   trei   copii
        a   father   of   three   children
        'a father of three children'

  (ii) Am   dat   cadouri la trei   copii
        have.1SG given presents to three children
        'I gave presents to three children'

4.   *Al* is also used to build ordinal numerals, but in this environment it has somewhat different syntactic properties: the prenominal position is fully acceptable (compare the marginal acceptability of (11a)), and *al* is obligatorily present after the suffixal article (compare (ii) with (8a–b))):

  (i)   a doua   casă
        al second house
        'the second house'

 (ii) cas-a a doua
    house-the *al* second
    'the second house'

Because of these syntactic differences, we consider ordinal *al* as a different functional item.

5. *al*-genitives can also be found, in the second member of coordinations, as complements of nouns which have an idiomatic use as spatial prepositions – such as *în spatele* 'in back-the' = 'behind', *în faţa* 'in face-the' = 'in front of'. Interestingly, as noticed by Grosu (1994), by analogy with these nouns, some prepositions which are not derived from nouns, but end in the same form as the definite article (-*a*, the feminine singular form of the article) select genitive complements and agreeing possessors – e.g. *contra* 'against', a modern borrowing from Latin, or *înaintea* 'before' < *în* 'in' + *ainte* < Lat. *ab-ante* 'of-before':

 (i) contra mea / Mari-ei
   against my.FSG / Maria.OBL-the.OBL

Note that in this case too, *al* can appear in the second member of conjunctions. Since these prepositions are not based on nouns, an analysis of *al* as N+D is very unlikely:

 (ii) contra Germaniei şi a Italiei
    against Germany-the.GEN and *al*.FSG Italy-the.GEN
    'against Germany and Italy'

6. On Romanian nominalizations, see Cornilescu (1999). PP agents as in (a), dative complements as in (c) and locative PPs without *de*, as in (b), are only possible in complex event nouns.

7. For a detailed presentation of noun ellipsis in Romanian, see Giurgea (2008, 2010).

8. Note, however, that overt fronting is not necessary for *wh*-genitives. They can also stay in situ and still pied-pipe the matrix DP, in which case a covert *wh*-feature in SpecDP needs to be assumed:

 (i) Cartea cui ai   cumpărat-o?
   book-the who.GEN have.2SG bought-CL.ACC
   'Whose book did you buy'

9. The initial vowel *a*-, which distinguishes these forms from the strong forms of the personal pronoun, also derived from *ille* (*el, ea, ei, ele*), probably developed in unaccented forms (see Tiktin 1895, Puşcariu in DAR, Găzdaru 1929). Miklosich (1881), followed by Tiktin and Găzdaru, proposed that the development *e>a* is regular in pretonic forms (cf. *acel* 'that one' < lat. *ecce illum, arici* 'hedgehog' < lat. *ericius, aoace* 'there' < lat. *illac-ce* etc.).

10. In old Romanian, preposed forms of the definite article (derived from *ille*) can be found in the oblique singular: m.sg. *lui*, f.sg. *ei*, mainly used before proper nouns and pronominal possessors. In the present-day language, only the form *lui* survived, and became a prefixal oblique marker used with proper nouns which do not have an oblique inflection:

 (i) I l- am   dat lui Dumitru
   CL.DAT- CL.ACC-have.1SG given OBL Dumitru
   'I gave it to Dumitru'

 (ii) O carte a   lui Dumitru
    a book *al*.FSG OBL Dumitru
    'a book of Dumitru('s)'

The loss of the initial vowel in these forms is very old (it is found in the corresponding strong pronouns and suffixal articles – *lui* 'he.OBL, the.MSG.OBL', *ei* 'she.OBL, the.FSG.OBL' – and in other Romance languages, see It. *lui, lei,* Fr. *lui, leur*). The vowel disappeared because it was unstressed (the stress was on the *-ui, -ei, -or* endings, cf. lat. Acc. *íllum,* Gen. sg. *illíus,* pl. *illórum,* arom. *aéstu/aiştúi* 'this' etc.).

11.   Romanian double definites have the form N+def – Def – Adj/PP; old Romanian also had the patterns N+def – A+def and N+def – Dem – A+def.

12.   The distal demonstrative tends to become the equivalent of a definite article in the context of noun ellipsis (see fr. *celui,* it. *quello,* engl. *that* used for *the one,* modern Rom. *acela, ăla* for *cel*). For an explanation of this pattern, see Giurgea (2009, 2010).

13.   In Meglenoromanian, the genitive marker *a* disappeared by aphaeresis, but left a trace in the genitive markers *ăl* (used in Umă) and *ău* (used in Țărnareca), which derive from *a* + the genitive-dative preposed definite article *lui* (*lu*). In the other varieties, *lu* became a preposed genitive marker (used for both genders and numbers). Aphaeresis of *a-* is also found in other forms (e.g. *vea<avea* 'have').

14.   Scandinavian languages resemble Romanian in this respect. For instance, in Norwegian, pronominal possessors (both genitive-marked and agreeing) can appear in postnominal position, where non-pronominal DPs marked by possessive *-s* are excluded (see Taraldsen 1990):

(i)   huset   mitt   /   hans   /   *guttens

house-the   my.NSG   /   he-GEN   /   boy-the-GEN

15.   Pronominal possessors can also appear postnominally, in the same position as genitives headed by lexical nouns:

(i)   prima   întâlnire   a   noastră/a   lor   / a   profesori-lor

first-the   meeting(F)   al.FSG   our.FSG/al.FSG   they.OBL / al.FSG   professors-the.OBL

'our/their/the professors' first meeting'

16.   There are several ways to formalize this involvement: (i) the Poss head which attracts weak pronominal possessors (which do not contain *al*) is selected by the definite D; (ii) *al* is always present in pronominal possessors, and the requirement that SpecPoss should be occupied only by weak forms is computed at PF, after *al* deletion has applied. So the syntax can generate (59)–(60), but these orders are excluded by a PF-filter; (iii) if the suffixation of the article is analyzed as a PF-displacement rule (see Dobrovie-Sorin & Giurgea 2006), it might be assumed that pronominal possessors cliticize to D and then are lowered together with the definite article:

(i)   [$_{DP}$ [$_D$-a mea] [$_{NP}$ prietenă]] → prieten-a mea

17.   Note that in this case, the co-referential PRO or relative pronoun has the φ-features which characterize the referent of the pronoun: for instance, if the speaker is a male, a secondary predicate will be masculine, as in (65a), even if the agreeing possessor co-indexed with its subject has a feminine form.

18.   A similar alternation can be found in many other Indo-European languages, e.g. Albanian, Latin, Slavic languages, Gothic and Scandinavian languages. The only difference is that in these languages, 3rd person agreeing forms are restricted to the reflexive pronoun.

19.   The vocalic form of the root is actually pronounced ̯ie-, which is not reflected in spelling. This ̯i- also appears in the feminine singular oblique, where it is the only phoneme corresponding to the root.

20. Deletion of *-l-* before *-i* (which is a semivowel) is also found in some nouns (e.g. cal_{sg}/cai_{pl} 'horse(s)') and adjectives (e.g. with the diminutive suffixe *-el*: $bunicel_{msg}/bunicei_{mpl}$ 'quite good'). Deletion of *-l-* before fem.sg. *-ă*, which becomes *-a* after a semivowel, is particular to pronouns and determiners, but used to be more widespread (in nouns, the plural *-le-* was reinterpreted as a plural ending; adjectives in *-el* used to have the form *-ea* in the feminine, e.g., *bunicea –*, but now this form is replaced by suffixal suppletivism – *bunicică* 'quite good (feminine)').

21. The weak form of the definite article is a suffix and has inflectional-like properties, although its root *-l-* is still visible in some forms (see especially the oblique forms *-l-ui, -l-or*).

22. Absence of inherent inflectional features on reflexives is also found in the other Indo-European languages which have the same alternation as Romanian (see note 18).

23. We use the D label for pronominal roots because pronouns have the external distribution and referential properties of DPs. This is not meant to imply that pronouns necessarily contain an NP (see Abney 1987, who treats pronouns as 'intransitive determiners').

24. Baker (2008) also assumes an internal structure of the three major lexical categories (N, Adj, V) which contains a Functional slot that governs the root. A crucial difference between our proposal and Baker's is that we do not allow the establishment of an Agree relation between the features in IFM and the features of the root itself (otherwise, agreeing personal possessors containing lexical number would be impossible: inflectional number would always copy the lexical number). When the features in IFM give indications regarding the referent of the pronoun (as in 3rd person pronouns), this is because these features are already valued at the beginning of the derivation.

De: A genitive marker in French?

Its grammaticalization path from Latin to French

Anne Carlier, Michèle Goyens and Béatrice Lamiroy
University of Lille 3, CNRS UMR 8163 STL and University of Leuven

This paper deals with the evolution of the genitive case from Latin to Old
and Middle French, and from Middle French to Modern French. The loss
of morphological case inflection in French raises the question whether the
category of the genitive is still a relevant notion. The authors claim it is, by
showing that the prepositional phrase *de* + NP, which gradually spread from
Latin to Modern French, fundamentally marks the dependency of a nominal
constituent with respect to another nominal expression, just like the adnominal
genitive did in Latin. They show that the preposition *de* underwent a pervasive
grammaticalization process from a full-fledged preposition introducing adjuncts
expressing spatial origin to a structural marker of arguments of verbal and
(especially) nominal heads.

Keywords: Latin, Old and Middle French, Modern French, preposition,
head-marking vs. dependent-marking, Romance, morphological case,
grammaticalization, adjunct vs. argument

1. Introduction

1.1 Is the category of the genitive relevant for Romance languages?

With the exception of Romanian, all Romance languages have lost nominal case inflection.[1] The lack of case inflection raises the question whether the category of the genitive case is even relevant for a language like French. Two options seem available:

– Latin, the ancestor of French, had specific morphological marking for the genitive case. A first option would be to study the decay of the genitive and its replacement in the evolution from Latin to French. However, as noted by Schøsler (2008: 428), there never was a general replacement of the genitive, but rather a replacement of specific uses of the genitive by specific prepositions or syntactic functions. For instance, for the verb *accusare* 'accuse' the genitive argument in Latin is expressed by a PP headed by *de* in Modern French, but for *damnare* and *condemnare* the genitive in Latin corresponds to a PP headed by the preposition *à* (Latin: *capitis condemnare*/Mod. Fr. *condamner à mort* 'sentence to death'), and for *oblivisci* 'forget' the genitive argument in Latin corresponds to an accusative in Modern French, etc. Hence, the set of expressions replacing the Latin genitive in Modern French does not form a natural class and is too heterogeneous to be a relevant object of study.

–   The second option is to devote a study exclusively to the preposition *de* in French. This option can be motivated as follows. In Latin as well as from a cross-linguistic viewpoint, the genitive is fundamentally an adnominal case: it marks the dependency of a nominal constituent with respect to another nominal expression.[2] It turns out that the trivial expression of this relationship corresponds in French to the preposition *de* 'of'. The study of this preposition can be conducted both from a synchronic and a diachronic viewpoint.

The present study will explore the second option, and will thus focus on NPs and VPs introduced by *de*. The perspective will be diachronic: we will analyze the evolution of *de*, from Classical Latin to Modern French. Our study is also synchronic as it intends to shed new light on the conditions of use of *de* in each stage of the evolution.

The diachronic perspective raises a problem: *de* cannot be considered as a genitive marker in Latin. It governs the ablative case and, although occasionally used for the expression of adnominal complements, it basically expresses spatial distancing from a source or an origin, typically in adverbal position (e.g. *de digito anulum detraho* 'I remove the ring from the finger', Terentius, *Heautontimoroumenos* 4, 1, 37), where no alternation with the genitive case is possible. This observation leads us to consider the complex relationship between genitive and ablative in a long-term perspective.

1.2   The complex relationship between genitive and ablative in a long-term perspective

The development of the prepositional phrase headed by *de* at the expense of the genitive has to be conceived in the larger context of the relationship between genitive and ablative case and its long-term evolution, from Indo-European to Latin and from Latin to Romance. Generally speaking, the case marking conveyed by a constituent expresses its syntactic and semantic dependency relation with respect to a head (Malchukov & Spencer 2008). In Latin, the genitive and the ablative case are quite close from a semantic viewpoint. According to Serbat (1996), the genitive conveys the values of 'inclusion', 'extraction'[3] and 'origin'. The two latter values, i.e. 'extraction' and 'origin', have also been attributed to the ablative. In spite of this semantic proximity, the ablative and the genitive are nevertheless distinct cases, not only morphologically – with different case endings – but also with respect to their syntactic properties.

Table 1. Distribution of the genitive in function of the morpho-syntactic nature of the head (based on Serbat 1996: 254)

	Noun/pronoun	Verb	Adjective	Total number of occurrences
Classical Latin	95,7%	2,4%	1,9%	2889
Late Latin	98,7%	0%	1,3%	525

From a syntactic viewpoint, there appear to be two major differences between the genitive and the ablative.

a. A first difference concerns the morpho-syntactic nature of the head.
    – In the case of the genitive, the head can be a noun, a pronoun, a verb or an adjective. However, the statistics offered by Serbat (1996: 254) for Classical Latin, summarized in Table 1, show that genitives overwhelmingly depend on a noun or a pronoun. This predominance of a (pro)nominal head will even increase in Late Latin.
    – On the contrary, a constituent in the ablative without preposition can never be adnominal. Rather, it typically stands in a relationship with the verb and has the status of an adjunct. According to Pinkster's figures (1984: 49), established on the basis of Cicero, *Orator*, I. 1–73, this is the case in 72% of its occurrences.
b. This syntactic difference entails another one, related to the presence of an adposition. As shown by Pinkster (1990) by means of the figures in Table 2, in Latin, case-marking is generally sufficient for the expression of the syntactic and semantic relationship of a nominal constituent with respect to its head and no adposition is needed to specify this relationship. As is shown in the same table, the frequency of adpositions will increase steadily in the evelution from Latin to Romance.

Crucially, however, as is shown in Table 3, the frequency of the adposition in Latin is dependent upon the syntactic function: whereas the presence of an adposition is exceptional in the adnominal position, which is the characteristic context of use of the genitive, it is common for syntactic functions characteristic of the ablative, i.e. adjuncts related to the verb. The frequent use of adpositions with the ablative, i.e. to mark adjuncts, is coherent with the cross-linguistic tendency to use oblique case more readily for non-core relations with respect to the verb (Nichols 1986: 78).

Table 2. Proportion of NPs without adposition and with adposition in Nepos, *Miltiades* 1–2, Latin & modern translations (Pinkster 1990: 197)

	NPs without adposition	NPs with adposition
Latin	85%	15%
Italian	40%	60%
French	50%	50%

Table 3. Distribution of NPs without adposition and with adposition in Sallustius, *History of Rome*, Or. Lep. 1–7 (Pinkster 1990: 197)

		1st argument	2nd argument	3rd argument	Adjunct	Adnominal Complement	Total
Latin	NP without adposition	25	13	6	16	15	75
	NP with adposition	0	0	2	10	0	12
Italian	NP without adposition	18	16	1	0	0	35
	NP with adposition	0	2	6	21	21	50

Given the global tendency of a one-to-one correspondence between meaning and form, those strong syntactic contrasts are at odds with the semantic affinity between genitive and ablative. Serbat (1996: 429) accounts for this discrepancy between syntax and semantics by formulating a hypothesis about the origin of the ablative. On the basis of the morphological markings of the genitive and the ablative in the old Indo-European languages such as Latin, Greek, Hittite, Sanskrit, Tocharian B, Germanic, Old Slavonic or Armenian, he rejects the widely held view that the ablative is a full-fledged case which disappeared in certain branches of the Indo-European family. Instead, he assumes that there was a set of different morphemes, close in meaning, all of which expressed in one way or another extraction, exclusion and origin. In the Indo-European family, this set arguably evolved in two different directions:

- Some branches of Indo-European, like Latin and Sanskrit, have introduced a two-fold distinction between morphemes which specialized in the meanings of 'extraction' and 'inclusion', typical of adnominal constituents, on the one hand, and others expressing the meaning 'origin', more likely to affect constituents which are adjoined to the verbal phrase, on the other hand.
- Other branches of the Indo-European family, such as Greek and Balto-Slavic, did not introduce this distinction and, hence, did not develop a separate case corresponding to the ablative.

According to Serbat (1996: 430), Latin, which belongs to the first group, has systematized the formal opposition between genitive and ablative, and gives the ablative the status of an autonomous and internally homogeneous case. Still, even in Latin, the ablative case is characterized by a large allomorphy, which shows that it is the result of syncretism or fusion of different 'cases', among which the ablative in a strict sense, meaning 'removal', the instrumental and the locative (Serbat 1996: 5–6). Moreover, in comparison with the other cases, the ablative case has a more peripheral status, as it is primarily used for adjuncts.

This imbalance between ablative and genitive is radically reversed during the evolution from Latin to Romance: as shown by Väänänen (1981), from Late Latin on, the ablative case leaves its marginal position and enters into competition with the genitive case under the form of the adpositional phrase "*de* + ablative". Crucially, it is no longer used dominantly for the expression of origin, in adverbal position (e.g. *de foro discedere* 'leave the market-place', lit. go away <u>from</u> the market-place), but it comes to be used as a marker of extraction and even inclusion in adnominal position (e.g. possession: *pedes de pecatore* 'the sinner's feet', lit.: the feet <u>of</u> the sinner).

1.3   Central hypotheses of the paper

The development of the prepositional construction with *de* at the expense of the genitive case will be the central topic of this paper. It will be studied from Latin to French, the central hypothesis being that *de* went through a pervasive grammaticalization process in which semantic bleaching and syntactic decategorization went hand in hand. Semantically, *de,* which had the referential meaning of indicating spatial origin at first, came to be used as a marker of several metaphorical meanings deriving from its original 'source' meaning, which we describe in detail in the Typology sections (§§ 2.3, 3.1, 4.1). From there it bleached further and eventually attained, according to Spang-Hanssen (1963) and Cadiot (1997), the stage of an element which is semantically "empty" and has a purely syntactic role.[4] Advanced bleaching can already be observed in some uses of *de* in Old and Middle French, but it significantly spreads in Modern French. Syntactically, the grammaticalization chain consists in the evolution from a full-fledged preposition capable of case marking and introducing adjuncts, to a purely structural element which marks what Haspelmath & Michaelis (2008) call genitive objects, i.e. arguments "lexically specified as marked by a case or an adposition (called 'genitive') that has as an additional function that of the possessor in an adnominal possessive construction."

Haspelmath & Michaelis (2008) observe a striking contrast between the rarity of genitive objects in Latin and their widespread use in Modern Romance. Genitive objects, though not impossible, were indeed rare in classical Latin, as shown in (1), whereas, as we will see in § 4, they are widespread in a modern Romance language like French.

(1)   Latin: *Flavi-us*   *indig-et*   **libr-orum**   **nov-orum**
      Flavius-NOM.M.SG lack-PRS.3SG book-GEN.M.PL new-GEN.M.PL[5]
      'Flavius needs new books'   (quoted in Lehmann 2002a)

On the basis of this observation, Haspelmath & Michaelis (2008) suggest that Romance and Latin genitive objects are "independent of each other to a large extent". Taking issue with this view, we will argue here that they are linked to each other by a grammaticalization chain which occasioned a massive extension of the preposition *de* in a way analogous to that observed for the French preposition *à* (Goyens et al. 2002, see also Spang-Hanssen 1963, Cadiot 1997, Marchello-Nizia 1997: 340 and 2006: 119). It will be shown that Modern French *de* + NP has a much larger range of uses than the Latin preposition *de* from which it originated, and that it particularly spread, with respect to Old and Middle French, as a marker of nominal and verbal arguments. These uses in which "*de* + NP" simply marks a "genitive" or even, as we will show, a "pseudo-genitive" object, have become predominant and correspond to the prototypical uses of *de* in Modern French, which is all the more striking as genitive objects seem to be quite rare in the world's languages (Haspelmath & Michaelis 2008: 150). As a corollary, its use as the introductory preposition of an adjunct, though sporadically attested in Modern French, significantly decreased and has become marginal. In sum, as will be shown, *de*'s main function in Modern French is no longer that of a full preposition introducing a locative adjunct but rather that of a totally grammaticalized element selected by a lexical head.

De + NP not only progressively invaded the argument zone of the VP but also massively extended its adnominal use. Whereas the genitive case prevailed in the nominal domain in Latin, thus constituting an area of resistance against the emergence of *de* + ablative, we will show that the competition between case and *de* + NP, still ongoing in Old French, steadily weakens in Middle French, so that by the time we reach Modern French, only fossilized remnants of case marking remain in a few totally lexicalized nominal compounds. In other words, *de* not only underwent bleaching and decategorization, it also displays another crucial property of grammaticalized items, viz. that of a massive extension (Heine & Narrog 2010), not only from the domain of adjuncts into that of arguments of the verb, but also from the verbal into the nominal domain.

As a corollary of this massive extension, *de* came to be used in a very wide variety of functions, some of which our study does not take into account:

–   lexicalized uses of *de* in compounds, e.g. *tremblement de terre* 'earthquake', *vert de rage* lit. green of rage 'furious', *afin de* 'in order to' etc.
–   predicative uses, like the so-called *historical infinitive* (Melis 2000), which is only found in a formal register (cf. ex. 2), and two nominal structures, one in which a predicative noun is followed by *de* + bare N, e.g. *ton imbécile de frère*, lit. your stupid of brother 'your stupid brother' (Milner 1978; Ruwet 1982) and one in which a noun is followed by *de* + a predicative adjective, e.g. *une chaise de libre*, lit. a chair of free 'a free seat' (cf. Lagae 1998):

(2) Il   s'   en   all-a   pass-er   sur le bord d'un
     He REFL.3 from there go-PST SIMPLE-3SG pass-INF.PRS on the side of a
     étang //Grenouilles aussitôt   **de** saut-er   dans les ondes
     pond frogs   immediately of jump-INF.PRS into the waves
     'He passed near a pond which made the frogs jump into the water'
     (La Fontaine, *Le lièvre et les grenouilles*)

– adjectival complements introduced by *de*, e.g. *Paul est fier **de** sa fille* 'Paul is proud of his daughter', *Paul est content **de** partir* 'Paul is glad to leave'.

Our paper is organized chronologically. Three major periods are outlined here: Latin, Old and Middle French, and Modern French. For each of the periods under study, three topics will be addressed: (1) a typology of the different meanings and functions of *de* both in the domain of the VP and that of the NP, (2) the competition between (genitive) case marking and prepositional marking by *de* and (3) the grammaticalization path of *de*.

2. *De* + NP in Latin

The first part of the paper is devoted to the prepositional phrase *de* + NP in Latin. The two first sections will deal with preliminary questions. In Section 2.1., we will consider the morpho-syntactic status of the preposition in Latin in an evolutionary perspective and identify some traces of earlier stages. In Section 2.2., it will be examined why "*de* + ablative" comes to be used instead of the ablative without preposition. The subsequent sections will offer a typology of the uses of *de* + NP-ABL in Latin (§ 2.3.) and determine in which contexts this PP enters into competition with the genitive (§ 2.4.). Finally, Section 2.5. will analyze the stage of grammaticalization of *de* in Latin by applying Lehmann's (2002b) parameters.

2.1 The morpho-syntactic status of the preposition in an evolutionary perspective

According to Meillet & Vendryes (1948: § 782), Latin prepositions originate from adverbs. This adverbial origin is still perceivable in some weakly grammaticalized prepositions in Latin. For instance, *clam* is used both as an adverb 'secretly' and as a preposition 'without the knowledge of', e.g.: *clam suom patrem* 'without his father knowing' (Plautus, *The Captives*, 1032). Weakly grammaticalized prepositions such as *clam* often show some fluctuation with respect to case, e.g. *clam* governs either the accusative or the ablative. Several of these adverbs derive from fossilized inflected nouns, e.g. *causā* 'because of' is the ablative form of *causa* 'cause'; *fini* 'until' corresponds to the ablative of *finis* 'end', etc.

Latin also has more grammaticalized prepositions, such as *per, in, ab, de, ex*, which are inherited from Indo-European. Meillet & Vendryes (1948: § 784) hypothesize that they also derive from fossilized inflected nouns that turned into adverbs[6] before reaching the stage of the preposition. In comparison with less grammaticalized prepositions such as *clam*, this subset has the specific property of having a double role in Latin. On the one hand, they have the status of a preposition combining with a nominal complement and governing its case (3a). But, on the other hand, they preserve the faculty to establish a relationship with the verb (3b). The tightening of this relationship turns them into verbal prefixes (Meillet & Vendryes 1948: § 843):

(3) a. ***Ex***   *urb-e*   *profisc-or*
         out-of city-ABL.SG leave-PASS.PRS.1SG
         'I leave the city'

     b. ***Ex-***   *eo*
         out-of- go-PRS.1SG
         'I go out'

This double status, of preposition and verbal prefix, is an inheritance from Indo-European. According to Meillet & Vendryes (1948: §§ 786–842), these elements have an adverbial status in Indo-European, with a high degree of syntactic autonomy and no fixed position. They are basically used to add some information to verbs or nouns or even adjectives: they specify for instance if the verbal action occurs within a certain place (*in*), together with other persons (*cum*), etc. Some of them still appear in this type of construction in Latin and are labeled as adverbs or as particles in the grammatical tradition (e.g. *ad, ante, per, post, prope, propter, extra, intra, super,* ... cf. Ernout & Thomas 1951: § 138). For most of them, however, the bond with the verb or the nominal constituent is strengthened and they eventually evolve into either prepositions or prefixes.

From a diachronic point of view, the evolution from adverb to preposition may be conceived as a reanalysis, in the sense of a rebracketting (Langacker 1977, Vincent 1999; Luraghi 2009): the adverb becomes a preposition and takes the nominal constituent as its complement: [Adv] [NP] → [Prep NP]. Since most of the former adverbs becoming prepositions repeatedly occur in combination with one and the same case, the correlation between a certain preposition and a certain case is analyzed in terms of syntactic dependency: the preposition is considered as governing the case of its nominal complement. In Classical Latin, there are still prepositions that do not strictly govern case but allow two cases with a difference in meaning (e.g. *in* + ablative 'within' (locational); *in* + accusative 'towards' (directional)), which points to an incomplete reanalysis (cf. also Luraghi 2009). Further evolution tends to establish a one-to-one correlation between a certain preposition and a certain case: as is evidenced by the Pompeii inscriptions (cf. Ernout & Thomas 1951: § 144), prepositions compatible with two cases are already eliminated in spoken Latin during the Classical period and the accusative case is generalized at the expense of the other cases.

2.2   *De* + ablative versus ablative without preposition

The core meaning of the Latin ablative case is that of 'removal', involving a starting point and a separation from that point. The question can be raised why the preposition *de*, meaning also 'removal', is used, rather than the ablative alone. Two reasons can be invoked.

–   Typologically, Latin is a dependent-marking language (Nichols 1986): both case inflection and adpositions are markers of grammatical relations that appear on the dependent constituent. It could be hypothesized that this grammatical relation needs a stronger and a more explicit expression when the dependency relation with respect to the verbal predicate is loose. Since the ablative case is predominantly used for constituents with the syntactic status of adjuncts with respect to the verb or the verbal predicate, the relationship expressed by this case is often strengthened and specified by a preposition.

–   A second reason is put forward by Ernout & Thomas (1951: § 100). The ablative in Latin is the result of the fusion of three Indo-European cases: the ablative properly speaking, the locative and the instrumental (cf. § 1.2.). Hence, according to these authors, prepositions came to be used in order to separate more specific meanings within this syncretic case. *De*, in competition with *ab* and *ex*, is used in order to distinguish the uses formerly expressed by the ablative properly speaking, i.e. the removal from a starting point.

However, sometimes the preposition is not used: this is in particular the case with nouns referring to stereotypical places typically associated with an activity such as *domo* 'from home', *rure* 'from the countryside', *venatu (redire)* (Plautus) '(come back) from hunting', *opsonatu redeo* (Plautus, *Menaechmi* 2,2) 'come back from the market' and with nouns which are names of cities or small islands, e.g. *Romā* 'from Rome'. These nouns thus somehow form an area of resistance to the spread of the preposition.[7]

De + NP-ABL inherits the distributional tendencies of the ablative case, as described in § 1.2. Thus, it typically stands in relationship with the verb as an adjunct and is rarely dependent on a nominal head, i.e. a noun or a pronoun. As we will see, both of these characteristics will dramatically change over time: in Modern French, *de* + NP is rarely an adjunct, and it is first and foremost a complement of the NP.

2.3   Typology[8]

The typology of the uses of *de* in Latin, in Medieval French and in Modern French will be organized as follows. A first distinction is related to the morpho-syntactic nature of the head: verbal or nominal. As to the uses depending on a verb, it may seem useful to distinguish *de* heading a PP that has the status of an adjunct from *de* + NP as an argument. We will first raise the question whether the distinction between argument and adjunct has the same relevance for the different language stages studied here.

2.3.0   *Preliminary remarks on the distinction between argument and adjunct*

In establishing the distinction between argument and adjunct, we have to take into account the typological specificities of the language or language stage under study. This can be illustrated by a comparison between Latin and French.

The typical tests to distinguish arguments from adjuncts, listed by Lazard (1994), are constraints related to (i) the presence, (ii) the form and (iii) the (syntagmatic) position of the constituent. As has been noted by Lehmann (2002a), the verb in Latin:

i.   does not require the presence of any argument;
ii. does not impose clear constraints on its arguments as it allows, for one and the same argument position, a case-marked noun phrase without a preposition or a prepositional phrase;
iii. does not strictly determine the sequential order of the arguments.

In other words, the boundary between arguments and adjuncts is fuzzy in Latin. By contrast, in Modern French, the constraints of the verb on its arguments are very strict on all these points.

Another typological parameter, highlighted by Nichols (1986), that distinguishes Latin and French is the opposition between head-marking and dependent-marking. Latin is a dependent-marking language: the syntactic function and semantic role of the NPs with respect to the verb is marked by case affixes on NPs. French, on the other hand, has features of a head-marking language: in spoken French, the argument structure can be marked under the form of clitics on the verbal head:

(4) *Marie, ce livre, il*   *le*   *lui*   *a donné, Pierre.*
     Mary, this book, he-NOM.M.SG it-ACC.M.SG her-DAT.SG has given, Peter
     'This book, it's to Mary that Peter gave it.'

Nichols (1986: 78) argues that dependent-marked constituents tend to have a higher degree of autonomy with respect to the verb than head-marked constituents. As a consequence, the constructional force of the verb is weaker and the boundary between arguments and adjuncts is less clear-cut. Applying this hypothesis to Latin and French, the typological difference between the two languages could explain why it is difficult to distinguish between adjuncts and arguments in Latin, whereas this distinction is less problematic in the French data. Since the general distinction between argument and adjunct is fuzzy in Latin, we decided not to consider this distinction for the organization of the Latin data.

The typology presented in the following section offers an overview of the different uses of *de* in Latin. The comparison with Medieval French and Modern French will allow us to highlight the major evolutionary tendencies of *de* in the history of the French language. We would like to point out that this typology is not intended as a detailed lexical study of the preposition *de*. There are two major conceptions of the lexical meaning of prepositions like *de*: according to the first conception, space is a concrete source domain from which the other more abstract meanings such as time are consistently derived by metaphorical mapping (e.g. Lakoff & Johnson 1980, see also Fagard 2010 for a diachronic perspective on French); the second approach, argued for by Jackendoff (1983) (cf. Honeste (2005) for *de* in French), gives less weight to the spatial domain and postulates a more abstract structure that can be suitably applied to different domains. Our diachronic study does not offer strong evidence for the chronological primacy of the spatial meaning: the Latin preposition *de* does not correspond to a hypothetical primitive stage where it can only be used to express a spatial relationship. *De* already has a variety of abstract meanings in Latin. The spatial meaning of 'movement away from a starting point' appears nevertheless to be the 'core meaning' in this sense that most of the other menings can be conceptually linked to this spatial meaning. Hence, we will adopt the working hypothesis that the spatial meaning of *de* is its primitive meaning.

A second preliminary remark concerns the relationship between intrinsic meaning of *de* and context-induced meaning. It is often difficult or even artificial to distinguish between the proper meaning of *de* and the meaning inferred from the context, for two reasons: in a synchronic perspective, the context of use helps us to identify the intrinsic meaning; in a diachronic perspective, the context of use can also create a new meaning by the mechanism of invited inferencing (cf. Traugott & Dasher 2002: 34–40).

The Latin data will be presented in two subsections: as mentioned before, *de* is principally used to mark a dependency on a verb or a VP (§ 2.3.1.); its use in relation with a noun or an NP (§ 2.3.2.) is less frequent and less diversified from a semantic viewpoint.

2.3.1   *Verbal domain*

A.   *Spatial meaning: movement or perspective away from a starting point*

From a semantic viewpoint, a preposition is a two-sided relator. It consists of (i) a reference point or "landmark", (ii) a *locatum* or "trajector", corresponding to the entity being located and (iii) a relationship between the landmark and the trajector. According to Langacker's view (1987), the landmark is an entity with reference to which the "trajector" is evaluated. The terms "landmark" and "trajector" are equivalent to Talmy's (1975, 2000) "figure" and "ground".

The NP governed by the preposition *de* defines the landmark or reference point, whereas *de* specifies the relationship with the landmark and characterizes this relationship as a schematic path, the beginning of which is highlighted. Insofar as the landmark or reference point corresponds to a spatial location, *de* marks a physical movement or an oriented action away from a starting point located in space.

A.1.   *Vertical movement*

Prepositions and prefixes have a common origin (§ 2.1.) and, hence, also a common primitive meaning. Cross-linguistically, prepositions exhibit a lower degree of fusion or agglutination with the NP they govern, while prefixes tend to agglutinate to the verb (Bybee 1985, Svorou 2010).

As for the Latin verbs indicating movement without intrinsic orientation, when *de* combines with this type of verb, it adds the feature of downward path to the verbal meaning (e.g. *descendere* 'go down', *defluere* 'flow down', *deicere* 'throw downwards', *de muro desilire* 'jump down from the wall', *despicere* 'look downwards, despise'), which implies that the starting point is a location situated higher. If we admit that the meaning of the prefix is less sensitive to semantic evolution than the preposition, because of its high degree of fusion with the verb, the feature of downward path could be part of the primitive spatial meaning of *de*. This meaning is still common in Classical Latin:

(5)   Major-es=que   cad-u-nt   *alt-is*   *de*   *mont-ibus*
      greater-NOM.P=and fall-PRS.3PL high-ABL.PL from mountains-ABL.PL
      umbr-ae [Class. Latin]
      shadow-NOM.PL
      'And the greater shadows fall from the lofty mountains.'(Virgil, *Eclogue* (I, 84))

A.2. Spatial movement without vertical orientation

As a result of desemantization, *de* is already used in Classical Latin to express a movement or perspective away from a starting point, without vertical orientation:

(6)   *Cum* *de* *fenestr-a*   corv-us   rapt-um   case-um
      when from window-ABL.SG raven-NOM.SG steal-PST.PTCP cheese-ACC.SG
      come-sse   vell-et
      eat-INF.PRS want-SBJV.IMPF.3SG
      'At the moment when a raven wanted to eat some cheese, stolen from a window, ...'   (Phaedrus, *Fabulae* 1, 13: *Vulpes et corvus*) [Class. Latin]

The same spatial meaning is attested in combination with deverbal nouns:

(7)   Comple-to   ann-o   profection-is   fili-orum
      finish-PST.PTCP.ABL.M.SG year-ABL.SG departure-GEN.SG son-GEN.PL
      Israhel *de* *terr-a*   Egypt-i
      Israel of land-ABL.SG Egypt-GEN.SG
      'One year after the exodus of the sons of Israel from the land of Egypt.'
                                              (*Peregr. Aeth.* 37, 2) [Late Latin]

A.3. Origin and lineage

The reference point or landmark expressed by the NP can refer to humans rather than being strictly spatial, which yields the meaning of origin. When the NP refers to a species (8), an ethnic group, a family or even an individual (9), we obtain the meaning of lineage:

(8)   *De*   *tigrid-e*   nat-us
      From tiger-ABL.SG born-NOM.M.SG
      'Born from a tiger'   (Ovidius, *Metamorph.* 9, 613) [Class. Latin]

(9)   Fili-um   habe-re   *de aliqu-a*
      son-ACC.SG have-INF.PRS of someone-ABL.F.SG
      'Have a son from someone'

A.4. From origin to partition

With verbs meaning 'eat', 'drink', 'take', 'give', the starting point or landmark is conceived as a contextually defined partition set, and *de* indicates the removal of a part of this set (Carlier 2007; Carlier & Lamiroy, forthc.):

(10) Ed-ere   ***de***   *arbor-e*   *uit-ae*
      eat-INF.PRS from tree-ABL.SG life-GEN.SG
      'Eat from the tree of life'

This partitive use of *de* + NP as a complement of the verb is not attested in Classical Latin. It emerges in Late Latin, in the popularizing texts written in Gaul from the 4th C. onwards, especially in the writings of Christian authors. Example (11) offers a bridging context between the meaning of spatial movement away from a reference point, on the one hand, and extraction or partition, on the other hand (cf. Luraghi forthc.): whereas *de calice* has only the first meaning, *de pane illo* is compatible with the meaning of spatial movement away from a reference point and with the meaning of partition.

(11) Et sic ***de pan-e***   ***ill-o***   *ed-a-t*   *et*   *de calic-e*
      and so of bread-ABL.SG that-ABL.SG eat-SBJV.PRS.3SG and of-chalice-ABL.SG
      bib-a-t
      drink-SBJV.PRS.3SG
      'And so let him eat **of the/that bread** and drink **of the chalice**'
                                                    (*Vulgate*, I *Corinthians* 11, 28) [Late Latin]

Interestingly, as has been noted by Väänänen (1981), the contextual anchorage of the partition set is mostly explicitly marked, by a demonstrative or a possessive determiner, as is the case in example (11) above, or by a relative clause (12):

(12) nam et   catell-i   ed-u-nt   ***de mic-is***
      for   and little-dog-NOM.PL eat-PRS.3PL of crumbs-ABL.PL
      quae   *cadunt*   *de* *mensa*   *dominorum*   *suorum*
      that-NOM.F.PL fall-PRS.3PL from table-ABL.SG master-GEN.M.PL his-GEN.M.PL
      'Yet the dogs eat **of the crumbs** which fall from their master's table'
                                                            (*Vulgata, Matthew* 15: 27)

B. Metaphorical meanings

A metaphor is defined as a kind of analogy that describes a subject by stating that it is, by some feature(s), the same as another unrelated object. Following Lakoff & Johnson (1980), we consider a metaphor as "understanding and experiencing one kind of thing in terms of another". One of the obvious metaphoric extensions of space is time, which we will analyze hereafter.

B.1. Temporal meaning

B.1.1. Movement away from a temporal starting point, especially an event

The reference point or landmark can be conceptualized as located in time, rather than in space, especially when it is an event. Given the linearity and the intrinsic directionality of time, predominantly conceived as moving from past to future in Indo-European languages,[9] *de* indicates that the *locatum* or the trajector occurs after the landmark:

(13) Non bon-us   somn-us   est   *de*   *prandi-o*
      Not good-NOM.M.SG nap-NOM.M.SG be-PRS.3SG from meal-ABL.SG
      'A nap after the meal is no good'   (Plautus, *Mostellaria*, 3) [Class. Latin]

We also find this meaning for the ablative without *de*:

(14) Rom-am   *mult-is*   *ann-is*   non veni-t
      Rome-ACC.SG many-ABL.PL years-ABL.PL not come-PRF.3SG
      'He has not come to Rome for many years'
                     (Cicero, *Pro Sex. Roscio Amerino Or.*, 74) [Class. Latin]

B.1.2. Partition within a time interval

When the landmark is a time interval, *de* can isolate a part of this time interval and locate the trajector, i.c. the event, with respect to this subinterval. This often yields the meaning of 'during':

(15) *De mens-e*   *Decembr-i*   navig-are
      of month-ABL.SG December-GEN.SG navigate-INF PRS
      'To navigate during December'
                     (Cicero, *Ep. ad Quintum Fratem* 2. 1. G) [Class. Latin]

The location within the subinterval can be specified, as is illustrated by (16):

(16) *Mult-a*   *de noct-e*
      much-ABL.F.SG of night-ABL.SG
      'In the middle of the night'   (Cicero, *Oratio pro P. Sextio* 75) [Class. Latin]

B.2. Movement away from a starting point, neither spatial nor temporal

The landmark can be neither purely spatial nor temporal, but can nevertheless be conceived metaphorically as if it were a spatial location or a time interval. *De* indicates that the *locatum* or trajector, in this case the event, can be conceived spatially as a movement away from the landmark and/or temporally as coming after the landmark:

(17) Aliqu-em   *de*   *somn-o*   excitare
      someone-ACC.M.SG from sleep-ABL.SG wake up-INF PRS
      'To wake up someone'   (Cicero, *Pro Sulla Or.* 24) [Class. Latin]

In combination with verbs indicating the transfer of a material object or information, this landmark indicating the starting point or origin can even be a human being:

(18) Nav-es   regi-ae,   cap-t-ae   *de*
      ship-NOM.PL royal-NOM.F.PL take-PST.PTCP.NOM.F.PL from
      Macedonibus
      Macedonian-ABL.PL
      'The royal ships, taken from the Macedonians'
                              (Livius, *Ab urbe condita* 14, 42) [Class. Latin]

(19) Hoc   audi-v-i   *de part-e*
      this-ACC.N.SG hear-PRF.1SG of father-ABL.SG
      'I heard this from my father'   (Cicero, *de Orat.* 3, 33, 133) [Class. Latin]

B.3. Objects of verbs of saying, thinking and feeling

In combination with verbs referring to an activity of saying, thinking or feeling, the NP governed by *de* indicates the entity at the origin of this activity, i.e. the one that triggers it. This entity is at the same time the object of this activity (20–22). In line with this meaning, *de* develops its use as a topic marker (23). This use is attested in more informal speech, for instance in theatre texts and letters:

(20) *De aliqu-o*   teme-re
      of something-ABL.N.SG fear-INF PRS
      'Be afraid of something'   (Cicero, *Pro Sestio Or.* 1) [Class. Latin]

(21) *De*   *nobis*   [...] cogita-bi-s
      about us-ABL   think-FUT.2SG
      'You will think about us' (Cicero, *Ep. ad Att.* VII, 1, 1) [Class. Latin, Letters]

(22) *De*   *ill-a*   ergo   ego   dic-o   tibi
      about her-ABL.F.SG therefore I-NOM talk-PRS.1SG you-DAT
      'It is about her that I am talking to you'
                              (Plautus, *Mercator* 899) [Old Latin, oral register[10]]

(23) *De*   *Pompei-o*   et   fac-i-o   diligen-ter,   et   fac-ia-m
      about Pompeius-ABL and do-PRS.1SG accurate-ADV and do-FUT.1SG
      quod   mone-s
      what-ACC.N.SG advise-PRS.2SG
      'As to Pompeius, I execute accurately what you ask me and I will continue to
      do so'   (Cicero, *Ep. ad Q.*, 3,1,9) [Class. Latin, Letters]

B.4. From origin to manner, instrument and cause

As we mentioned before, the ablative case in Latin is the result of the fusion of three Indo-European cases: the ablative case properly speaking indicating separation, the locative case and the instrumental case (§ 1.2.). The different meanings grouped in this subsection were formerly expressed by the instrumental case. The notions of cause or instrument are compatible with the meaning of "*de* + ablative case", since origin and temporal precedence are often source domains for the expression of causality (Heine & Kuteva 2002). In the following examples, the NP governed by *de* corresponds to an instrument:

(24)   Percuss-am [...]   *su-a* [...]   *de cuspid-e*   terr-am
       hit-PST.PTCP.ACC.F.SG his-ABL.F.SG of spear-ABL.SG ground-ACC.SG
       'The ground hit with his spear'   (Ovid, *Metamorphoses* 6, 80) [Class. Latin]

These uses become more common in Late Latin (Adams 2011):

(25)   *De   man-ibus   su-is*   summitat-es [...] prem-e-t
       with hands-ABL.PL his-ABL.PL edge-ACC.PL   squeeze-FUT.3SG
       'He will squeeze with his hands the edges'   (*Peregr. Aeth.* 37, 2) [Late Latin]

The NP governed by *de* can also express the cause, at the origin of the event:

(26)   Fle-ba-t   uterque   non *de   su-o*
       weep-IMPF-3SG each-of-both.NOM.SG not about his-OWN-ABL.N.SG
       supplici-o,   sed pater   *de   fili*   *mort-e,*
       punishment-ABL.SG but father.NOM.SG about son-GEN.SG death-ABL.SG,
       de   part-is   fili-us
       about father-GEN.SG son-NOM.SG
       'They were both weeping, not because of their own punishment, but the father because of the death of his son, the son because of the death of his father.'
                                        (Cicero, *In Verr.* I, 30, 76) [Class. Latin]

Manner readings are attested only in frozen expressions:

(27)   a.   *De audito* 'on the basis of hearsay' (Plautus, *Mercator* 903)
       b.   *De integro* 'again', lit. starting from an intact basis
       c.   *De industria* 'intentionally'

2.3.2   *Nominal domain*

In Classical Latin, *de* + NP-ABL is by no means the catch-all adnominal complement. In all its uses, *de* retains traces of its meaning of removal or origin.

A.   *Origin and lineage*

In Classical Latin, the adnominal *de* + NP-ABL can be used with the meaning of origin when the NP it governs indicates a place. *Ab* is mostly used for names of cities, whereas *ex* is used when the NP refers to a region or a country:

(28)   Turn-us   Herdoni-us   *ab   Arici-a*
       Turnus-NOM.SG Herdonius-NOM.SG from *Aricia*-ABL
       'Turnus Herdonius, from Aricia'
       (Livius, *Ab urbe condita* I, 50, 3, quoted from Ernout & Thomas, 1951: 71)
       [Class. Latin]

(29) Quint-us   Iuni-us   *ex Hispani-a*   quidam
Quintus-NOM.SG Iunius-NOM.SG from Hispania-ABL a certain-NOM.M.SG
'A certain Quintus Iunius, from Spain'
(Caesar, *De Bello Gallico*, 5, 27, 1, quoted from Ernout & Thomas, 1951: 71)
[Class. Latin]

In Late Latin, *de* is extended at the expense of *ab* and *ex* and, hence, occurs for all types of places:

(30) Ibi null-i   ali-i   commane-nt nisi *cleric-i*
here nobody-NOM.M.PL other-NOM.M.PL stay-PRS.3PL except clergy-NOM.PL
de ips-a ecclesi-a
of the church-ABL.F.SG
'Here nobody else stays except the clergy of the church'
(*Peregrinatio*, 21, 3) [Late Latin]

From Classical Latin onwards, the adnominal *de* + NP-ABL can also be used with the meaning of origin when the NP governed by *de* indicates a social or ethnic group:

(31) Atque e-o-dem   tempor-e   *accusator*   *de pleb-e*
and   same-ABL.N.SG time-ABL.SG accuser-NOM.SG of plebs-ABL.SG
L. Caesulen-us   fu-i-t
L. Caesulenus-NOM be-PRF.3SG
'And there was in this same period an accuser coming from the plebs, named
L. Caesulenus'   (Cicero, *Brutus* 34, 131) [Class. Latin]

In Late Latin, the NP governed by *de* can also refer to an individual rather than a group and in this way becomes a marker of parentage:

(32) Fili-os   *de fili-o*   *me-o*   *Childebert-o*
son-ACC.PL of son-ABL.SG my-ABL.SG Childerbert-ABL.SG
'The sons of my son Childebert'
(Gregorius Turensis, *Hist. Franc.* 9, 11) [Late Latin]

B.   *From origin to extraction and partition*

As is illustrated by the following Classical Latin examples, the pattern NP + *de* + NP-ABL is commonly used to indicate the notion of extraction: the NP governed by *de* indicates the whole from which a part is isolated.

(33) Suc-us   *de quinquefoli-o*
juice-NOM.M.SG of cinquefoil-ABL.N.SG
'Juice of cinquefoil'   (Plinius, *Natural History* 26, 23) [Class. Latin]

This use of NP + *de* + NP-ABL becomes more frequent in Late Latin:

(34) Virg-am   *de*   *arbo-re*   Abraham in Ausoni-o
off-shoot-ACC.SG from tree-ABL.SG Abraham in Italian-ABL.SG

planta-sse   littor-e
plant-INF.PRF coast-ABL.SG
'You have planted on the shores of Italy an offshoot of the tree of Abraham'
(St-Hieronymus, *Epistola* LXVI. AD PAMMACHIUM, end 4th C.)

This pattern is extended to contexts without extraction. In the following examples, *de* no longer means 'taken from' but rather 'being a part of':

(35)   Pariet-es   *de cellol-a*   in qu-a   Joseph tene-ba-tur
       wall-NOM.PL of cell-ABL.F.SG in which-ABL.F.SG Joseph hold-PASS.IMPF.3SG
       'The walls of the cell in which Joseph was emprisoned'
       (Greg. Tur. *Historia Francorum I 21*, quoted from Väänänen 1981: 93, 6th C.)

(36)   Ped-es   *de peccator-e*
       foot-ACC.PL of sinner-ABL.SG
       'The sinner's feet'
       (Venance Fortunat, *Vita s. Maart.* 2, 369, quoted by Väänänen 1981: 94, end 6th C.)

As a partition marker, the prepositional structure *de* + NP-ABL occurs frequently, from Classical Latin onwards, in combination with quantifying expressions, determiners or pronouns, in particular when there is a strictly partitive meaning, i.e. when the partition set is definite:

(37)   Nemo   *de nobis*
       nobody of us-ABL
       'None of us'   (Cicero, *Tusculanae Disputationes* 5, 36) [Class. Latin]

(38)   Un-us   *de mult-is*
       one-NOM.M.SG of many-ABL.PL
       'One of the populace/of the mass'
                                (Cicero, *De officiis,* I, 30 (109)) [Class. Latin]

C.   From origin to property

The NP governed by *de* can also indicate the substance from which an entity is made (39a). In this use, the prepositional complement enters into competition with the corresponding adjective (39b):

(39)   a.   Templ-um   *de marmor-e*   (Vergilius, *Georgica*, 3, 13) [Class. Latin]
            temple-ACC.SG of marble-ABL.SG
            'Temple made of marble'

       b.   *marmore-o*   thalam-o
                                (Vergilius, *Aeneas*, 4, 390, quoted by Väänänen 1981) [Class. Latin]
            marble-ADJ.ABL.SG room-ABL.SG
            'Room made of marble'

This alternation between the PP and the adjective shows a meaning shift from 'taken from' towards 'having the property of'.

D.   From origin to object of deverbative nouns of thinking and feeling

In combination with nouns referring to thinking or feeling, *de* + NP expresses the entity – a person or a thing – which triggers the activity indicated by the noun, and which is at the same time the object of this activity:

(40)   Admiratio   *de fili-o*
       admiration-NOM.SG of son-ABL.SG
       'The admiration for his son'
       (Terentius, *Heauton*, 424, quoted by Väänänen 1981: 100) [Old Latin, conversational style]

As noted by Väänänen (1981: 100), the expression of the adnominal complement by a PP, rather than in the genitive, is unambiguous: whereas the genitive in (41b) can have an object or a subject reading, only the object reading is available in (41a):

(41)   a.   Metus *de fratr-e*
            fear   of brother
            'The fear inspired by his brother'
                                          (Cicero, *Epistulac ad Atticum* 3,8,4) [Class. Latin]

       b.   Metus   *fratr-is*
            fear- NOM.SG brother-GEN.SG
            'His brother's fear' or 'The fear inspired by his brother'

This use of *de* develops considerably in Late Latin:

(42)   Desideri-um *de ill-o*   *paradys-o*
       desire-NOM.SG of that-ABL.M.SG paradise-ABL.SG
       'The longing for Paradise'
                (MGH, *Leg.* V, *Formulae*, p. 203, 25, quoted by Väänänen 1981: 101)

The following example shows a bridging context (Heine 2002), since it allows two syntactic analyses: *de triumpho* can be linked to *cupiditas* as an object genitive; given its initial position, it can also be interpreted as the expression of the topic:

(43)   *De*   *triumph-o*   autem null-a   me   *cupiditas*
       about triumph-ABL.SG however no-NOM.F.SG me-ACC desire-NOM.SG
       ten-ui-t
       hold-PRF.3SG
       Object reading: 'I felt no desire for triumph'
       Topic marker: 'As for the triumph, I felt no desire.'
       (Cicero, *Epistulae ad Atticum.* 7, 2, 6 quoted by Väänänen 1981: 90) [Class. Latin]

E.   From origin to possession

Cross-linguistically, the meaning 'taken from' often shifts towards 'belonging to'. However, Classical Latin does not offer clear examples of NP + *de* + NP-ABL indicating a possessive relationship. Even in Late Latin, few instances with a possessive meaning can be retrieved:

(44)   Res   *de mulier-em   su-am*   exinde   em-eri-t
        things of wife-ACC.SG his-ACC.F.SG from there buy-PRF.FUT.3SG
        'He will have bought his wife's things'
        (MGH, *Edictus ceteraeque Langobardorum leges Edictus Rothari*, 133, 7th C.,
        quoted by Väänänen 1981) [Late Latin, cf. confusion between accusative and
        ablative: *muliere(m) sua(m)*]

The possessive relationship is thus an area of resistance to the development of the prepositional construction *de* + NP-ABL. Due to this resistance, a non-prepositional construction will persist to a certain extent until Old French, but will gradually decrease from Middle French onwards.

2.4   Competition between genitive case and "*de* + ablative" in Latin

In Classical Latin, the ablative, governed by a preposition or not, is mostly an adverbal case, whereas the genitive is used for adnominal complements. Hence, there is no real competition between genitive and ablative, but rather a global complementary distribution.

Nevertheless, *de* + NP-ABL is sometimes used as a non-standard expression of NP dependency. In Classical Latin, there is at least one case where "*de/ex* + NP-ABL" is well-established: as a complement of quantifiers, determiners or pronouns, the prepositional pattern is frequently used instead of the genitive when the partition set is definite, for instance when the partition set is expressed by a pronoun (e.g. *multi de nobis* (many of us-ABL) instead of *multi nostrum* (many us-GEN) (Menge 2000: 375). *De* + NP-ABL is used as adnominal complement with other meanings such as 'lineage' or 'extraction'. (cf. § 2.3.2.), provided that the primitive meanings of 'origin' and 'removal, movement away from this origin' are still relevant.

Two global tendencies characterize the development of the prepositional construction *de* + NP-ABL at the expense of the genitive:

–   *De* + NP-ABL is more frequent when the noun in the adnominal complement refers to an inanimate entity. Conversely, the genitive is often maintained when the adnominal complement refers to a specific human being. In particular, for the expression of the possessive relationship, the genitive resists the extension of the prepositional construction (cf. § 2.3.2.E. & Väänänen 1981: 107). This area of resistance can still be observed in medieval French.

– *De* + NP-ABL is more readily used when the adnominal complement contains a morpho-syntactically complex NP. In the following example, the use of the prepositional construction (45a) rather than the genitive (45b) could have been favored by the presence of the relative clause:

(45) a. ***De** taur-o*   qu-em   Hercules […] immola-ra-t
of bull-ABL.M.SG that-ACC.SG Hercules-NOM immolate-PLQPRF.3SG
cori-um   *protuli-t*
hide-ACC.SG bring-PRF.3SG
'He brought the hide of the bull that was immolated by Hercules'
(Caius Valerius Flaccus, *Hyg. fab.* 195, quoted from Väänänen 1981: 90,
1st C.)

  b. *Taur-i*   *cori-um*   *protuli-t*
bull-GEN.M.SG hide-ACC.SG bring-PRF.3SG
'He brought the hide of the bull'

In the following section, we will recapitulate some characteristics of *de* in order to evaluate its degree of grammaticalization in Classical and Late Latin.

2.5 Degree of grammaticalization of the preposition *de* in Latin

As mentioned above (§ 2.2.), in comparison with prepositions such as *causā* 'because of' or *fini* 'until', which still have clear traces of their lexical origin, *de* belongs to the subset of prepositions inherited from Indo-European that are already in a rather advanced stage of grammaticalization. In this section, we will evaluate its degree of grammaticalization with respect to the six parameters put forward by Lehmann (2002b).

INTEGRITY

The integrity or paradigmatic weight of a sign consists of its substance, both formal and semantic, which defines its identity, from a paradigmatic and syntagmatic viewpoint (Lehmann 2002b: 112). For instance, with respect to its numeral origin *one*, the indefinite article *a(n)* displays both formal and semantic erosion (Carlier 2001 and 2013).

Table 4. Lehmann's (2002b) parameters of grammaticalization

Axis / Parameter	Paradigmatic	Syntagmatic
Weight	Integrity	Scope
Cohesion	Paradigmaticity	Bondedness
Variability	Paradigmatic variability	Syntagmatic variability

Even in its spatial meaning, the preposition *de* in Classical Latin has already undergone some bleaching. When used as a prefix or a preverb, the movement indicated by *de-* is mostly vertical, from a higher to a lower position (e.g. the verbs cited above in §2.3.1.A.1. *descendere* 'go down'). This semantic feature is weakened in the prepositional use, as observed in Classical Latin. Hence, the preposition *de* can also be used for movement without vertical orientation and even for upward movement, e.g. *de terra ad sidera mundi* 'from the earth to the stars of this world' (Lucretius, *De rerum natura*, 1, 788). This loss of integrity, both formal and semantic, will continue in the evolution from Latin to French.

In Late Latin, *de* tends to combine with other prepositions (Ernout & Thomas 1951: § 144). These combinations give rise to new prepositions, not only in French (*de ex* 'of out' > *dès* 'from', *de retro* 'of behind' > *derrière* 'behind', *de sub, de subtus* > *dessous, ab ante* > *avant* 'before (temporal)' integrated into *de ab ante* > *devant* 'before (spatial meaning)'), but also in other Romance languages (e.g. *de post* > *doppo* (It.), *per ad* > *para* (Sp., Port.)). This tendency could also be linked to the loss of integrity.

The evolution is even clearer for the corresponding pronoun indicating 'removal'. In Late Latin texts, *inde* 'from that place' is very often strengthened by *ex-* or *de-*, also indicating distancing. For example, in the 4th Book of Fredegarius' *Chronicle* and its *Continuations*, according to our counts, 26 of the 33 instances, i.e. 79%, are strengthened by a prefix.

Paradigmaticity

Paradigmaticity or paradigmatic cohesion is the degree to which the individual members of the paradigm are linked to each other by clear-cut paradigmatic relations of opposition and complementarity. A tightly integrated paradigm typically has a small number of members, showing formal and functional similarity (Lehmann 2002b: 118–120).

As mentioned in § 2.1., the paradigm of Latin prepositions as a whole is heterogeneous with respect to the degree of grammaticalization of its members and their integration in the paradigm. In comparison with prepositions like *causā* 'because of' or *fini* 'until', which still show their lexical origin, *de* belongs to the subclass of highly grammaticalized prepositions. It enters into competition with two other prepositions indicating a movement away from a starting point, *ex* and *ab*.

- In the case of *ex*, the landmark is conceived as a containing space, and the preposition indicates a movement out of this containing space, e.g. *profluit ex monte* 'it flows out of the mountain'.
- In the case of *ab*, the starting point of the movement is located outside of the landmark, e.g. *aps te abire* 'go away from you' (Plautus, *Miles gloriosus* 4,1), *caput a cervice revulsum* 'the head pulled off from the neck' (Vergilius, *Georgica* 4, 523).
- *De* does not specify the relationship with its landmark but at least in its primitive meaning, it describes the pathway as a downward movement with respect to the landmark.

As *de* loses its feature of verticality and becomes a general marker of a movement away from a landmark, without specifying the relationship with this landmark, it can be used in alternation with *ex* or *ab*. That the three prepositions partly share the same meaning is suggested by examples such as (46b) where there is no formal correspondence between the prefix/preverb and the preposition:

(46)   a.   ***Ex***   *oppid-o*   *ex-ire*
            out-of city-ABL.SG out-go-INF
            'To go out of the city'   (Caesar, *De Bello Gallico*, 33 1)

       b.   ***De***   *civitat-e*   *e-icere*
            from city-ABL.SG out-throw-INF
            'To drive out of the city'   (*Arch.* 22)

More generally, the distinction between the three prepositions is blurred, since we also find examples of non-correspondence between preverb and preposition in the cases of *ex* and *ab*:

(47)   ***Ex***   *eo*   *loc-o*   ***ab***-*esse*
       out-of that-ABL place-ABL be-absent-INF
       'To be absent from that location'   (Caesar, *De bello Gallico*, 5, 21, 2)

The following examples, corresponding to three different translations of the same bible verse, offer strong evidence of the loss of the semantic distinction in Late Latin: at least in some contexts, *de, ab* and *ex* alternate freely.

(48)   a.   ***De*** *ligno* quod est scientiae boni et mali non editis
       b.   ***A(b)*** *ligno* sciendi bonum et malum non manducabitis
       c.   ***Ex*** *arbore* diagnoscentiae boni et mali ne tangerent
            'From the tree of the knowledge of good and evil you shall not eat'
            (*Genesis* 2: 17, *Vetus Latina*, Ed. Bonifatius Fischer (Beuron), Freiburg: Heider, 1951)

Paradigmatic variability

Paradigmatic variability is the freedom of choice between different members of the same paradigm (intraparadigmatic variability) or the freedom to specify or to leave unexpressed the grammatical category corresponding to the paradigm (transparadigmatic variability of 'obligatoriness') (Lehmann 2002b: 123–124).

As mentioned in § 2.2., in Classical Latin, the ablative case as such expresses 'removal' and does not really need the reinforcement of a preposition. In Late Latin, the prepositionless ablative decreases and *de* + NP-ABL becomes more frequent. Moreover, as we have just pointed out, *de* is extended at the expense of *ex* and *ab*. A first explanation for this particular evolution is phonological. As to *e(x)* and *a(b(s))*, their consonantal ending is already unstable in Classical Latin: it can be dropped before a consonant other than *h*. *De*, on the other hand, takes advantage of its consonantal initial (Vaännänen

1981: 89). Secondly, its semantic neutrality with respect to the opposition "internal *versus* external with respect to the landmark" may also have played a role.

The progressive loss of the paradigmatic variability of the three prepositions is very slow. In Fredegarius' *Chronicle of Frankish History* (4th Book) and its *Continuations,* written in the 7th and 8th C., the three prepositions are still attested. Their frequency is as follows: 262 occurrences for the preposition *de*, 61 occurrences for the preposition *e(x)* and 230 occurrences for the preposition *a(b)*. Note that *ab* is less common in its spatial meaning but frequent for the expression of the agent in passive constructions, where there is no real competition with *de* or *ex*.

STRUCTURAL SCOPE

Structural scope or the syntagmatic weight of a grammatical expression is the structural size of the construction this expression helps to form, or the grammatical level on which it operates (Lehmann 2002b: 128). For instance, a definite article can bear on the NP or its scope can be reduced to the noun.

In Classical Latin, a preposition can take scope over a coordinated NP and, hence, is normally not repeated in the case of two NPs coordinated by *et, atque* or *-que* 'and':

(49)   Misericordi-am ***ad** op-em   fer-e-nd-am   et   calamitat-es*
    pity-ACC.SG   to help-ACC.SG give-GER.ACC.F.SG and calamity-ACC.PL
    homin-um   indign-orum   subleva-nd-as
    man-GEN.PL not-worth-GEN.M.PL lighten-GERUND.ACC.F.PL
    'Pity [is useful] in order to help those who are in need, and who suffer undeservedly'   (Cicero, *Tusculanae Disputationes*, 4, 46)

A preposition can even have scope over a complement in another proposition without being repeated:

(50)   *Stult-i   scriptor-is   esse   non posse   omn-ibus **de***
    foolish-GEN.M.SG writer-GEN.SG be-INF not can-INF all-ABL.PL of
    *re-bus   caue-re,   [**de**] qui-bus   ueli-t   [cauere].*
    things-ABL.PL foresee-INF PRS [of] which-ABL.PL want-SBJV.PRS.3SG foresee
    'A foolish writer cannot foresee all the cases that he had the intention to foresee'   (Cicero, *De Inventione*, II, 50, 153, quoted by Menge 2000: 251)

(51)   ***A**   re-bus   ger-e-nd-is   senect-us   abstrahi-t.*
    From affairs-ABL.PL manage-GER.ABL.PL old-age-NOM.SG draw-away-PRS.3SG
    *[**A**]Qui-bus?   An [**ab**] iis   qu-ae   iuventut-e*
    From which-ABL.PL Q from those-ABL.PL who-NOM.F.PL youth-ABL.SG
    ger-u-ntur   et   vir-ibus?
    manage-PASS.PRS.3SG and strength-ABL.PL
    'His old age has turned him away from business management. From which business? From the business run by the youth in its vigor?'
    (Cicero, *Cato Maior De Senectute* 15, quoted by Ernout & Thomas, 1951: § 143)

In Late Latin, the structural scope of the preposition is shrinking. The preposition is sometimes repeated in the case of NPs coordinated by *et* 'and' (53), although not systematically (52):

(52) **De** *imperi-o*   *Constant-is,*   *et*   *vastation-e*   *Saracen-orum*
     about reign-ABL.SG Constant-GEN.SG and devastation-ABL.SG Saracen-GEN.PL
     'About the reign of Constant and the devastation of the Saracens'
                               (Fredegarius, *Chronicle*)

(53) **De** *fili-o*   *Theuderic-i*   *nat-o,*   *et*   ***de***
     about son-ABL.SG Theudericus-GEN.SG born-ABL.SG and about
     Agilan-e   *patrici-o*   *interfect-o*
     Agilanus-ABL.SG patrician-ABL.SG killed-ABL.SG
     'About the birth of Thierry's son and about the murder of Agilanus, the patrician'   (Fredegarius, *Chronicle*) [Late Latin]

The construction exemplified by (50) and (51), where the preposition takes scope over a complement in another proposition, is no longer attested in Late Latin.

BONDEDNESS

Bondedness or syntagmatic cohesion is the closeness of the relationship that links an expression to another expression. An increase of bondedness is called coalescence. According to Lehmann (2002b: 132), the different degrees of coalescence correspond to: juxtaposition, cliticization, agglutination and merging.

In Classical Latin, the preposition stills shows a high degree of autonomy, insofar as it can be separated from the noun

–   by an adverb or a conjunction of adverbs:

(54) **De** *bene beate=que*   ***uiu-e-nd-o***
     about well happily=and live-GERUND.ABL
     'On the virtuous and happy way of living'
                 (Cicero, *De finibus bonorum et malorum*, [1,2] II. (5)

–   by a genitive complement (55) or even an object (56):

(55) **De** *Galli-ae*   *German-iae=que*   ***mor-ibus***
     about Gallia-GEN.SG Germania-GEN.SG=and customs-ABL.PL
     'About the customs of Gallia and Germania'
                   (Caesar, *Commentarii de Bello Gallico* 6, 11)

(56) Nec in *constitu-e-nt-ibus*   *re-m public-am*   *nec*   ***in*** *bell-a*
     Not in constitute-PTCP.PRS.ABL.PL republic-ACC.F.SG neither in war-ACC.PL
     ger-e-nt-ibus
     make-PTCP.PRS.ABL.PL
     'Not while constituting a state nor while making war'   (Cicero, *Brutus* 12, 45)

In Late Latin, this type of construction tends to disappear. For instance, the genitive is no longer inserted between the preposition and the noun: the sequence "Prep + N + genitive" is used rather than "Prep + genitive + N", as is shown in (57).

(57) ***De   victori-a   Heracli-i   super Pers-as***
about victory-ABL.SG Heraclius-GEN.SG over Persian-ACC.PL
'About the victory of Heraclius over the Persians'   (Fredegarius, *Chronicle*)

SYNTAGMATIC VARIABILITY

Syntagmatic variability is the positional freedom of an expression, i.e. its position with respect to another expression with which it has some grammatical relation. As to the adpositions in Classical Latin, they are normally adjacent to their nominal complement (Ernout & Thomas 1951: § 142; Matthews 1981: 256). There is, however, still some positional freedom: (a) adpositions can be to the left or, more marginally, to the right of the NP (preposition + NP/NP + postposition); (b) they can be adjacent to the N rather than to the NP as a whole (i.e. "Det/Adj + Prep + N" instead of "Prep + Det/Adj + N") (Ernout & Thomas 1951: § 141).

a.   Preposition and postposition

In Classical Latin, adpositions like *de, in, ex, ab* are placed before the NP and are thus prepositions. Hence, there is some reduction of syntagmatic variability in comparison with Indo-European, where these elements still had an adverbial status and no fixed position.[11] There is however still fluctuation between preposition and postposition in some cases. Specifically, postposition is possible

–   when the adposition governs a relative pronoun, since relative pronouns tend to be in the initial position of the proposition:

(58) ***De***   qu-a   post loqu-e-mur
about which-ABL.F.SG after talk-PASS.FUT.1PL
'Of which we will talk afterwards'   (Cicero, *De Inventione*, II, 23, 70)

(59) Qu-a   *de* ante dict-um est
which-ABL.F.SG of before spoken be-PRS.3SG
'Of which has been spoken before'   (Cicero, *De Inventione*, II, 23, 70)

–   for less grammaticalized adpositions, closer to the stage of inflected noun or adverb:

(60) ***Delectation-is   caus-a***
pleasure-GEN.SG because-of (or: cause-ABL)
'Because of the pleasure'   (Cicero, *De Oratore* XI)

(61) ***Tiberi-m   iuxta***
Tiber-ACC.SG next
'Next to the Tiber'   (Tacitus, *Annales*, 2, 41)

–   for *cum* 'with' when it governs a relative or personal pronoun:

(62)   *Te=**cum**=que*   apud te   ambula-re quam cum eo
        you-ABL=with=and near you-ACC.SG walk-INF than with him-ABL.M.SG
        *Qu-o=**cum**   uide-o   esse   ambula-nd-um*
        whom-ABL.M.SG=with see-PRS.1SG be-INF walk-GERUND.ACC
        '[I prefer] to walk with you and in your company than with this man with
        whom I have to walk, I see'   (Cicero, *Ep. ad Atticum*, 4)

b.   Even in the case of adpositions which are strictly prepositional, there is some po-
     sitional fluctuation: the preposition can be to the left of the NP as a whole or it can
     be inserted between the adjective or determiner and the noun:

(63)   a.   *Omn-ibus **de** re-bus*   (Cicero, *Ep. ad Fam.* 7)
            all-ABL.PL of thing-ABL.PL

       b.   ***De** omn-ibus re-bus*   (Cicero. *Ep. ad Atticum* 6, 5, 1)
            Of all-ABL.PL thing-ABL.PL
            'About all things'

(64)   *Cuius **de**   itiner-e*   (Cicero, *Ep. ad Atticum* 15, 23)
        whose about trip-ABL.SG
        'About whose trip'

Some of these structures still occur in Late Latin, but invariably with the same lexical
items, *e.g. se**cum**/qua **de** causa*. This tends to indicate that there is fossilization.

As pointed out in the beginning of this section, *de* in Classical Latin belongs to the
subset of prepositions that are in a rather advanced stage of grammaticalization, in
contrast with prepositions that still exhibit their adverbial or nominal origin. The evaluation of its degree of grammaticalization with respect to Lehmann's parameters shows
that *de* is indeed already grammaticalized to a certain extent. We should, however, bear
in mind that in Classical Latin, syntactic function is to a very large extent expressed by
case-marking rather than by adpositions (cf. Table 2). In this context, even the most
grammaticalized prepositions are, on the continuous scale from lexicon to grammar,
nearer to the lexicon. They do not really have the function of marking a structural
relationship. They rather specify semantically a relationship that is expressed by the
case-marker as such and they are also used to express semantically more complex relationships, for instance *sine* + ablative 'without' (Pinkster 1990: 197).

This general consideration allows us to understand the restricted distribution of
de: it is rather infrequent for adnominal complements, unless the concept of 'origin'
and/or movement away from this origin is relevant. As to the verbal domain, *de* is infrequent for core arguments but is only used to specify less cohesive relationships with
the VP, characteristic of adjuncts (cf. Table 3).

This disintegration of the case system will confer a structural role to the subset of
the most grammaticalized prepositions, a process which is ongoing in Late Latin and
will be pursued in Old and Middle French.

3.   *De* + NP in Old and Middle French

3.1   Typology

3.1.0   *Preliminary remarks on the distinction between adjunct and argument status*
It has been argued for Latin that the distinction between adjuncts and arguments is fuzzy (cf. *supra* § 2.3.0.): the tests generally used for Modern French do not yield clear results for the Latin data. The fuzziness of the boundary has been related to the fact that Latin is a dependent-marking language: dependent-marked constituents have a high degree of autonomy with respect to the verb and, hence, the constructional force of the verb is weaker. Spoken contemporary French, on the contrary, shows some features of a head-marking language, which makes the distinction between arguments and adjuncts less problematic. With respect to this typological evolution, Old and Middle French have an intermediate position and, consequently, the distinction between arguments and adjuncts is still somewhat problematic.

Old French still has a case system, consisting of the nominative case, marking the subject of the sentence, and the oblique case, for the other arguments and for adjuncts. This system is defective, however, since only masculine nouns have case, whereas feminine nouns do not.[12] In Middle French, case-marking is completely lost and syntactic function is expressed by the position with respect to the verb for core arguments, and by prepositions for more peripheral arguments and adjuncts.

The Modern French system is not yet in place, however: unlike Modern French, which allows head-marking by means of clitics attached to the verbs, Old and Middle French have pronouns like *en* whose status has not yet reached the stage of a purely grammatical marker attached to the verbal head.

In our typology, we will distinguish only two major categories for the use of *de* in Old and Middle French, as we did for Latin: as a verbal complement (§3.1.1.) and as a nominal complement (§3.1.2.).[13]

3.1.1   *Verbal domain*

A. Spatial meaning

A.1. Vertical movement

In Old and Middle French, we find *de* + NP with verbs expressing a vertical movement (*cheoir* 'fall down' etc.). The NP expresses the reference point situated on a higher spatial level and *de* refers to a downward path starting from the reference point:

    (65)   Pruec que *de son diestrier* ne   cai-e
            Let's.hope off his   horse   not fall-SBJV.PRS.3SG[14]
            'Let's hope he does not fall from his horse'
                                  (Chrétien de Troyes, *Perceval* 32380; 12th C.)

This feature of downward movement is also attached to the verbal prefix *de-*. Witness the following example in Middle French, where *decouler* still has its concrete meaning of vertical motion ('run down from'). Verbs of this type combine naturally with a PP headed by the preposition *de* and activate the primitive spatial meaning of *de*:

(66) une playe luy   fist   en la cuisse sy grande que
      a   wound to.him make-PST SIMPLE.3SG in the thigh so big   that
      le sanc luy   *decoul-a*   jusques en   terre
      the blood to.him glide.down-PST SIMPLE.3SG on.to   in.the earth
      'He wounded him so seriously in his thigh that his blood flowed on the
      ground.   (*Gérard de Nevers*, 110; 15th C.)

A.2. Spatial movement without vertical orientation

The preposition *de* is used, as was the case in Latin, to express a movement away from a starting point without a vertical direction, in combination with motion verbs (67) (e.g. *aller* 'go', *returner* 'come back', *geter* 'throw') or verbs expressing an oriented action (68) (e.g. *apercevoir* 'perceive'):

(67) **De** port en port se   vu-nt   turna-nt
      from port to port REFL-3 go-PRS.3PL leave-PRS PTCP
      'They slip off from port to port'   (Wace, *Le Roman de Rou* I, 325; 12th C.)

(68) Or   puis   je apparcevoir *d'* icy La maison de monsieur mon
      now can-PRS.1SG I see   from here the house of sir   my
      pere
      father
      'Now I can see, from here, my father's house'
                          (Andrieu de La Vigne, *Le Mystère de saint Martin*, 288; 15th C.)

De + NP occasionally appears with other verbs (e.g. *plurer* 'cry') and suggests that the verbal process involves a movement away from the reference point or landmark expressed by the NP:

(69) Plur-ent   **des**   *oil-z* de doel e   de tendrur
      cry-PST SIMPLE.3PL from.the eyes of grief and of tenderness
      'They cried out of grief and tenderness'   (*Chanson de Roland* 1446; 12th C.)

Moreover, *de* + NP is used in contexts where the verb refers to a movement <u>towards</u> the reference point or landmark expressed by the NP. This is the case for *aprochier de*, exemplified in example (70), which alternates with the construction *aprochier a* (71) or even *aprochier* without preposition (72):

(70) Et   quant il approach-a   *de* *la di-ct-e*   *fontaine,*
      and when he approach-PST SIMPLE.3SG from the say-PST PTCP.F.SG fountain

il entr-ouy   une voix qui chant-oit
he hear-PST SIMPLE.3SG a   voice that sing-IMPF.3SG
'And when he approached the fountain, he heard a voice singing'
(Jean d'Arras, *Mélusine*; end 14th C.)

(71) Ke tuit cil   k'   enlumin-eit   vo-rroi-ent   estre
      that all those which enlighten-IMPF.3SG want-COND.PRS.3PL be-INF.PRS
      aproch-essent   *a lui*
      approach-PRS PTCP to him
      'That all those enlightened by him wanted to be close to him'
      (*Traduction des sermons de Saint Bernard*; quoted in Godefroy 1880–1902,
      VIIIb: 158b; BNF fr. 24768, fol. 71; 12th C.)

(72) [...] il aproch-ier-ent   Le chastel de Pesme   Avanture
      they approach-PST SIMPLE.3PL the castle of Very.Bad Adventure
      'They approached the castle of Very Bad Adventure'
      (Chrétien de Troyes, *Le Chevalier au lyon*, 5108; 12th C.).

The fact that *de* + NP can be used in contexts expressing a movement <u>towards</u> the
landmark rather than <u>away from</u> the landmark shows clearly that there is semantic
weakening in comparison with the Latin preposition *de*.

A.3. Origin and lineage

The use of *de* referring to an origin or lineage is also found in Old and Middle
French:

(73) Est-ei-t nez   *de Senz*
      be born-IMPF.3SG from Senz
      'He was native of Senz'
      (Guernes de Pont-Sainte-Maxence, *La vie de saint Thomas Becket*, ed.
      Wahlberg 1922, 4741; end 12th C.)

(74) Né-s   *de* [...] *haut parentet*
      born-PST PTCP.NOM.M.SG   out.of noble lineage
      'Of noble lineage'   (*La vie de saint Alexis*, 26; 11th C.)

A.4. Partition

As has been shown by Carlier (2007), the partitive use of *de* + NP as a complement of
the verb, already attested in Late Latin in combination with verbs meaning 'eat', 'drink',
'give', 'take' (cf. § 2.3.1.A.4.), remains sporadic in Old French. Moreover, it is used with
the same meaning as in Late Latin: it isolates a part of a contextually determined set. It
is also subject to the same distributional constraints: it is used in the object position of
verbs meaning 'eat', 'drink', 'give', 'take' and occurs only in combination with concrete
nouns:

(75) Donc pren-t   li   padre *de ses meilors serjanz*
      thus take-PRS.3SG the father of his best   servants
      'So the father chooses from his best servants'
                                          (*La vie de saint Alexis*, 23a; 11th C.)

Its frequency dramatically increases in Middle French, in particular during the 15th century. At that stage, *de* + NP no longer presupposes a contextually determined partition but simply marks indefiniteness and acquires the status of an article. It is combined with a wider range of verbs, but remains restricted to concrete nouns. This distributional constraint disappears in the 17th century.

B. Metaphorical meanings

B.1. Temporal meaning

B.1.1. Movement away from a temporal starting point

The reference point or landmark can be a time interval. In that case, *de* indicates a movement away from this temporal reference point and can be glossed as 'since': the situation expressed by the verb (i.e. the *locatum*) started at some point in the past, defined by the NP headed by *de*:

(76) La dame que *d'   enfance*   av-oi-t amee
      the lady that since childhood love-PST PRF.3SG
      'The lady whom he loved since his childhood'
                          (*Fabliaux et contes*, ed. Méon 1823, II 157, 111; 12th -15th C.)

This use of *de* still exists in Middle French, in expressions like *de long temps* 'since long', and also occurs in combination with other temporal complements:

(77) Et   aux quelz heraulz   promptement et   *de ce mesmes matin*
      and to   which messengers promptly   and of this same   morning
      furent bailiees   lettres de responce
      give-PASS.PST SIMPLE.3PL letters of answer
      'And to which messengers were given promptly and this same morning letters
      that served as replies'
        (*Jean Maupoint* §98, p. 62; quoted in Martin & Wilmet 1980: §303; 15th C.)

B.1.2. Partition within a time interval

In Old French, *de* + NP can refer to an inclusion in a time interval:

(78) *De nuit* est   a la curt   priveement ale-z
      of night is-PRS.3SG to the court alone   go-PST PTCP.NOM.M.SG
      'During the night, he went alone to the court'
      (Guernes de Pont-Sainte-Maxence, *La vie de Saint Thomas Becket*, ed.
      Wahlberg 1922, 2053; end 12th C.)

(79) *De trente ans*   n'   i   fut trovez
      of thirty years NEG there find-PASS.PST SIMPLE.3SG
      'He was not found there for 30 years'
      (Guillaume de Saint-Pair, *Le Roman du Mont Saint-Michel* 2125; 12th C.)

These examples illustrate two differences in comparison with Modern French (cf. *infra*, § 4.1.1. B.1.2.)

– The pattern is still productive, since it can occur in combination with different types of time intervals.
– Although it is already frequent in negative contexts (79), it also occurs in affirmative contexts (78).

This temporal use of *de* + NP is still attested in Middle French, in affirmative (80) as well as in negative contexts (81):

(80) Ilz   mainn-ent bien leur ost XX [...] liewes loing, que *de jour* que
      They lead-PRS.3PL well their army XX [...] miles far,   as.well of day as
      de nuit
      of night
      'They take well their army XX [...] miles further, during the day as well as during the night'   (Jean le Bel, *Chroniques*; mid-14th C.)

(81) Le bon homme ne menge-a   *de tout* le jour
      the good man   NEG eat-PST SIMPLE.3SG of whole the day
      'The gentleman did not eat during the whole day'
      (*Quinze Joies de Mariage*, ed. Rychner 1957: 21; 15th C.)

As will be shown below, in Modern French its distribution is restricted to negative sentences (e.g. *Il n'a pas fermé l'œil de la nuit* 'he did not close the eye for the whole night > he did not sleep all night long').

B.2. Movement away from a starting point: neither spatial nor temporal

In the same way as in Latin, the reference point expressed by the NP headed by the preposition can be conceived as if it were a spatial location or a time interval, even if it refers to a rather abstract notion. *De* locates the event by conceiving it as a movement away from the landmark. This use is common in Old French:

(82) Ensi fu   Adrenoble delivr-ee   *del* siege
      so   be-PST SIMPLE.3SG Adrenoble deliver-PST PTCP.F.SG of.the siege
      'In this way Adrenoble was delivered from the siege'
      (Geoffroi de Villehardouin, *La conquête de Constantinople* 121, 1; early 13th C.)

In combination with verbs indicating a transfer of information (e.g. *oïr* 'hear'), the landmark is often a human being. The following example shows that the verb *oïr* allows not only the preposition *de* but also *a*:

(83) Dire   l' ai oï   *a*   plusurs Qui le oïr-ent
      say-INF.PRS it hear-PRS PRF.1SG from several who it hear-PST SIMPLE.3PL
      des   ancesurs
      from.the ancestors
      'I heard it from several people, who in their turn heard it from their ancestors'
                                    (Wace, *Le Roman de Rou* III, 342, ed. Andresen 1877; 12th C.)

In Middle French, a verb like *dependre* can take an NP introduced by *de* with the
meaning of a metaphorical starting point:

(84) Car   ta   science   despent   *des*   *choses* que tu
      Because your knowledge depend-PRS.3SG of.the things that you
      sçai-s   de luy, et   les choses qu' il sçai-t
      know-PRS.2SG of him, and the things that he know-PRS.3SG
      despend-ent   *de sa   science.*
      depend-PRS.3PL of his knowledge
      'Because your knowledge depends on the things you know of him, and the
      things that he knows depend on his knowledge'
                            (Alain Chartier, *Livre de l'espérance*, 160, quoted in *DMF* 2010; 15th C.)

B.3. Objects of verbs of saying and thinking

In Old and Middle French, *de* + NP combines with verbs of intellectual activity, such
as verbs of saying and thinking, in order to express the object discussed or thought
about.

(85) Puis le Roy lui demand-a   *de la   prise* d' Escallon
      then the king him ask-PST SIMPLE.3SG of the taking of Escallon
      'Then the king asks him about the taking of Escallon'
                            (*Jouvencel* II, 135; quoted in Martin & Wilmet 1980: §303; 15th C.)

Moreover, a constituent introduced by *de* can have the function of framing the topic of
an utterance, as was already the case in Latin (cf. § 2.3.1. B.3. ex. 23):

(86) *Del   rei   paien*, sire, par veir cre-ez,   Ja   ne ve-rr-ez
      of.the king pagan Sire by   truth believe-IMP.2PL never NEG see-FUT.2PL
      cest premer meis pass-et   Qu' il vos siv-ra-t   en
      this first   month pass-PST PTCP.M.SG that he you follow-FUT.3SG in
      France le   regnet
      France the kingdom
      'Regarding the pagan king, Sire, please believe it, you will not see this first
      month pass that he will follow you in the kingdom of France'
                                            (*Chanson de Roland* 692; 12th C.)

The topic defined by *de* + NP can combine with the presentative *veez, vez* ('see here'):

(87)   Vez *del   deable* com a   la   teste lee
       see of.the devil   how have-PRS.3SG the head amazed
       'Look at the devil, what an amazed expression he has' (*Aliscans* 3246; 12th C.)

Although more expressive prepositional phrases such as *quant à* 'as for' develop, this topical use of *de* is conserved in Middle French (Prévost 2003):

(88)   [« Combien a il que vous ne veïstes vostre dame par amours?
       – Ma dame, je n'en ai point] [...]
       – Mais *de   celle*   que vous   plus   am-ez   et   voul-dri-és
       but   as.to that-F.SG that you-PL more love-PRS.2PL and want-COND-2PL
       qui   fus-t   vostre dame, puis quand ne   la
       who be-PST SIMPLE-3SG your   lady,   since when not her
       ve-ist-es   vous? »
       see-PST SIMPLE-2PL you-PL
       ['For how long haven't you seen your lady-love?
       – My lady, I don't have one.]
       – But as to the woman that you preferred and that you would like to have as
       your lady, since when didn't you see her?'   (*Jehan de Saintré*; 15th C.)

B.4. Manner and instrument, cause and agent

Like Latin, Old French expresses the four meanings described in this paragraph by means of an adjunct introduced by *de*. *De* + NP indicating manner, which, in Modern French, is infrequent and mainly occurs in lexicalized expressions (e.g. *de bon/mauvais gré* 'willingly/unwillingly', *de bonne/mauvaise humeur* 'in a good/bad mood'), is still widespread and productive in Old French:

(89)   Le   servi-r-a   *de bone volenté*
       him serve-FUT.3SG of good will
       'He will serve him willingly'
                           (Wace, *Le Roman de Rou*, II 2498, ed. Andresen 1877; 12th C.)

(90)   Mor-ir   *de mort honteuse,*
       die-INF.PRS of death shameful
       'to die in a shameful way'
       (Jean Froissart, 14th C.; quoted in Tobler & Lommatzsch 1915ff.: vol. II, col.
       1216).

A related meaning is the expression of the instrument. In the following example, we would expect the preposition *avec* 'with' in the Modern French equivalent:

(91)   *De lur   espee-s*   I   fier-ent   demaneis
       of their sword-PL there strike-PRS.3PL without-delay
       'They strike immediately with their sword'
                           (*Chanson de Roland* 3419, 12th C.; quoted in Buridant 2000: 471)

Both uses, manner and instrument, remain frequent in Middle French (Marchello-Nizia 1997: 343):

(92) Ledit   d'Alençon leur   aide-r-oi-t   *de ses places,*   *de son*
      the-said d'Alençon them-DAT help-COND.PRS.3SG of his fortresses, of his
      artillerie, et *de tout*   ce que en monde lui   seroit
      artillery, and of everything this that in world him-DAT be-COND.PRS.3SG.
      possible
      possible
      'The said d'Alençon would help them with his fortresses, his artillery and eve-
      rything in this world he could possibly do'
      (Jean Chartier, *Chronique de Charles VII,* 102; 15th C.; quoted in Martin &
      Wilmet 1980: §303)

A third use is the causal value:

(93) *De paör* me   tre-s   arriere
      of fear REFL-1SG draw-PRS.1SG back
      'I step back in fear'   (Chrétien de Troyes, *Le Chevalier au lyon* 285; 12th C.)

Again, in Modern French, this use is restricted to lexicalized expressions like the conjunctions *de peur de* (+ inf., 'lest/for fear that') and *de ce que* 'because'. The alternation
between *de ce que* and *pour ce que* 'because of' in the following example reveals the
causative meaning:

(94) Molt fu   nostre Sires [...]   merci-és,
      much be-PST SIMPLE.3SG our   Lord-NOM.M.SG thank-PST PTCP.NOM.M.SG
      pour ce que il les   av-oi-t   en tele maniere
      because   he them rescue-PST PRF.3SG-AUX in such way
      secoru-s   et *de ce que* il   est-oi-ent mis   au desor de ce   dont
      PST PTCP.M.PL and because they put-PASS.IMPF.3PL above   that what
      il   sol-oi-ent   estre   au desous
      they use-IMPF.3PL be-INF.PRS beneath
      'Our Lord received many thanks, because he had rescued them in such a
      way, and because they were placed as sovereigns of what they used to be sub-
      jugated to'
      (Geoffroi de Villehardouin, *La conquête de Constantinople* 84, 10; early 13th C.)

A final related meaning is the expression of the agent. In Latin, the agent was marked
by *ab* + NP. Because of the replacement of *ab* by *de* (§ 2.5.), *de* + NP takes over this
role. In the competition between the prepositions *par* and *de* for the expression of the
agent, *de* combines with a wider range of verbs than is the case in Modern French:
whereas the expression of the agent by *de* + NP is restricted to stative contexts in Modern French (cf. § 4.1.1.B.4.), it is available for all aspectual categories of verbs in Old

French. Witness the following examples, containing the verbs *regarder* 'look at' and *contredire* 'contradict':

(95) Il   fur-ent[...] regardé   ***de maintes gens***
      they watch-PASS.PST SIMPLE.3PL of many   people
      'They were watched by many people'
      (Geoffroi de Villehardouin, *La conquête de Constantinople*16, 4; early 13th C.)

(96) Li   plais fu [...] contredit   ***de ceus***   qui ...
      the plea contradict-PASS.PST SIMPLE.3SG of those who ...
      'The plea was questioned very much by those who...'
      (Geoffroi de Villehardouin, *La conquête de Constantinople* 38, 16; early 13th C.)

The extension of *de* + NP for the expression of the agent in passive constructions is also observed in Middle French (Martin & Wilmet 1980: §303; Marchello-Nizia 1997: 343). According to Marchello-Nizia (1997: 344), *de* is more frequent than *par* for this function in certain Middle French texts:

(97) Les dis   des   anciens doiv-ent   estre desclairiez   amiablement
      the words of.the Ancients must-PRS.3PL explain-PASS.INF.PRS kindly
      de leur   successeurs
      of their successors
      'The words of the Ancients must be explained kindly by their successors'
                       (*La Chirurgie de Maître Henri de Mondeville*, I, §11; early 14th C.)

C. "Empty" preposition

In some examples, *de* does not seem to have a clear semantic value any more. For instance, some verbs taking a direct object have a pronominal construction expressing the same argument as an oblique complement headed by *de*, e.g. *apercevoir quelque chose, s'apercevoir **de** quelque chose* ('realize something'):

(98) Onques ***de rien***   ne   m'   aparçu-i
      ever   of nothing NEG REFL.1SG remark-PST SIMPLE.1SG
      Ne   ***de sa fille***,   ne   ***de lui***
      neither of his daughter, neither of him
      'I never remarked anything, nothing regarding his daughter, neither anything
      concerning him'   (Chrétien de Troyes, *Le Chevalier au Lyon*, 563; 12th C.)

It is worth noting that this type of pronominal construction has been analyzed as an 'antipassive' (Creissels 2006: 34). Contrary to the passive construction, the antipassive construction does not affect the subject, but rather the object. In the case of pairs like *apercevoir X/s'apercevoir de X*, the direct object of the non-pronominal transitive construction is 'demoted' to the status of an oblique complement in the pronominal construction. Interestingly, in combination with certain verbs, the other empty preposition, viz. *à*, can also fulfil the function of introducing the oblique complement in the antipassive construction (e.g. *attendre des critiques, s'attendre à des critiques* 'expect criticism'; *agripper la main de sa mère/s'agripper à la main de sa mère* 'grab his mother's hand').

De + infinitive can even correspond to a direct objet (99) or to a subject (100):

(99) *de* deu serv-ir   ne cess-et
      of God serve-INF.PRS NEG stop-PRS.3SG
      'He does not stop to serve God'   (*La vie de Saint Alexis* 17e; 11th C.)

(100) En cuer et en pensé li vint   *De* vendre   Eracle,
      in heart and in thought him come-PST SIMPLE.3SG of sell-INF.PRS Eracle
      son enfant
      his child
      'In his heart and in his mind it dawned on him to sell Eracle, his child'
                                              (Gautier d'Arras, *Eracle* 389; 12th C.)

In Middle French, according to Marchello-Nizia (1997: 341), the uses of *de* with an "empty" meaning become even more numerous. In particular, she mentions the case where *de* + NP corresponds to the thematic subject of a copular sentence:

(101) a. Dure cose est   *de* mariage[15]
          hard thing be-PRS.3SG of marriage
          'Marriage is a difficult thing'
                                         (Eustache Deschamps, IX, v. 4128; end 14th C.)

      b. *De povreté* est lais mehains
          of poverty is ugly wound
          'Poverty is an ugly wound'   (*Guillaume d'Angleterre* 1972; 12th C.)

The "emptiness" of the preposition is even more evident when *de* appears before another preposition or before an adverb prefixed by *de-*, e.g. *devant (= de + avant)* in (102):[16]

(102) Un suen ami a fait   venir   *de devant sei*
      a his friend make-PRS PRF.3SG come-INF.PRS of before him
      'He has one of his friends brought before him'
                                  (Benoît de Sainte-Maure, *Le roman de Troie* 17749; 12th C.)

De is regulary used as a prefix for the formation of adverbs and adverb-prepositions: e.g. *hors/de-hors, fors/de-fors* ('ouside'), *sor/de-sor* ('on/on him, her, it, them'), *suz/de-suz* ('under/under him, her, it, them'), *riere/derrière (< de retro)* ('after/behind'), *lez/de-lez* ('next (to)') and in the oldest texts even *de-de-vant* (*Chanson de Roland*, v. 2192, [ca 1100]), *de-de-suz* (*Chanson de Roland*, v. 2705), *de-de-fors* (Guillaume de saint Pair, *Chronique rimée de saint Michel* [ca 1155]):

(103) Lur cheval-s lais-ent   *dedesuz* un olive.
      their horses let-PRS.3PL under   a olive tree.
      'they leave their horses under an olive tree'   (*Chanson de Roland*, v. 2705)

This tendency towards desemantization and even loss of the status of preposition fore-shadows the further evolution towards Modern French (cf. §4.1.1. C.).

3.1.2   *Nominal domain*

A. *Origin and lineage*

The adnominal PP *de* + NP has the primitive value of origin when the NP refers to a place (104) or to a social or ethnic group (105), as was the case in Latin (§ 2.3.2.A.).

(104)   Un chevalier d' Escoce
      a   knight   of Scotland
      'A knight from Scotland'   (*La Mort le Roi Artu* 67.32; 13th C.).

(105)   Frans   hons   *de bon   linage*
      noble-NOM.M.SG man-NOM.M.SG of good lineage
      'A noble man of good lineage'   (*Li Bastars de Buillon*, 84; 14th C.)

B. *From origin to extraction and partition*

In Old and Middle French, adnominal *de* + NP is also used to indicate extraction or partition. The NP headed by *de* indicates the whole from which a part is extracted. It can be combined with quantity expressions – nominal (108), adverbial (e.g. *assez de* 'enough of', ex. 106) or pronominal (107) – with indefinite, interrogative or demon-strative pronouns and with comparative or superlative constructions. In comparison with Latin, *de* is used not only to express a partition within a contextually defined set (106–107), but also when no contextual set is available (108):

(106)   *De ses denier-s* assez   li   baill-e   Por achat-er   de la
      of his pennies enough him-DAT give-PRS.3SG for buy-INF.PRS PART.ART
      vitaille
      food
      'He gives him enough of his pennies to buy food'
          (*Fabliaux et contes*, ed. Barbazan & Méon, 1808, I 251, 268; 12th – 15th C.)

(107)   chascun-e *de nous*
      each-F.SG of us   (Alain Cartier, *La Belle Dame sans Mercy*, 358; 15th C.)

(108)   Dis muis   *de vin*
      Ten measures of wine
      'Ten mesures of wine'   (quoted in Godefroy II: 428b)

C. *From origin to property*

In the same way as in Latin, the NP governed by *de* can indicate the substance from which an entity is made (109). However, it can also indicate a more abstract property (110):

(109) Un perron   *de marbre*
A   platform of marble
'A platform made of marble' (*Chanson de Roland* 112; 12th C.)

(110) Ceste deffense ne   voul-ons   nous qu' elle se   estend-e
this   defense NEG want-PRS.1PL we   that it   REFL-3 spread-SBJV.PRS.3SG
aus   prevos,   ne   aus   autres *de meneur office*
to.the provost marshals, neither to.the others of lesser   office
'We do not want this defense to spread towards the provost marshals, neither to
others of a lesser office' (Jean de Joinville, 13th C.; quoted in Godefroy II: 430b)

The qualifying meaning of *de* + NP also occurs in the equivalent of the Latin genitive
of quality (e.g. *vir summae virtutis*, 'man of the highest courage'). As is shown by the
following example, this adnominal NP can be separated from its head by the copular
verb *estre* 'be':

(111) Riche-s hom fu   *de grant nobilitet*
rich   man be-PST SIMPLE.3SG of great nobility
= fu riches hom de grant nobilitet
'He was a rich man, of great nobility' (*La vie de Saint Alexis* 3a; 11th C.)

D. From origin to agent or patient

Medieval French more readily allows the nominalized use of infinitives marked by the
presence of a nominal determiner, as is the case in the following example, where the
infinitive combines with a definite article:

(112) Mainte   larme i   est plour-e-e   au   departir   *de lor*
numerous tear   there weep-PASS.PRS.3SG.F at.the leave-INF.PRS of their
gens   et   *de lor   amis*
people and of their friends
'Lots of tears were shed at the departure of their people and their friends'
(Geoffroi de Villehardouin, *La conquête de Constantinople* 30, 5; early 13th C.)

In this nominalized use, the arguments of the infinitive are expressed by means of a PP
headed by *de*. This is also the case with deverbative nouns:

(113) Il met-r-a   tot   l' enpire de Romanie a la <u>obedience</u> *de Rome*
he put-FUT.3SG whole the empire of Romania at the obedience of Rome
'He will subject the whole empire of Romania to Rome's obedience'
(Geoffroi de Villehardouin, *La conquête de Constantinople,* 93; early 13th C.)

In comparison with Latin, there is an extension with respect to the conditions of use of
the adnominal PP headed by *de*. In the pattern $NP_1 + [de + NP_2]_{PP}$, the PP in Latin
could only refer to the object of the verbal process expressed by the deverbative noun

in NP$_1$ (cf. §2.3.2.D. and *infra* §3.2.), whereas in Old and Middle French the PP can refer to the object or the subject of this verbal process.

E. From origin to possession

The possessive meaning, now one of the core features of the genitive, is already very frequent in Old and Middle French. *De* + NP can refer to body parts or kinship relations and in this use it alternates with the bare adnominal NP (cf. *infra*, § 3.2.):

(114)   Puis pren-t   la teste *de Jurfaleu le blund*
        then take-PRS.3SG the head of Jurfaleu the blond
        'Then he takes Jurfaleu the blond's head' (*Chanson de Roland* 1904; 12th C.)

It can, however, also express alienable possession, as illustrated in the following example:

(115)   Si   a trové   *de Richier* l'esperon
        then find-PRS PRF.3SG of Richier the spur
        'Then he found Richier's spur'   (*Aspremont* 2011; end 12th C.)

These values of possession are also found in Middle French (Marchello-Nizia 1997: 342), sometimes with personal pronouns:

(116)   Il sembl-oi-t [...] que il ve-oi-t ...   un gros crapaut sur le   cuer *d'* elle
        it seem-IMPF.3SG that he see-IMPF.3SG a big   toad   on the heart of her
        'It seemed that he saw a big toad on her heart'
                        (*Landry*, p. 203, 14th C.; quoted by Marchello-Nizia 1997: 342)

F. "Empty" preposition

In Old and Middle French, we find contexts where the semantic value of *de* is rather "empty", which testifies to the gradual bleaching of the preposition:

(117)   El   meis *de* fevrier
        In.the month of February
        'In February'   (Philippe de Taon, *Comput* 2275; early 12th C.)
(118)   En la riviere *de* Garonne
        in the river   of Garonne
        'In the river Garonne'
        (Guillaume Guiart, *Branche des royaux lignages, Chronique métrique de Guillaume Guiart*, I 5577; early 14th C.)

Buridant (2000: §380–a) qualifies this use as identificational. Martin & Wilmet (1980: §246, NB) emphasize the abstract nature of the preposition *de* (cf. also Marchello-Nizia 1997: 342).

3.2   Non-prepositional vs. prepositional adnominal complements
in Old and Middle French

As has been shown in § 2, the genitive in Latin is fundamentally an adnominal case, and exceptional in adverbal position. In Late Latin, the use of *de* + NP-ABL is extended in adverbal position, where it replaces the prepositionless ablative NP, as well as PPs introduced by *ex* 'out of' or *ab* 'from'. Moreover, in adnominal position it spreads at the expense of the genitive-marked NP without preposition. For the expression of the possessive relationship, however, the genitive-marked NP still prevails and resists the extension of *de* + NP-ABL.

This area of resistance can still be observed in Old French. As mentioned in § 3.1.0, Old French has a two-case system, consisting of the nominative case and the oblique case. However, this system was already defective, since most feminine nouns had no case marking, and, as a corollary, other markers of syntactic functions, such as word order and prepositional phrases, developed.[17] For the expression of the possessive relationship by means of an adnominal complement, Old French allowed not only PPs headed by *de* (§ 3.1.2.E.) but also the more conservative structure, i.e. prepositionless NPs in the oblique case,[18] reminiscent of the Latin genitive case, as in the following examples:

(119) la   fille   *son*   *oste*
       the   daughter his   guest
       'The guest's daughter'   (Chrétien de Troyes, *Erec* 744; 12th C.)

(120) Ci   feni-st   l'   uevre *Crestïen*
       here end-PRS.3SG the work Chrestien
       'This is where Chrestien's work ends' (Chrétien de Troyes, *Cligés* 6664; 12th C.)

With respect to the frequency of the non-prepositional adnominal complement, in comparison with the adnominal PP, statistics vary in the different studies devoted to the topic. According to Palm (1977), who studied those constructions in literary texts of the second half of the 12th century and the beginning of the 13th century, the genitive construction without preposition appeared in 55,2% of the adnominal NPs of his corpus. Westholm's older study on the genitive construction in Old French (1899) lists an even more overwhelming majority of non-prepositional adnominals in texts before the 13th century, viz. 1645 cases against 120 cases with the preposition *a*, and 79 constructions with *de* (see the comments of Väänänen 1981: 104, fn 46). The 13th century charters from the Vosges analyzed by Holman (1991) also show a high degree of non-prepositional constructions, which is however attributed to the eastern dialect (Lorrain).

As to the conditions of use of the non-prepositional adnominal complement for the expression of the possessor, the classical hypothesis is based on the degree of individuation of NP_2 (Gamillscheg 1957: 16ff., Foulet 1965: §19–36, Palm 1977, Väänänen 1981: 105, Jensen 1990: §50ff.). When NP_2 refers to a distinct individual, often designated by a proper noun, a nobility title or a parent name, it is usually attached without a preposition to NP$_1$ (cf. examples 119–120 above). The prepositions *a* or *de* are used when NP$_2$ is less individuated, viz. plural, indefinite or generic and inanimate and, in more recent texts, even human. A different hypothesis, based on the nature of NP$_1$, is put forward by Herslund (1980), who argues that the non-prepositional adnominal complement occurs when the noun contained in NP$_1$ selects the NP$_2$ as its complement or its argument. This is the case when N$_1$ is a relational noun, for instance a kinship term (cf. example 119 above) or a body part term, or when it is a deverbative noun:

(121)   le   respons Lancelot
       the answer Lancelot
       'Lancelot's answer'   (*La Mort le roi Artu* 146.5; 13th C.)

Herslund analyzes the non-prepositional adnominal complement as a "lexical genitive", which establishes a more cohesive link with NP$_1$. The prepositional genitive, by contrast, has to be conceived as an "extended genitive", where NP$_2$ is in a more "detached" relation with NP$_1$. Other prepositions are also found, among which *a*,[19] *envers* and *contre*:

(122)   Fai-re   trahison ... *vers*   *mon droit*   *seignor natural*
       make-INF PRS treason   toward my righteous lord   natural
       'To betray my natural lord, who is righteous'
                                 (*La Chastelaine de Vergi* 94; 13th C.)

In Middle French, the case system further declines and eventually vanishes: even though some texts still show traces, it is no longer used in a systematic way, which proves that authors and copyists do not understand it anymore (Martin & Wilmet 1980: § 291, Zink 1990: 29ff., Marchello-Nizia 1997: 137, Buridant 2000: §66). Nevertheless, the non-prepositional adnominal complement is still sometimes used, in the same distributional conditions as in Old French. But the competition with *de* NP is clearly increasing, in particular from the 15th century onwards: even when all the conditions for the non-prepositional construction are met, the prepositional construction, which was rather exceptional in Old French, appears more often than the non-prepositional NP (Marchello-Nizia 1997: 407ff.).

It should be noted that most of the studies mentioned above, for Old French and for Middle French, are based on literary texts, which present a conservative register. Foulet (1965: 21–22) characterized the use of the non-prepositional NP in Old French as "quelque chose de sentimental et d'aristocratique" ('something sentimental and aristocratic'). Non-literary texts offer a different picture. In an earlier study, Goyens (1994) conducted a corpus analysis of a Late Old French translation of two Latin rhetorical treatises (Cicero's *De Inventione* and the *Rhetorica ad Herennium*), entitled *Rectorique de Marc Tulles Cyceron* and written by Jean d'Antioche in 1282. In the first 400 adnominal NPs of this text, there was only one single occurrence of a non-prepositional adnominal complement, which satisfies the distributional constraints described in the

Table 5. Adnominal complements in *La Rectorique de Marc Tulles* Cyceron translated by Jean d'Antioche, Late Old French (13th C.)

NP$_1$ *de* NP$_2$	391
NP$_1$ *sans* NP$_2$	5
NP$_1$ *a* NP$_2$	3
NP$_1$ ø NP$_2$	1
Total	400

literature: N$_1$ is relational (Herslund 1980) and NP$_2$ is definite, refers to a human being and, as such, has a motivated gender and number (Palm 1977):

(123) (Est acusé)   dou murtre *sa mere*
       (is   accused) of   murder his mother
       '(He is accused) of having murdered his mother'

Yet Jean d'Antioche's text reveals 10 further occurrences that correspond to the distributional constraints, but in all these cases the preposition is used.

Moreover, this corpus shows the dominance of the preposition *de* for PPs in adnominal position: as shown in Table 5, the translator uses *de* in 391 cases, i.e. 97,75% of the occurrences studied.

The NP$_2$ listed above are mostly translations of a Latin genitive adnominal case (78%) or of another case-marked NP.[20] This means that, at least in the non-literary register, the replacement of the Latin genitive case by *de* + NP is largely accomplished at the end of the Old French period.

3.3 Degree of grammaticalization of de in Old and Middle French

The degree of grammaticalization of *de* in Old and Middle French will be evaluated with respect to Lehmann's (2002b) parameters, in the same way as for Latin.

INTEGRITY OR PARADIGMATIC WEIGHT

From a formal point of view, *de* undergoes phonetic attrition as it reduces to *d'* when followed by a vowel.

On the semantic side, the bleaching process begun in Latin, continues in Old and Middle French. The original spatial meaning of *de*, referring to a movement away from a landmark or reference point, is still present, but – as was the case in Latin – we also find uses where this reference point is no longer spatial, i.e. *de* + NP often has a metaphorical interpretation. The diversity of nuances is even larger than in Latin. In addition, with respect to the pathway expressed by *de*, we find contexts where this preposition does not express a movement away from the reference point, but the opposite movement of coming closer to the reference point. In this case, *de* is still in competition with another preposition, *a* (cf. ex. 70–71 above: *aprochier de* vs *a* 'come closer to'). The example of *aprochier de* shows that the meaning of *de* has become so tenuous that it is very sensitive to context or, to put it more strongly, that it is the context (the VP or the NP of which *de* + NP is a complement) that creates the meaning.

Signs of further loss of integrity of *de* in Old and Middle French are found in the fact that *de* appears more frequently in combination with other prepositions or adverbial expressions in order to express spatial movement. *De* often appears to the left of another preposition.[21] In such cases, it conserves its dynamic spatial meaning of movement away from a starting point or extraction. The second preposition, which has a static meaning, indicates the initial position of the trajector or *locatum* with respect to the reference point or landmark, as was the case for *ex* and *ab* in Latin.

(124) a. Nus   n'   eschap-oi-ent   *d'*   *entre*   lor   mains
  none NEG escape-IMPF.3PL from between their hands
  'No one escaped from them'   (*Le roman d'Eneas* 12; 12th C.)

  b. vous   ne   laiss-i-és   a   oster   vostre   chaperon [...]
  you-PL NEG let-SBJV.PRS.2PL to remove your-POSS small-hat,
  de <u>sur</u> vostre   chief
  of on your-POSS head
  'Do not let anybody remove your hat from your head'
              (Jean de Saintré, p. 41; 15th C.).

In some cases, *de* even seems redundant, since it is followed by a preposition that etymologically includes *de*, together with another preposition (e.g. *avant* and *hors*):

(125) Il   voi-t   le   conte, si   li   vien-t   *de <u>devant</u>*
  he see-PRS.3SG the count, and he-DAT come-PRS.3SG of before
  'He sees the count, and goes towards him'
          (*Auberi*, cf. Tobler, *Mitteilungen*, 1870, 23, 10; 13th C.)

Recall that the formation of an adverb or an adverb-preposition by means of the prefix *de* is a common derivation (e.g. *de-avant* > *devant* and even *de-de-avant* > *dedevant* or *de-hors* > *dehors* and *de-dehors* > *dedehors*).

A highly desemanticized use of *de* is the pattern *de* + adjective. For the expression of manner, *de* is often found in phrases like *de brief, de legier* or *de vrai* in Middle French (Marchello-Nizia 1997: 343), where its only function is apparently to indicate the idea of "manner", the specification of that manner being expressed by the following adjective.

As to the pronoun *en* (< INDE), which can often replace the complement construed by *de*, it can still have its strong meaning of spatial movement away from a starting point 'from there' in Medieval French, as in the following example:

(126) Et   encore detin-t   le   dit   brigand   le   dit   chastel [...],
  And still   keep-PST SIMPLE.3SG the said infantryman the said castle,

et *en*   guerroy-a   le pays
and from-there invade-PST SIMPLE.3SG the land
'And still, the said infantryman kept the castle, and from there invaded the whole land' (Jean Froissart, 14th C.; quoted in Greimas & Keane 2001^2: 228)

This use is common with motion verbs such as *issir* ('go out of'), expressing movement out of a certain space, where *de* + NP or its corresponding pronoun *en* has the status of an argument:

(127) En ceste tur   sui   en prisun, Ja   n' *en*   is-tr-ai
       in this tower be-PRS.1SG in prison, never NEG from.there leave-FUT.1SG
       se par mort nun
       if by death NEG
       'I am imprisoned in this tower, and will never leave it, if not dead'
                                  (Marie de France, *Lais, Yonec* 74; 12th C.)

Interestingly, with these verbs, Early Old French already allows dislocation structures, where *en* can co-occur with *de* + NP:

(128) Donc *en*   e-ist   fors *de* la chambre de son pedre
       so   from.there leave-PST SIMPLE.3SG out of the room   of his father
       'So he leaves his father's room'   (*La vie de Saint Alexis* 15d; 11th C.)

En has also several of the metaphorical meanings listed above for *de* + NP, for instance separation (129), and manner or instrument (130–131):

(129) L' un des   enfan-z me baill-i-ez   ça; Jeo vus *en*
       The one of.the children me give-SBJV.PRS.2PL now; I   you from-them
       Deliv-err-ai   ja,   Si que honi-e   n' en
       deliver-FUT.1SG immediately, so that shame-PST PTCP.F.SG NEG of.it
       ser-ez
       be-FUT.2PL
       'Give me this instant one of the children; I will deliver you from them, so that you will not be dishonored'   (Marie de France, *Lais, Fraisne* 110; 12th C.)

(130) Les escu-z ... Trai-ent   avant   et si s'   *an* cuevr-ent
       the shields bring-PRS.3PL forward and so REFL-3 by.it cover-PRS.3PL
       'They bring forward their shields and cover themselves with them'
                    (Chrétien de Troyes, *Le Chevalier de la Charrette* 871; 12th C.)

(131) Elle s'   arrach-a   d' alentour de la teste son bandeau
       She REFL-3 rip-off-PST SIMPLE.3SG of around   of the head her headband
       royal, et, se   le nou-ant   a l'entour du   col, s' *en*
       royal, and, REFL-3 it tie-PRS PTCP around   of.the neck, REFL-3 with.it

pend-it

hang-PST SIMPLE.3SG

'She ripped off her royal headband from her head, tied it around her neck and hung herself with it'

(Jacques Amyot, *Plutarque, Vie des hommes illustres – Lucullus,* 32; 16th C.)

En can, moreover, also have a purely quantitative value:

(132) .M. *en i treuv-e qui fo-nt dore-e-s*

Thousand PRO.GEN there find-PRS.3SG who make-PRS.3PL gilded-F.PL

sellee-s

saddle-PL

'He found one thousand of them who gild saddles'

(*La Chevalerie Vivien,* 966; end 12th C.-early 13th C.)

En displays a wide arrange of values, characterized by different degrees of semantic bleaching. Since it can still express removal from a starting point, even without a motion verb (cf. ex. 126), and still has derived metaphorical meanings, it cannot be regarded as a purely grammatical marker, unlike the clitic *en* in Modern French. (cf. *infra*, § 4.1.1.).

Paradigmaticity & Paradigmatic variability

In Old and Middle French, *de* + NP still displays an important paradigmatic variability, alternating with other PPs and with the prepositionless genitive NP.

– In adnominal position, Old French has a competition between *a, de* and the non-prepositional genitive, according to certain rules that have been described above (§ 3.2.). Later on, the non-prepositional genitive is abandoned – in Middle French it is used far less often – and, *a* competes with *de* for the expression of possession.

– In adverbal position, *de* can be replaced by new prepositions: in Old French, *dès* 'from' expresses a movement away from a spatial or temporal reference point (cf. § 3.1.A1., A2. & B1.1.), *(de)puis* 'since' is used when the reference point is temporal (cf. § 3.1.B1.1.); the present participles *durant/pendant* 'during' become prepositional from Middle French onwards (cf. § 3.1.B1.2.). But above all, medieval French develops prepositional phrases in abundance, some of which undergo progressive lexicalization (Fagard 2010).

Structural scope

With respect to the structural scope of the preposition, Old and Middle French show an intermediate situation between Latin and Modern French. When combined with a coordinated NP, *de* can be omitted in front of the second element of the coordination (Buridant 2000: § 404). This pattern is attested in Middle French, but becomes less frequent:

(133) Mais [...] don-r-ons   les comandemen-s *de l' exorde   ou*
       but   give-FUT.3PL the rule.PL   of the exordium or
       commencement
       beginning
       'But we will give the rules concerning the exordium or beginning [of a dis-
       course]' (Jean d'Antioche, *Rectorique de Marc Tulles Cyceron*, I, 12; end 13th C.)

BONDEDNESS

From Latin to Old and Middle French, there is an increase in bondedness between the
preposition *de* and the NP it heads. This bondedness is reflected in the fusion of the
preposition and the definite article, which is the most frequent initial element of the NP:

Singular: *de* + *le* > *del* > *deu* > *dou/du*
Plural: *de* + *le* > *dels* > *deus/des*

SYNTAGMATIC VARIABILITY

In Old and Middle French, *de* no longer has any positional freedom with respect to the
NP it governs: it is at the left of this NP and adjacent to it. But the adnominal PP *de* +
NP has some positional freedom with respect to the NP to which it is a complement:
de + NP can be separated from this NP and can even linearly precede it. For instance,
adnominal *de* + NP with a possessive or partitive meaning is often found in initial
position, separated from the NP to which it is a complement and at the left of it, as in
the following Old French example:

(134) *De* noz ostage-s fe-r-at   trench-er   les teste-s
       of our hostage-s do-FUT.3SG cut-INF.PRS-off the head-PL
       'He will have the heads of the hostages cut off'
                                              (*Chanson de Roland* 57; 12th C.)

Even in Middle French, the adnominal NP was less "attached" to the NP_1 than is the
case for Modern French (cf. Martin & Wilmet (1980: §§ 246 ff.) and *infra* §4.3.), as is
shown in the following example:

(135) Icy se   clos-t   le testament Et finis-t   *du   povre*
       here REFL-3 close-PRS.3SG the will   and finish-PRS.3SG of.the poor
       Villon
       Villon
       'Here concludes and ends the last will of the poor Villon'
                                      (François Villon, *Testament* 1996–7; 15th C.)

A final difference with respect to Modern French is the potential for the prepositional
adnominal NP to be coordinated with a possessive determiner:

(136)   Mon honneur saulf et *du   duc   Gerard*
        my   honor   saved and of.the duke Gerard
        'my saved honor and that of the duke Gerard'
                    (*Chroniques et conquestes de Charlemaine* I, 378; 15th C.)

4.   *De* + NP in Modern French

The far reaching grammaticalization in which the preposition *de*, expressing the spatial meaning of downward motion at its origin, gradually desemanticized, continues from medieval to Modern French, so much so that in Modern French *de* may have two opposite meanings:

(137)   a. s'approcher *de N*   ↔   s'éloigner *de N*
           'to come closer to N'   'to get further from N'

        b. manquer *de N*   ↔   déborder *de N*
           'for N to be lacking'   'for N to be plentiful'

        c. le train *de Paris*   ↔   le train *de* Paris
           'the train from Paris'   'the train to Paris'

In this section, we will account for the empirical data of Modern French by analyzing *de* as the result of this grammaticalization process. We will show that the semantic evolution from a spatial meaning of distancing towards a structural meaning went hand in hand with the syntactic evolution from a full-fledged preposition introducing adverbial complements and capable of case marking, to an "empty" preposition which introduces the argument of a verb (§ 4.1.1.) or a preceding noun (§ 4.1.2.). This grammaticalization process had a number of consequences which contrast Modern French with the stages outlined so far, both with respect to the typology of *de* (§ 4.2.) and the competition between the preposition and the genitive case (§ 4.3.).

4.1   Typology

4.1.0   *Preliminary remarks on the distinction between adjuncts and arguments*
A crucial property of *de* + NP in Modern French, which is the result of a massive extension of *de*, is that it pops up in all kinds of functions, ranging from spatial adjuncts (ex. 138) to oblique arguments (ex. 139) and even to direct objects (ex. 140). When it introduces an adjunct, *de* is still a preposition which establishes a relation both with its head (S or VP) and with the following noun. However, when *de* introduces an argument, i.e. a "genitive object" (Haspelmath & Michaelis 2008), it mainly establishes a syntactic link between the verb and the following noun. Hence, *de* + NP belongs to the VP. Finally, in quantified NPs, *de* is no longer a preposition but simply introduces the noun as a determiner, i.e. it fully belongs to the NP (cf. Kupferman 1996).

(138)   ***De***   *la*   *tour de guet* on   pouv-ai-t   control-er   l'ennemi
        from the watchtower one pouv-IMPF.3SG control-INF.PRS the enemy
        'From the watchtower you could control the enemy'

(139)   Cela dépend   ***de*** *ta*   *decision*
        this   depend-PRS.3SG of your decision
        'This depends on your decision'

(140)   a.   Paul mange   volontiers   ***de la*** *salade*
           Paul eat-PRS.3SG with pleasure of the salad
           'Paul likes salad'

        b.   Qu'est-ce qu' il   mange   volontiers?   ***De*** *la*   *salade*
           what-Q   he eat-PRS.3SG with pleasure of the salad
           'What does he like? Salad'

Two remarks are in order here. First, as we have seen, the distinction between adjuncts and arguments is not a clear-cut boundary in Latin (Lehmann 2002a), nor in Old and Middle French. Although this distinction can remain fuzzy even in Modern French, one of the consequences of the grammaticalization of *de* and of the corresponding pronoun *en* is that the distinction between adjuncts and arguments progressively became clearer. Thus, in Modern French, the genitive pronoun *en*, which goes back to the Latin adverb *inde* 'from there' and is mainly used with this meaning in Old French (ex. 126, 127, 128), has turned into a mere clitic and only patterns with arguments (ex. 141b–c), and not with adjuncts (ex. 141a). From a semantic point of view, it only has its original (spatial) meaning when used with motion verbs (e.g. *Marie en revient, de l'école* 'Mary comes back from school'). It has metaphorical meaning when it introduces a genitive object (cf. 141b). It no longer indicates any configuration, be it spatial or metaphorical, in a quantified NP (cf. 141c):

(141)   a.   ***De la tour de guet*** on pouvait contrôler l'ennemi

        a'. *On pouv-ait   **en**   control-er   l'ennemi
            one can-IMPF.3SG PRO.GEN control-INF.PRS the enemy

        b.   Cela dépend *de ta décision*

        b'. Cela **en**   dépend
            it   PRO.GEN depend-PRS.3SG

        c.   Paul mange *de la salade*

        c'. Paul **en**   mange
            Paul PRO.GEN eat-PRS.3SG

Moreover, Lazard's (1994) constraints for arguments also apply to examples b and c, and not to example a.

- Regarding mobility, the order of *de* + NP is free in (142a), and fixed in (142b) and (142c):[22]

(142)   a.   On pouvait contrôler l'ennemi *de la tour de guet*
     b.   **De ta décision* cela dépend
     c.   **De la salade* Paul mange

- Regarding subcategorization, *de* alternates with other prepositions in (143a), but not in (143b) or (143c):

(143)   a.   *De / depuis / à partir*   *de la tour de guet* on pouv-ait
        of / from   / to leave-INF.PRS of the watchtower one can-IMPF.3SG
        control-er   l'ennemi
        control-INF.PRS the enemy

     b.   **Cela dépend*   *de / *depuis / * à partir de*   *ta   décision*
        this depend-PRS.3SG of / from   / to leave-INF.PRS of your decision

     c.   Paul mange   *de / *depuis / * à partir de*   *la   salade*
        Paul eat-PRS.3SG of / from   / to leave-INF.PRS of the salad

Secondly, among the arguments introduced by *de*, both oblique complements and quantified direct objects alternate with the genitive clitic *en*. However, when followed by an infinitive, *de* is pronominalized by the accusative clitic *le* for some verbs, i.e. the argument no longer is an oblique complement in spite of the presence of *de*. Instead, it has really acquired the status of a pseudo-genitive object:

(144)   a.   Paul a décidé   / envisagé   *de partir*
        Paul decide-PRS PRF.3SG / think of-PRS PRF.3SG of leave-INF.PRS
        'Paul has decided to leave/has thought of leaving'

     b.   Paul *l'*   a décidé   / envisagé
        Paul PRO.ACC decide-PRS PRF.3SG / think of-PRS PRF.3SG

Summing up, *de* + NP appears in four different functions in Modern French, as shown in Table 6.

Although adverbial uses of *de* + NP are still attested in Modern French, in what follows we will argue that these are decreasing in favour of uses in which *de* introduces genitive (clitic *en*) and pseudo-genitive objects (clitic *le*).

Table 6. Syntactic functions of *de* + NP or infinitive

Syntactic function	Corresponding clitic	Example
Adjunct	** en*	*De la tour de contrôle* on guette l'ennemi
Genitive object	*en*	Paul sort *de la réunion*
		Cela dépend *de ta décision*
		Paul le persuade *de venir*
Quantified direct object	*en*	Paul mange *de la salade*
Direct object	*le*	Paul a décidé *de partir*

4.1.1 *Verbal domain*

A. Spatial meaning

A.1. Vertical movement

As shown by the following examples, the original use of *de* can still be found with motion verbs which indicate vertical movement away from a starting point:

(145) Après cela je vis   descendre *du*   *ciel*   un ange
        after   that I see-PST SIMPLE.1SG come.down of.the heaven an angel
        'After that I saw an angel coming down from heaven'
                               (*Apocalypse* 20: 1, Ostervald translation-French Bible online)

However, strikingly, examples containing *de* + NP often sound literary (ex. 146a), or *de* + NP enters into semi-idiomatic PPs (ex. 146b). Both of these facts suggest that this use has become less productive over time:

(146) a. Un rat, mont-é   *de la rivière*, saute   par   la
           a   rat   come up-PST PTCP of the river   jump-PRS.3SG through the
           fenêtre
           window
           'A rat which climbed out of the river jumps through the window'
                                     (Guyotat, *Frantext*)

        b. Un skieur un peu trop confiant   ou seulement imprudent,
           a   skier a   bit too confident or only   not.careful
           a chuté   *du*   *haut d'* une montagne / ? *d'*une montagne
           fall-PRS PRF.3SG of.the top of a   mountain / of a   mountain
           'A skier who was a little too confident or simply not careful enough fell from the top of a mountain' (Google, 6.12.2011)

In complements indicating a movement or perspective away from a spatial reference point, *de* alternates with more expressive prepositions such as *à partir de* or *de-puis*, which contain the element *de* and also mean 'from', as in (147). These confirm the original spatial meaning of *de*, but they also suggest that *de* has bleached: if not, there would be no need to reinforce it.

(147) a. *A partir de*   Castres, nous descend-ons   vers   Montauban
           leaving   from Castres we   go.down-PRS.1PL towards Montauban
           'From Castres we travel down towards Montauban' (Guyotat, *Frantext*)

        b. Je mont-ai-s   jusqu'à la station Pasteur *depuis le* *lycée*
           I   go.up-IMPF.1SG until   the station Pasteur from   the high.school
           Buffon
           Buffon
           'I used to go up to the station Pasteur from the Buffon high school'
                                     (Lucot, *Frantext*)

A.2. Spatial movement without vertical orientation

Locative adjuncts without a vertical orientation typically occur with perception verbs:

(148) ***Du***   *seuil*, il hum-a   l'odeur   pestilentielle de la chambre
of.the sill   he smell- PST SIMPLE.3SG the smell pestilent   of the room
'From the doorstep he could already smell the stink of the room'
(J. Kessel, quoted TLF)

With motion verbs, *de* can only be used to introduce adjuncts indicating spatial origin if the endpoint of the spatial movement is also defined:

(149) a. Elle err-ai-t   *de château **en** château, de Windsor à Osborne,*
she wander-IMPF.3SG of castle   in castle,   of Windsor to Osborne,
d' Osborne à Balmoral
of Osborne to Balmoral
'She wandered from castle to castle, from Windsor to Osborne, from Osborne to Balmoral'   (Maurois, *Disraëli*, 1927, p. 234)

b. Elle s'est promenée   *de la plage **au***   château / *de la plage*
she walk-PRS PRF.3SG of the beach to.the castle / *of the beach
'She has been walking from the beach to the castle'

When the NP indicating the landmark or reference point has a human referent, *de* is currently reinforced by *chez*,[23] which again points to the desemantization of *de*:

(150) a. Elle revien-t   *du*   *médecin* / *de chez* le *médecin*
she come-PRS.3SG of.the doctor / of at   the doctor
'She comes from the doctor'

More generally, *de*, as an indication of the pathway, is often followed by another preposition that specifies the initial location of the trajectory with respect to the landmark. In Latin, prepositions such *ex* and *ab* expressed both the pathway and the initial location with respect to the landmark (cf. § 2.5.).

(151) a. ***De sous*** les paupières obstiné-ment clos-e-s,   l'eye-liner
Of under the eyelids   stubborn-ly   close-PST.PTCP.F.PL, the eye-liner
ruissel-ait.
stream-IMPF.3SG
'From under the stubbornly closed eyelids, the eye-liner was streaming'
(M. Embareck, *Sur la ligne blanche*, 1985)

b. [Bonsoir, que tu as été longue! soupira le père]
en voy-ant   sa   femme débouch-er   ***d'entre***
[...] see-GERUND his-F.SG wife   appear.suddenly-INF PRS of between

les arbre-s
the.PL tree.PL
'Good evening, you are late! sighed the father, when seeing his wife appear
suddenly from between the trees'   (B. Clavel, *Les fruits de l'hiver*)

A restricted number of motion verbs have a locative (directional) argument of the
form *de* + NP in their argument structure. Unlike with locative adjuncts, the expression of this argument is not stylistically marked or constrained by the presence of a
second complement indicating the endpoint of the movement.

(152) Elle sor-t   ***de la*** réunion / ***de bureau***
       she leave-PRS.3SG of the meeting / of office
       'She comes out of the meeting/back from work'

There is an interesting parallel to be noted here between Latin and Modern French. In
Latin, the prepositionless ablative was typically used with nouns referring to stereotypical places associated with a social activity such as *domo* 'from home' or *rure* 'from the
countryside', as well as with proper names of well-known places, e.g. *Romā* 'from
Rome'. These nouns resisted the spread of the more expressive form, viz. *de* + ablative
(or did not need to be reinforced by the preposition *de*). What we observed so far in
Modern French is that spatial *de* + NP is in turn competing with more expressive
prepositions such as *à partir de*, except with nouns referring to social activities that
typically take place in particular locations (such as meetings, or work in offices, as in
(152)). In other words, it is the same type of locative that seems to constitute an area of
resistance (in this case against loss of *de* in its meaning of 'spatial origin').

Unlike *de* + NP with the status of an adjunct (cf. Table 6), in this case the locative
argument can be pronominalized into the genitive clitic *en*:

(153) a. Chaque fois que Lalla revien-t   ***des***   ***dunes*** (...), son
           each   time that Lalla come.back-PRS.3SG of.the dunes,   her
           coeur se   serre
           heart REFL-3 close-PRS.3SG
           'Every time Lalla comes back from the dunes, she is moved'
                                              (Le Clézio, *Désert, Frantext*)

       b. Chaque fois que Lalla ***en***   revien-t, ...
           each   time that Lalla PRO.GEN come.back-PRS.3SG

A.3. Origin and lineage

Modern French maintains the use of *de* + NP to indicate lineage, which already existed
in Latin (cf. ex. 8–9):

(154) Alors dans Besançon, vieille ville espagnole, (...)
       then in   Besançon, old   town Spanish, (...)

> Naquit   **d'** un sang breton   et   lorrain à la
> be-born-PST SIMPLE.3SG of a   blood from.Brittany and Lorraine to the
> fois Un enfant sans   couleur, sans   regard et   sans   voix
> time a   child without color, without look and without voice
> 'At that time in Besançon, an old Spanish town, a colorless, voiceless and blind
> child was born out of blood both from Brittany and Lorraine' (V. Hugo, *TLF*)

A.4. Partition

In Modern French, as opposed to Latin and Old and Middle French, *de* + NP has become a full-fledged partitive article (for a detailed analysis, see Carlier 2007, Carlier &
Lamiroy, forthc.). As such, it can introduce the NP in any syntactic function, including
that of subject (155) or direct object (156) and, unlike what has been observed for
medieval French, it can refer to any kind of N, including abstract nouns (156):

(155) **Des   gens** arriv-ent   de partout
       Of.the people arrive-PRS.3PL of everywhere
       'People arrive from everywhere'

(156) Paul ressent   **de la haine** pour son patron
       Paul feel-PRS.3SG of the hatred for   his boss
       'Paul hates his boss'

B. Metaphorical Meanings

B.1. Temporal meaning

B.1.1. Movement away from a temporal starting point

Temporal *de* indicating the origin or beginning of a state-of-affairs is still attested, but
only in combination with a limited set of temporal nouns such as *moment* 'moment',
jour 'day', *nuit* 'night', *année* 'year', which once again points to lexicalization. Moreover,
this temporal use of *de*, illustrated by the examples in (157) clearly belongs to a literary
register:

(157) a. En effet, **de ce   jour**, dev-ai-t   commenc-er pour moi
           indeed, of this day, must-IMPF.3SG begin-INF.PRS for   me
           une autre existence
           another existence
           'Indeed, from that day on, a new life would begin for me'

                                                          (M. Havet, *Frantext*)

       b. Car, **de ce   moment**, il se   laiss-a   all-er
           since of this moment, he REFL.3 let-PST SIMPLE.3SG go-INF
           davantage à la   conversation et   y   prit
           more   to the conversation and to.it take-PST SIMPLE.3SG

visible-ment du   goût
visib-ly   of.the   taste
'Since from that moment he indulged more in conversation and clearly
enjoyed it'   (Gobineau, *Frantext*)

Usually, however, other prepositions will be preferred in Modern French to indicate
temporal origin, such as *depuis*, *dès* or *à partir de*, which again suggests that *de* is to a
large extent desemanticized. Thus, in the following example, simple *de* would be ungrammatical with a temporal meaning:

(158) Philippe me   reconnaî-t   ***à partir***   ***de*** ***là***   /
       Philippe me-PRO.DAT.1SG recognize-PRS.3SG starting to leave from there /
       ****de**** *là*   le droit d'écri-re[24]
       from there the right of write-INF PRS
       'Philip allows me from then on to write'   (C. Arnaud, *Frantext*)

Note that *de* + NP can still be used to indicate temporal origin provided the endpoint
of the time span is also mentioned, as shown by the following contrast in (159a–b). The
fact that another prepositional phrase such as *à partir de* is needed when the endpoint
is not marked (159c), once again suggests that *de* in itself no longer has sufficient semantic content:

(159) a. Paul ser-a   absent ***de mardi*** ***à*** ***vendredi***
           Paul be-FUT.3SG absent of Tuesday to Friday
           'Paul will be away from Tuesday till Friday'

       b. *Paul ser-a   absent ***de mardi***
           Paul be-FUT.3SG absent of Tuesday

       c. Paul ser-a   absent ***à partir de*** *mardi*
           Paul be-FUT.3SG absent from   Tuesday
           'Paul will be away from Tuesday on'

B.1.2. Partition within a time interval

The temporal use of *de* to indicate a particular point in time did not survive, except
when *de* + NP is in the scope of negation, as in (160a), as well as in a large series of
lexicalized (idiomatic) expressions, e.g. *de son vivant* 'in his lifetime', *de mémoire
d'homme* 'as far as mankind can remember', *de bonne heure* 'early', *du temps de X* 'in X's
time', *de jour* 'during daytime', *de nuit* 'at night', etc. as in (160b):

(160) a. Je ne dorm-i-s   pas ***de la*** *nuit*, mon état d'
           I not sleep-PST SIMPLE.1SG neg of the night, my state of
           effervescence ne laiss-ai-t   aucune place au   repos
           excitement   not leave-IMPF.3SG any   place to-the rest
           'I did not sleep all night long, my state of excitement did not leave me any
           rest'   (Guibert, *Frantext*)

b. Madame ét-ai-t   folle, capricieuse, infernale *de jour* comme *de*
   Madam be-IMPF.3SG mad, whimsical, horrible   of day   as   of
   nuit
   night
   'Madam was mad, whimsical, horrible, both during the day and at night'
   (Boudard, *Frantext*)

Both facts – the survival of temporal *de* in lexicalized expressions and the existence of
constraints that did not hold for Old or Middle French such as the presence of a negation,- suggest that *de* has lost most of its vitality in this use.

B.2. Movement away from a starting point: neither spatial nor temporal

Sentences such as (161) are perfectly comparable to the equivalent examples in Latin
(cf. ex. 19) and Old French (cf. ex. 83):

(161) a. J'ai entendu   cela *de mon père*
         I   hear-PRS PRF.1SG this of my   father
         'I heard this from my father'

      b. Nous av-ons appris   la   terrible nouvelle *des*   *voisins*
         we   learn-PRS PRF.1PL the terrible news   of.the neighbors
         'We heard the terrible news from our neighbors'

Whereas *de* + NP in such examples corresponds to an adjunct, the following examples
show that a whole series of French verbs[25] have an argument position for a genitive
object introduced by *de* that patterns with the clitic *en*, and in which a spatial metaphor of origin can often still be perceived. The degree to which this is the case obviously varies according to the verb. Compare the following examples:

(162) a. Tout le problème (pro)vient / découle / dérive   *d'* *un*
         all the problem   come   / flow   / derive-PRS.3SG of a
         malentendu
         misunderstanding
         'The whole problem is due to a misunderstanding'

      b. Paul a déduit / conclu   *des*   *paroles de Marie* qu' elle
         Paul deduce / conclude-PRS PRF.3SG of.the words   of Mary that she
         le   quitt-ai-t
         him-ACC leave-IMPF.3SG
         'Paul deduced/concluded from Mary's words that she was leaving him'

      c. On a séparé   l' enfant *de sa mère*
         one separate-PRS PRF.3SG the child   of his mother
         'The child was separated from his mother'

Genitive objects also include those that are subcategorized by verbs of locative alternation (Boons, Guillet & Leclère 1976: 41, Haspelmath & Michaelis 2008, Salkoff 1983),

i.e. verbs which have two constructions. The theme is either indicated as a genitive object introduced by *de* (163a/164a) or it occurs as the subject (163b) or the object (164b) of the sentence. Verbs of locative alternation can be intransitive (ex. 163) or transitive (ex. 164):

(163) a. Le jardin grouille　　　　*d' abeilles*
　　　　　the garden swarm-PRS.3SG of bees
　　　　　'The garden is swarming with bees'

　　　　b. *Les abeilles* grouillent　　　dans le jardin
　　　　　the bees　　swarm-PRS.3PL in　　the garden
　　　　　'The bees are swarming in the garden'

(164) a. Max a chargé　　　　le camion *d' oranges*
　　　　　Max load-PRS PRF.3SG the truck　of oranges
　　　　　'Max has loaded the truck with oranges'

　　　　b. Max a chargé　　　　*les oranges* dans le camion
　　　　　Max load-PRS PRF.3SG the oranges in　　the truck
　　　　　'Max has loaded the oranges in the truck'

B.3. Objects of verbs of saying, feeling and thinking

Many verbs in this category take genitive objects introduced by *de* that alternate with the clitic *en*, e.g. *blaguer* 'joke', *discuter* 'discuss', *deviser* 'speak', *juger* 'judge', *parler* 'talk', *traiter* 'treat', etc.

Interestingly, many of these verbs allow two constructions: they take either an oblique complement introduced by *de*, or a direct object NP. Although there may be subtle nuances between the two constructions, there is no significant meaning change for the verb. This alternation between *de* (165a) and zero (165b) clearly points towards a desemantization of *de*, e.g.:

(165) a. On discut-a　　　　　　　jadis　　　*de la conviction et de*
　　　　　one discuss-PST SIMPLE.3SG in-former-days of the conviction and of
　　　　　l' honorabilité des　　directeurs de journaux
　　　　　the respectability of.the directors of newspapers
　　　　　'People used to argue about the convictions and the respectability of
　　　　　newspaper directors'　　　　　　　　　　　　　(Maurras, *TLF*)

　　　　b. Deux personnages peu définis entr-èrent　　　　　　et　　se
　　　　　two persons　　little defined come.in-PST SIMPLE.3PL and REFL.3
　　　　　partag-èrent　　　　une chopine　　en discut-ant　　*le coup*
　　　　　share-PST SIMPLE.3PL a　　little.beer discuss-GERUND the event
　　　　　'Two undefined people came in and shared a little beer while discussing
　　　　　the event'　　　　　　　　　　　　　　　　(R. Queneau, *TLF*)

In comparison with Latin and medieval French, *de* as a topic marker is subject to heavy constraints, which once again shows its desemantization. For instance, as shown by Lagae (2003), *de* + NP occurs only when it is linked to an argument of the verb that is in the focus of a restriction (166) or a negation (167a). Hence, *de* + NP as a topic marker is ungrammatical without restriction or negation (167b).

(166)　**De couleur authentique** il n'　　y　　　a　　　　　　que　le　gris
　　　　of　color　　authentical　it　RESTR　PRO.LOC　have-PRS.3SG　RESTR　the　grey
　　　　pierre des　　yeux.
　　　　stone　of.the eyes.
　　　　'As authentic color, there is only the stone-grey color of his eyes.'
　　　　　　　　　　　　　　　　　　　　　　　　(R. Crevel, *Êtes-vous fous*, 1929)

(167)　a.　**D'aéroport**,　il n'　　y　　　en　　　a　　　　　pas　dans cette
　　　　　　of airport,　　it　NEG　PRO.LOC　PRO.GEN　have-PRS.3SG　NEG　in　　this
　　　　　　capitale
　　　　　　capital
　　　　　　'As to an airport, there is none in this capital.'

　　　　b.　*D'aéoroport*,　il y　　　en　　　a　　　　　　dans chaque capitale
　　　　　　of airport,　　it　PRO.LOC　PRO.GEN　have-PRS.3SG　in　　each　　capital

Topical *de* + NP is also excluded when there is no referential link with an argument of the verb. In such cases, it is replaced by more expressive prepositional phrases such as *quant à, à propos de, en ce qui concerne* or *pour ce qui est de.*

(168)　*Quant à mon voyage,* il faut　　　　que je me　　　décide
　　　　De　　mon voyage, il faut　　　　que je me　　　décide
　　　　of　　my　trip　　it must-PRS.3SG that I　REFL-1SG decide
　　　　'As to my trip, I have to decide'

B.4. Manner and instrument, cause and agent

For *de* introducing manner or instrument complements, the same remarks can be made as for the spatial and temporal adjuncts. On the one hand, they are still attested, but mainly occur in lexicalized semi-idiomatic expressions, e.g. *de la sorte,* lit. 'of the sort', *de (d'une) manière X* lit. 'of a X manner', *de (d'une) façon X* lit. 'of a X way', as in (169–170). On the other hand, other prepositions like *par* or *avec* will often be preferred to indicate manner, as shown in (171):

(169)　Tu n'　au-r-ai-s　　pas dû　　　　　agir **de la sorte** / **de cette façon**
　　　　you not should have NEG must-PST PTCP act　of the sort / of this　way
　　　　'You should not have acted that way'

(170)　Il la　suiv-ai-t　　　**du**　　regard
　　　　he her follow-IMPF.3SG of.the view
　　　　'He followed her with his eyes'

(171) Il ten-ai-t   l' enfant ? *de la main* / *par* la main
      he hold-IMPF.3SG the child of the hand / by the hand
      'He held the child by its hand'

Cases in which *de* + NP indicates the cause or the agent of an action (in passive sentences) can also be subsumed under the metaphorical meanings. As suggested by Hettrich (1990), they can be analyzed as the source of the process indicated by the verb:

(172) a. Il est mort   *d' une crise cardiaque*
         he die-PRS PRF.3SG of a   heart attack
         'He died of a heart attack'

      b. Elle pleure   *de chagrin*
         she cry-PRS.3SG of sorrow
         'She is crying with sorrow'

      c. Ce professeur est aimé / apprécié   *de ses élèves*
         this teacher   is loved / appreciated-PST PTCP of his pupils
         'This teacher is loved/appreciated by his pupils'

Note, however, that this use of *de* + NP is also more restricted than in Old and Middle French. Its use is limited to psychological verbs (Martin 2002) like *aimer* or *apprécier* (cf. ex. 173) and to resultative (ex. 174) or iterative aspect (ex. 175). Once again, this use only occurs in a more formal, written register.

(173) Jean est aimé   *de* tous
      John is love-PST PTCP of all
      'John is loved by everyone'

(174) a. Jean est surveillé   ***par** Marie / *de Marie*
         John is watch-PST PTCP by   Mary / *of Mary
         'John is watched by Mary'

      b. Jean est surveillé   *de* tous
         John is watch-PST PTCP by all
         'John is watched by everyone'   (Authier 1972: 133)

(175) a. Jean est pâli   *par* / ***de* la peur qu' il ressent
         John is turn-pale-PST.PTCP by / of the fear that he feel-PRS.3SG
         'John turns pale because of the fear he feels' (Authier 1972: 131)

      b. Jean est pâli   *par* / *de la peur qu' il a*
         John is turn-pale-PST PTCP by / of the fear that he has feel
         ressentie
         -PST PTCP.f.SG
         'John has become pale because of the fear he felt'   (Authier 1972: 131)

C. "Empty" preposition

A large number of French verbs take a genitive object introduced by *de* in which the preposition has completely lost its original meaning and simply introduces an oblique complement. Compare, for instance, the following pairs of verbs that are synonyms or quasi-synonyms, one of which takes *de* + NP, while the other takes a direct object:

(176) a. Max se rappelle très bien *cette soirée*
            Max REFL-3 remember-PRS.3SG very well that evening

     b. Max se souvient très bien *de cette soirée*
            Max REFL-3 remember-PRS.3SG very well of that evening
            'Max remembers that evening very well'

(177) a. Max aime *le* ridiculiser
            Max like-PRS.3SG him ridicule-INF.PRS

     b. Max aime rire / se moquer *de lui*
            Max like-PRS.3SG laugh / REFL-3 ridicule of him
            'Max likes to laugh at him'

(178) a. Les militaires ont pris *le pouvoir*
            the military take-PRS PRF.3PL the power

     b. Les militaires se sont emparés *du pouvoir*
            the military REFL-3 become master-PRS PRF.3PL of.the power
            'The army took the power'

Similarly, as shown for Middle French, a number of verbs that take a direct object have a corresponding anti-passive pronominal construction, where the object takes the form of *de* + NP without a significant difference in meaning, e.g. *apercevoir* vs. *s'apercevoir*, or *saisir* vs. *se saisir*.

(179) a. Il sais-i-t *l' arme*
            he take-PST SIMPLE.3SG the weapon

     b. Il se sais-i-t *de l' arme*
            he REFL-3 take PST SIMPLE.3SG of the weapon
            'He took the weapon'

In several verbal structures that take an object of the form *de* + V-INF, *de* can no longer be analyzed as introducing an oblique object from a syntactic perspective, since the corresponding clitic has the accusative form (i.e. *de* introduces a pseudo-genitive object in this case). Such structures clearly show that the preposition *de* has also undergone decategorization (Heine & Narrog 2010), i.e. it no longer displays one of the typical properties of its prepositional category, viz. that of constructing oblique objects:

(180) a. Max a décidé / essayé / suggéré / évoqué / envisagé *de*
            Max decide / try / suggest / evoke / envisage-PRS PRF.3SG of

partir
leave-INF.PRS
'Max has decided/tried/suggested/suggested to leave/thought of leaving'

b. Max l'   a décidé / l'   a essayé / l'   a suggéré /
   Max PRO.ACC decide   / PRO.ACC try   / PRO.ACC suggest   /
   l'   a évoqué / l'   a envisagé
   PRO.ACC suggest   / PRO.ACC consider-PRS PRF.3SG
   'Max has decided/tried/suggested/suggested it/thought of it'

Certain verbs take either a bare infinitive or an infinitive introduced by *de,* without any clear semantic difference. Both infinitives correspond to the accusative clitic. Interestingly, of the two variants, the one introduced by *de* sounds more archaic or literary (Grevisse-Goosse 2008: 1119), suggesting that bare infinitives are extending:[26]

(181) a. Cette ceinture d' officier dans laquelle j' av-ai-s espéré   ***de***
      this   belt   of officer in   which I hope-PST PRF.1sg of
      mour-ir
      die-INF PRS
      'This officer's belt in which I had hoped to die'

                                                (Grevisse-Goosse 2008: 1119)

   b. Elle espér-ai-t   mourir   dans son pays   natal
      she hope-IMPF.3SG die-INF.PRS in   her country native
      'She hoped to die in her home country'

      Elle l'   éspér-ai-t
      she PRO.ACC hope-IMPF.3SG
      'She hoped so'

A similar remark can be made for infinitival subject complements: with *de,* the sentence sounds archaic or literary, as in (182a). When the infinitive is extraposed, the complementizer *de* is obligatory, but it has a mere structural function and its meaning is totally "empty", as in (182b):

(182) a. *(De) partir*   *en vacances* est   agréable
      (of) leave-INF.PRS on holidays be-PRS.3SG pleasant
      'To leave on holidays is pleasant'

   b. C' est   agréable ***de*** *part-ir*   *en vacances*
      it be-PRS.3SG pleasant of leave-INF.PRS on holidays
      'It is pleasant to leave on holidays'

4.1.2 *The nominal domain*

A. Origin and lineage

Ever since Latin, *de* can introduce an adnominal NP to indicate origin or lineage:

(183) a. Un homme *de province*
           a   man   of province
           'A man with a provincial origin'

       b. *De son père*, certes, il av-ai-t   le front   et les yeux
           of his father, sure, he have-IMPF.3SG the forehead and the eyes
           'He had for sure his father's forehead and his eyes'   (Zola, *Frantext*)

As mentioned, *de* is desemanticized, as the following ambiguous structure shows: *de* +
NP may indicate origin here, but also destination.

(184) le train *de Vintimille*
       the train of Vintimiglia
       'the train from Vintimiglia' or 'the train to Vintimiglia' (Kupferman 1996)

B. From origin to extraction and partition

As a partitive adnominal complement, *de* + NP is still occasionally used to indicate the
whole to which something or someone belongs. Yet, while *de* can express this meaning
on its own in medieval French, Modern French *de* will be reinforced by a second preposition or will be simply replaced by another preposition when it really refers to a part-
of-a-whole.

(185) a. *Qui de vous* connaî-t   la réponse?
           who of you know-PRS.3SG the answer?

       b. *Qui d' entre*   vous / *parmi vous* connait   la réponse?
           who of between you / among you know-PRS.3SG the answer?

By contrast, partitive *de* is not reinforced when combined to quantifiers like *beaucoup
de*, precisely because *de* no longer refers to a part-whole relation and has become a
mere determiner of the following N.

C. From origin to property

In many cases, as a result of a pervasive bleaching process, the function of *de* as an
adnominal marker is to indicate all kinds of abstract relations with the following noun,
ranging from physical (186) or abstract (187) properties to part-whole relations (188)
(for an overview cf. Bartning 1996, Honeste 2005):

(186) Cette table est   *de marbre*
       this table be-PRS.3SG of marble
       'This table is made out of marble'

(187) Enfin   il vi-t   la gravité *du regard que maître Biard*
       eventually he see-IMPF.3SG the strength of.the look   that lawyer Biard
       posait   sur lui
       put-IMPF.3SG on him
       'Eventually he saw how seriously lawyer Biard looked at him' (quoted Bartning
       1996)

(188)   Il habite   au   coin *de la rue*
he live-PRS.3SG at.the corner of the street
'He lives around the corner'

D. From origin to agent or patient

The analysis of the genitive as being able to indicate both the *agent* and the *patient* of a deverbative noun has a tradition going back as far as Sanskrit grammar (for details, see Daladier 1999). Both can in fact be related to the primitive meaning of origin: in *the fear of the devil, the devil* is the source of the fear, being the one who generates it, whereas in *the fear of the faithful, the faithful* identifies the persons who are fearful. In Latin, the genitive was compatible with both readings, whereas *de* + NP-ABL was restricted to the patient reading (cf. § 2.3.2.D.). Obviously, French *de* + NP can also have either meaning. In the following example *les parents* can either be those who are afraid or the object of fear for the children:

(189)   La peur *des*   parents frustre   les enfants
the fear of.the parents frustrate-PRS.3SG the children
'To fear your parents is frustrating for children'
'[To have] fearful parents is frustrating for children'

Note that patient NPs can also refer to abstract notions:

(190)   Car Bérénice av-ai-t   le goût *de l' absolu*
since Bérénice have-IMPF.3SG the taste of the absolute
'Since Bérénice loved the absolute'   (Aragon, quoted Bartning 1996)

E. From origin to possession

According to Hettrich (1990), the agent/patient genitive was gradually extended, starting in Sanskrit and Ancient Greek, and became a marker of possession, a function which French *de* + NP obviously also has, like in *la maison des parents* 'the parent's house'. Note that several structures are ambiguous, not only between an agentive and a patient reading but also between an agentive and a possessive reading, as in (191).

(191)   La photo *de Pierre*
the picture of Pierre
= the picture that Pierre took
= the picture that was made of Pierre
= the picture that belongs to Pierre

F. "Empty" preposition

As is the case with *de* + NP in the verbal domain, *de* + NP also occurs in adnominal structures with a bleached meaning, its only function being to establish a formal link with a following N in a relation of equivalence:

(192) a. La ville *de Paris* est en deuil
           the city of Paris is in mourning
           'The city of Paris is mourning'

       b. Le thème *de la culpabilité* est typiquement chrétien
           the theme of the guilt   is typically   Christian
           'Guilt is a typically Christian issue'

4.2   Competition between "case" and "*de* + NP"

As a consequence of the massive extension of *de* + NP, the remnant of the former
genitive case which French inherited from Latin and which was still partly alive in Old
and Middle French in bare adnominal constructions, only remains in a number of
fully lexicalized compounds in Modern French, i.e. fossilized expressions as exemplified in (193a) and in dialectal variants, for example in Walloon (193b):

(193) a. l' Hôtel-Dieu
           the House-God
           'The hospital'

       b. l fiye   Pipin
           the daughter Pipin
           'The daughter of Pipin'

For indefinite non-singular NPs, the partitive article has become obligatory in Modern
French in all syntactic positions except within the PP (Carlier 2007) and in some non-
referential syntactic positions such as the nominal predicate position:

(194) a. Marie a fait   ça   avec amour / avec *de* l'   amour
           Mary do-PRS PRF.3SG this with love   / with of the love
           'Mary has done this with love'

       b. Ses   fils   sont   *médecins.*
           His-PL son-PL be-PRS.3PL doctor-PL
           'His sons are doctors'

4.3   Degree of grammaticalization of *de*

From Medieval to Modern French, the grammaticalization process affecting *de* continued.

Integrity

Several facts of Modern French usage testify to a further loss of integrity of *de*:

–   In a number of uses, in particular as an adjunct, *de* appears more frequently in
    combination with other prepositions, cf. examples (147, 149, 150, 151, 158, 159c);

– In certain uses as a genitive object, its meaning is bleached even though it still corresponds to a genitive clitic, cf. examples (176b, 177b, 178b, 179b);

– For some instances of *de* + infinitive, labeled "pseudo-genitive" objects, the meaning is so strongly bleached that the corresponding clitic is no longer the genitive *en,* but the accusative *le,* cf. examples (180, 181).

Paradigmaticity

Whereas *de* was a full-fledged preposition in Latin, competing with other prepositions that indicated spatial origin such as *ex* and *ab,* in Modern French *de* usually competes with other "empty" prepositions such as *à,* and even "zero" (cf. Spang-Hanssen 1963). This implies that *de* left its original paradigm of locative prepositions to enter a new paradigm of semantically "empty" prepositions whose only function is structural, viz. relating an argument to its head. It should be recalled here that several verbs such as *discuter* 'discuss', *parler* 'talk' or *traiter* 'deal with' can take either *de* + NP or a direct NP without significant meaning change, cf. example (165). It is also worth mentioning that in those cases where an infinitival complement can either be introduced by *de* or by "zero" (*espérer* 'hope', *aimer* 'love', *préférer* 'prefer', etc.), the latter option is the newer one, suggesting that *de* is slowly being phased out here.

Paradigmatic variability

The transformation of *de* into an element whose main function is to introduce an argument selected by a verbal or a nominal head, also implies that there is no choice between *de* and any other preposition, and hence no paradigmatic variability. In other words, *de* + NP belongs to the argument structure of the verb (or the noun) and, as such, is constrained as to its formal expression. In some cases, alternation with zero is still possible, without a significant meaning difference, as has been illustrated by examples (165) and (181).

Structural scope

Another consequence of the same evolution is that its structural scope is also reduced: originally introducing an adjunct with scope over the whole sentence, *de* progressively reduced its weight or structural size, ending up as a structural element within the VP or NP, or as a mere determiner within the (quantified) NP. One of the results of this reduction in scope is that *de* can no longer introduce an NP that consists of two coordinated nouns in Modern French, which was still possible in Middle French:

(195) a. Max parle   *du*   *vin*   *et* *de* la *bière*
           Max speak-PRS.3SG of.the wine and of the beer

      b. *Max parle   *du*   *vin*   *et* *la* *bière*
           Max speak-PRS.3SG of.the wine and the beer
           'Max talks about the wine and beer'

In this respect, *de* differs from less grammaticalized prepositions, which can take scope over two coordinated NPs, even in Modern French, as shown by the following example:

(196)   Il   proteste **contre** *Pierre et   son voisin.*
    'He protests against Peter and his neighbor'

Bondedness

If *de* can still be separated from a following infinitive by certain adverbs, its autonomy is obviously not as great as it used to be. This can be shown by the comparison of the Latin example given in (54), with its Modern French equivalent in (197d):

(197)   a.   Il vécu-t   bien et   longtemps
        he live-PST SIMPLE.3SG well and long
        'He lived a long and happy life'

    b.   Il ét-ai-t   content **de** *bien viv-re*
        he be-IMPF.3SG happy   of well live-INF.PRS
        'He was happy to live well'

    c.   *Il ét-ai-t   content **de** *longtemps viv-re*
        he be-IMPF.3SG happy   of long   live-INF.PRS
        'He was happy to live long'

    d.   *Il ét-ai-t   content **de** *bien et   longtemps viv-re*
        he be-IMPF.3SG happy   of well and long   live-INF.PRS
        'He was happy to live a long and happy life'

Syntagmatic variability

In contrast with what we observed for Latin and Old and Middle French, the positional freedom of *de* is totally constrained, except when *de* + NP is an adjunct, which, as we have seen, is less and less the case in Modern French. Compare example (135) with its Modern French equivalent; as shown in (198a–b), *de* + NP can no longer be separated from its head:

(198)   a.   *Ici se   ferme   le testament et   fini-t   **du**
        here REFL-3 close-PRS.3SG the will   and finish-PRS.3SG of.the
        pauvre Villon
        poor   Villon
        'Here concludes and ends the will of poor Villon'

    b.   Ici se   ferme   et fini-t   le testament **du**
        here REFL-3 close-PRS.3SG and finish-PRS.3SG the will   of.the
        pauvre Villon
        poor   Villon

It comes as no surprise that the coordination of adnominal *de* + NP with an NP introduced by a possessive determiner is no longer possible. Compare example (136) with the following example from Modern French:

(199) a. *Mon honneur et   du   duc Gérard
           my   honor   and of.the duke Gérard
           'My honor and that of duke Gérard'

       b. Mon honneur et   celui du   duc Gérard
           my   honor   and that of.the duke Gérard

To sum up, then, two major facts seem to characterize Modern French. On the one hand, although *de* still functions as a full-fledged preposition that can introduce adjuncts in a number of cases, it is so strongly bleached that it often has to be reinforced by other prepositions when introducing an adjunct. Its major syntactic function seems to be a structural one, viz. linking arguments to their verbal or nominal head. On the other hand, the competition which used to exist in Middle French between *de* and genitive case has completely disappeared, since *de* is massively present to express possession in NPs, while traces of the old genitive are only to be found in totally lexicalized, i.e. fossilized, expressions such as *hôtel-Dieu*.

5.   General conclusion

The main question addressed in this paper is to what extent the Latin preposition *de* evolved into a genitive case marker in Modern French. Since *de* governs the ablative case in Latin, our study also takes into account the peripheral status of the ablative in the Latin case system and the change in balance between ablative and genitive from Latin to Modern French. The main results of our study can be summarized as follows.

First, our diachronic study of *de* + NP as a genitive marker provides ample evidence for the well-known fact that case marking and prepositional marking are two formally different grammatical devices which by and large serve the same function, viz. indicating the syntactic and semantic roles of NPs (Hewson & Bubenik 2006). In the same way as they vary typologically, they can vary through the history of a language, as is the case here, showing once more that synchronic and diachronic variation run along the same lines. Latin was above all a case marking (synthetic) language, while French is an analytic language in which prepositional marking plays a major role, case marking being reduced to a number of remnants found in lexicalized compounds. However, there is no strict causal link between the erosion of the declension system and the emergence of prepositions. On the one hand, as pointed out by Pinkster (1990), and shown by the data presented here, prepositions such as *ad* and *de* are used in Latin for enhanced expressivity rather than for functional disambiguation. It is only in a later stage that they became grammatical tools. On the other hand, case endings were not unambiguous, even in Latin (Pinkster 1993), and the identification of syntactic function and semantic role also relied on the lexical meaning of the verb and its (rather loose) syntactic constraints and selectional restrictions on the nominal constituents (Pinkster 1984, Schøsler 2008).[27]

A second, even more important observation, is that the transition from a system based on case inflection to a system where prepositions mark functions does not consist in a simple replacement of one formal tool by another. Along the way, there is a series of complex and unpredictable collateral changes. Thus we have seen that while *de* + NP was used rather marginally in the verbal domain in Latin, and hardly at all in the nominal domain, its massive extension entailed not only its spread in the verbal domain but also in the nominal domain, where it is now omnipresent, and probably even predominant compared to the verbal domain.[28] Another significant aspect of the historical evolution of *de* + NP is that it moved from a peripheral status, essentially used for adjuncts in Latin, to a central status in the sentence in French. As we have shown, once a full-fledged preposition introducing an adjunct expressing spatial origin, *de* and the corresponding clitic *en* gradually came to be used as structural markers of arguments depending on a verbal or a nominal head. This evolution went along with two important syntactic changes: (i) while Latin is dependent-marking, contemporary French shows features of a head-marking language; (ii) as a corollary, the distinction between adjuncts and arguments, which was fuzzy in Latin, became sharper in the evolution towards Modern French. With respect to this distinction, *de* is only sporadically attested in Modern French as a preposition introducing an adjunct, and moreover this adjunct does not correspond to the clitic *en*. Instead, the prototypical role of *de* is that of a structural marker of arguments.

A third conclusion is that there is overwhelming evidence for our hypothesis of a pervasive grammaticalization process for *de*: whether one applies Lehmann's (2002b) parameters or Heine & Narrog's (2010) criteria, *de* fulfills all the conditions for a highly grammaticalized element. As we have seen, the bleaching process of the preposition, which started in Latin, went on relentlessly. *De* showed the first signs of an "empty" preposition in Old and Middle French, and in certain structures in Modern French no longer confers the status of oblique argument to the constituent of which it is the head. Thus, for instance, it functions as a complementizer for several verbs introducing an infinitive whose syntactic function is that of direct object (the corresponding clitic being the accusative *le* rather than the genitive *en*). This amounts to saying that *de* not only underwent semantic bleaching, but also that it decategorized: prepositional phrases which no longer yield oblique pronouns but accusative pronouns can no longer be considered as displaying the normal behavior of their category. It has also been shown that *de*, whose grammaticalization path parallels that of another preposition, viz. *à* (Goyens et al. 2002, Kilroe 1994), presents the typical symptoms associated with the final stages of the grammaticalization process, viz. coalescence (*du, des*) and phonetic attrition (*d'* in front of a vowel). However, the grammaticalization of *de* does not imply, of course, that none of its original meaning(s) remain. As we have seen, *de* may still express an array of more 'substantial' meanings such as the spatial downward meaning and several metaphorical meanings.

A final point we would like to make here is that our study can also shed new light on how language change takes place: the transition from one stage to another operates unevenly (De Mulder & Lamiroy 2012, Lamiroy & De Mulder 2011) because certain areas of the language resist more than others to the expansion of the new form. Not surprisingly, our data show that, in the competition between the conservative pattern of case marking without preposition and the innovative pattern of PP, those uses that formed the core meaning of the old form were also more robust with respect to change. With regard to the ablative case in Latin, a case in point is that of stereotypical places typically associated with human activities, which maintained the conservative structure of the prepositionless ablative until Late Latin (e.g. *opsonatu redeo* 'I come back from the market') and resisted the spread of the "new" *de* + (ablative) NP. Interestingly, the same category now resists the disappearance of *de* as a marker of adverbial elements in Modern French. As to the genitive case in Latin, it resisted the development of the prepositional construction *de* + NP-ABL for the expression of the possessive relationship. Interestingly, the very same area of possessive genitives is where we find most prepositionless adnominal complements in Old and Middle French, i.e. remnants of the old genitive marking in Latin. Although this area of resistance eventually succumbs to *de* + NP in Modern French, the possessive genitive, corresponding to the core meaning of genitive case, proves to be more robust with respect to linguistic change. Since the same tendency has been observed for meaning changes in the lexicon (Geeraerts 1997), this hypothesis is a promising line of research that should, of course, be verified by independent data.

References

Corpora

CLASSICAL LATIN
Itinera Electronica (Université catholique de Louvain)
Stroebel, E. ed. 1965 (19151). *Rhetorici libri duo qui vocantur De Inventione. Editio strereotypa editionis prioris (MCMXV). (M. Tulli Ciceronis scripta quae manserunt omnia 2. Bibliotheca scriptorum Graecorum et Romanorum Teubneriana)*. Stuttgart: Teubner. XXII-170 p.
Bornecque, Henri. ed. s.d. [1932] *Cicéron. De l'invention (De Inventione). Texte revu et traduit avec introduction et notes. (Classiques Garnier)*. Paris: Garnier.

LATE & MEDIEVAL LATIN
Monumenta Germaniae Historica. Turnhout: Brepols. (http://www.brepolis.net)
Fredegarii Chronicarum liber quartus cum continuationibus/The Fourth Book of the Chronicle of Fredegar, translated from the Latin with Introduction and Notes by J.M. Wallace-Hadrill, London: Thomas Nelson & Sons, 1960.

EARLY OLD FRENCH
Base du projet ANR « Corptef » (ENS-Lyon, CNRS UMR 5191 ICAR)

OLD FRENCH
Base du français médiéval (ENS-Lyon, CNRS UMR 5191 ICAR)

Godefroy, Frédéric. 1880–1902. *Dictionnaire de l'ancienne langue française et de tous ses dialectes du IXe au XVe siècle, composé d'après le dépouillement de tous les plus importants documents manuscrits ou imprimés qui se trouvent dans les grandes bibliothèques de la France et de l'Europe et dans les principales archives départementales, municipales, hospitalières ou privées.* Paris: Vieweg.

Greimas, Algirdas Julien & Keane, Teresa Mary. 2001² (1992¹). *Dictionnaire du moyen français.* Paris: Larousse.

Pignatelli, Cinzia & Gerner, Dominique. éds. 2006. *Les traductions françaises des* Otia imperialia *de Gervais de Tilbury par Jean d'Antioche et Jean de Vignay. Édition de la troisième partie.* (*Publications romanes et françaises* CCXXXVII). Genève: Droz.

Stein, Achim et al. Eds.: *Nouveau Corpus d'Amsterdam. Corpus informatique de textes littéraires d'ancien français (ca 1150–1350), établi par Anthonij Dees (Amsterdam 1987), remanié par Achim Stein, Pierre Kunstmann et Martin-D. Gleßgen, Stuttgart.*

Tobler, A. & Lommatzsch, E. 1915ff. *Altfranzösisches Wörterbuch. Adolf Toblers nachgelassene Materialien bearbeitet und herausgegeben von E. Lommatzsch.* Berlin: Weidman – Wiesbaden: Steiner.

Van Hoecke, Willy. Ed. *"La Rectorique de Marc Tulles Cyceron". La traduction par Jean d'Antioche (1282) du "De Inventione" de Cicéron et de la "Rhetorica ad Herennium" éditée d'après le manuscrit unique.* Unpublished edition.

Guadagnini, Elisa. Ed. 2009. *La* Rectorique de Cyceron *tradotta da Jean d'Antioche. Edizione e glossario.* Pisa: Edizione della Normale.

MIDDLE FRENCH
Dictionnaire du Moyen Français, version 2010. ATILF CNRS – Université de Lorraine. Site internet: http://www.atilf.fr/dmf.
Godefroy 1880–1902 cited for Old French.

CLASSICAL & MODERN FRENCH
Frantext (CNRS UMR Atilf, Nancy – Université de Lorraine. Site internet: www.frantext.fr.

Linguistic studies

Adams, James. N. 2011. Late Latin. In: J. Clackson Ed. *A Companion to the Latin Language.* Wiley-Blackwell, 257–283.

Authier, Jacqueline. 1972. Étude sur les formes passives du français. *Drlav* 1: 1–145.

Bartning, Inge. 1996. Eléments pour une typologie des SN en *de* en français. *Langue française,* 109: 29–44.

Bauer, Brigitte L.M. 1995. *The Emergence and Development of SVO Patterning in Latin and French. Diachronic and Psycholinguistic Perspectives.* Oxford: Oxford University Press.

Boons, Jean-Paul, Guillet, Alain & Leclère, Christian. 1976. *La structure des phrases simples en français. Constructions intransitives.* Paris: Droz.

Buridant, Claude. 2000. *Grammaire nouvelle de l'ancien français.* Paris: Sedes.

Bybee, Joan L. 1985. *Morphology: A Study of the Relation between Meaning and Form.* Amsterdam: John Benjamins.

Cadiot, Pierre. 1997. *Les prépositions abstraites du français.* Paris: A. Colin.

Carlier, Anne. 2001. La genèse de l'article *un. Langue française* 130: 65–88.

Carlier, Anne. 2007. From Preposition to Article. The Grammaticalization of the French Partitive. *Studies in Language,* 31/1: 1–49.

Carlier, Anne. 2013. Grammaticalization in progress in Old French: indefinite articles. In: Arteaga-Capen D. Ed. *Research in Old French: The State of the Art.* Dordrecht, Heidelberg: Springer, 45–60.

Carlier, Anne & Lamiroy, Béatrice. forthc. The grammaticalization of the prepositional partitive in Romance. In S. Luraghi and T. Huumo. Eds. *Partitives.*

Clairin, Paul. 1880. *Du génitif latin et de la préposition 'de'.* Paris: F. Vieweg.

Creissels, Denis. 2006. *Syntaxe générale: une introduction typologique* 2. Paris: Lavoisier, Hermes.

Daladier, Anne. 1999. Origine adverbiale du génitif indo-européen, extractions, possessifs, anaphore associative et interprétations grammaticalisées dans les GN français. *Langue française* 122: 101–125.

De Mulder, Walter & Lamiroy, Béatrice. 2012. Gradualness of grammaticalization in Romance. The position of French, Spanish and Italian. In: Davidse, K., Breban, T., Brems, L. & Mortelmans, T., Eds. *Grammaticalization and language change.* Amsterdam: John Benjamins, 199–227.

Ernout, Alfred & Thomas, François. 1951. *Syntaxe latine.* 2nd edition, 1972. Paris: Klincksieck.

Fagard, Benjamin. 2010. *Espace et grammaticalisation. L'évolution sémantique des prépositions dans les langues romanes.* Sarrebruck: Editions Universitaires Européennes.

Foulet, Lucien. 1965³. *Petite syntaxe de l'ancien français.* Paris: Champion.

Gamillscheg, Ernst. 1957. *Historische französische Syntax.* Tübingen: Niemeyer.

Geeraerts, Dirk. 1997. *Diachronic Prototype Semantics.* London: Clarendon Press.

Goyens, Michèle. 1994. *Émergence et évolution du syntagme nominal en français.* (*Sciences pour la communication* 43). Bern: P. Lang.

Goyens, Michèle, Lamiroy, Béatrice & Melis, Ludo. 2002. Déplacement et repositionnement de la préposition *à* en français. *Linguisticae Investigationes*, 25/2: 275–310.

Granvik, Anton. 2012. *De "de": estudio histórico-comparativo de los usos y la semántica de la preposición "de" en español.* Helsinki: Société Néophilologique.

Greenberg, Joseph H. 1963. Some universals of grammar with particular reference to the order of the meaningful elements. In: J. Greenberg Ed. *Universals of Language.* Cambridge/Ms.: MIT Press, 73–113.

Grevisse, Maurice & Goosse, André. 2008. *Le Bon Usage.* Bruxelles: Deboeck – Duculot.

Gross, Maurice. 1975. *Méthodes en Syntaxe.* Paris: Hermann.

Guillemin Anne-Marie. 1921. *La préposition 'de' dans la littérature latine et en particulier dans la prose latine de Lucrèce à Ausone.* Chalon-sur-Saone: E. Bertrand, Paris: Honoré Champion.

Haspelmath, Martin & Michaelis, Susanne. 2008. Leipzig fourmille de typologues – Genitive objects in comparison. In: Corbett, G. & Noonan, M.. Eds. *Case and Grammatical Relations.* Studies in honor of Bernard Comrie. Amsterdam: J. Benjamins, 149–166.

Heine, Bernd & Kuteva, Tania. 2002. *World Lexicon of Grammaticalization.* Cambridge: Cambridge University Press.

Heine, Bernd & Narrog, Heiko. 2010. Grammaticalization and Linguistic Analysis. In: Heine, B. & Narrog, H. Eds. *The Oxford Handbook of Linguistic Analysis.* Oxford: Oxford University Press, 401–423.

Heine, Bernd. 2002. On the role of context in grammaticalization. In: Wischer, I. & Diewald, G. Eds. *New reflections on grammaticalization.* (Typological Studies in Language, 49). Amsterdam. Benjamins, 83–101.

Herslund, Michael. 1980. *Problèmes de syntaxe de l'ancien français. Compléments datifs et génitifs.* (*Revue Romane* n° spécial 21). Akademisk Forlag.

Hettrich, Heinrich. 1990. Der Agens in passivischen Sätzen altindogermanischer Sprachen. *Akademie der Wissenschaften*. Göttingen: Vandenhoeck & Ruprecht.

Hewson, John & Bubenik, Vit. 2006. *From Case to Adposition: the Development of Configurational Syntax in Indo-European*. Amsterdam: J. Benjamins.

Holman, Robyn A. 1991. The syntax of the genitive structure in thirteenth century Vosgian charters. *Romance notes* 32/2: 141–149.

Honeste, Marie Luce. 2005. Rendons à César ... Critique de la polysémie prépositionnelle: le cas de *de*". In: P. Dendale. Ed. *Le mouvement dans la langue et la métalangue*. Metz: Université de Metz, 271–298.

Jackendoff, Ray. 1983. *Semantics and cognition*. Cambridge: MIT Press.

Jagemann, Hans C.G. von. 1884–5. On the Genitive in Old French. *Transactions of the Modern Language Association of America* I. 64–83.

Jensen, Frede. 1990. *Old French and Comparative Gallo-Romance Syntax. (Beihefte zur Zeitschrift für Romanische Philologie* 232). Tübingen: Niemeyer.

Kemmer, Suzanne & Bat-Zeev Shyldkrot, Hava. 1995. La grammaticalisation des prépositions: concurrence et substitution. *Revue romane*, 30/2: 205–226.

Kemmer, Suzanne & Bat-Zeev Shyldkrot, Hava. 1996. The semantics of "empty prepositions" in French. In: E.Casad (ed.) *Cognitive Linguistics in the Redwoods: the expansion of a new paradigm in linguistics*. Berlin: De Gruyter, 347–389.

Kilroe, Patricia. 1994. The Grammaticalization of French *à*. In: W. Pagliuca (ed.) *Perspectives on Grammaticalization*. Amsterdam: J. Benjamins, 49–61.

Kühner, Raphael & Stegmann, Carl. 1912². *Ausführliche Grammatik der lateinischen Sprache*. II. *Satzlehre*. Hannover: Hahn (Reprint 1974).

Kupferman, Lucien. 1996. Un bien grand mot: *de*. De la préposition au mode de quantification. *Langue française* 109, 3–9.

Lagae, Véronique. 1998. *Les constructions en 'de' + adjectif*. Louvain: Presses Universitaires de Louvain.

Lagae, Véronique. 2003. Quant aux livres/De livre, il n'en a lu aucun: Etude syntaxique de deux constructions détachées. *Lingvisticae investigationes* 26/2: 235–58.

Lakoff, George & Johnson, Mark. 1980. *Metaphors we live by*. Chicago: University of Chicago.

Lamiroy, Béatrice & De Mulder, Walter. 2011. Degrees of grammaticalization across languages. In: Heine, B. & Narrog, H. Eds. *Handbook of Grammaticalization*. Oxford: Oxford University Press. Chapter 24, 302–318.

Langacker, Ronald W. 1977. Syntactic reanalysis. In: Ch. N. Li Ed. *Mechanisms of Syntactic Change*. Austin, London: University of Texas Press, 57–139.

Langacker, Ronald W. 1987. *Foundations of Cognitive Grammar*, Volume 1, *Theoretical Prerequisites*. Stanford: Stanford University Press.

Lazard, Gilbert, 1994. *L'Actance*. Paris: Presses Universitaires de France.

Lehmann, Christian. 2002a. Latin valency in a typological perspective. In: Bolkestein, M. et al. Eds. *Theory and Description in Latin linguistics*. Amsterdam: Gieben, 183–203.

Lehmann, Christian. 2002b. *Thoughts on Grammaticalization*. 2nd revised edition. Erfurt: Seminar für Sprachwissenschaft. (on-line version).

Luraghi, Silvia. 2009. The internal structure of adpositional phrases. *In* Helmbrecht, J. et al. *Form and function in Language Research. Papers in Honour of Christian Lehmann*. Berlin: Mouton de Gruyter, 231–254.

Luraghi Silvia. forthc. Partitives and differential marking of core-arguments: a cross-linguistic survey.

Malchukov, Andrej & Spencer, Andrew. 2008. *The Oxford Handbook of Case*. Oxford: Oxford University Press.

Marchello-Nizia, Christiane. 1997. *La langue française aux XIVe et XVe siècles*. Paris: Nathan. (réimpression 2005: Armand Colin).

Marchello-Nizia, Christiane. 2006. *Le français en diachronie: douze siècles d'évolution*. Paris: Ophrys.

Martin, Fabienne. 2002. La préposition *de* du complément d'agent des verbes psychologiques causatifs: un génitif. *Scolia* 15: 57–70.

Martin, Robert & Wilmet, Marc. 1980. *Manuel du français du moyen âge. 2. Syntaxe du moyen français*. Bordeaux: Sobodi.

Matthews, Peter H. 1981. *Syntax*. Cambridge: Cambridge University Press.

Meillet, Antoine & Vendryes, Joseph. 1948² (1924¹). *Traité de grammaire comparée des langues classiques*, Paris: Honoré Champion.

Melis, Ludo. 2000. L'infinitif de narration comme prédication seconde. *Langue française* 127: 36–48.

Menge, Hermann. 2000. *Lehrbuch der lateinische Syntax und Semantik*. Darmstadt: Wissenschaftliche Buchgesellschaft.

Milner Jean-Claude. 1978. *De la syntaxe à l'interprétation*. Paris: Seuil.

Nichols, Johanna. 1986. Head-marking and dependent-marking grammar. *Language* 62: 56–119.

Palm, Lars. 1977. *La construction* li fiz le rei *et les constructions concurrentes avec* a *et de* étudiées dans des oeuvres littéraires de la seconde moitié du XIIe siècle et du premier quart du XIIIe siècle. (*Acta Universitatis Upsaliensis. Studia Romanica Upsaliensia* 17). Uppsala: Almqvist & Wiksell.

Pinkster, Harm. 1984. *Latijnse syntaxis en semantiek*. Amsterdam: B.R. Grüner.

Pinkster, Harm 1990. The development of cases and adpositions in Latin. In: Pinkster, H. & Genee, I. Eds. *Unity in Diversity*. Papers presented to Simon C. Dik on his 50th birthday. Dordrecht: Foris. 195–209.

Pinkster, Harm. 1993, Chronologie et cohérence de quelques évolutions latines et romanes. In: *XXe Congrès international de linguistique et philologie romanes*, Vol. III, Section IV – *Typologie des langues romanes*, 239–250.

Pope, Mildred K. 1952² (1934¹). *From Latin to Modern French, with especial consideration of Anglo-Norman. Phonology and Morphology*. (*Publications of the University of Manchester* 229, French Series VI). London: Manchester University Press.

Prévost, Sophie. 2003. Détachement et topicalisation: des niveaux d'analyse différents. *Cahiers de Praxématique* 40: 97–126.

Ruwet, Nicolas. 1982. *Grammaire des insultes et autres études*. Paris: Seuil.

Salkoff, Morris. 1983. Bees are swarming in the garden: a systematic study of productivity. *Language* 59, 2: 288–346.

Sävborg, Torsten. 1941. *Etude sur le rôle de la préposition "de" dans les expressions de lieu relatives en latin vulgaire et en ancien gallo-roman*. PhD Thesis, Uppsala.

Schøsler, Lene. 1984. *La déclinaison bicasuelle de l'ancien français. Son rôle dans la syntaxe de la phrase, les causes de sa disparition*. (*Etudes romanes de l'Université d'Odense* 19). Odense: University Press.

Schøsler, Lene. 2008. Argument marking from Latin to Modern Romance languages: an illustration of 'combined grammaticalisation processes'. In: Thórhallur Eythórsson Ed. *Grammatical Change and Linguistic Theory. The Rosendal Papers*. Amsterdam: Benjamins, 411–438.

Serbat, Guy. 1996. *Grammaire fondamentale du latin*. Tome VI. *L'emploi des cas en latin*. Vol. 1: *Nominatif, Vocatif, Accusatif, Génitif, Datif*. (*Bibliothèque d'études classiques*). Leuven, Paris: Peeters.

Spang-Hanssen, Ebbe. 1963. *Les prépositions incolores du français moderne*. Copenhague: Gads Verlag.

Svorou, Soteria. 2010. Relational Constructions in Cognitive Linguistics. In: D. Geeraerts and H. Cuyckens. Eds. *The Oxford Handbook of Cognitive Linguistics*. Oxford: Oxford UP.

Talmy, Leonard. 1975. Semantics and syntax of motion. In: J. P. Kimball Ed. *Syntax and Semantics*, vol. 4. London: Academic Press, 181–238.

Talmy, Leonard. 2000. *Toward a Cognitive Semantics*. Cambridge: MIT Press.

Traugott, Elizabeth Closs & Dasher, Richard B. 2002. *Regularity in Semantic Change*. (*Cambridge Studies in Linguistics* 97). Cambridge: Cambridge University Press.

Väänänen, Veikko. 1981. La préposition latine *de* et le génitif. *Recherches et récréations latino-romanes*. Napoli. Bibliopolis.

Vincent, Nigel. 1999. The evolution of c-structure: prepositions and PPs from Indo-European to Romance. *Linguistics* 37: 1111–1153.

Westholm, Alfred. 1899. *Etude historique sur la construction du type 'li filz le rei' en français*. PhD Thesis, Uppsala.

Zink, Gaston. 1990. *Le moyen français (XIVe et XVe siècles)*. Paris: Presses Universitaires de France.

Endnotes

1.   Clitics, however, show a formal variation according to their syntactic function.

2.   Cf. amongst others Kühner & Stegmann (1912[2]: § 82), Ernout & Thomas (1951: § 52), Pinkster (1984: 50) and Serbat (1996: 253).

3.   Although the notions of 'inclusion' and 'extraction' can seem contradictory at first sight, they are similar insofar as they both involve the part-whole relationship (Serbat 1996: 424).

4.   In their study devoted to the contrast between the prepositions *à* 'to' and *de* 'of', Kemmer & Bat-Zeev Shyldkrot (1995, 1996) at first sight take the opposite viewpoint: according to these authors, the use of the preposition *de* has always a semantic motivation, both in a synchronic and a diachronic perspective. The meaning of *de* is nevertheless a very subtle one. They argue that *de* expresses an abstract-schematic relationship: it is used to make explicit an "intrinsic relationship" when no other more specific relationship is relevant. We consider that the option of defining *de* as having this abstract relational meaning rather than analyzing it as a marker of a purely syntactic relationship is based on a theoretical choice rather than on empirical evidence.

5.   We adopt the Leipzig Glossing Rules for the interlinear glosses.

6.   For the preposition *de*, the adverbial use is still attested in the expression *susque deque* 'both up and down, with indifference' especially with the verbs *habere, ferre* (e.g. Plautus *Amphitryon* 3, 2, 5; Cicero *Att*. 14, 6, 1).

7.   As we will see in § 4., Modern French shows a similar phenomenon: when the noun refers to places stereotypically associated with a regular activity, the conservative structure is still in use.

8. Guillemin (1921) offers a detailed typology of the uses of *de* in Classical Latin and in Late Latin until the 4th C. Clairin (1880) describes the evolution of the genitive and the preposition from Latin to French. See also the excellent overview of Väänänen (1981).

9. The inverse direction is also attested. Witness examples like *Time will come when there are no more typewriters. The deadline is approaching.* Cf. Lakoff & Johnson (1980: 143).

10. Titus Maccius Plautus (c. 254–184 BC) is a comic playwright, known for his colloquial style.

11. Given the dominant OV order in Latin, adpositions would be expected to be postpositional (Greenberg 1963). On the basis of this observation, Bauer (1995) argues that the few instances of postpositions (examples (59–62)) are traces of an archaic language stage, where postpositions rather than prepositions were normal. In accordance with Meillet & Vendryes (1924) and Vincent (1999), we do not assume an earlier stage of postpositions but rather a stage of adverb-like expressions that can figure in different positions (cf. § 2.1.).

12. For the case system in Old French and its further evolution, see, for instance, Pope (1952²: §806), Schøsler (1984), Buridant (2000: §§36–52), Marchello-Nizia (2006: 82–90).

13. The evolution of *de* from Latin to French has been studied by several authors, a.o. Jagemann (1884–5), who focuses on the situation in Old French from the point of view of the values of the Latin genitive (*genitivus subjectivus, objectivus, qualitatis,* etc.) and the Latin ablative. In his study of the relationship in Latin between the genitive and the preposition *de*, Väänänen (1981: 104–107) analyzes the outcomes in French from the point of view of the possessive meaning. For Old French, see especially Buridant (2000: §376ff.), who gives an excellent overview of the different values of *de* in this stage of the language. For Middle French, see Martin & Wilmet (1980: §246ff., 303) and Marchello-Nizia (1997: 341ff.).

14. With respect to the two-case system of Old French, the oblique case is considered as the unmarked case. Hence, it will not be indicated in the interlinear glosses.

15. This example could be analyzed as an elliptic construction such as "Dure cose est (cose) de mariage"; in this case, the meaning of *de* is identifiable as an adnominal genitive. We thank one of the reviewers for this suggestion.

16. Regarding this "double" use of *de*, see also Sävborg (1941: for example 241ff.).

17. See above, Footnote 12.

18. Old French still has some lexicalized residues of the Latin genitive case, such as the following forms:

(i) Iovis die > *juesdi* ('Thursday')
 Veneris die > *vendresdi* ('Friday')

(ii) Lat. -orum > caballu mille solidorum ('a horse which is worth a thousand *sous*') > *milsoudor* ('horse of great value; warrior horse')

(iii) il est escrit en la geste *Francor* (*Chanson de Roland,* 1443)
 'it is written in the epic poem of the Franks'

As to the genitive of the pattern illustrated in (iii), it behaves as an ordinary adjective, since it agrees morphologically with the head noun, taking the plural ending -*s* (*livre-s paienour-s* / book-PL heathen-[GEN.M.PL]-PL 'books of heathens' (*Floire et Blancheflor,* 231) (Buridant 2000: § 43).

19. There is an important competition between *a* and *de* for the expression of the possessive relationship, which persists until today in popular French and in some dialects (*la fille à/de ma* *soeur* 'my sister's daughter'). For details, see Herslund (1980), Martin & Wilmet (1980: § 251) and Marchello-Nizia (2006: 81).

20.   Except for *sans* NP$_2$, which always translates a prepositional construction with *sine*.

21.   *De* can also be at the right of an adverb or preposition. In this configuration it no longer has its spatial meaning of movement away from a reference point:

> Quant il   sont   <u>hors</u> *de* la   cité
> when they be-PRS.3PL out   of the city
> 'When they are outside the city'   (Jean Renard, *Escoufle*; 13th C.)

22.   Sentences such as (142b–c) are ungrammatical in a neutral reading, but they are acceptable when the argument introduced by *de* is topicalized.

23.   The fact that *chez* occurs after *de* when it introduces human referents (rather than with in-animate referents) may be due to the fact that the preposition *chez* (etymologically derived from Latin *casa* 'house') is mainly used with animate NPs, e.g. *On a observé cela chez l'homme/chez les girafes/ *chez le plomb* 'This was observed with humans/with giraffes/*with lead.'

24.   *De là* is acceptable here as a fixed expression which indicates a logical relation between two elements, as in the following (constructed) example *De là la police a déduit qu'il était coupable* 'From this (lit.: there) the police deduced he was guilty.' The same use can be found in the conjunction *de là que*, e.g. *Il occupa ces fonctions jusqu'en avril 1897. De là que bien souvent, dès que je sus marcher, je flânai dans les couloirs et les coulisses de ce théâtre, petit garçon curieux et timide...* (Paul Léautaud, *In memoriam*, 1905, *Frantext*). 'He carried out this function until April 1897. Therefore, as a curious and shy little boy, as soon as I could walk, I often strolled in the corridors and wings of this theatre.'

25.   Gross (1975: 313ff)'s Table 8 which only represents intransitive French verbs followed by *de* + NP contains 284 verbs.

26.   The construction with *de* is also a regional variant, used in Belgian French for example.

27.   Similarly, Schøsler (1984) questions the causal relationship between erosion of the Old French two-case system, on the one hand, and the fixation of word order and the development of prepositions, on the other hand, by pointing to a redundancy between several markers of syntactic function, only one of which was case marking.

28.   Interestingly, the same observation was made regarding the evolution of Spanish *de* by Granvik (2012: 506).

The Bantu connective construction

Mark Van de Velde
LLACAN – CNRS

The Bantu equivalent of a genitive construction, a construction in which a nominal constituent modifies another one, is part of a family of constructions commonly called the *connective construction*. This paper analyses the family of Bantu connective constructions from a perspective inspired by canonical typology. I first define a canonical type and subsequently discuss departures from this type along five dimensions. The resulting picture shows a functionally extremely versatile construction type in a grammatical space that lacks clear-cut boundaries between genitives, adjectives and relative clauses. Connective constructions are a frequent source of lexicalisation, and of grammaticalisation patterns that often lead to agreement in unusual places.

1. Introduction[1]

When two nominal constituents are in a relation of dependency in the Bantu languages, the syntactically dependent constituent is usually introduced by a relator. In Bantu studies this relator is called *connective* (also *associative, genitive* or *connexive*) *element* (or *pronoun, clitic, prefix, marker* or *particle*). The order is HEAD (R1) – RELATOR (REL) – DEPENDENT (R2). R1 and R2 are short for first and second relatum. Dependency relations are not always unproblematic, as we will see in Section 5.1. The terms *relator* and *relatum* are from Dik (1989). I will use the term *connective construction* to refer to the entire construction, i.e. R1 REL R2, rather than to REL R2, as is sometimes done in the literature. A typical example is provided in (1).[2]

(1) Kagulu   (Tanzania; Petzell 2008: 86)
     m-eji   *g-a*   *mu-nyu*
     6-water VI-CON   3-salt
     R1   REL   R2
     'salt water'

This paper provides an overview of the variation in connective constructions throughout the Bantu languages. It will be shown that connectives form a category with fuzzy boundaries, for which no definition in terms of necessary and sufficient conditions can be provided. In order to deal with the variation in connective constructions I will adopt an approach inspired by canonical typology, as developed most notably by Corbett (2007). That is, I will define a canonical connective construction and then describe the formal variation found among connective constructions in terms of departures from the canon along several dimensions. Note that a canonical approach makes no claims whatsoever regarding the status of the canonical type as either being frequent or diachronically primary. The canon is simply a starting point for mapping the variation among related constructions. Section 2 introduces the canonical type. Sections 3 to 7 each discuss departures from the canon along a single dimension, viz. departures from the canonical R2 (Section 3), from the canonical connective relator (Section 4), from the canonical dependency relation (Section 5), from the canonical R1 (Section 6), and from the canonical arrangement of constituents (Section 7).

Depending on how one counts, there are between 300 and 600 Bantu languages, spoken in an area south of a line between Cameroon in the west and Kenya in the east. The internal classification of the Bantu languages is problematic, but by and large the Bantu languages can be subdivided in an eastern, a western and a north-western group. The north-western Bantu languages, spoken in Cameroon, Gabon, Equatorial Guinea, parts of the two Congos and the Central African Republic, are closest to what is generally accepted to be the Bantu homeland. Not surprisingly, linguistic fragmentation is highest in the northwest.

The typological characteristics of the Bantu languages most relevant for this chapter are their noun class system and extensive noun class agreement. Typically, Bantu languages have somewhere between ten and twenty noun classes, which are overtly marked on the noun with a prefix. The noun classes are numbered and usually come in pairs in which the odd numbered class contains the singular nouns and the even numbered class the plurals. Such noun class pairings are traditionally called *genders*. Nominal modifiers, pronominals and verbs agree in gender with nominal controllers. See Maho (1999) for an overview of Bantu noun classes and agreement.

This study is based on a convenience sample of about forty areally differentiated Bantu languages. This sample sufficed to find most, if not all, logically possible departures from the canonical type, but it does not allow us to determine how recurrent each of these departures is within the entire family.

2. The canonical connective construction

The definition of the canonical connective construction in this section is to serve as a point of reference for an overview of the variation in connective constructions within the Bantu family. The characteristics of the canonical type proposed here are based on knowledge of what is typical in the Bantu languages. In a sense, the canonical connective construction is what is the prototypical connective construction, not in the mind of the speaker of a Bantu language, but in the mind of the Bantu linguist.

The canonical connective construction relates nominal constituents headed by a canonical Bantu noun by means of an overt relator. A canonical Bantu noun can be characterized as a lexeme that can function as an argument of a lexical verb and that has a unique gender specification, i.e. that does not derive its gender marking from another element in the context. Canonically there is a uniform element that relates R1 to R2. We will call this element the *connective stem* and gloss it as CON (but if a connective relator lacks a stem, i.e. if it consists solely of an agreement marker, the agreement marker that serves as a connective relator will be glossed CON). The connective stem canonically takes a prefix (AG) that indexes R1. This prefix belongs to a paradigm called *pronominal prefixes* in Bantu studies. In Meeussen's (1967) reconstruction of Proto-Bantu grammar the connective stem is reconstructed as – ˜*a*, where the tilde symbolizes a tone that is harmonic with that of the preceding prefix. I will incorporate this form of the connective stem in the canonical construction (but without the tonal specification). The canonical form of the connective relator is thus AG-*a*. In the canonical connective construction, the connective relator is placed iconically in between R1 and R2. Since it marks R2 as being syntactically dependent on R1, it is more closely linked to R2 than to R1 and this is reflected in a relatively high degree of morphological bonding between the relator and R2. In all descriptions that I consulted and that discuss this issue explicitly, the degree of bonding between the relator and R2 is higher than that between separate words. Moreover, in the Bantu languages that have pre-head modifiers in the NP that I am aware of, the connective relator precedes the first element of R2 and therefore behaves as a phrasal affix. This is shown in the example from Songye in (2).

(2) Songye   (DRC; Stappers 1964: 81)
  ba-ntu b-aá=[ky-ǎbu   kí-pîndi]
  2-people II-CON=VII-their 7-neighbourhood
  'the people of their neighborhood'

Due to the strong phonological integration between the connective relator and the following word, the relator is not analyzed as a separate word in Stappers (1964). In many of the languages in my sample, the degree of bonding between REL and R2 can be described as intermediate between that of a word boundary and that of an affix boundary. Therefore, typically, the Bantu connective relator is a proclitic and I will integrate this formal characteristic in the canonical type used in this study.

Semantically, some further characteristics of the canonical construction are that R2 modifies R1 and that the two nominal constituents are not co-referential.

The connective construction is not dedicated to the expression of a specific relation. The examples in (3–8) illustrate equally typical uses of the canonical connective construction. In (3) and (4) the connective construction is used to express linguistic possession. That is, the number of potential referents of R1 is restricted to those that have a privileged relationship with the (prototypically human) individual denoted by R2.

(3)   Kinyamwezi   (Tanzania; Maganga and Schadeberg 1992: 89)[3]
      m̂-zuna   w-aa-m̂-kɪíma
      1-younger_sister I-CON-1-woman
      'the younger sister of the woman'

(4)   Swahili   (Tanzania; Hawkinson 1979: 86)
      ni-li-tafuta   zawadi   y-a=m-toto
      1SG-PST-seek [9]present IX-CON=1-child
      'I sought a present to give to the child.' (recipient)
      'I sought a present on behalf of the child.' (benefit)
      'I sought the child's present (i.e. that he misplaced).' (ownership)

R2 frequently qualifies (5–6) or classifies (7) R1, or locates it in space or time (8). Note that the head noun of R2 can be property denoting (5) or entity denoting (6) in a qualifying canonical connective construction.

(5)   Mongo   (DRC; Hulstaert 1966: 246)
      ntando ěy=o-lindó
      [9]river IX.CON=3-depth
      'a deep river'

(6)   Mongo   (Hulstaert 1966: 247)
      e-kútu   ě-a=n-dɔsɔ́
      7-calabash VII-CON=10-pores
      'a porous calabash'

(7)   Swahili   (Welmers 1963: 433)
      nyumba   z-a=ma-we
      [10]houses X-CON=6-stones
      'houses made of stone'

(8)   Mongo   (Hulstaert 1966: 255)
      m-pótá ě-a=lo-kolo
      9-injury IX-CON=11-foot
      'a foot injury'

3.   Departures from the canonical R2

This section discusses departures from the canonical R2. The two departures discussed first involve an R2 that has formal characteristics of an adjective (Section 3.1) and a verb (Section 3.2). These departures move gradually from almost canonical connective constructions to typical adjectival and relative constructions respectively. It will be shown that any clear cut-off point between connective constructions on the one hand and adjectival and relative constructions on the other hand is arbitrary. Section 3.3 deals with possessive pronouns, which are often connective constructions with a pronominal R2, if not synchronically, then historically. Section 3.4, finally, provides a brief overview of miscellaneous departures in which the R2 position is occupied by members of minor word classes.

3.1   R2 has adjectival features

Morphosyntactic departures from the canonical R2 will be increasingly important as we move through this section. In (5) we saw an example of a qualifying canonical connective construction, in which R2 is a canonical noun that denotes a quality. A first departure from this situation is illustrated in (9), where R2 has the morphological properties of a noun, but the distributional potential of an adjective. In contrast to canonical adjectives in Makwe, which "agree in class with the noun on which they syntactically depend" (Devos 2008: 115), the word *kibúúli* 'silent' is inherently of class 7. In contrast to canonical nouns, *kibúúli* cannot be used as the head of a referential phrase. It occurs only as R2 in a connective construction or as a predicate following a copula. Moreover, it does not have a morphological plural (Maud Devos, p.c.).

> (9)   Makwe   (Mozambique; Devos 2008: 136)
>   muú-nu   w-á=ki-búúli
>   1-person I-CON=7-silent
>   'a silent person'

Hulstaert's Mongo grammar (1966: 30–32) distinguishes three types of quality-denoting R2s that do not agree in gender. The first type are those that do not agree with R1 at all, they always appear in the singular. This type includes words for 'black', 'white', 'careful' and 'respectful'.

> (10)   Mongo   (Hulstaert 1966: 32)
>   bi-longi by-ǎ=w-ĭlo
>   8-faces   VIII-CON=3-dark/black_color
>   'black faces'

The second and third type illustrate a further departure from the canon, in that the number of R2 depends on that of R1. R2 always agrees in number in the second type (11). Nouns that do not denote a quality, strictly speaking, but rather an entity defined by a quality, are always of the second type (12).

> (11)   Mongo   (Hulstaert 1957: 1176 (a) & 1966: 30 (b))
>   a.   bo-nto   o-ǎ=li-nsimí
>   1-person I-CON=5-taciturn
>   'a taciturn person'
>
>   b.   ba-nto   b-ǎ=ba-nsimí
>   2-persons II-CON=6-taciturn
>   'taciturn persons'

(12) a. ba-álí b'=â-fokú
2-wife II.CON=6-beautiful_women
'beautiful wives' (lì-fòkú 'beautiful woman' (cl.5))

b. bà-ékòlì b-ǎ=bi-séngà
2-pupil II.CON=8-stupid_persons
'stupid pupils' (è-séngà 'stupid person' (cl.7))

In the third type, a plural R1 licenses, but does not require a plural R2. A plural R2 has a distributive meaning in this case.

(13) Mongo   (Hulstaert 1966: 31)
a. ntɛkɛ   y-ǎ=bo-salangano
[10]parties x-CON=3-cheerful
'cheerful parties' (for one person or one occasion)

b. ntɛkɛ   y'=ê-salangano
[10]parties x.CON=4-cheerful
'cheerful parties' (for several occasions)

(14) a. b-ámàtò b'=ô-tsélé
2-women II.CON=3-implacable
'women relentless at quarrel' (in group)

b. b-ámato b'=ê-tsélé
2-women II.CON=4-implacable
'women relentless at quarrel' (considered individually)

When R2 also agrees in gender, the resulting construction could be characterized as a connective construction with an adjective in R2 position. R2 is doubly marked for the function of modification: by means of an agreement prefix and by means of the (equally agreeing) connective relator. This type of construction can be found in Koongo of Boko (15).

(15) Koongo of Boko   (Congo; Bouka 1994: 14)
a. di-nkondi di-a=di-nené
5-banana   V-CON=V-big
'a big banana'

b. bw-atu   bw-a=bu-nené
14-canoe   XIV-CON=XIV-big
'a big canoe'

c. m-atu   m-a=ma-nené
6-canoes   VI-CON=VI-big
'big canoes'

In some other varieties of the Koongo dialect cluster the same quality denoting lexemes can be employed in two different constructions with the same meaning, but possibly different pragmatics (Bouka does not provide any information on this). Both construction types involve a connective relator, but in only one of them does R2 have an agreeing prefix (16a). In the other type of connective construction R2 is invariant (16b).

(16) Suundi   (Congo; Bouka 1994: 16)[4]
    a. ki-salu ky-a=kí-kèèke 'a small job'
       bi-salu by-a=bí-kèèke 'small jobs'
       zi-ngasi z-a=zí-kèèke 'small palm nuts'
    b. ki-salu ky-á=n-kèèke 'a small job'
       bi-salu by-á=n-kèèke 'small jobs'
       zi-ngasi z-á=n-kèèke 'small palm nuts'

The presence of the connective relator can be optional too. This is the case in Bakueri, also known as *Kpe* or *Mokpwe* (17). Since I found no other examples than the one in (17), it is impossible to know whether R2 should be analyzed as a class 9 noun or as an agreeing adjective.

(17) Bakueri   (Cameroon; Kagaya 1992: 12, 16, 151)
    a. mgbá   y-a=ndɛ́nɛ
       [9]dog IX-CON=[9]big
       'a big dog'
    b. mgbâ   ndɛ́nɛ
       [9]dog IX.big
       'a big dog'

In Lingala of Kinshasa the use of the invariant connective relator *ya* (historically agreement pattern IX) is optional for a closed class of quality-denoting lexemes when they modify a noun. These lexemes never agree in gender with the head noun and only four or five of them agree in number. According to Michael Meeuwis (p.c.) the presence versus absence of CON marks a subtle pragmatic difference in that the connective relator tends to be used when the head noun is topical (and the qualification new), whereas the absence of CON correlates with a non-topical nominal constituent. Hulstaert (1966: 291) describes a similar distinction for a number of qualifying nouns in Mongo.

(18) Lingala   (DRC; Meeuwis 1998: 15; p.c.)
    lo-pángo   (ya=)mo-ké
    11-compound (CON=)3-small
    'a small compound'

We will come back to connective constructions with a property-denoting modifying noun in Section 5.1, which discusses dependency reversal.

3.2   R2 has verbal characteristics

This section provides a brief overview of connective constructions in which R2 has verbal characteristics. Thus, it explores the grammatical space in between the canonical connective construction and typical relative constructions. In the simplest case, R2 is a non-finite verb form consisting of a verb stem and a nominal prefix, such as the infinitive, which in many languages has a prefix of class 15, or the non finite verb form called *gerund* (*gérondif*) in Hulstaert (1966), illustrated in example (19). In the canonical case the verb stem denotes an event (19), but often it denotes a property, so that an infinitival R2 can have adjectival characteristics (21). Note in passing the difference in coordinating multiple R2s between (19b) and (20). The connective relator is repeated in the latter, not in the former.

(19)   Mongo   (Hulstaert 1966: 251)
    a.   i-síni   y-ǎ=n-kɔ̌~kɔt-a
         19-machine XIX-CON=9-GER~write-FV
         'writing machine'

    b.   ba-éfa b-ǎ=n-kǐ~kis-a   la   m-bétám-á
         6-days VI-CON=9-GER~sit-FV and 9-lie-FV
         'days off' (lit. 'days of sitting and lying down')

    c.   b-ɔlɔ́tsi   w-ǎ=n-dekól-á
         3-goodness III-CON=9-surpass-FV
         'really very good' (lit. 'goodness of to surpass')

(20)   Ruwund   (DRC; Nash 1992: 369)
      mà-d   ma-kùnd m-à=ku-kùn   âap m-à=ku-dà?
      VI-COP 6-beans VI-CON=15-plant or   VI-CON=15-eat
      'Are they beans to plant or to eat?'

(21)   Makwe   (Devos 2008: 136)
      muú-nu w-á=ku-dóóba
      1-person I-CON=15-be_lazy
      'a lazy person'

Bantu infinitives can be expanded in many ways that make them more typically verbal (see Hadermann 1994 for an overview), and all kinds of expanded infinitives can be found in the R2 position of connective constructions. In the following Ruwund examples the infinitive has an object (22) or a subject (23).

(22)   Ruwund   (Nash 1992: 367)
    a.   m-es   m-à=kù-tekàp   ordinateur
         6-table VI-CON=15-put computer
         'computer table' (lit. 'table of to put computer')

b. mi-jik   y-à=kù-sangar-esh   a-ntu
4-music IV-CON=15-rejoice-CAUS 2-people
'music to make people happy'

(23) Ruwund   (Nash 1992: 370)
tu-kìmb-in   n-dônd y-à=kù-laal   mw-ânt
1pl-search-PRS.PROG 9-place IX-CON=15-sleep 1-chief
'We are looking for a place for the chief to sleep.'

In (24) the R2 position is occupied by an infinitive that has more verbal properties in that it has passive morphology and is preceded by the negative adverb *bílá*.

(24) Makwe   (Devos 2008: 405)
ǹ-táama   w-á=bílá   ku-kálángí-iw-a
3-sorghum III-CON=NEG 15-fry-PASS-FV
'sorghum that has not been fried'

R2 is more typically verbal (and the resulting construction more typically relative) if it is finite, i.e. when it has a subject prefix. The example in (25) is from Makwe, where the subject prefix is preceded by a connective relator in all non-subject relatives.[5]

(25) Makwe   (Devos 2008: 394)
vií-nu   vy-á=á-yúm-íite
8-thing VIII-CON=I-buy-PRS.PFV.REL
'the things that he has bought'

If the non-subject relative clause has a nominal subject, this follows the verb form in Makwe (26). In Konzo, the nominal subject is in its usual preverbal position, preceded by the connective relator (27).[6]

(26) Makwe   (Devos 2008: 396)
ku-nyéenje k-a=jí-péele   ji-ng'úúnde
17-side   XVII-CON=X-grow.PRS.PFV.REL 10-bean
'at the side where the beans grow'

(27) Konzo   (Uganda; Tucker 1960: 27)
o-mu-ndú   e-y-a=a-ba-ndú   bá-lángíra
AU-1-person AU-I-CON=AU-2-people II-saw
'the person whom the people saw'

The connective relator can also introduce a clause that functions as a complement or an adjunct of a noun and that often cannot be analyzed as a relative clause, since the antecedent (R1) does not necessarily have a role in it (28a, b). The clause in R2 position can be complex (28c, d). In (28b), the connective relator is followed by an optional subordinating conjunction.

(28) Mongo   (Hulstaert 1946 (a,b) 1966: 278 (c,d))

a. ts-ók-a   ɛɛfɛ́   é-â=w-ăné   w-ăné tɔ-tá-l-á   y-ŏmba
    1PL-feel-FV   [7]pain   VII-CON=3-day   3-day 1PL-COND-eat-FV   19-thing
    'We suffer because we haven't eaten anything all day long.'
    (lit. 'we feel pain of day day we didn't eat thing')

b. bo-tsó   bó-ki   w-ílima   w-ǎ=(te)   á-ongan-e nkɔlɛ
    3-night III-COP.PST 3-darkness   III-CON=(SUB)   I-hurt-SBJV [9]injury
    'The night was so dark that he hurt himself.'

c. ba-nto   bǎ=mpángá ba-kit-áká   ko bǎol-ékel-á
    2-people II-CON=next II-arrive-RPST and II.HPST-accustom-FV
    ba-móng'ése
    2-native
    '(foreign/European) men who adapt easily to native customs' (lit. 'men of
    they-have-hardly-arrived-and-they-are-already-accustomed-to-the-
    natives')

d. bo-támbá w-ǎ=ngá   w-ô-tumb-a   bó-fó-longól-é
    3-tree   III-CON=if 2SG-III-set_fire-FV III-PRS.NEG-burn-FV
    'a tree that does not burn if you set fire to it'

Finally, in a rather idiosyncratic departure from the canon, Mongo has a connective
construction in which R2 consists of a fully reduplicated verb stem that characterizes
R1 in terms of an action that is either repeated or futile.

(29) Mongo   (Hulstaert 1966: 256)

a. bo-támbá w-ǎ=kɔtá   kɔtá
    3-tree   III-CON=cut cut
    'a tree impossible to cut down'

b. bɔ-lɔkɔ́ w-ǎ=sangá   sangá
    3-speech III-CON=talk talk
    'an endless speech'

3.3   R2 is pronominal

Possessive pronouns often originate in a connective construction in which R2 is a pronoun. This origin is fully transparent in some Bantu languages, but has become opaque
in many others, to the extent that sometimes a connective origin cannot be demonstrated. A consequence of the connective origin of possessive pronouns is that they
index both the possessor and the possessed. In other words, they agree with two controllers. The canonical paradigm of possessive pronouns has a form for every possible
combination of possessor and possessed. The Namibian Bantu language Herero provides an example of this canonical situation. It has eighteen noun classes, which can
each control R1 and/or R2. This produces a paradigm of 18 x 22 = 396 forms (22, since

the discourse participants can occur in R2 position too). Examples of possessive pronouns with two non-human controllers are given in (30). The possessive pronouns in
this example are glossed as connective constructions (AG-CON-AG-PPR). Elsewhere I will
gloss them as AG-POS, without making explicit their internal morphological structure.

(30)　Herero　　　　　　　　　　　　　　　　　(Namibia; Möhlig et.al. 2002: 60)
　　　a.　òmù-tí n-òví-yàò　　vy-á-⤓w-ó
　　　　　3-tree　and-8-leaves VIII-CON-III-PPR
　　　　　'the tree and its leaves'

　　　b.　òtjì-kúnìnò n-òmí-tí　　vy-á-⤓ty-ó
　　　　　7-garden　　and-4-trees IV-CON-VII-PPR
　　　　　'the garden and its trees'

There are at least three ways in which paradigms of possessive pronouns can depart
from regular connective constructions with a pronominal R2. First, the connective
relator used in the possessive pronoun can differ from that used in connective constructions with a nominal R2. For instance, in the north-western Mongo dialects the
connective stem is *-ka* when R2 is pronominal and *-a* elsewhere. Second, frequency of
use can lead to a stronger morphological integration of CON and a pronominal R2,
often accompanied by reduction and idiosyncratic phonological changes. Third, in
many languages the paradigm of possessive pronouns is reduced, often to six stems:
two (singular and plural) for each discourse participant and two for the third person,
as in the Kagulu paradigm reproduced in Table 1 (Petzell 2008: 87).

3.4　Miscellaneous other departures

So far we have seen departures from the canonical R2 in the direction of adjectives and
verbs, as well as pronominal R2s. It turns out that many other types of elements can
occur in R2 position too. What follows is a brief enumeration.

　　In the majority of Bantu languages, ordinal numbers are introduced by the connective relator (Bynon-Polak 1965: 134).

(31)　Eton　　　　　　　　　　　　　　　(Cameroon; Van de Velde 2008: 182)
　　　lèwòl lé ⤓báà
　　　|lə̀-wòl lə́=bǎà|
　　　5-hour v.CON=second
　　　'the second hour'

Table 1. Kagulu possessive pronouns

1SG	-angu	1PL	-etu
2SG	-ako	2PL	-enu
3SG	-agwe	3PL	-ao

Another recurrent departure from the canon is with R2 as a locative noun, derived from another noun by means of a locative prefix. In the following Ruwund examples the class 18 nominal prefix *mù-* is a locative marker.

(32)   Ruwund   (Nash 1992: 357)
    a.   ci-kùmbu c-à=mù-Zaïre
        7-house   VII-CON=18-Zaire
        'Zairian house' (lit. 'house of in Zaire')

    b.   yi-twaamu y-à=mu-ci-kùmbu
        8-chairs   VIII-CON=18-7-house
        'house chairs' (lit. 'chairs of in the house')

R2 is an ideophone in (33) and a prepositional phrase in (34–35). Cardinal numbers too are construed as R2 in a connective construction in Bafia (34).

(33)   Mongo   (Hulstaert 1966: 246)
    ba-úta b-ǎ   sɛ́njɛlɛ
    6-oil   VI-CON pure
    'pure oil'

(34)   Bafia   (Cameroon; Guarisma 2000: 208)
    ɓʌ-yíp   ɓʌ=↓ɓɛ̀ɛ̀   ɓʌ=á   bɛ̀y
    2-women   II.CON=two II.CON=LOC [9]past
    'the two women of before'

(35)   Mongo   (Hulstaert 1966: 270)
    bo-búngá w-ǎ=la   j-ángo
    3-error   III-CON=with 5-plan
    'an intentional error'

4.   Departures from the canonical connective relator

There is considerable variation in the form of the connective relator. Some of this variation is unconditioned, i.e. a number of languages and dialects have a single connective relator that deviates from the canonical Bantu AG-*a* form. Other languages have several connective relators, the choice of which can be conditioned by factors such as prosody, morphological and/or pragmatic-semantic characteristics of R1 and/or R2, the type of relation between R1 and R2 and/or tense. This section provides an overview, starting with examples of unconditioned variants of AG-*a* (4.1), followed by some types of conditioned variation (4.2–4.4).

4.1   Unconditioned variants

In many north-western Bantu languages, such as Eton, Basaa and Bafia, the connective relator has no stem. It consists solely of an agreement marker, which does not necessarily correspond to an agreement prefix used in other modifiers or pronouns. Sometimes the form of this connective relator is similar or identical to a demonstrative, e.g. in Basaa (Hyman 2003: 266).

In languages where the connective relator does have a stem, this is not always -*a*. Thus, some northern dialects of Mongo have a connective stem *'-ká* rather than -*a*. This variant is found in literary registers in the other dialects, where it also serves in the formation of the possessive pronoun (see Section 3, Hulstaert 1965: 171). Another, more frequent, alternative for -*a* as the only connective stem in Mongo dialects is -*na* or -*nda* (Hulstaert 1993: 336). Some languages have an AG-V relator, where the stem is a vowel other than *a*. This is the case for Bodo (D332), where the connective stem is -*o* (Asangama 1983: 253). Interestingly, the Bodo reflex of the Proto-Bantu comitative relator **na* (Meeussen 1967: 115) 'and, with' is *no* (Asangama 1983: 399). In languages where the stem of the connective relator is a vowel other than *a*, this vowel may be a trace of the pre-prefix or augment of R2 (Nzang Bie 1995: 50–53). The augment is a prefix found in many Bantu languages, whose function differs from language to language. Often it can be characterized as what Greenberg (1978) calls a stage 2 or non-generic article, i.e. a further development of a definite (stage 1) article, in that its use has been generalized to most contexts, excluding generic utterances and inherently definite nominals such as proper names.

In Kol (Cameroon), we find a peculiar departure from the canonical AG- in the connective relator. One of the three different series of connective relators, the so-called "qualificative associative", has the canonical connective stem -*a* (Henson 2007: 114), but this stem is preceded by a paradigm of agreement prefixes that usually appears before consonant initial stems, which may point to a -C*a* (possibly -*na*) origin of the stem.

4.2 "Amplexives"

A well known example (Welmers 1963, Güldemann 1999) of conditioned variation in the form of the connective relator is that in which the AG-*a* connective is followed or replaced by a so-called amplexive morpheme, often *ka* or *kwa* (but many other forms can be found throughout Bantu), when R2 belongs to class 1a.[7] Class 1a usually contains proper names, kinship terms, borrowings and some other nouns. These nouns lack a class prefix and/or an augment and trigger class 1 agreement. Usually class 1a is analyzed as a subclass of class 1, but see Van de Velde (2006) for an alternative analysis that argues that these nouns lack a gender specification.

In Zulu, for instance, the amplexive *ka* replaces the connective stem *a*. Moreover, it is preceded by the subject agreement prefix, rather than by the so-called pronominal prefix. According to Doke (1997: 120), the *ka*-relator appears before class 1a nouns, obligatorily when they have animate reference (37), optionally when they do not (38). Example (36) illustrates the default connective relator before an animate R2 that does not belong to class 1a.

(36) Zulu   (South Africa; Doke 1997: 120)
      i-zi-hlalo   z-o=m-lungu
      AU-10-chairs X-CON.1.AU=1-white_man
      'the white man's chairs'

(37) i-zi-hlalo   zi-ka=baba
      10.AU-10-chairs X-CON=father
      'father's chairs'

(38) a. u-bu-khulu   bu-ka=tamatisi
          14.AU-14-size XIV-CON=tomato
          'the size of the tomato'

      b. u-bu-khulu   bo=tamatisi
          14.AU-14-size XIV.CON=tomato
          'the size of the tomato'

Apparently, animacy is not the only relevant factor for the obligatory use of the *ka*-connective, since Doke points out that names of coins, such as *umpondwe, usheleni, umfagolweni* and *uzuka* "take only the construction with -*ka*" (1997: 120). This may mean that the *ka*-connective is obligatory if R2 is a class 1a proper name (or kinship term) and that names for different types of coins are construed as proper names in this construction. Several hypotheses concerning the origin of *ka* have been put forward: a contraction of the connective relator *kwa*, which contains the locative class 17 agreement prefix *ku*- (Van Eeden 1956), a reflex of a proto-Niger-Congo connective stem **ka* (Welmers 1963), a reflex of the often diminutive class 12 prefix *ka*-, a grammaticalization of the Proto-Bantu noun **ka* 'wife' (Bosch 1997), and finally an origin in a Southern Bantu locative prefix *ka*- (Güldemann 1999).

Specific connective relators for an R2 belonging to class 1a do not always involve an amplexive morpheme. In Oshindonga the connective relator is AG-*a* before a class 1a noun and AG elsewhere (Fivaz 1986: 85).[8]

4.3   Different relators for different relations

The choice between multiple connective relators can be conditioned by the function of the modifier, i.e. whether CON R2 classifies, qualifies, quantifies or anchors R1. Thus, the north-western Bantu language Kol has three paradigms of connective relators (Henson 2007: 113). The connective relator that Henson calls *basic* consists of AG (^{H} in class 3, Ø in classes 1, 9 and 10). The connective relator called *possessive* consists of the stem *mə̀*, preceded by a floating high tone in classes 2–8. Finally, there is a nearly canonical AG-*a* relator (see 4.1) called *qualificative*. Henson's description does not make clear how these connectives differ from each other functionally, and the descriptive labels are not very revealing of their function. Nevertheless, it seems clear that the choice for one of the three types of connective construction in Kol depends on the nature of the relation expressed by the connective.

There are several cases in which a non-canonical relator is used to mark a (type of) possessive relation, as defined in Section 2, while a canonical relator is used for any other relation. For instance, several Mongo dialects have more than one connective stem, usually *-a* and another one, viz. *-ná, -ká, -áká, -náká, -ánáká* or *ˇ-lĕka*. In these variants the *-a* connective tends to be the more general one, whereas the other stem usually expresses possession or some kind of focus on R2 (Hulstaert 1993). The exact functional difference between the two connective relators is not always clear. The following examples (39–40) are from the Bombwanja dialect (Hulstaert 1965: 172).

(39) m-pɔ́ngɔ y-á=n-sombo
     9-fat   IX-CON=9-pig
     'pork fat'

(40) m-pɔ́ngɔ i-ná   n-sombo
     9-fat   IX-CON 9-pig
     'the fat of the pig'

The connective relator *ˇ-lĕka* historically derives from a relative form of the copula *le* 'be' followed by the preposition *ĕka* 'at (somebody's place)'.[9] It is used to express ownership (and contrastive focus on the owner). Consequently, R2 must have human reference.

(41) Mongo   (Hulstaert 1965: 178)
     a. w-áto   bŏ-lĕka Mbangó
         3-canoe III-CON Mbango
         'Mbango's canoe (not sb. else's)'
     b. bi-tóo   bĭ-lĕka wê
         8-clothes VIII-CON 2SG
         'your own clothes'

In Makwe, if R2 is human and singular, i.e. if it is a prototypical possessor, the connective relator takes the form of a possessive pronoun (42a). The canonical connective relator cannot be used (42b).[10]

(42) Makwe   (Devos 2008: 136)
     a. ki-táabu c-áke=mw-áana
         7-book VII-I.POS=1-child
         'The book of the child.'
     b. *ki-táabu c-á=mw-áana
         7-book VII-CON=1-child

There is prosodic evidence for the claim that the possessive pronoun functions as a relator in this construction. Devos (2008: 136) points out that "[w]hereas the possessive [pronoun] normally occurs in a single phonological phrase with the possessed it now occurs in a single phonological phrase with the possessor, the possessed forming a phonological phrase on its own." The possessive pronoun can also have a specific tone pattern and some phonological reduction in the construction exemplified in (42a). Compare (42a) to (43). In (43) the possessive pronoun has phrase final penultimate lengthening, not R1. In (42a) it is the other way around.

(43)   ki-tabú cáa-ke (mw-áana) 'his/her book, (the child's)'

Similar constructions can be found in other Bantu languages (46–47), where the exact conditions for its use may differ. Petzell (2008) does not discuss the Kagulu construction in example (44), which I found in a text, but note that R2 is human and singular, which may mean that Kagulu is similar to Makwe in this respect. In Ruwund R2 does not need to be singular and the use of a possessive pronoun relator is optional (45).

(44)   Kagulu   (Petzell 2008: 197)
     di-sina dy-akwe   mw-ana-angu
     5-name v-3SG.POS 1-child-1SG.POS
     'My child's name'

(45)   Ruwund   (Nash 1992: 364)
     ci-kùmbu c-èndaay-Yâav   / ci-kùmbu c-a-Yâav
     7-house   VII-3SG.POS-Yaav / 7-house   VII-CON-Yaav
     'Yaav's house'

4.4   Tense

In a number of Bantu languages, such as Tetela and Mongo, the connective construction has a past versus non-past tense distinction. In order to express that the (usually possessive) relation does no longer hold or that the relation between R1 and R2 is due to a past event, these languages use a relative past tense form of the copula as a connective relator (46). In this construction, the copula replaces the canonical connective relator, which is the main argument for analyzing it as a connective relator. Note in this respect that REL=R2 can follow a copula as a non-verbal predicate in Mongo, see example (78a) in Section 6.2.

(46)   Mongo   (Hulstaert 1966: 145)
     a.   li-sála lǐ-kí   ngóya
          5-field v-CON.PST my_mother
          'the field that my mother planted'

     b.   ts-ǎ   tǒ-kí   'mí
          13-fire XIII-CON.PST 1SG
          'the fire I lighted'

In their typological overview of nominal tense, Nordlinger and Sadler (2004: 781) point out that in constructions like the Bantu connective construction there are two semantic predicates with respect to which the tense marker may be interpreted: "One possibility is that the tense marker temporally locates the nominal referent itself (e.g. 'former house'). Another possibility is that the tense marker does not refer to the nominal, but rather provides the time at which the possessive relation holds (e.g. 'formerly possessed')." The interpretation of nominal tense in such constructions is ambiguous in the majority of the languages of their sample (which does not include Bantu languages). I do not have sufficient data for an analysis of the preferred interpretation of tense in Bantu connective constructions. The examples I found contain no clear illustrations of a cancelled possession interpretation. By contrast, examples (46a) and (46b) illustrate a third possible interpretation, viz. a temporal location of the establishment of the possessive relation.

5. Departures from the canonical dependency relations

5.1 Dependency reversal: R1 is the attribute

Several Bantu languages show examples of so-called dependency reversal in connective constructions, in that the morphosyntactic head (i.e. R1) modifies the morphosyntactic dependent (R2), as illustrated in the Eton examples in (60–61). Similar constructions have been identified in languages as diverse as Basque, Hausa, Latin and some Oceanic languages of northwest Melanesia (see, for instance, Malchukov 2000, Ross 1998). Within Bantu, this construction type is common only in the north-west. A short survey suggests that dependency reversal is an areal phenomenon that can be found in the core of the so-called Macro Sudan belt, comprising Nilo-Saharan, Niger-Congo and Afroasiatic languages (see Güldemann 2008). More research is needed to confirm this.

(47) Eton   (Van de Velde 2008: 218)
     ì-ŋgúŋgwál í=m-ôd
     7-miserable VII.CON=1-person
     'a miserable person'

(48) m̀-púm ndá
     3-white III.CON.[9]house
     'a white house'

R1 determines external agreement (49a), at least when agreement is syntactic. In languages that have semantic agreement, agreement will be determined by R2. In Eton, semantic agreement occurs on pronominal targets when the controller is a noun with human denotation (including personified animal characters in fairy tales), that does not belong to gender 1/2 (49b).

(49) Eton   (Van de Velde 2008: 402)
   a. dɔ́   mìŋ-kɔ́d mí=mbú   mí-↓bá mí-ŋgá-sɔ́
       then 4-skinny IV.CON=[10]dog IV-two IV-RP-come
       'Then two skinny dogs came.'

   b. bɔ́   èèy bɔ́   nâ: ["íí yɔ̂ byàkê."]
       II.SUBST with II.SUBST CMP
       'They (the dogs) said to them (the animals): ["This one (road) we will
       go."]'

Languages in which the same property noun can be construed either as R2 or as R1
may provide insight in the way dependency reversal originated. In Mongo dependency
reversal is rather rare. When it occurs, the property-denoting noun acquires an aug-
mentative reading, as seen in the examples in (50) from Hulstaert (1966: 247). Rodegem
(1970) proposes a similar analysis for some property nouns in Kirundi.

(50) a. e-sus'   é-a=n-sombo
          7-bigness VII-CON=9-wild_boar
          'a huge boar'

      b. n-sombo   ě'=e-susá
          9-wild_boar IX.CON=7-bigness
          'a big boar'

Some Mongo nouns expressing superlative qualities can only appear in R1 position in
connective constructions, e.g. ekóla 'tremendous, splendid' in (51).

(51) e-kóla   ě-a=i-lɔmbɛ
      7-tremendous VII-CON=5-house
      'a tremendous house'

Note that the dependency reversal constructions discussed here should be distinguished from binominal constructions in which R1 and R2 both refer to objects (rather
than properties), such as in English *this crook of a servant*. This type is more common
in the languages of the world and can be found throughout the Bantu family, not only
in the north-west. It departs from the canonical dependency relations too, in that R1
and R2 are co-referential (see Section 5.2). It is very frequently used to express 'male'
(R1 = 'husband'), 'female' (R1 = 'wife') or 'small/young' (R1 = 'child') (52).

(52) Eton   (Van de Velde 2008: 220)
      ɲ̀-ɲóm   mbú
      3-husband III.CON.[9]dog
      'male dog'

5.2   R1 and R2 are coreferential

Another set of connective constructions depart from the canonical construction in
that R1 and R2 are coreferential. Modification in these constructions is either restrictive

or non-restrictive, depending on the type of relata, the position of the more general term with respect to the more specific one, and the presence or absence of a connective relator. In this section, I have to rely heavily on examples found in Hulstaert's description of Mongo.

5.2.1 Non-restrictive modification

When R2 is a proper name for an individual of the category expressed by R1, the connective construction expresses the relation of 'being called'. This can be compared to prepositional constructions like *the city of London* and *the month of August* in English. As in English, the construction is used with some types of proper names (e.g. place names), not with others (e.g. personal names), where mere juxtaposition is used (see below, Section 5.2.2.).

(53) Mongo   (Hulstaert 1966: 250)

    a. i-bonga y-ǎ=Mbándáká
        5-town v-CON=Mbandaka
        'the town of Mbandaka'

    b. batswá   b'=Îkéja
        2-pygmee II.CON=Ikeja
        'Ikeja pygmies'

In languages like English, the possibility of occurring as the second member in a close appositional construction of the type *the city of London* can be used as a formal criterion for proper name status (Van Langendonck 2007: 87). In at least some Bantu languages this criterion is not valid, since we find examples of connective constructions very similar to those in (53), in which R2 can hardly be analyzed as a proper name.

(54) Orungu   (Gabon; Odette Ambouroue, p.c.)[11]

    a. òŋwáŋgà   w=ókwárà
        3.iron.tool.DEF III.CON=3.machete.INDF
        'the iron tool called/of the type *machete*'

    b. nyámà   y=ínyárè
        9.animal.DEF IX.CON=9.cow.INDF
        'the animal called/of the type *cow*'

(55) Mongo   (Hulstaert 1966: 250)
    li-kɔngá j-ǎ=bo-ntómbá
    5-lance v-CON=3-type.of.lance
    'a lance of the type *bontomba*'

I have no examples of such constructions in context and therefore do not know how they should be interpreted. They may be equivalent to the Eton construction illustrated in (56–58), where the function of the semantically redundant more general term is reminiscent of noun classifiers in some Australian languages (see Rijkhoff 2002: 74). They do differ formally, in that the more general term occupies R2 position in Eton

(Van de Velde 2008: 222), whereas R2 is occupied by the more specific term in the Orungu and Mongo examples (54–55).

(56) ὲ-yáŋ   ὲ=↓ɲɔ́y
      5-green_mamba v.con=[9]snake
      'green mamba'

(57) bé-↓té wɔ̂   yòlò   mé-↓bádná   mé=mwé
      II-PR 2SG.PPR INF-bestow LT.6-nickname VI.CON=6-name
      'They give you a nickname.'

(58) ì-sòm   í=m-úɲá
      7-toddler vii.con=1-child
      'a toddler'

Modification is necessarily non-restrictive when R1 is pronominal, especially with first and second person pronouns. The presence of a connective relator is optional in such appositive constructions with a pronominal R1. According to Hulstaert (1966: 290) the presence of a connective relator highlights the relevance of the modification.

(59) Mongo   (Hulstaert 1966: 242)
      a. emí ǒ-a=bo-laki
          I   I-CON=1-instructor
          'I, the instructor'

      b. ísó b-ǎ=tuu
          we II-CON=black
          'we, blacks'

5.2.2 Restrictive modification

In Mongo, unlike in English, the order in the appositional construction involving a place name illustrated in (67) can be reversed. The resulting construction is used to restrictively modify the place name in R1 position, for instance to distinguish places of different categories that bear the same name (60). Another type of restrictive modification of a place name can be seen in (61), where the village name *Batsina* has a fully transparent etymology in the plural noun *batsína* 'origins'. The connective construction with the basic level term 'village' in R2 position is used to disambiguate between the village name and its etymology. Note that, strictly speaking, R1 is not construed as a proper name in (60–61), but rather as a deproprial noun, i.e. a noun meaning 'individual called *x*'. See Van de Velde and Ambouroue (2011) for a discussion of the distinction between proper names and deproprial nouns in the Bantu language Orungu.

(60) Mongo   (Hulstaert 1966: 250)
      Mbándáká ěa=i-bonga
      Mbandaka IX-CON=5-town
      'Mbandaka the *town* (not the indigenous village)'

(61) Mongo   (Hulstaert 1966: 251)
      Batsína b'=ŏ-moto
      Batsina VI.CON=3-village
      'Batsina the village'

In another set of Mongo constructions, the presence of a connective relator signals restrictive modification, whereas non-restrictive modification is signaled by means of mere juxtaposition. The function of R2 in the connective construction is to disambiguate between two or more possible referents of R1.

(62) Mongo   (Hulstaert 1966: 289)
      a. n-kanga   Ikánya
         9-fetishist Ikanya
         'the fetishist Ikanya'

      b. i-kánya   y-ǎ=n-kanga
         19-Ikanya XIX-CON= 9-fetishist
         'Ikanya *the fetishist* (not another person called Ikanya)'

(63) Mongo   (Hulstaert 1966: 289)
      a. n-doí   ě-kám   bo-laki
         9-friend IX-my 1-instructor
         'my friend, the instructor'

      b. n-doí   ě-kám   ě-a=bo-laki
         9-friend IX-my IX-CON=1-instructor
         'my friend, *the instructor* (not another friend).'

Interestingly, Mongo has another means of distinguishing between a restrictive, disambiguating and a non-restrictive reading in connective constructions of the type discussed here. In (64) agreement marks the difference between the two readings. In (64b) the use of agreement pattern I signals that the agreement controller is not in need of referential disambiguation (see Van de Velde 2006). Therefore, it is non-restrictively modified by CON R2. It is not clear whether the use of alternative agreement patterns described here is restricted to personal proper names in R1 position.

(64) Mongo   (Hulstaert 1966: 7)
      a. Ilumbé   y-ǎ=bo-kúnji
         [19]Ilumbe XIX-CON=1-harpist
         'Ilumbe *the harp player* (not another person called Ilumbe)'

      b. Ilumbé   ŏ-a=bo-kúnji
         Ilumbe   I-CON=1-harpist
         'Ilumbe the harp player'

5.2.3 X1 *con* X1 '*a real X*'

In the extreme case R1 and R2 are identical, rather than merely co-referential. The non-compositional meaning of the construction is 'a real x'. I found examples in Mongo and Kinyarwanda.

(65) Mongo   (Hulstaert 1966: 257)

    a. nsósó   ĕa=nsósó
        [9]chicken IX-CON=[9]chicken
        'a real chicken (not a similar bird)'

    b. t-o-n-jél-ák-é   bo-sáánga   w'=ô-sáánga,
        PROH-2SG-1SG-bring-PF-SBJV 3-spiral_ginger III.CON=3-spiral_ginger
        o-n-jêl-ak-a   bo-sáánga   w'=ĕ-sukúlu
        2SG-1SG-bring-PF-IMP 3-spiral_ginger III.CON=7-owl(sp.)
        'Don't bring me a *Costus afer* (spiral ginger) proper, bring me one of the esukulu variety.'[12]

(66) Kinyarwanda   (Rwanda; Kimenyi 1989: 54)
    umugore nya mugore 'a real wife'
    umugabo nya umugabo 'a real man'
    umuntu nya muntu ' a real person'

The Kinyarwanda examples show a number of peculiarities not discussed by Kimenyi. First, *nya* is analyzed as a connective relator by Kimenyi, but it is not the connective form of class 1 (which is *wa*). Second, in two of the three examples the augment of R2 is dropped and third, all examples are with human nouns, which may or may not be a coincidence.

    In a rather extreme departure from the canon, Makwe has a connective construction with two identical infinitival relata. I have no data regarding this construction other than the example in (67).

(67) Makwe   (Devos 2008: 136)
    mámáá-ye   kú-m-móona kw-á=kú-m-móona ku-fúláái
    [9]mother-3SG.POS 15-I-see   XV-CON=15-I-see   15-be_happy
    'His mother became happy the very minute she saw him.'

5.3 The connective construction has a non-compositional meaning

The meaning of the canonical connective construction can normally be derived from the meaning of its constituents, R1 and R2. Semantically opaque connectives abound in the Bantu languages, however. The meaning of the entire construction can be partly (68a) or fully (68b) opaque.

(68) Eton   (personal field data)

    a. ì-só í-bégî
       |ì-só   ^H=ì-bègì|
       7-plate VII.CON=7-tear
       'breakable/porcelain plate (as opposed to the traditional wooden plate)'

    b. kpèkpàg   à=njì
       toothbrush I.CON=gorilla
       'first glass of palm wine in the morning'

Names of biological species, especially those low on the (folk) taxonomy, are often partly opaque connective constructions (69).

(69) Mongo   (Hulstaert 1966: 250)
     e-káá   ĕa=bo-ntamba
     7-anabas VII-CON=1-slave
     'mottled ctenopoma, *Anabas oxyrhynchus* (fish species)' (lit. 'Anabas of slave')

Sometimes, a non-compositional meaning is formally signaled. In Mongo, for instance, idiomatic connective constructions can have a relator that consists solely of the stem *a*, i.e. without AG (Hulstaert 1965: 173).

(70) a. ba-tói b-ǎ=njɔku
       6-ears VI-CON=[9]elephant
       'the ears of the elephant'

    b. ba-tói 'ǎ=njɔku
       6-ears CON=[9]elephant
       'mushrooms with large caps (probably a species)'

In Makwe, some semantically opaque connective constructions have a tone bridge between the first high tone of R1 and the last one of R2 (Devos 2008: 112), which points to their univerbation, since tone bridge formation is a rule that applies within the lexical domain in Makwe. However, these compounds retain morphological characteristics of full syntagms, in that the connective relator agrees in number with R1.

(71) Makwe   (Devos 2008: 112)
    a. li-kójóojo (class 5) 'sea cucumber'; luú-zi (class 11) 'thread'

    b. li-kójójó-ly-á-lúú-zi
       5-sea_cucumber-V-CON-11-thread
       'sea cucumber (sp.)'

    c. ma-kójójó-y-á-lúú-zi
       6-sea_cucumber-VI-CON-11-thread
       'sea cucumbers (sp.)'

(72) ǹ-kóngá-w-á-n-néembo
      3-trunk-III-CON-1-elephant
      'banana (sp.)'

Other semantically opaque connective constructions in Makwe have an irregular tone pattern or contain words that do not exist in isolation.

6.   Departures from the canonical R1

The connective relator marks R2 for the function of modification and it is prosodically and morphosyntactically closely linked to R2. In contrast, R1 is much less affected by the connective construction. Therefore, departures from the canonical R1 are less relevant for this overview and I will pay less attention to them. Section 6.1 provides a brief and incomplete enumeration of constructions in which R1 is not a canonical noun. The most relevant departure from the canon is that in which there is no R1, i.e. in which CON R2 is used independently, discussed in Section 6.2.

6.1   R1 is not a canonical noun

In R1 position we find more or less the same range of variation as in R2 position: infinitives, ideophones, pronominals, numbers, and so on. An infinitive R1 is illustrated in (73–74). The connective relator can introduce a diverse set of verbal complements and adjuncts, such as adverbials (73) and agents/notional subjects (74).

(73) Kete   (DRC; Kamba Muzenga 1980: 187)
      kù-cìmb kù-a=mánkâm
      15-walk XV-CON=nothing
      'a pointless walk'

(74) Shona   (Zimbabwe; Perez 1985: 120)
      kù-chémà kw-é=mw-àná
      17-cry   XVII-CON=1-child
      'the crying of the child'

In Mongo, when a gerund is followed by its object, the latter is introduced by a connective relator if and only if the gerund heads a constituent that functions as a clausal subject. In all other cases the object follows the gerund without extra marking. Hulstaert's interpretation of this is that the gerund is more nominal in character when in subject position and more verbal in other positions.

(75) Mongo   (Hulstaert 1966: 294)
      a. n-ká~kúnd-a   ě-a=b-ɔ́na [éfosóngi la wê]
          9-GER~beat-GER   IX-CON=1-child
          'Beating the child [doesn't suit you].'

b. n-ganja ě-a=n-ká~kúnd-a   b-ɔ́na
   9-stick IX-CON=9-GER~beat-GER 1-child
   'a stick for beating a child'

When R1 is a locative noun derived from a non-locative noun by means of one of the locative class prefixes, many Bantu languages allow alternative agreement patterns. That is, the connective relator can agree with the inherent noun class of R1 (76a, 77a) or with the locative class (76b, 77b).

(76) Ruwund   (Nash 1992: 357)
   a. ku-ci-kùmbu c-à=Yâav
      17-7-house   VII-CON=Yaav
      'at Yaav's house'

   b. ku-ci-kùmbu kw-à=Yâav
      17-7-house   XVII-CON=Yaav
      'at Yaav's house'

(77) Makwe   (Devos 2008: 135)
   a. pa-li-pááta   ly-á=n-náandi
      16-5-stump   V-CON=3-tree
      'at the stump of the tree'

   b. ǹ-nyúumba mw-á=íimba
      18-[9]house XVIII-CON=[1a]lion
      'in the house of the lion'

6.2   R1 is absent

In many Bantu languages the connective relator can be used pronominally. It then either agrees endo- or exophorically, or it selects a default agreement pattern. Agreement on the pronominalized connective relator is anaphoric in the Mongo examples in (78) and exophoric with an intended class 5 controller in the Ruwund example (79a). The connective relator acts as an independent pronoun in (79b), where it selects agreement pattern VII, the default pattern for the singular in Ruwund (the plural is VIII).[13]

(78) Mongo   (Hulstaert 1966: 240)
   a. b-ɔ́n'   ɔ-né á-fa   ǒ-a=bo-laki
      1-child I-this I-COP.PRS.NEG   I-CON=1-instructor
      'This child is not that of the instructor.'

   b. i-lɔmbɛ ǐ-tútsí   la y-ǎ=ntúndu
      19-house XIX.REL-be_close with XIX-CON=[9]edge
      'the house that is close to that at the edge'

   c. by-ili   ngá by'=ô-senge
      4-roots like IV.CON=3-uapaca
      'roots like those of an *Uapaca guineensis*'

(79)   Ruwund   (Nash 1992: 359)

    a.   Ni-kàt-in   d-à=Yâav
        1sG-like-prs.prog   v-con=Yaav
        'I like Yaav's.' (referring to a class 5 controller)

    b.   Tù-kwet-àp   c-à=kù-mw-ink
        1pl.neg-have-neg   vii-con=15-i-give
        'We don't have anything to give him/her.' (lit. 'We don't have of to give him.')

In such languages there can be a difference between coordinated R2s and coordinated rel=R2s, such that coordinated R2s together modify one R1 (80a), whereas coordinated rel=R2s involve different referents (80b).

(80)   Mongo   (Hulstaert 1966: 286)

    a.   i-lɔmbɛ   y-ǎ=Boliá   la   Bolínga
        19-house   xix-con=Bolia and Bolinga
        'the house of Bolia and Bolinga'

    b.   i-lɔmbɛ   y-ǎ=Boliá   la   y-ǎ=Bolínga
        19-house   xix-con=Bolia and xix-con=Bolinga
        'the house of Bolia and that of Bolinga'

If a pronominalized connective construction modifies a constituent that is itself R2 in a connective construction, the result is a succession of two connective relators (81b).

(81)   Tswana   (Botswana; Creissels 1993: 349)

    a.   m̀-híɲánà w-á=sì-lépè   s-á=mɔ̀-ńná
        3-handle iii-con=7-axe vii-con=1-man
        'the handle of the axe of the man'

    b.   m̀-híɲánà w-á=s-á=mɔ̀-ńná
        3-handle iii-con=vii-con=1-man
        'the handle of the one of the man'

We saw in Section 3.2 that the subject prefix is preceded by a connective relator in all non-subject relatives in Makwe. The antecedent of the relative clause occupies the R1 position. A headless relative clause can be formed by leaving out R1. Note that the resumptive demonstrative pronoun *kuuyá* is optional in (82) (Maud Devos, p.c.).

(82)   Makwe   (Devos 2008: 394)

    ǹ-ní-úuma   k-a=ni-li-piy-íite   kuu-yá
    1sG-prs.pfv-come_out   17-con=1sG-refl-hide-prs.pfv.rel   17-dem
    'I came out from where I was hiding.'

In languages that have an augment, this often functions as a pronominalizer when prefixed to modifiers such as the connective relator (83b).

(83) Kete (Kamba Muzenga 1980: 111, 113)

   a. o-mw-aːn   y-aː=kú-m-pal
      1.AU-1-child I-CON=17-9-face
      'the first child'

   b. ó-y-aː=kú-m-pal
      I.AU-I-CON=17-9-face
      'the first one'

(84) Bemba (Zambia/DRC; Tsibashu Balekelay 1985: 34)

   a. u-mw-ana   w-a=ma-somo
      1.AU-1-child I-CON=6-school
      'the child from school'

   b. ù-w-ǎ=ma-somo
      I.AU-I-CON=6-school
      'the one from school'

(85) Dzamba (DRC; Bokamba 1971: 224)

   o-Salomi tɛɛnɛki   o-mw-ana   w-a=m-bongo   emba, kasi
   1.AU-Sally did_not_see 1.AU-1-child I-CON=9-elephant NEG   but
   o-w-a=n-gbeya
   I.AU-I-CON=9-pig
   'Sally did not see the baby-elephant, but that of a pig.'

The combination of CON and R2 is a common source of word formation. Often the target is a (pro-)adverbial. As can be seen in (87) the agreement prefix on the connective relator is often that of the locative agreement pattern XVII (*ku-*).

(86) Mongo (Hulstaert 1966: 236)

   ǒ-a=n-sɔ́mí
   I-CON=9-first_born
   'firstborn'

(87) Makwe (Devos 2008: 135)

   a. kwa cáani 'why?'
   b. kwa úyóovi 'therefore'
   c. kwa kílá siíku 'everyday'
   d. kwa yaámbi 'as for now'
   e. kwa siíku jámbééle 'in the future'

The Ruwund interrogative pro-adverbial meaning 'what for' consists of a pronominalized connective relator followed by the interrogative 'why'. The relator agrees with the noun for the entity the purpose of which is questioned.

(88) Ruwund   (Nash 1992: 372)
   a. lêt   ci-twààmu
       bring 7-chair
       'Bring a chair!'

   b. c-áa-k
       VII-CON-why
       'What for?'

Certain patterns of lexicalization of CON R2 are so recurrent that the connective relator involved in them can be analyzed as a derivational morpheme. In Zulu, patro-
nyms are regularly derived from personal names by means of the connective relator
ka, which does not contain an overt agreement marker in agreement patterns I, III, IV,
VI and IX (89).

(89) Zulu   (Doke 1997: 119)
   a. *uNtengo kaJojo* 'Tengo, son of Jojo'
   b. *uMpande kaSenzangakhona* 'Mpande, son of Senzangakona'
   c. *wena kaJojo!* 'Thou, son of Jojo!'

In Langi, many nominals consist of a connective relator of agreement pattern VII –
apparently agreeing with the class 7 word *ki-ntʊ* 'thing' – and a full noun, e.g.
tʃaamʊtɔndɔ 'breakfast' (< *mʊtɔndɔ* 'morning', cl.9) (Dunham 2005: 114).

Pronominalized connective relators, followed or not by a fixed R2, are a very common source of closed class elements such as prepositions, subordinators and adverbs.[14]
In some cases the distinction between derivational morpheme and preposition is not
self-evident, for instance where a connective relator of a locative agreement pattern
preceding a personal noun expresses the notion of 'at somebody's place' (90–91). In
many languages locative nouns cannot be directly derived from personal proper names
by means of a locative class prefix.

(90) Ha   (Tanzania; Harjula 2004: 65)
   a. Ng-end-é   kw-a=Máriámu
       1SG-go-SBJV 17-CON=Mariamu
       'Let me go to Mariamu.'

   b. mw-a=Chíisohoye
       18-CON=Chiisohoye
       'at Chisohoye's'

(91) Songye   (Stappers 1964: 56)
       kwamúkají 'at the woman's place'
       kwǎmfumú 'at the chief's'

In Ruwund the connective relator of agreement pattern V (*dà*) developed into the
preposition 'via' or 'through' and that of agreement pattern XI (*rà*) into a preposition

meaning 'by (means of transportation)' (92). Something similar is found in Mongo, where 'via' is expressed by the connective relator of agreement pattern I (93). Another recurrent preposition that develops from connective relators is 'for' (94–95).

(92) Ruwund   (Nash 1992: 382)
    a. dà masuku
       'through the bush'

    b. dà kûns
       'by side path'

    c. rà nking
       'by bike'

    d. rà pânsh
       'on foot' (pânsh 'on the ground')

(93) Mongo   (Hulstaert 1966: 239)
    to-ó-y-é   ŏa ntando
    1PL-HAB-come-FV via [9]river
    'We come via the river.'

(94) Ha   (Harjula 2004: 65)
    b-a-rim-a   kwa Tunguhore
    II-PRS-cultivate-FV for Tunguhore
    'They cultivate for Tunguhore' (*kwa* < *ku-a* XVII-CON)

(95) Lwalwa   (DRC, Ndembe-Nsasi 1972: 120)
    bwáamí
    'for me' (< *bu-a=mi*; XIV-CON=1SG.PPR)

When R2 is a non-finite verb form, a pronominalized connective relator functions as a subordinator introducing an adverbial clause.

(96) Makwe   (Devos 2008: 135)
    ńníiída kw-a=ku-lífúunda ki-máakwe
    I.came XV-CON=15-study 7-Makwe
    'I came to study Makwe.'

(97) Kete   (Kamba-Muzenga 1980: 112)
    bw-aː=kú-cwu-mon
    XIV-CON=15-1PL-see
    'in order to see us'

In the Lwalwa example in (98), *bwáamí* (see ex. 95) introduces a purpose clause. This is another example of agreement in an unusual place: a subordinator indexing the object of the adverbial clause it introduces.

(98) Lwalwa   (Ndembe-Nsasi 1972)
    bwáamí kumóno 'in order to see me'

7.   Departures from the canonical arrangement of constituents

7.1   R1, CON and R2 are not adjacent

Canonically R1, the connective relator and R2 are adjacent. In a common departure from the canon, CON R2 is separated from R1 by other modifiers of R1 (99). Example (99) also illustrates that CON R2 can be preceded by modifiers that have scope over it.

> (99)   Kagulu   (Petzell 2008: 196)
>   i-mu-ana   yu-ya   u-a=i-chike
>   AU-1-child I-DEM I-CON=AU-feminine
>   'that young girl'

7.2   The order of elements is not R1 CON R2

The connective relator is placed iconically between R1 and R2 in the canonical construction. Departures from the canon on this dimension are rarely mentioned in the literature. One partial departure can be found in Mongo in the case of coordinated R1s, where CON R2 can be placed either after the second R1 (100a), or, non-canonically, in between the coordinated R1s (100b).

> (100)   Mongo   (Hulstaert 1966)
>   a.   bo-ngángo l'   a-kulá   w-ǎ   mbengi
>   3-bow   and 6-arrow III-CON 9.hunter
>
>   b.   bo-ngángo w-ǎ   mbengi   l'   a-kulá
>   3-bow   III-CON 9.hunter and 6-arrow
>   'the bow and arrows of the hunter'

Also in Mongo, CON R2 can be placed in front of R1 in order to express contrastive focus.

> (101)   Mongo   (Hulstaert 1966: 284)
>   y-ǎ=fafá   nyama   y-ɔl-ɔtsw-a   nd' é-lóngó
>   x-CON=my_father [10]animals x-PST-enter-FV in   7-barn
>   '*My father's* animals have entered the barn (in contrast to the others).'

8.   Conclusions

The main typological characteristics of a typical connective construction, the construction used to express adnominal possession in the Bantu languages, are well known and can be summarized as follows:

> (102)   a.   two nominal constituents are in a relation of dependency
>   b.   the dependent nominal follows the head nominal

    c. the dependent nominal is marked by a dedicated connective relator, which
        agrees with the head nominal

    d. the connective construction is not dedicated to the expression of posses-
        sion, nor of any other relation

Even the minimal characteristics in (102a–c) prove to be too strong as necessary
definitional criteria for the connective construction. They do not apply to several
construction types, illustrated in this paper, that one would wish to classify as connective constructions on the basis of their family resemblance with typical instances
of the construction. Thus, we saw several construction types in which a connective
marker links a head nominal to a clearly non-nominal dependent and there is not
always a clear cut-off point between a clearly nominal and a clearly non-nominal
dependent. For instance, as we saw in Section 3.2, nominalized verb forms like infinitives that are marked by a connective relator, can be gradually elaborated with
more and more verbal features, which creates a continuum of construction types
between a typical connective construction on the one hand and a typical relative
clause construction on the other, with no non-arbitrary cut-off point in between
them.

    The aim of this paper was to provide an overview of the formal and functional
variation in construction types that show a family resemblance to typical connective
constructions. In order to do this, I defined a canonical type and then described the
formal variation found among connective constructions in terms of departures from
the canon along several dimensions. The canonical type reflects the prototypical connective construction in the mind of the Bantuist. No claims are made regarding the
higher frequency or the diachronic primacy of the canonical type as opposed to other
types. That being said, the canonical construction is the only one that was found in
every description that I consulted, at least if we ignore the form of the connective relator in the definition of the canonical type. This may be due to the fact that many grammarians do not go beyond discussing the construction type that they perceive as
prototypical. It may also mean that the canonical type *is* diachronically primary (with
some uncertainty regarding the form of the connective relator in the proto-language).
The variation described in this paper could then be explained in terms of extensions
from the original use of the connective relator. With respect to departures from the
canonical second relatum (R2) it should be pointed out that no Bantu language 'extended' the use of the connective relator to become a generalized marker of adnominal
modification.

    At several points in the discussion of departures from the canon, it became clear
that a canonical approach is useful for the description of parts of speech categories in
individual languages too. In Section 3.1, for instance, I referred to canonical Makwe
adjectives in order to distinguish them from some of the non canonical adjective types
that can occur in R2 position, which can equally well be characterized as non-canonical
nouns. Thus, *kibúúli* 'silent' has the distributional potential of an adjective, but the
morphological characteristics of a noun.

Many of the departures from the canonical connective construction appear to be crosslinguistically rare and theoretically interesting. Examples are dependency reversal (Section 5.1), nominal tense (Section 4.4) and the classifier-like constructions in Section 5.2.1. A connective origin explains a number of unusual agreement phenomena, like the fact that Bantu possessive pronouns have two agreement controllers, or some instances of agreement in unusual places, e.g. on the non selective interrogative 'what for' in Ruwund. Also, we have seen hints of the role of the connective relator in coding information structure within the nominal constituent. Where its presence is optional, the connective relator appears to foreground its second relatum, as with the Lingala adjectives in Section 3.1 and the examples of optional connective relators in Section 5.2. I was often unable to go beyond enumerating these typologically interesting phenomena, since, due to the scarcity of detailed grammatical descriptions of Bantu languages, my knowledge of them is based on a small number of examples and their translation equivalent. For the same reason I do not know how recurrent the different departures from the canonical connective construction are throughout the Bantu family. An overwhelming majority of the departures from the canon can be found in Hulstaert's detailed description of Mongo, a large and rather diverse dialect cluster, which Gustaaf Hulstaert tried to unify in an effort of standardization. The availability of more thorough grammatical descriptions of other Bantu languages is likely to make Mongo seem less exceptionally rich. The canonical typology put forward here could serve as a questionnaire for future descriptive work.

References

Ambouroue, Odette. 2007. *Eléments de description de l'orungu, langue bantu du Gabon* (B11b). PhD Dissertation, Université Libre de Bruxelles. (available at http://theses.ulb.ac.be/ETD-db/collection/available/ULBetd-07162007-152714/unrestricted/TheseAmbouroue.pdf)

Asangama, Natisa. 1983. *Le budu: langue bantu du nord-est du Zaïre. Esquisse phonologique et grammaticale*. PhD Dissertation, INALCO/Paris III.

Bokamba, Georges D. 1971. Specificity and definiteness in Dzamba. *Studies in African Linguistics* 2–3, 217–237.

Bosch, Sonja E. 1997. Possible origins of the possessive particle -ka- in Zulu. *South African Journal of African Languages* 17, 1, 1–5.

Bouka, Léonce Yembi. 1994. L'accord des adjectifs du protobantou en zone H. *Africana Linguistica* 11, 13–18.

Bynon-Polak, Louise. 1965. L'expression des ordinaux dans les langues bantoues. *Africana Linguistica* 2, 127–160.

Corbett, Greville G. 2007. Canonical typology, suppletion and possible words. *Language* 38, 1, 8–42.

Creissels, Denis. 1993. Description du tswana. Unpublished manuscript. Grenoble: Université Stendhal.

Devos, Maud. 2008. *A Grammar of Makwe*. München: LINCOM.

Dik, Simon. 1989. *The Theory of Functional Grammar.* Dordrecht: Foris.

Doke, Clement Martyn 1997. *Text book of Zulu grammar.* (sixth edition). Cape Town: Maskew Miller Longman.

Dunham, Margaret. 2005. *Elements de description du langi, langue bantu F33.* Leuven/Paris: Peeters.

Fivaz, Derek. 1986. *A Reference Grammar of Oshindonga.* Windhoek: Bureau for Research, University of Namibia.

Guarisma, Gladys. 2000. *Complexité morphologique – simplicité syntaxique. Le cas du Bafia, langue bantoue périphérique (A50) du Cameroun.* Leuven/Paris: Peeters.

Greenberg, Joseph H. 1978. How does a language acquire gender markers? In *Universals of Human Language,* III: *Word Structure,* Joseph H. Greenberg, Charles A. Ferguson and Edith A. Moravcsik (eds), 47–82. Stanford: Stanford University Press.

Güldemann, Tom. 1999. The *ka*-possessive in southern Nguni. *Journal of African Languages and Linguistics* 20, 157–184.

Güldemann, Tom. 2008. The Macro-Sudan belt: towards identifying a linguistic area in northern sub-Saharan Africa. In *A Linguistic Geography of Africa,* Bernd Heine and Derek Nurse (eds), 151–185. Cambridge: Cambridge University Press.

Hadermann, Pascale. 1994. Aspects morphologiques et syntaxiques de l'infinitif dans les langues bantoues. *Africana Linguistica* 11, 79–91.

Harjula, Lotta. 2004. *The Ha Language of Tanzania. Grammar, Texts and Vocabulary.* Köln: Rüdiger Köppe Verlag.

Hawkinson, Annie K. 1979. Homonymy versus unity of form: the particle -a in Swahili. *Studies in African Linguistics* 10, 1, 81–109.

Henson, Bonnie. 2007. *The Phonology and Morphosyntax of Kol.* PhD Dissertation, University of California, Berkeley.

Hulstaert, Gustaaf. 1946. Connectieve bijzinnen in Lomongo. *Aequatoria* 5, 135–137.

Hulstaert, Gustaaf. 1957. *Dictionnaire lɔmɔ́ngɔ-français.* Tervuren: Royal Museum for the Belgian Congo.

Hulstaert, Gustaaf. 1965. *Grammaire du lɔmɔ́ngɔ. Deuxième partie. Morphologie.* Tervuren: Royal Museum for Central Africa.

Hulstaert, Gustaaf. 1966. *Grammaire du lɔmɔ́ngɔ. Troisième partie. Syntaxe.* Tervuren: Royal Museum for Central Africa.

Hulstaert, Gustaaf. 1993. Connectif et possessif dans les dialectes mongo. *Annales Aequatoria* 14, 334–344.

Hyman, Larry M. 2003. Basaá (A43). In *The Bantu Languages,* Derek Nurse and Gérard Philippson (eds), 257–282. London: Routledge.

Idiatov, Dmitry. 2008. Antigrammaticalisation, antimorphologization and the case of Tura. In *Theoretical and Empirical Issues in Grammaticalisation,* Elena Seoane, María José López-Couso and Teresa Fanego (eds), 151–169. Amsterdam/Philadelphia: John Benjamins.

Kagaya, Ryohei. 1992. *A Classified Vocabulary of the Bakueri Language.* Tokyo: ILCAA.

Kamba Muzenga, Jean-Georges. 1980. *Esquisse de grammaire kete.* Tervuren: Royal Museum for Central Africa.

Kimenyi, Alexandre 1989. *Kinyarwanda and Kirundi Names: a semiolinguistic analysis of Bantu onomastics.* Lewiston NY: Edwin Mellen Press.

Maganga, Clement and Schadeberg, Thilo C. 1992. *Kinyamwezi: Grammar, Texts, Vocabulary.* Köln: Rüdiger Köppe Verlag.

Maho, Jouni Filip. 1999. *A Comparative Study of Bantu Noun Classes* (= Orientalia et Africana Gothoburgensia 13). Göteborg: Acta Universitatis Gothoburgensis.

Malchukov, Andrej L. 2000. *Dependency Reversal in Noun-Attributive Constructions: Towards a Typology.* München: LINCOM.

Meeussen, Achilles E. 1967. Bantu grammatical reconstructions. *Africana Linguistica, 3,* 81–121.

Meeuwis, Michael. 1998. *Lingala.* München: LINCOM.

Möhlig, Wilhelm, Marten, Lutz and Kavari, Jekura. 2002. *A Grammatical Sketch of Herero (Otjiherero).* Köln: Rüdiger Köppe Verlag.

Nash, Jay Arthur. 1992. *Aspects of Ruwund grammar.* PhD Dissertation, University of Illinois at Urbana-Champaign.

Ndembe-Nsasi, Damase. 1972. Esquisse phonologique et morphologique de la langue lwalwa. Mémoire de licence, Université Nationale du Zaïre, Lubumbashi.

Nordlinger, Rachel and Sadler, Louisa. 2004. Nominal tense in crosslinguistic perspective. *Language* 80, 4, 776–806.

Nzang Bie, Yolande. 1995. Le connectif dans les langues bantu: analyses synchroniques et perspectives diachroniques. PhD Dissertation, Université Libre de Bruxelles.

Petzell, Malin. 2008. *The Kagulu Language of Tanzania. Grammar, texts and vocabulary.* Köln: Rüdiger Köppe Verlag.

Perez, Carolyn Harford. 1985. *Aspects of Complementation in three Bantu Languages.* PhD Dissertation, University of Wisconsin-Madison.

Rijkhoff, Jan. 2002. *The Noun Phrase.* Oxford: Oxford University Press.

Rodegem, Firmin M. 1970. Syntagmes complétifs spéciaux en rundi. *Africana Linguistica* 4, 181–207.

Ross, Malcolm. 1998. Possessive-like attribute constructions in the Oceanic languages of northwest Melanesia. *Oceanic Linguistics* 37, 2, 234–276.

Stappers, Leo c.i.c.m. 1964. *Morfologie van het Songye.* Tervuren: Royal Museum for Central Africa.

Tshibasu Balekelay. 1985. *Les formes pronominales en bemba (approche structurale).* MA thesis, Institut Supérieur Pédagogique de Lubumbashi.

Tucker, Archibald N. 1960. Notes on Konzo. *African Language Studies* 1, 16–41.

Van de Velde, Mark L.O. 2006. Multifunctional agreement patterns in Bantu and the possibility of genderless nouns. *Linguistic Typology* 10, 2, 183–221.

Van de Velde, Mark L.O. 2008. *A Grammar of Eton.* Berlin: Mouton de Gruyter.

Van de Velde, Mark L.O. and Ambouroue, Odette. 2011. The grammar of Orungu proper names. *Journal of African Languages and Linguistics* 32, 113–141.

Van Langendonck, Willy. 2007. *Theory and Typology of Proper Names.* Berlin: Mouton de Gruyter.

Van Eeden, B.I.C. 1956. *Zoeloe-grammatika.* Stellenbosch: Universiteitsuitgewers en boekhandelaars.

Welmers, William Everett. 1963. Associative *a* and *ka* in Niger-Congo. *Language,* 39, 3, 432–447.

Endnotes

1.   The research for this chapter was carried out while I was a postdoctoral researcher at the Center for Grammar, Cognition and Typology at the University of Antwerp, funded by a grant

from the Research Foundation – Flanders. I am very grateful for generous comments on earlier versions of this chapter by Koen Bostoen, Dmitry Idiatov, Larry Hyman, Dan Ponsford, Jan Rijkhoff, Jean-Christophe Verstraete and an anonymous reviewer.

2.   Most sources do not provide glosses, so glossing is generally mine. Where glosses are provided in the sources, I adapted them for the sake of homogeneity. I use the Leipzig glossing rules, with the following additions: AG agreement marker, AU augment, CON stem of the connective relator, FV final vowel (a TAM morpheme), GER gerund, HAB habitual, HPST hodiernal past, PF pre-final (a multifunctional TAM-morpheme), POS stem of a possessive pronoun, PPR personal pronoun, R1 first relatum, RP remote past, RPST recent past, SUB subordinator. Arabic numbers gloss overt noun class markers on nouns and roman numbers gloss class/number agreement prefixes.

3.   Maganga and Schadeberg analyse the connective stem as a prefix in Kinyamwezi. However, they point out that the tonal behaviour of the connective relator resembles that of a prefix in some contexts and that of a word in others, which could be used as an argument to analyse the connective relator as a proclitic.

4.   Bouka (1994) cites Jean Baka (p.c.) as the source of these examples. The tonal difference on the connective relator between the examples in (15a) and (15b) is said to be due to rules of tone displacement. Still according to Bouka, the construction exemplified in (15b) is historically derived from that in (15a) by means of a generalisation of agreement pattern IX in R2 position.

5.   There is a formal difference between the connective relator when it is followed by a noun (including infinitives) or by a finite verb form: only in the former case does the relator have a structural high tone. Devos (2008: 261) suggests that this tonal difference is due to a difference in degree of morphological bonding. In relative verb forms the connective relator is analysed as a (complex) prefix, elsewhere as a proclitic. The morpheme *á* glossed as I is the third person subject prefix of agreement pattern I.

6.   Note that the augment is used in Konzo to pronominalise a connective relator (see Section 6.2). The connective relator in Konzo non-subject relative clauses always takes the augment.

7.   The exact conditioning for the appearance of the "amplexive" may be more intricate than that in many languages, e.g. involving only proper names or only class 1a nouns with human reference, or proper names whether they belong to class 1a or not. Better descriptive work is needed on this issue.

8.   It may be that the presence versus absence of an augment is the real conditioning factor here, rather than class 1a membership. Class 1a nouns typically lack an augment and since the augment is vocalic in Oshindonga, the absence of the connective stem *-a* before other nouns might be due to a phonological rule of vowel hiatus resolution. Since Fivaz does not explicitly mention the connective construction in his overview of where vowel hiatus resolution rules apply, we can assume that he analyses the connective relator as lacking a stem except before class 1a nouns. An example of a connective construction with an R2 of class 8 could show which analysis is correct, since the augment of class 8 is *i-* and vowel hiatus resolution in the case of *a* + *i* involves coalescence to *e*. Unfortunately, there is no such example in his grammar.

9.   According to Hulstaert (1965: 178) native speakers are not aware of this origin, i.e. they do not recognise the preposition 'at (somebody's place)' as a constituent part of the connective relator.

10.   Interestingly, the canonical connective construction is used (obligatorily) if a singular, human R2 is itself modified by a possessive pronoun: *ki-táabu c-á=mw-áná w-áa-ngu* (7-book VII-CON=1-child I-CON-1SG.POS) 'the book of my child'.

11.   It is very unusual for Bantu languages to have a formal distinction between definite and indefinite nominals. See Ambouroue (2007) for a description.

12.   Esukulu is a species of owl (*Ciccaba woodfordi Smith*), whose cry is seen as a bad omen. In *Costus afer* and other plants it refers to a type of malformation which the Mongo attribute to the fact that the plant was planted too late in the evening, after the owl's cry (Hulstaert 1957: 606).

13.   In Nash's (1992: 359) words "Without specific contextual referents, cl 7 and cl 8 associative phrases refer automatically to implicit *côm* 'thing' and *yôm* 'things' respectively."

14.   It would be interesting to know whether this evolution is sometimes accompanied by anti-morphologisation, i.e. an evolution towards a lower degree of morphological bonding (see Idiatov 2008).

PART 2

Case studies

Word order restrictions in adnominal constructions

The case of the German pre- versus postnominal genitive

Petra Campe
University College Gent[1]

This paper focuses on variation between pre- and postnominal genitives of proper names in German. It refines and completes previous studies, in that it provides a systematic corpus study of all factors described in the existing literature and offers a thorough analysis of factors that may hamper genitive variation. The two constructions are not 'equivalent', since (1) the prenominal genitive has a specifying, determinative function, (2) certain factors exclude variation and (3) a variety of other factors hamper the alternation in so-called 'choice' contexts, such as the semantic factor 'Agent/Patient role', the syntactic factor of prosodic weight and a number of pragmatic factors like minor relevance of N1, further elaboration of N2, contrastive meaning, and higher participant identifiability of the genitive proper noun.

1. Introduction

To express adnominal relations in German a number of alternating constructions are available, such as prepositional phrases, appositions or bare morphological cases, in particular the genitive case. In previous research we concentrated on the constraints underlying the alternation between these constructions (e.g Campe 1997, 1998, 2010) and thus illustrated the idea that paradigmatic variation, the network of different constructions expressing a similar meaning, can be used as a heuristic tool to pinpoint the individual semantics of a grammatical construction.

The genitive construction itself, however, also displays variation, viz. between the prenominal and the postnominal genitive, as in example (1).[2] Through offering a corpus-based case-study of German pre- and postnominal genitive variation, this paper aims to provide further evidence supporting the idea of paradigmatic variation as a heuristic tool.

(1) **der Unfalltod**   Diana-s   (...) Diana-s   **Söhne** (DW 08.04.08)[3]
     the accidental.death Diana-GEN   Diana-GEN sons
     'the accidental death of Diana''Diana's sons'

The existing literature on the pre- and postnominal use of the German genitive reveals the importance of a number of factors. Some of these factors exclude variation between the two genitives and are therefore of minor relevance for this paper. The discussion of these factors is limited to a brief overview in Section 3. In this case, extra data from our corpus are only included if they provide counterexamples or additional information for claims in the existing literature. The factors which the existing literature mentions as relevant for genitive variation and for which it does not offer a systematic and detailed analysis, are elaborated in Section 4. First, it is shown that the semantic factor 'Agent/Patient role' plays a more important role in the pre-/postnominal variation than has previously been assumed (Section 4.1). Second, the importance of the syntactic factor of prosodic weight is demonstrated (Section 4.2). Finally, it is shown that the decomposition of the third and most important factor of pragmatic status (Section 4.3) reveals a number of interesting subfactors, such as minor relevance of N1 (first noun of the NP; 4.3.1.1), further elaboration of N2 (4.3.1.2), contrastive meaning (4.3.1.3), and higher participant identifiability of the genitive proper noun (Section 4.3.2).

Before we embark on the overview of factors identified by the existing literature, some more detailed comments are in order on the exact topic of the paper, and on the composition of the corpus of empirical data we used (Section 2). This topic has received relatively little attention in grammars or recent linguistic literature, unlike, for instance, the (rather common) variation between the prenominal genitive and the genitive-like, postnominal *of*-construction in English (e.g. Rosenbach 2003, Stefanowitsch 2003, Rosenbach 2005, Jäger & Rosenbach 2006, Hinrichs & Szmrecsanyi 2007). This is probably due to the fact that the prenominal genitive is restricted to unmodified proper names. Only Rozen (1988), Marillier (1992), Teuber (2000) and Hartmann & Zimmermann (2003) focus on this type of genitive variation in German. It does receive more attention in recent historical studies (e.g. Lanouette 1996, Prell 2000, Demske 2001: 215–232, Ebert 2003), since in earlier stages of German the prenominal genitive was much more frequent and not limited to proper names (see Section 2). The same applies to generative studies, which often focus on the question how the essentially identical pre- and postnominal genitives get to their specific positions and whether these genitive positions are base-generated or derived respectively (e.g. Lindauer 1995, Ehrich & Rapp 2000, Krause 2000, Demske 2001).

2. Topic of the paper and composition of the corpus

2.1   Unmodified proper names as pre- or postnominal genitives[4]

The variation between pre- and postnominal genitives in German is mainly restricted to unmodified proper names: humans – as *Diana* in example (1) above – or geographical names (2) (cp. for instance Marillier 1992: 47; Eisenberg 1994: 250; Teuber 2000: 175, 179; Demske 2001: 210; Leys 2007; Duden 2009: 826).[5]

(2) **die Tibet-Politik** <u>China-s</u> (...) <u>China-s</u> **Vorgehen in Tibet** (DW 27.03.08)
the Tibet.policy China-GEN China-GEN actions in Tibet
'the Tibet policy of China' 'China's actions in Tibet'

The restriction of genitive variation to *unmodified* proper names is illustrated in (3). Though the name *Maria* is prototypically used without an article, it can also be modified by a definite article in colloquial speech. In postnominal position, both constructions are possible as a genitive (3a). When used prenominally, the construction with the definite article is marked (^m), if used at all (3b). This claim about markedness (Neef 2006) is corroborated by the fact that empirical examples are rare: (3c) is the only example found in our corpus (admittedly of written German). Names that have to be accompanied by the definite article, such as *Türkei* in *die Türkei*, do not to occur prenominally (3d).[6] No such examples could be found in our corpus. The prenominal use of such proper names *without* an article is also claimed to be ungrammatical (3e), but journalistic article headlines do occasionally contain examples of such 'shortened' prenominal genitives, thus complying with the norm of unmodified proper names (3f).

(3) a. **die Röcke** <u>Maria-s</u> / **die Röcke** <u>der</u> <u>Maria</u> (Neef 2006: 287)
the skirts Maria-GEN the skirts the.GEN.F Maria
'the skirts of Maria' 'the skirts of Maria'

   b. <u>Maria-s</u> **Größe** >< ^m<u>der</u> <u>Maria</u> **Größe** (Neef 2006: 295)
Maria-GEN length the.GEN.F Maria length
'Maria's length' 'Maria's length'

   c. <u>des</u> <u>Pai-s</u> **Geschmack** (Ks:141)
the.GEN.M Pai-GEN taste
'Pai's taste'

   d. Er wohnt in *Türkei / der Türkei. (Lattewitz 1994: 139)
he lives in Turkey the.DAT.F Turkey
'He lives in Turkey'.

   → *<u>der</u> <u>Türkei</u> **Gastarbeiter**
the.GEN.F Turkey migrant.workers
'Turkey's migrant workers'

   e. *<u>Rhein-s</u> **Ufer**; *<u>Türkei-s</u> **Gastarbeiter**
(Neef 2006: 284) (Lattewitz 1994: 139)

   Rhine-GEN banks Turkey-GEN migrant.workers
'the Rhine's banks' 'Turkey's migrant workers'

   f. <u>Jemen-s</u> **Präsident** bei Merkel (DW 02.03.08)
Yemen-GEN president with Merkel
'Yemen's president visits Merkel'

>< mit **dem Präsidenten** <u>des</u>   Jemen   (ibid.)
with the president   the.GEN.M Yemen
'with the president of Yemen'

Proper names *with* an article resemble 'normal' full noun phrases, and unlike in English (*the mother's car*) such full NPs are rarely used prenominally in German. A prenominal genitive NP sounds marked nowadays, highly formal, archaic or ironic (4a) (e.g. Lanouette 1996: 97, Ballweg 1998: 162, Teuber 2000: 171, Demske 2001: 210, Duden 2009: 823). The only unmarked use of the prenominal genitive NP seems to be in fixed expressions. In this case, however, variation with a postnominal genitive is hardly possible (4b). It is significant in this respect that all prenominal genitive NPs in our corpus are examples from the novel *Das Parfum* by Süsskind, which is written in a rather archaic style (4c). When used prenominally, the genitive NP is almost always singular and/or definite, with an animate referent (Marillier 1992: 48) – singularity, definiteness and animacy being exactly the characteristics of proper names as well. Indefinite prenominal NPs are rare (4d), as are plural NPs (which do not occur in our corpus; 4e). NPs that are themselves modified postnominally are excluded from the prenominal position (4f) (Demske 2001: 212). Moreover, Hartmann & Zimmermann (2003: 10–11) claim that "the first phonological word in the sequence" of prenominal genitive NPs "must be marked unambiguously as genitive", which reduces the possibility of prenominal genitive NPs more or less to masculine and neutral singular NPs.[7] Though all examples of prenominal NPs in our corpus are single masculine or neutral definite singular NPs (4c), Marillier (1992: 48) does provide a few examples of feminine definite singular NPs (4g) (see also Lattewitz' example given in 5).

(4) a. <u>des</u>   Kaiser-s   **neue Kleider**   (Neef 2006: 292)
the.GEN.M emperor-GEN new   clothes
'the Emperor's new clothes'

<u>der</u>   Sehnsucht **Widerhall** (ibid.)
the.GEN.F craving   echo
'the craving's echo'

b. Simbabwe stehe   "auf <u>des</u>   Messer-s **Schneide**"
(DW 07.04.08)
Zimbabwe stand.SBJV on   the.GEN.M knife-GEN edge
'Zimbabwe is on a knife's edge.'

c. <u>des</u>   Mörder-s   **Hand** (Pf:282)
the.GEN.M murderer-GEN hand
'the murderer's hand'

<u>des</u>   herrlichen Mädchen-s **Betrachtung**   (Pf:255)
the.GEN.N gorgeous   girl-GEN   observation
'the observation of the gorgeous girl'

    d. <u>eines</u>   <u>Menschen</u>   **Duft**   (Pf:239)
        a.GEN.M human.being.GEN.M odour
        'a human being's odour'

    e. Appelle an <u>anderer</u>   <u>Leute</u> **Mitgefühl** (KM 104, Marillier 1992: 48)
        appeals to other.GEN.PL people compassion
        'appeals to other people's compassion'

    f. *<u>des</u>   <u>Kaiser-s</u>   <u>von</u> <u>China</u> **neue Kleider**   (Neef 2006: 292)
        the.GEN.M emperor-GEN of China new clothes
        'the Emperor of China's new clothes'

    g. zu <u>der</u>   <u>hilfsbereiten</u> <u>Bibliothekarin</u> **ungläubigen** [sic] **Staunen**
                               (KM 79, Marillier 1992: 48)
        to the.GEN.F helpful   librarian   disbelieving   surprise
        'to the helpful (female) librarian's disbelieving surprise'

The existing literature offers two claims about the prototypical semantic contexts for prenominal genitive NPs, neither of which is based on empirical data. Firstly, Lattewitz (1994: 121) claims that some prenominal genitive NPs are grammatical due to the use of a superlative (5). We were not able to verify this claim due the lack of similar examples in our corpus, but we believe the uniqueness expressed by the superlative corresponds to what we argue is the specifying function of the prenominal genitive (see Section 3.1.1), which may be the reason why prenominal superlatives are less marked than other prenominal genitive NPs.

  (5) <u>der</u>   <u>Welt</u> **teuerste**   **Briefmarke**   (Lattewitz 1994: 121)
        the.GEN.F world most.expensive stamp
        'the world's most expensive stamp'

     / **die teuerste**   **Briefmarke** <u>der</u>   <u>Welt</u>   (ibid.)
        the most.expensive stamp   the.GEN.F world
        'the most expensive stamp in the world'

A second prototypical context offered by the existing literature is that of 'generic expressions'. According to Hartmann & Zimmermann (2003: 10), prenominal genitive NPs are restricted to 'generic expressions', which are "reanalysed as proper names" (6a). If, however, "the statement is changed such that a generic interpretation is suppressed (...) a prenominal genitive is impossible" (6b).

  (6) a. <u>Des</u>   <u>Blauwal-s</u>   **Lebensraum** ist der Ozean.   (ibid.)
          the.GEN.M blue.whale-GEN habitat   is the ocean
          'The blue whale's habitat is the ocean.'

       b. *<u>Des</u>   <u>vor Boston gesichteten</u> <u>Blauwal-s</u>   **Lebensraum**
          that.GEN.M near Boston spotted   blue.whale-GEN habitat

ist der Ozean.
is the ocean
'The habitat of the blue whale that was spotted near Boston is the ocean.'

Again, we were not able to verify this claim due to a lack of similar examples in our corpus. In any case, many of the examples in (4) above provide counterexamples for the claim that prenominal genitive NPs usually have a generic character. Hartmann & Zimmermann (2003: 11) do add that so-called 'function descriptions' (title and position holders) seem to be exceptions to the rule (cp. 4a: the Emperor's new clothes).

Finally, demonstrative pronouns also occur as pre- and postnominal genitives (7). However, in this case variation between pre- and postnominal genitives is excluded. Two different constructions are involved: prenominal pronouns systematically refer to the last mentioned noun or NP (anaphoric: 7a), postnominal pronouns to a following one (cataphoric: 7b).

(7) a. Sikorski und <u>dessen</u>   **Frau** Anne Appelbaum (DW 07.04.08)
         Sikorski and the.GEN.M.DEM wife Anne Appelbaum
         'Sikorski and his wife Anne Appelbaum'

     b. [der Thron ist] Symbol für (...) **den   Reichtum**   <u>dessen</u>,
         [the throne is] symbol for the wealth the.GEN.M.DEM,
         der ihn bestiegen hat   (DW-world 25.07.07)
         who him ascended has
         '[the throne is] symbolic of the wealth of he who has ascended it'

Since the use of prenominal genitives NPs is clearly marked (3–6) and demonstrative pronouns do not display variation between pre- and postnominal genitives (7), this paper will focus only on the variation between pre- and postnominal unmodified proper nouns, as illustrated in examples (1–2) above.[8]

2.2   Corpus

The corpus used is a collection of genitive proper names excerpted from three different sources: a compilation of six weeks of the daily electronic news reports of *Deutsche Welle* (March-April 2008) and two fairly recent novels (Ks, Pf, cp. References). In these sources, the pre- and postnominal genitives of the kind illustrated in (1–2) were manually selected, copied with sentence context to a database and coded according to a number of linguistic parameters using the corpus research tool *Abundantia Verborum* (Speelman 1997). Interestingly, in the novels included in the corpus (Pf, Ks), the ratio of pre- vs. postnominal genitives is far less balanced than in the news reports of Deutsche Welle (Table 1). This might be an indication of the fact that pre-/postnominal genitive variation typically occurs in journalistic language. Register and style have clearly been identified as determining genitive choice in English (e.g. Altenberg 1982, Hinrichs & Szmrecsanyi 2007).

Table 1. Ratio prenominal genitive/postnominal genitive

	PRE- (453)	POST- (246)	(total) (699)
DW (news reports)	132	158	(290)
Pf (novel)	97	53	(150)
Ks (novel)	224	35	(259)

Table 2. DW-corpus – pre-/postnominal genitives

DW	PRE- (132)	POST- (158)	(total: 290)
Variation possible	76 (58%)	106 (67%)	(182)
Semantic/syntactic factors excluding variation	56 (42%)	52 (33%)	(108)

Because of the relative balance between pre- and postnominal genitives, we will focus on the *Deutsche Welle*-subcorpus (DW) in this paper. Occasionally, examples will be used from the other subcorpora and from Google searches. As mentioned, pre- and postnominal genitives that vary in relation to each other (cp. (1): *Dianas Unfalltod* ≈ *der Unfalltod Dianas*) are of particular interest for this paper. In the DW-corpus, 60% of the prenominal genitives can alternate with a postnominal genitive and about 70% of the postnominal genitives with a prenominal construction. The other genitives in the corpus cannot alternate due to the (semantic or syntactic) restrictions described in Section 3 (Table 2).

2.3   Postnominal genitive versus von-phrase

Some linguists claim that prenominal genitives alternate with postnominal *von*-phrases, rather than with postnominal genitives, which they consider to be stylistically marked (8a), archaic (8b) or even ungrammatical (8c) (see also Section 4.1 below). This prepositional alternative for the postnominal genitive of proper nouns is commonly accepted by grammars (e.g. Zifonun et al. 1997: 1971, Duden 2009: 828, 970). The high number of postnominal genitive examples in our corpus (Table 1 above), however, indicates that constructions like (8c) cannot be considered ungrammatical. Some linguists accept the postnominal genitive as marked (e.g. Bhatt 1990: 159, Teuber 2000: 171), many others, moreover, accept this genitive without further discussion (e.g. Zifonun et al. 1997: 1971; Neef 2006: 287; Spencer 2009: 182).

(8) a. ʔ**die Grammatik** Peter-s   (Teuber 2000: 171)
         the grammar   Peter-GEN

   → die Grammatik von Peter
     the grammar   of   Peter
     'the grammar of Peter'

  b. **die Stadt** <u>David-s</u>   (Teuber 2000: 171)
      the city   David-GEN
      → die Stadt von David
        the city of   David
        'the city of David'

  c. *__die Schrift__   <u>Otto-s</u>   (Harweg 1967, in Lauterbach 1993: 67)
      the handwriting Otto-GEN
      → die Schrift   von Otto
        the handwriting of   Otto
        'the handwriting of Otto'

  d. *__die Museen__   <u>Rom-s</u> (Demske 2001: 267) → von Rom
      the museums Rome-GEN   of   Rome
      'the museums of Rome'

As mentioned above, the ratio of pre- vs. postnominal genitives is far less balanced in the novels included in our corpus (Pf, Ks) than in the news reports (Tables 1 and 3). One could interpret this as evidence for Teuber's claim (2000: 171–72) that *von* rather than the postnominal genitive alternates with the prenominal genitive, but *von* is far less frequent than the prenominal genitive in these novels as well (Table 3).

    The *von*-phrases in the novels and in DW are, moreover, mainly restricted to specific constructions such as fixed names, authors, localizations, titles and coordinated names (Table 4). These are all semantic contexts for which grammars point out the predominance of *von* over the genitive (cp. for instance Zifonun et al. 1997: 1971, Ten Cate et al. 2004: 289–290, Duden 2009: 828). *Von*-phrases illustrated in subcategory 1 of Table 4 (fixed names) exclude variation with pre- *and* postnominal genitives. The examples in subcategories 2–5 clearly show a tendency towards postnominal coding with *von*, though theoretically pre- and postnominal genitives are also possible (Campe 1997). The examples in subcategories 2 ('author') and 3 ('localization') show a higher incidence of the *von*-phrase because of the agentive and spatial meanings of this preposition (compare the English translation with 'by' in case of an author relation). In none of the three corpus examples of subcategory 2 is a prenominal genitive possible.

Table 3. Ratio prenominal genitive/postnominal genitive/*von*-phrase

	PRE- (453)	POST- (246)	VON (202)	(total) (901)
DW (news reports)	132	158	110	(400)
Pf (novel)	97	53	40	(190)
Ks (novel)	224	35	52	(311)

This is due to the syntax or the semantics of the structure. As to subcategory 4, which constitutes more than half of our *von*-corpus, we could not find any pre- or postnominal genitive proper names in similar structures ('title + first name + family name'). This observation is corroborated by a number of random Google checks: whereas *Kurs von Parteichef Kurt Beck* yields 50 hits, both *Parteichef Kurt Becks Kurs* (prenominal genitive) and *(der) Kurs Parteichef Kurt Becks* (postnominal genitive) yield no hits at all. A Google check with a better-known name yields similar results: *(die) Rede von Bundeskanzlerin Angela Merkel* (279 hits)/*(die) Rede Bundeskanzlerin Angela Merkels* (5 hits)/*Bundeskanzlerin Angela Merkels Rede* (4 hits).[9] The same manifest preference for the *von*-phrase was observed for the examples of subcategory 5. Here the combination of names plays an important role in the choice of the postnominal position (see also Section 4.2.2).

Since the number of instances of possible variation between *von*-phrases and pre-/postnominal genitives is thus very small (about 10%: subcategory 6 in Table 4), we chose not to take the *von*-phrase into consideration as a genitive alternative, though we will point out the resemblance of the examples in subcategories 2–6 with postnominal

Table 4. DW-corpus – adnominal *von*-phrases (proper names)

DW	(110)	VON
1. Fixed name, e.g. der Vertrag von Lissabon (DW 02.03.08) (/ *der Vertrag *Lissabon-s*/**Lissabon-s* **Vertrag**) 'the Treaty of Lisbon'	16	14.54%
2. Author, e.g. die Filme 'Kirschblüten' von Doris Dörrie und 'Die Welle' von Dennis Gansel (DW 28.03.08) 'the films 'Cherry Blossoms' by Dorris Dörrie and 'The Wave' by Dennis Gansel'	3	2.73%
3. Localization, e.g. in der Nähe von Mossul (DW 13.03.08) 'in the neighbourhood of Mossul'	14	12.73%
4. Title incorporated in NP, e.g. den Kurs von Parteichef Kurt Beck (DW 03.03.08) 'the policy of party leader Kurt Beck'	62	56.36%
5. Coordinated names, e.g. in Teilen von Frankreich und Großbritannien (DW 10.03.08) 'in parts of France and Great Britain'	4	3.64%
6. Variation, e.g. Milizionäre von al Sadr (DW 28.03.08) / **Milizionäre** *al Sadr-s*/mit Vertretern von *al Sadr-s* **Miliz**) (ibid.) 'militia of al Sadr'	11	10%

genitives vis-à-vis prenominal genitives in the relevant parts of section three. The identity of this particular *von*-phrase with proper names is, moreover, an interesting topic
for further research.

3. Factors excluding variation between pre- and postnominal genitives of proper names

3.1   Semantic factors

3.1.1 *Specifying function and referentiality of the prenominal genitive*
A first semantic factor excluding genitival variation is the fact that the prenominal genitive has a determinative (specifying, defining) function, similar to that of the definite
article or the possessive pronoun (Demske 2001: 209ff). According to Brinkmann
(1971: 76) the prenominal genitive *Goethes Werke* is to be interpreted as 'all of the works
that have been written by Goethe', whereas the postnominal genitive *Werke Goethes*
pertains to an undetermined number of works by Goethe. The prenominal genitive has
a defining function even when it is itself accompanied by an indefinite determiner (9a).
However, definiteness does not necessarily imply uniqueness (9b). This defining function of the prenominal genitive is the reason why all indefinite head nouns take a postnominal genitive.[10] Approximately 25% of the postnominal genitives in the corpus are
of this kind and are therefore excluded from this analysis (see Table 2 above).

(9) a.   eines   Menschen   **Duft**   (Pf:239)
          a.GEN.M human.being.GEN.M odour
          'a human being's odour'
          = der Duft eines   Menschen
          the odour a.GEN.M human.being.GEN.M
          'the odour of a human being'

     b.   Goethe-s   **Roman** = der Roman Goethe-s
          Goethe-GEN novel   the novel   Goethe-GEN
          'Goethe's novel'   'the novel by Goethe'
          ≠ der einzige Roman Goethe-s
          the only   novel Goethe-GEN
          'the only novel by Goethe'

Due to this specifying function, only an appositive relative clause is allowed in semantic
contexts such as those illustrated in (10a): a specific Italian invasion is introduced, which
happened to take place in the 19th century. Postnominal genitives do not have this
specifying function: the relative clause in (10b) can therefore either be interpreted as an
appositive or as a restrictive relative clause (Hartmann & Zimmermann 2003: 32).

(10) a.   Italien-s **Invasion,** die im   19. Jahrhundert stattfand,
           Italy-GEN invasion   that in.the 19th century   took.place

war sehr blutig.   (ibid.)
was very bloody
'Italy's invasion, which took place in the 19th century, was very bloody.'

   b. **Die Invasion** <u>Italien-s</u>, die im   19. Jahrhundert stattfand,
the invasion Italy-GEN that in.the 19th century   took.place
war sehr blutig.   (ibid.)
was very bloody
'The invasion of Italy, which took place in the 19th century, was very
bloody.'

For the same reason, only a postnominal construction is possible when specific, individual reference is to be avoided, as in (11a). Unlike in (11b), it is not the beard of the
historic individual King Edward that is meant here, but a generic type of beard, an
Edward-like beard (11a) (Rozen 1988: 34, in: Marillier 1992: 56–57).

(11) a. Männer (...) ließen sich   **den Spitzbart**
        men   let   themselves the pointed.beard
        <u>Eduard-s</u>   <u>VII.</u>   wachsen. (ibid.) (→ what kind?: type)
        Edward-GEN VII[.GEN] grow
        'Men of position grew the pointed beard of Edward the 7th.'

     b. Alle Damen (...) liebten <u>Eduard-s</u>   <u>VII.</u>   *Spitzbart.*
        all   ladies   loved   Edward-GEN VII[.GEN] pointed.beard
        (→ whose?: instance)
        'All ladies loved Edward the 7th's pointed beard.'

The specifying function of the prenominal genitive also explains why only the postnominal and not the prenominal genitive can alternate with a compound (12), in
which the head is essentially non-referential and generic (Campe 2010: 207ff).

(12) Er ließ sich   einen / den Eduard VII.-Spitzbart   wachsen.
      he let himself a   / the Edward the.7th.pointed.beard grow
      'He grew an/the Edward the 7th pointed beard.'

3.1.2 *Type of semantic relation expressed*

The use of the prenominal genitive is limited to so-called possessive (13a), subjective
(13b) and objective genitives (13c) (Marillier 1992: 53; Demske 2001: 247). Explicative
genitives (13d) do not occur prenominally. This constraint can be explained in the
light of the specification/referentiality discussion in 3.1.1: unlike the postnominal genitive, the prenominal genitive always has a specific, individual reference (13e; cp. (11)).
Partitive (quantitive) prenominal genitives seem to be excluded by the same specificity
constraint, since they usually have an indefinite head noun (13f). Partitive genitives
(13g) are, moreover, never unmodified proper nouns, since the referent of the head
noun instantiates the referent of the genitive: whereas 'one' of 'bars' is indeed a 'bar', the

'rest' of 'Germany' is not 'Germany as such' (13g). Similarly, qualitative genitives are never unmodified proper nouns (13h).

(13) a. <u>Frankreich-s</u> **Atomwaffenarsenal**   (DW 21.03.08)
      France-GEN   atomic.weapons.arsenal
      'France's atomic weapons arsenal'

  b. <u>China-s</u>   **Vorgehen in Tibet**   (DW 27.03.08)
      China-GEN actions   in Tibet
      'China's actions in Tibet'

  c. <u>Amerika-s</u>   **Entdeckung**   (Zifonun et al. 1997: 1971)
      Amerika-GEN discovery
      'America's discovery'

  d. **die Figur** <u>Gretchen-s</u>   (Campe 1999: 209)
      the role   Gretchen-GEN
      'the role of Gretchen' (theatre role = 'Gretchen')

  e. <u>Gretchen-s</u>   **Figur**   (ibid.)
      Gretchen-GEN figure
      'Gretchen's figure' (the body shape of a specific girl named Gretchen)

  f. in **einer** <u>der</u>   <u>Bars</u>   (Ks:142)
      in one   the.GEN.F bars
      'in one of the bars'

  g. der **Rest** <u>Deutschland-s</u>
      the rest Germany-GEN
      'the rest of Germany'

  h. **irgendein gesunder Mensch**   <u>seines</u>   <u>Alter-s</u>   (Pf:200)
      some   healthy   human.being his.GEN.N age-GEN
      'some healthy human being of his age'

Our corpus contains no examples of explicative, partitive or qualitative postnominal genitive proper names.

Possessive genitives can have either a relational head noun (inalienable possession) or a non-relational head noun (alienable possession). According to Hartmann & Zimmermann (2003: 30), non-relational heads cannot be construed with a postnominal genitive proper name (*die Tasche Peters 'the bag of Peter'). Since corpus evidence contradicts this ungrammaticality claim, we have included examples such as *die Tasche Peters* in our analysis (see also Sections 2.3 and 4.1).

3.1.3 *Agent/Patient role*

A third semantic restriction pointed out in the existing literature relates to a nominalised transitive verb with two genitives. In this case, the prenominal genitive unambiguously codes the Agent role, whereas the postnominal genitive codes the Patient role (14a) (e.g. Erben 1972: 155, Engel 1988: 611, Marillier 1992: 53, Lattewitz 1994: 119, Hartmann & Zimmermann 2003: 24). If the semantic context imposes a Patient interpretation of the prenominal genitive, the construction is considered to be ungrammatical (14b). While this construction with two genitives is amply discussed in secondary literature (e.g. Bhatt 1990, Lattewitz 1994, de Wit & Schoorlemmer 1996, Ehrich & Rapp 2000, Hartmann & Zimmermann 2003), it is very hard to find in empirical data (Ballweg 1998: 162). No example could be found in our corpus.

(14) a. <u>Vater-s</u>   **Unterstützung** <u>Juliane-s</u>
                                 (Hartmann & Zimmermann 2003: [24])
          father-GEN support   Juliane-GEN
          'father's support of Juliane'

      b. *<u>Dresden-s</u>   **Zerstörung** <u>Harrison-s</u>   (Lattewitz 1994: 124)
          Dresden-GEN destruction Harrison-GEN
          'Dresden's destruction by Harrison'

According to Hartmann & Zimmermann (2003: 21), the restriction and asymmetry disappears when pre- and postnominal genitive do not co-occur. In Section 4.1 we will investigate this claim further.

3.1.4 *Proper names as head nouns*
A final semantic constraint pertains to the impossibility of a postnominal genitive modifying a proper name (cf. Bhatt 1990: 138, Lattewitz 1994: 138) (15a). A prenominal genitive, by contrast, is possible (15b). This may be explained by the fact that the specifying function of the prenominal genitive matches the identifying character of the proper name head (cp. Section 3.1.1). In most examples of this kind in our corpus, the head is accompanied by the title or function of the person in question, as in (15c). In these examples, a postnominal genitive, if at all possible, would merely have a reference-limiting function (as if, for instance, there were another country in the world which had a president called Nicolas Sarkozy in (15d)). The example in (15c) can only be construed postnominally if the proper name is added between commas, as a nonrestrictive apposition, and the head is accompanied by the definite article (15e). In case the head constitutes a combination of a proper noun ('ZANU') and a common noun ('party'), the postnominal genitive can be used (15f).

(15) a. Das ist *<u>**Peter** Maria-s.</u>   (Bhatt 1990: 138)
          that is   Peter Maria-GEN
          'That is Peter of Maria.'

      b. Das ist <u>Maria-s</u>   **Peter.**   (ibid.)
          that is   Maria-GEN Peter
          'That is Maria's Peter.'

    c. <u>Frankreich-s</u> **Präsident Nicolas Sarkozy**   (DW 14.03.08)
        France-GEN   president Nicolas Sarkozy
        'France's president Nicolas Sarkozy'

    d. ^{??}**Präsident Nicolas Sarkozy** <u>Frankreich-s</u>
        president Nicolas Sarkozy France-GEN
        'president Nicolas Sarkozy of France'

    e. **der Präsident** <u>Frankreich-s</u>, Nicolas Sarkozy
        the president France-GEN, Nicolas Sarkozy
        'the president of France, Nicolas Sarkozy'

    f. **die ZANU-Partei** <u>Mugabe-s</u>   (DW 11.04.08)
        theZANU.party   Mugabe-GEN
        'the ZANU party of Mugabe'
        >< ^{??}ZANU   <u>Mugabe-s</u>
        ZANU Mugabe-GEN
        'ZANU of Mugabe'

Since pre-/postnominal variation is excluded in examples like (15), the relevant corpus examples (i.e. one third of all prenominal genitives) are excluded from the analysis in Section 4.

3.2   Syntactic factor: Modification of the head or genitive noun

The modification of the head noun sometimes excludes the use of a prenominal genitive. The head can, for instance, be modified by two genitives, one of which cannot occur as a prenominal genitive. In (16a), the indefiniteness of the second genitive blocks a prenominal construction (cp. 3.1.1 above). In (16b), the definite article of the genitive proper noun and the full genitive NP resp. have to be coded as postnominal genitives (cp. 2.1 above). Apposition to a possessive pronoun, by contrast, triggers the use of a prenominal genitive (Marillier 1992: 52). Our corpus provided ample evidence for this constraint (16c).

  (16) a. **den EU-Beitritt** <u>Albanien-s</u>   <u>und</u>
          the EU.entry   Albania-GEN and
          <u>aller</u>   <u>Nachfolgestaaten Jugoslawien-s</u>   (DW 14.04.08)
          all.GEN.M successor.states   Jugoslawia-GEN
          'the EU entry of Albania and of all successor states of Jugoslawia'

      b. **die mögliche Aufnahme** <u>der</u>   <u>Ukraine</u> <u>und</u>
          the possible   admission the.GEN.F Ukraine and
          <u>Georgien-s</u>   (DW 01.04.08)
          Georgia-GEN
          'the possible admission of Ukraine and of Georgia'

die Führungen	Israel-s	und	der	Palästinenser

(DW 05.03.08)

the governments Israel-GEN and the.GEN.M Palestinians
'the governments of Israel and the Palestinians'

c. sein, Grenouille-s, **Eigengeruch** (Pf:171)
his, Grenouille-GEN, own smell
'his, Grenouille's, own smell'

Similarly, genitive nouns which are themselves modified by a relative clause or an apposition, always appear postnominally (e.g. Marillier 1992: 50–51, Neef 2006: 292). Our DW-subcorpus provided only one such example, which was postnominal (17a). The other subcorpora, however, yielded ample corroboration of this constraint (17b).

(17) a. **die Freilassung** Betancourt-s (…), die auch die französische
the liberation Betancourt-GEN who also the French
Staatsbürgerschaft hat (DW 02.04.08)
nationality has
'the liberation of Betancourt, who also holds the French nationality'

b. nach **dem Tod** Nomuka'la-s, des Medizinmann-es
after the death Nomuka'la-GEN, the.GEN.M medicine.man-GEN
des Stamm-es (Ks:6)
the.GEN.M tribe-GEN
'after the death of Nomuka'la, the medicine man of the tribe'

Genitives like those illustrated in (16–17) are excluded from the analysis in Section 4.

4. Factors hampering variation between pre- and postnominal genitives of proper names

Whereas the factors listed in Section 3 exclude variation between pre- and postnominal genitives, other factors merely hamper this variation. In this section, these factors will be discussed and analysed in detail.

4.1 Semantic factor: Agent/patient role expressed by the genitive

Section 3.1.3 focussed on the Agent/Patient-role in semantic contexts which exclude variation between the pre- and postnominal genitive (14a, here repeated as 18a). As already mentioned, Hartmann & Zimmermann (2003: 21) claim that the restriction and asymmetry disappears when pre- and postnominal genitive do not co-occur. The prenominal genitive in (18b) can either be a subject- or an object-genitive, as can the postnominal genitive in (18c). These authors point out, however, that whereas prenominal genitives can have both interpretations (18b), this is not always the case for postnominal genitives (18d). Postnominal genitives can only have both interpretations when the relational head noun "does not contain a change of state predicate" (ibid.: 21), i.e. it expresses a 'process' (18c) rather than a 'change' (18d). If a 'change of state' is expressed, the only possible interpretation is the Patient one (18d) (ibid.: 22).

(18) a. Vater-s   Unterstützung Juliane-s

                                        (Hartmann & Zimmermann 2003: [24])

          father-GEN support   Juliane-GEN

          'father's support of Juliane'

     b. Hugo-s   Explosion   (ibid.: [6])

          Hugo-GEN explosion

          'Hugo's explosion'

          (Hugo causes an explosion [Agent]/Hugo explodes [Patient])

     c. die Berührung Peter-s   (ibid.: [20])

          the touching   Peter-GEN

          'the touching by/of Peter' (Peter touches [Agent]/ is touched [Patient])

     d. die Explosion Hugo-s   (ibid.: 6)

          the explosion Hugo-GEN

          'the explosion of Hugo'

          (Hugo explodes [Patient]/ not: Hugo causes an explosion [Agent])

Two remarks are in order here. First, we doubt Hartmann & Zimmermann's claim that both the Agent- and Patient-interpretation are equally plausible for prenominal genitives (18b: 'Hugo's explosion'). It is striking that in our corpus no examples could be found of prenominal genitives with a Patient reading: all objective genitives are realized as postnominal genitives (19a) (Table 5). Head nouns derived from a transitive verb induce an agentive interpretation of the prenominal genitive (19b). This observation seems to contradict Hartmann & Zimmermann's claim that the prenominal genitive expresses a free relation to the head noun, even if the head expresses a 'change of state'.

(19) a. die Loslösung Tibet-s   von   China   (DW 12.04.08)

          the separation Tibet-GEN from China

          'the separation of Tibet from China'

Table 5. Ratio Agent/Patient-role coded by genitives modifying a nominalised verb

DW Head = nominalization	Agent (43)	Patient (18)	(Total) (61)
PRE-	20 (100%)	0 (0%)	(20)
POST-	23 (56.1%)	18 (43.9%)	(41)

b. Wilder-s [sic] **Beleidungen**   (DW 28.03.08)
    Wilder-GEN   insults
    'Wilders' insults'

    Sarkozy-s   **Besuch**   (DW 27.03.08)
    Sarkozy-GEN visit
    'Sarkozy's visit'

Secondly, all 'agentive' postnominal genitives in our corpus (Table 5 above) have a
nominalised head derived from an intransitive verb, which completely lacks a Patient
argument position (20a), or they have a resultative[11] head noun, which incorporates
the Patient argument itself (20b). In both cases, a 'Patient' reading is impossible. In
other words, our corpus contains no examples of nominalised heads derived from
transitive verbs with an agentive postnominal genitive. All similar examples occur
with a patient postnominal genitive (20c). We do not wish to claim here that the agentive interpretation of postnominal 'process'-genitives like (18c) ('the touching by
Peter') are impossible, but merely that it is far less likely than the Patient interpretation
in real life language use, since the postnominal position is prototypically filled by the
most intrinsic argument of the transitive verb underlying the nominalised head noun,
i.e. the Patient argument. Interestingly, the 'agentive' postnominal genitives in our corpus can seldom be replaced by the agentive preposition *durch* (20a/b → 20d), whereas
the agentive prenominal genitives often can be (19b → 20e).

(20) a. **die Rückkehr** Frankreich-s in die NATO   (DW 08.04.08)
          the return   France-GEN in the NATO
          'the return of France to the NATO'

      b. **der Entwurf** Slowenien-s   (DW 11.03.08)
          the plan   Slovenia-GEN
          'the plan of Slovenia'

      c. nach **der Teilung**   Zypern-s   (DW 21.03.08)
          after the separation Cyprus-GEN
          'after the separation of Cyprus'

      d. **die Rückkehr** Frankreich-s
          the return   France-GEN
          'the return of France'

          → [??]die Rückkehr durch Frankreich
               the return   by   France
               'the return by France'

      der Entwurf Slowenien-s
      the plan   Slovenia-GEN
      'the plan of Slovenia'

→ ?der Entwurf durch Slowenien
the plan   by   Slovenia
'the plan by Slovenia'

e. **Beleidigungen** durch Minderjährige (www.juraforum.de 2010)
insults   by   minors
'insults by minors'

der **Besuch** durch den Vorsitzenden (www.agr.de 2006)
the visit   by   the chair
'the visit by the chair'

All of this suggests that, in contrast to what has been claimed before, pre- and post-nominal genitives occurring alone have the same default interpretation as pre- and postnominals occurring together: the prenominal position clearly prefers more extrinsic, agentive genitives, the postnominal position more intrinsic, objective genitives.

The agentive character of the prenominal genitive (agent as initiator) may also account for the fact that in the case of a human referent of the genitive, the prenominal genitive occurs slightly more frequently than the postnominal one, whereas geographical names are more frequently coded postnominally (Table 6).

The agentive character of the prenominal genitive may finally account for the fact that possessive genitives expressing an alienable relation are prototypically coded prenominally. As was mentioned above, possessive genitives can have either relational (inalienable relation) or non-relational head nouns (alienable relation). A relational noun inherently evokes a relation with another noun. Kinterms are typical relational nouns: 'mother', for instance, inherently evokes a relation to a 'child'. Non-relational nouns, such as 'book' or 'hat', do not relate inherently to another noun. This distinction resembles Hartmann & Zimmermann's distinction between R-nouns (relational nouns) and P-nouns (property nouns = non-relational nouns) (2003: 5). According to Hartmann & Zimmermann (ibid.: 30), non-relational heads cannot be construed with a postnominal genitive proper name (21a): *Peters* is a genitive 'modifier' rather than a genitive 'argument' of the head. They claim that only postnominal genitive 'arguments' (i.e. relating to a relational head noun) are grammatical (21b). While they do not offer corpus evidence for this claim, our corpus does provide a number of counterexamples: 'meal', for example, is a non-relational noun, which does seem to allow a postnominal genitive (21c). This example supports the view of the linguists who assess the post-nominal genitive after non-relational nouns as "only slightly marked" (21d) or who

Table 6. Ratio pre-/postnominal genitive referring to a human being or country

DW variation	Human being (50 = 100%)	Geographical name (132 = 100%)	(Total: 182)
PRE-	29 (58%)	47 (35.60%)	(76)
POST-	21 (42%)	85 (64.40%)	(106)

accept the pre- and postnominal use of proper nouns 'modifying' non-relational head nouns without further discussion (21e).

(21) a. *die Tasche <u>Peter-s</u>   (Hartmann & Zimmermann 2003: 30)
          the bag   Peter-GEN
          'the bag of Peter'

      b. die Ernennung <u>Martin-s</u>   (ibid.: 9)
          the appointment Martin-GEN
          'the appointment of Martin'

      c. von einer **Mahlzeit** <u>Runel-s</u>   (Pf:192)
          of   a   meal   Runel-GEN
          'of one of Runel's meals'

      d. <u>Peter-s</u>   **Buch** / [?]**das Buch** <u>Peter-s</u>   (Lattewitz 1994: 122)
          Peter-GEN book / the   book Peter-GEN
          'Peter's book/the book of Peter'

      e. **das Brot** <u>Erik-s</u>   (Zifonun et al. 1997: 1971)
          the bread Erik-GEN
          'the bread of Erik'

          die **Gemälde** <u>Picasso-s</u>   (Ten Cate et al. 2004: 289)
          the paintings Picasso-GEN
          'the paintings of Picasso'

          die Röcke <u>Maria-s</u>   (Neef 2006: 287)
          the skirts Maria-GEN
          'the skirts of Maria'

          die Kantaten <u>J S Bach-s</u>   (Spencer 2009: 182)
          the cantatas J S Bach-GEN
          'the cantatas of J S Bach'

Though we dispute Hartmann & Zimmermann's ungrammaticality claim with respect to examples such as (21a), we do not deny the fact that possessive genitives tend to occur prenominally. An alienable relation resembles an agentive relation in that it is an extrinsic relation (due to the absence of a relational head noun) and it involves an 'initiator'-meaning (the possessor can handle the possession as he/she likes). Although these genitives do not constitute a large part of our corpus examples, we believe that Table 7 shows that they are more likely to appear prenominally (22a) than postnominally (22b). This argumentation may account for the radical ungrammaticality judgement by Hartmann & Zimmermann.

(22) a. <u>Frankreich-s</u> **Atomwaffenarsenal**   (DW 21.03.08)
          France-GEN   atomic.weapons.arsenal
          'France's atomic weapons arsenal'

Table 7. Ratio pre-/postnominal genitive coding a relation

DW Variation	Possessive relation (24 = 100%)	(Total: 182)
PRE-	17 (70.80%)	(76)
POST-	7 (29.20%)	(106)

    b. **die ZANU-Partei** Mugabe-s   (DW 11.04.08)
        the ZANU party Mugabe-GEN
        'the ZANU party of Mugabe'

4.2   Syntactic factors

4.2.1   *Modification of the head noun*

In certain structures the modification of the head noun excludes the use of a pre- or postnominal genitive (see Section 3.2 above), but in others it merely induces the preference for either genitive. 'Heavy' modification of the head noun, for example, is one such factor mentioned by Marillier (1992). In English literature, this factor is often discussed as 'syntactic weight', including the relative weight of N(P)1 and N(P)2 and following Behaghel's 'Gesetz der wachsenden Glieder', which says that the 'shorter' of two constituents tends to precede the 'longer' one (Behaghel 1923–32: 6). In this respect, Marillier claims that 'heavy' postnominal modification of the head noun induces the prenominal use of the genitive (23a). This claim may hold in ambiguous cases (23b) – a number of prenominal genitives exemplifying Marillier's claim could be found in our corpus (23c) – but we also found a significant number of counterexamples to Marillier's claim (23d: postnominal genitive).

(23) a. <u>des</u>   <u>Vater-s</u>   **Nahkampfreglement, das** **er auswendig**
        the.GEN.M father-GEN fighting.rules,   which he by.heart
        aufsagen kann wie die "Glocke"   (KM 107, in: Marillier 1992: 50)
        recite   can   as   the "Glocke"
        'father's fighting rules, which he can recite by heart just like the "Glocke"'

     b. [der Geruch von] <u>des</u>   <u>Vater-s</u>   **grauem Überzieher,**
        [the smell of] the.GEN.M father-GEN grey   overcoat,
        in den   Nelly gewickelt ist   (KM 36, in: Marillier 1992: 50)
        in which Nelly wrapped is
        '[the smell of] father's grey overcoat, in which Nelly is wrapped'

     c. <u>Limbach-s</u> **Erfolge bei der Reform des**
        Limbach-GEN successes at   the   reform the.GEN.N
        Goethe-Institut-s   (DW 31.03.08)
        Goethe.institute-GEN
        'Limbach's successes in reforming the Goethe institute'

d. **den Sieg** Kibaki-s **bei der Präsidentenwahl**
the victory Kibaki-GEN at the presidential.election
Ende Dezember   (DW 21.02.08)
end December
'the victory of Kibaki in the presidential election at the end of December'

die offiziellen Gespräche Steinmeier-s **mit Sikorski**
the official talks Steinmeier-GEN with Sikorski
und auch mit Ministerpräsident Donald Tusk   (DW 06.04.08)
and also with Prime.Minister Donald Tusk
'the official talks of Steinmeier with Sikorski and also with Prime Minister
Donald Tusk'

The same holds for Marillier's claim (ibid.:51) that to avoid the clash of two attributes
to the right of a head noun [head + (PP = preposition + **noun** = 1; + *genitive attribute*
of the prepositional attribute = 2)], the genitive is often positioned in front of the head
of the PP (24a). Again, many counterexamples could be found in our corpus. In (24b),
the 'clash' of two attributes to the right of a head noun is not avoided.

(24) a. **auf der Stuhllehne** *an* des Bruder-s **Bett**(Marillier 1992: 51)
on the chair.back at the.GEN.N brother-GEN bed
'on the back of the chair near the brother's bed'

Vereinbarung *über* Mugabe-s **Rückzug**   (DW 01.04.08)
agreement on Mugabe-GEN retreat
'agreement on Mugabe's retreat'

b. **der Marsch** *für* **die Unabhängigkeit** Tibet-s   (DW 13.03.08)
the march for the independence Tibet-GEN
'the march for the independence of Tibet'

rund 34 Jahre nach der Teilung Zypern-s   (DW 21.03.08)
about 34 years after the separation Cyprus-GEN
'about 34 years after the separation of Cyprus'

Although it is not mentioned in the existing literature, our corpus examples seem to
provide evidence for the opposite situation: heavy prenominal modification of the
head noun induces the postnominal use of the genitive (25a). It should be added, however, that most of the prenominally modified head nouns in the corpus are modified
by one adjective only. In that case, both pre- and postnominal genitives occur. By contrast, all examples in which two or more adjectives or PPs prenominally modify the
head include a postnominal genitive (25a–b).

(25) a. **gegen die vom Präsidenten geplante vollständige Rückkehr**
against the by.the president planned full return
Frankreich-s   (DW 08.04.08)
France-GEN
'against the full return of France that was planned by the president'

   b. zu **den größten mittelalterlichen Domschätzen**   Europa-s
       to the largest   medieval   cathedral.treasures Europe-GEN
                                                    (DW 13.04.08)
       'to the largest medieval cathedral treasures of Europe'

We can conclude that our corpus data do not provide evidence for Marillier's syntactic factors. It is therefore more likely that other factors prevail in the variation between pre- and postnominal genitives (cp. 4.1, 4.2.2, 4.3).

4.2.2   *Prosodic weight*

A second syntactic factor pertains to the 'prosodic weight' of the genitive itself. In Section 4.1 we pointed out Hartmann & Zimmermann's ungrammaticality judgement of proper names as postnominal 'modifying' genitives (after non-relational head nouns, cf. (21a) **die Tasche Peters*). With respect to similar examples (26), these authors add that

> "if the postnominal proper name gets prosodically heavier, the acceptability of these genitive modifiers increases. While the monosyllabic and bisyllabic names (...) yield ungrammatical genitive expressions, the trisyllabic name *Ursula* (...) is only slightly marked. If the names contain more than three syllables, they are perfect postnominal genitive modifiers" (ibid.: 30).

(26) *der   Computer   Ulf-s
       *?der   Computer   Peter-s
       ?der   Computer   Ursula-s
       der   Computer   Alexander-s
       der   Computer   Katharina-s der Großen

We put our corpus examples to a prosodic weight test, counting the numbers of syllables of the pre- and postnominal genitives (irrespective of the relationality of the head noun and irrespective of the semantic relation expressed) (cp. Stefanowitsch 2003: 425), in an attempt to verify or refute Hartmann & Zimmerman's claim. The numbers in Table 8 seem to support their claim, although especially 2- or 3-syllable nouns occur in both constructions and so the markedness claim of the second and third examples in (26) can be questioned. The 1-syllable (shorter) nouns tend to be coded prenominally, as expected, and the 4-syllable (longer) nouns postnominally. Similarly, 'longer' structures with titles are coded with the postnominal *von*-phrase (see Section 2.3 above: *der Kurs von Parteichef Kurt Beck* 'the policy of party leader Kurt Beck').

Table 8. Prosodic weight of pre- and postnominal genitives

DW variation	1 syllable	2 syllables	3 syllables	4(+) syllables	Double name	(Total: 182)
PRE-	4	38	29	5	3	(76)
POST-	0	49	28	29	7	(106)

Moreover, prosodically 'heavier' double names are also preferably coded postnominally (Table 8; 27a). In addition, all three instances of double names as prenominal genitives in our corpus pertain to (shorter) double family names (27b), whereas all 7 instances of postnominal double names pertain to a (heavier) combination of first and family names (27a). This observation accords with Marillier's claim (1992: 52) that coordinated (double) genitives are preferably coded postnominally (cp. Demske 2001: 250, as in (27c)). No examples of coordinated prenominal genitives could be found in our corpus. In the case of coordinated names the postnominal genitive seems to alternate with the postnominal *von*-phrase (see Section 2.3 above). Moreover, in most of our corpus examples this involves at least one proper name with an article or a full NP (cf. 16b: 'the governments of Israel and the Palestinians'). As noted in Section 2.1 above, a prenominal genitive is then very unlikely.

(27) a. **der Sturz** <u>Sadam Hussein-s</u>   (DW 19.03.08)
          the fall   Sadam Hussein-GEN
          'the fall of Sadam Hussein'

          die Nachfolge <u>Bertie Ahern-s</u>   (DW 06.04.08)
          the succession Bertie Ahern-GEN
          'the succession of Bertie Ahern'

      b. <u>Bin Laden-s</u>   **Botschaft**   (DW 20.03.08)
          Bin Laden-GEN message
          'Bin Laden's message'

          <u>Al Sadr-s</u>   **Miliz**   (DW 27.03.08)
          Al Sadr-GEN militia
          'Al Sadr's militia'

      c. **die Präsidenten** <u>Israel-s</u>   und <u>Polen-s</u>   (DW 15.04.08)
          the presidents   Israel-GEN and Poland-GEN
          'the presidents of Israel and Poland'

          seit **dem Beitritt**   <u>Polen-s</u>   und <u>Tschechien-s</u>   (DW 01.04.08)
          since the accession Poland-GEN and Czechia-GEN
          'since the accession of Poland and Czechia'

4.3 Pragmatic factor: Information focus and participant identifiability

A final factor impeding pre-/postnominal genitive variation seems to be pragmatic. Marillier (1992: 54) draws attention to Sauter's (1983) and Rozen's (1988) observation that the position of the genitive could be related to the "communicative value" of the head or the genitive respectively, the second noun being the actual theme of the utterance. The only grammar which vaguely hints at this difference is Erben (1972: 155–6), who claims that the 'accent' is moved to the genitive in postnominal position. Marillier (1992: 54) comments on Rozen's examples in (28) as follows:

(28) a. Die Olympischen Spiele in Berlin waren schon   vor
         the Olympic   Games in Berlin had   already before
         <u>Hitler-s</u>   **Machtergreifung** an Deutschland vergeben worden.
         Hitler-GEN coup.d'état   to Germany   granted been
         'The Olympic Games in Berlin had already been granted to Germany be-
         fore Hitler's coup d'état.'

     b. daß 99% der   Stimmberechtigten **die Politik** <u>Hitler-s</u>   billigen
         that 99% of.the voters   the policy Hitler-GEN approve
         'that 99% of the voters approve of the policy of Hitler'

     c. Hindenburg, der   in **die Hände** <u>Adolf Hitler-s</u>
         Hindenburg, who in the hands   Adolf Hitler-GEN
         euer Schicksal legte
         your fate   put
         'Hindenburg, who put your fate into the hands of Adolf Hitler'

(28) a. – 'before Hitler's coup d'état' = before 1933:
         the date is the most important element here,
         'Hitler' functions as a time scale
         (Hitler's coup attempt/Hitler's coup d'état/Hitler's suicide)

     b. – that 99% of the voters approve of Hitler
     c. – that they entrusted Hitler with their fate

Although Marillier lists a few similar examples from his own corpus and stresses the importance of this factor (1992: 55, 57), he does not offer a detailed and systematic analysis of this information factor. The following subsections attempt to offer such an analysis.

'Thematic' information pertains to discourse structure and communicative relevant entities, and is therefore connected with phenomena such as information focus and information continuity. On the one hand, the thematic composition of the sentence or NP is relevant: which parts are thematic information and which parts are focussed (topic/focus- or theme/rheme-division) (Section 4.3.1). On the other hand, discourse information is composed thematically. There are three kinds of information continuity: theme-, action- and participant-continuity (Givón 1983). For the topic of this paper, participant-continuity is certainly the most important one. A participant can be introduced, reintroduced or disappear. A participant that has been introduced and re-introduced in the text is more identifiable than a participant that has not (Section 4.3.2).

4.3.1 *Information focus*

All examples in (29) are illustrations of the fact that on the discourse level, the second noun (N2 – head noun) is focussed in the NP with prenominal genitive (N1-N2). In (29a), the head noun (N2: 'substitute') provides new information and is therefore the focus of attention. The prenominal genitive (N1 – 'Wen's') repeats information given in one of the preceding sentences. (29b) is a similar example: the information focus pertains to the individuals involved in the caravan: first Richis, then the daughter, the maid, and finally the servants.

(29) a. Der Nationale Volkskongress hat den chinesischen **Regierungschef** Wen Jiabao (...) im Amt bestätigt. Einen **Gegenkandidaten** gab es nicht. Im Anschluss daran wählten die rund 3.000 Delegierten

<u>Wen-s</u>   **Stellvertreter.**   (DW 16.0308)
Wen-GEN substitute
'The National People's Congress officially confirmed the Chinese head of government Wen Jiabao (...). There was no opponent. Subsequently the approx. 3000 delegates elected Wen's substitute.'

      b. Richis ritt voran. (...) Ihm folgte seine **Tochter** (...) Dann (...) die **Zofe,** dann

<u>Richis'</u>   **Diener.**   (Pf:263)
Richis.GEN servants
'Richis rode first (...) his daughter followed him (...) then the maid, then Richis' servants.'

By way of contrast, in the examples in (30), the postnominal genitive (N2) is focussed, whereas the head often merely repeats what has been said before. In (30a) the whole paragraph is devoted to the cathedral treasure in the German town Halberstadt. Only at the end of the text is the perspective widened to Europe. In (30b), it is the postnominal genitive that uncovers the identity of the masked person involved, i.e. the information the reader is waiting for.

(30) a. Nach mehrjährigen Umbauarbeiten sind die neuen Räume des mittelalterlichen Halberstädter **Domschatzes** eröffnet worden (...). Er [Köhler, PC.] würdigte die Wiedereröffnung der **Domschatz**räume als bedeutenden Tag für ganz Deutschland. Die Halberstädter **Sammlung** gehört zu

den größten mittelalterlichen Domschätzen   <u>Europa-s.</u>
the   largest   medieval   cathedral.treasures Europe-GEN
                                                           (DW 13.04.08)
'After several years of building alterations the new treasure rooms of the medieval cathedral of Halberstadt have been opened (...). He paid tribute to the reopening of the cathedral treasure rooms as an important day for the whole of Germany. The collection of Halberstadt is among the largest medieval cathedral treasures of Europe.'

      b. Und Ron tauchte ein in die (...) Stille eines Operationssaals, vor dessen glänzenden gekachelten Wänden ihn drei vermummte Gestalten erwarteten. Eine dieser Gestalten kam lautlos auf ihn zu, beugte sich über ihn, und in dem Streifen Gesicht, den die Maske freigab, konnte er

die ruhigen, warmen Augen <u>Hendrik Merz'</u>   erkennen.
the calm,   warm   eyes   Hendrik Merz.GEN recognize

(Ks:271)

'And Ron dived into the (...) silence of the operation theatre. In front of its shiny, tiled walls, three masked figures waited for him. One of these figures came over to him soundlessly, bent over him and in the facial stripe, which the mask uncovered, he recognized the calm, warm eyes of Hendrik Merz.'

4.3.1.1 *Potential omission of N1.* A consequence of the difference in information focus between pre- and postnominal genitives is that it is often possible to omit N1 (rather than N2) without a major loss of meaning and/or to replace it by the definite article or a possessive pronoun, since it is not the real focus of attention. Potential omission of head or genitive can, in other words, be used as a test for thematicity. A large number of examples illustrating this observation can be found in our corpus.

FARC in (31a) stands for *Fuerzas Armadas Revolutionarias de Colombia*, or: Revolutionary Armed Forces of Columbia. Since the name of the revolutionary rebels contains 'Columbia', the prenominal genitive is added for those who are not familiar with *FARC* or who do not remember which country *FARC* is related to.

(31) a. <u>Kolumbien-s</u>   **FARC-Rebellen** lassen vier weitere Geiseln frei.

(DW 02.03.08)

Columbia-GEN   FARC.rebels
'Columbia's FARC rebels release four more hostages.'

→ <u>(Die)</u> FARC-Rebellen lassen vier weitere Geiseln frei.
'(The) FARC rebels release four more hostages.'

b. Osama bin Laden hat Europa wegen der erneuten Veröffentlichung von Karikaturen des Propheten Mohammed mit Vergeltung gedroht. (...)
<u>Bin Laden-s</u>   **Botschaft**
Bin Laden-GEN message
sei eine klare Bedrohung der EU-Mitgliedstaaten.   (DW 20.03.08)
'Osama bin Laden has threatened Europe with retribution on account of the cartoons of the prophet Mohammed which have been published again (...) Bin Laden's message is said to be a clear menace to the EU member states.'

→ <u>(Seine/die)</u> Botschaft sei eine klare Bedrohung der EU-Mitgliedstaaten.
'(His/the) message is a clear menace to the EU member states.'

c. (...) am letzten Tag des Staatsbesuches des französischen Präsidenten Nicolas Sarkozy in London (...) Brown ergänzte,
<u>Sarkozy-s</u>   **Besuch**
Sarkozy-GEN visit

sei Dokument für ein neues Bündnis zwischen London und Paris.

(DW 27.03.08)

'(...) on the last day of the official visit to London of the French president Nicolas Sarkozy (...) Brown added that Sarkozy's visit was a document for a new alliance between London and Paris.'

→   (Sein/der) Besuch sei ein Dokument.
   '(His/the) visit was a document.'

Similar examples are given in (31b–c). The prenominal genitive can be omitted without major loss of meaning and/or replaced by a definite article or possessive pronoun. As noted earlier (Section 3.1.1), prenominal genitives resemble possessive pronouns. Both have a high degree of thematicity (the possessive pronoun is almost always used anaphorically) and therefore a small degree of communicative-informative value.

In the examples with postnominal genitives in (32), on the other hand, N1 is the head of the NP and here as well, N1 can often be omitted without rendering the sentence ungrammatical and changing its contents radically. The South African 'summit' in (32a) happens to be held in Zambia; that it is held in the capital of Zambia is not the focus of attention and therefore somewhat less important. Although N1 'capital' certainly has its own function in adding more detail and individuating the concept denoted in N2, it could be omitted without any great loss of meaning. Some head nouns (N1) add little in terms of necessary information, as in the examples in (32b). In the headline, the noun 'countries' is not even mentioned. These countries *are* South America – South America is a conglomerate of countries. And Uhrlau is the person who estimates – N1 'words' adds little meaningful new information. Finally (32c) illustrates that words such as 'north' and 'south' (the points on the compass) are typically followed by a postnominal genitive. Although they give more detailed geographic information, the focus of attention is usually the region or country that is dealt with.[12]

(32)   a.   In **der Hauptstadt** <u>Sambia-s</u>
       in the capital   Zambia-GEN
       sind die Staaten der Südafrikanischen Entwicklungsgemeinschaft SADC
       zu einem Gipfel (...) zusammengekommen.   (DW 12.04.08)
       'In the capital of Zambia the states of the South African Development
       Union SADC have gathered for a summit.'
       →   In Sambia sind die Staaten (...) zusammengekommen.
          'In Zambia the states (...) have gathered.'

       b.   Rice ruft Südamerika zur Zusammenarbeit gegen Terror auf.
       [headline]
       BRASILIA – US-Außenministerin Condoleezza Rice hat bei einem Besuch in Brasilien
       die Länder   <u>Südamerika-s</u>
       the countries South.America-GEN

zur Zusammenarbeit (...) aufgerufen. (DW 14.03.08)
'Rice calls on South America for cooperation against terrorism.
Brasilia – At a visit to Brazil, US-Secretary of State Condoleezza Rice has
called on the countries of South America to cooperate.'
→   Rice hat (...) Südamerika zur Zusammenarbeit aufgerufen.
'Rice has (...) called on South America to cooperate.'

Die Zahl der gewaltbereiten islamistischen Extremisten in Deutschland
wird von den Sicherheitsbehörden
nach   **den Worten** Uhrlau-s
according.to the words   Uhrlau-GEN
auf einige hundert geschätzt.   (DW 24.03.08)
'The number of Islamic extremists in Germany willing to resort to vio-
lence is estimated at a few hundreds by the safety authorities, according to
the words of Uhrlau.'
→   Die Zahl (...) wird (...) nach Uhrlau auf einige hundert geschätzt.
'The number (...) is (...) estimated at a few hundreds, according to
Uhrlau.'

c.   Zwei venezolanische Rot-Kreuz-Hubschrauber waren zuvor an einen unbekannten Ort
im   Süden Kolumbien-s geflogen.   (DW 20.03.08)
in.the south   Columbia-GEN
'Two Venezuelan Red Cross helicopters had previously flown to an unknown location in the south of Columbia.'
→   Zwei Hubschrauber waren an einen unbekannten Ort in Kolumbien
geflogen.
'Two helicopters had flown to an unknown location in the south of
Columbia.'

As Table 9 shows, in the prenominal genitive construction, the genitive (N1) has more
'omission potential' than the head noun (N2), whereas for the postnominal genitive
construction, the omission test can more easily be applied to the head noun (N1).

Table 9. 'Omission potential' of head/genitive

DW variation	Potential omission of the head (+ loss of detail)	Potential omission of the genitive (+ loss of detail)	Neither head nor genitive can be omitted	(Total: 182)
PRE-	6 (7.89%)	25 (**32.90%**)	45 (59.21%)	(76) = 100%
POST-	54 (**50.94%**)	28 (26.42%)	24 (22.64%)	(106) = 100%

4.3.1.2   *Elaboration on N2.* The idea that the second noun of the NP is focussed is supported by the observation that the sentence context following the NP often provides more detailed information precisely on N2, be it the (prenominal genitive's) head (33) or the (postnominal) genitive itself (34).

At the end of (33a) (*Wilders' film*), the writer elaborates on the title ('Fitna') and contents ('terrorist attacks') of the film discussed (= N2 = head). Similarly, the last sentence of (33b) provides further information on N2 (= head), not on N1 (= prenominal genitive).

(33)   a.   Indonesische Internetprovider haben mit der Schließung von Webseiten begonnen, die den islamfeindlichen Film des niederländischen Rechts-populisten Geert Wilders zeigen. (...) Die indonesische Regierung hatte am Donnerstag angekündigt, Youtube im ganzen Land zu sperren, sollte

Wilder-s [sic] **Film**
Wilders-GEN film

nicht bis zum Wochenende aus dem Netz genommen werden. **Der Film mit dem Titel 'Fitna' (Zwietracht) kombiniert Bilder von Opfern ter-roristischer Anschläge in New York und Madrid mit Zeitungss-chlagzeilen und Koranversen.**   (DW 05.04.08)
'Indonesian internet providers have started the closure of websites that show the anti-islam film of the Dutch right-wing populist Geert Wilders (...) The Indonesian government announced on Thursday that it would deactivate Youtube throughout the country, if Wilders' film wasn't taken off the net by the weekend. The film titled 'Fitna' (disagreement) combines images of victims of terrorist attacks in New York and Madrid with newspaper headlines and verses from the Quran.'

b.   Nach elf Jahren im Amt ist der irische Premierminister Bertie Ahern zurückgetreten. Ahern hatte den Schritt bereits Anfang April unter dem Druck einer Korruptionsaffäre angekündigt.

Als Ahern-s   **Nachfolger**
As   Ahern-GEN successor

steht der 48-jährige bisherige Finanzminister **Brian Cowen** fest. **Seine Wahl durch das Unterhaus in Dublin ist für diesen Mittwoch geplant. Cowen hatte bereits mehrere Ministerposten bekleidet. Anfang der 90er Jahre führte er das Arbeitsressort, später war er für Verkehr und Gesundheit zuständig, bis er von 2000 bis 2004 Außenminister war.** (DW 07.05.08)
'After eleven years in office the Irish Prime Minister Bertie Ahern has re-signed. Ahern had already announced this step at the beginning of April, due to a corruption affair. It is clear that Ahern's successor will be the present Finance Minister, 48-year old Brian Cowen. His election by the House of Commons in Dublin is scheduled for this Wednesday. Cowen

has already held a number of ministerial posts. At the beginning of the 90's, he led the Ministry of Employment, later he was responsible for Traffic and Health, until he became Foreign Minister 2000–2004.'

The examples in (34) illustrate that also in constructions with a postnominal genitive, N2 (= postnominal genitive) rather than N1 (= head) is elaborated in the sentence context following the NP. (34a) is an announcement of the death of Annemarie Renger. The last two sentences provide a short description of who Renger was and her official positions, rather than of her life's work. The head noun could even be omitted without major loss of meaning (cp. Section 4.3.1.1 above). The second examples of (33) and (34) both pertain to Ireland and Bertie Ahern/Brian Cowen. They seem to be more or less each other's counterpart, however, in that the sentence context in (33b) concentrates on Cowen (N2: '[Ahern's] successor'), in (34b) on Ahern (N2: '[ascension of] Ahern').

(34) a.   Mit einem Staatsakt hat der Bundestag der früheren Parlamentspräsidentin Annemarie Renger gedacht. In ihren Trauerreden würdigten Bundestagspräsident Norbert Lammert und Altbundeskanzler Gerhard Schröder
das Lebenswerk <u>Renger-s.</u>
the life's.work   Renger-GEN
<u>Sie war die erste Frau und erste Sozialdemokratin an der Spitze des Bundestages, dem sie von 1953 bis 1990 angehörte. Renger war vergangene Woche im Alter von 88 Jahren nach schwerer Krankheit gestorben.</u>
(DW 13.03.08)
'With an act of state the Bundestag has commemorated the former President of Parliament, Annemarie Renger. In their funeral orations, the President of the Bundestag, Norbert Lammert, and the former Chancellor, Gerhard Schröder, paid tribute to the life and work of Renger. She was the first woman and first social democrat to be head of the Bundestag, of which she was a member from 1953 till 1990. Renger, aged 88, died last week after a serious illness.'

   b.   Der irische Finanzminister und Vize-Premierminister Brian Cowen wird voraussichtlich Irlands neuer Regierungschef. Nach Ablauf der parteiinternen Nominierungsfrist sei Cowen der einzige Kandidat
für **die Nachfolge** <u>Bertie Ahern-s</u>
for the ascension   Bertie Ahern-GEN
geblieben, teilte die Regierungspartei Fianna Fail in Dublin mit. (...) <u>Nach fast elf Jahren Amtszeit hatte Premierminister Bertie Ahern am Mittwoch unter dem Druck einer Korruptionsaffäre seinen Rücktritt angekündigt. Ahern wies die Vorwürfe zurück.</u>   (DW 06.04.08)

'The Irish Finance Minister and Vice President, Brian Cowen will probably be Ireland's new head of government. At the end of the intra-party
nomination deadline the government party Fianna Fail announced in
Dublin that Cowen was the only candidate left to assume the position of
Bertie Ahern (...). After almost 11 years in office, Prime Minister Bertie
Ahern had announced his resignation due to a corruption scandal. Ahern
rejected the accusations.'

Table 10 shows that in the sentence context following the NP, N2 is more likely to be
focussed, both for prenominal (N2 = head) and for postnominal genitives (N2 = genitive). The discrepancy between the figures for N2 (53.95% >< 25.47%) can easily be
explained by the fact that the postnominal genitive is a proper name, whose referent is
by definition identifiable. The elaborative context therefore merely provides additional
information. N2 head nouns, by contrast, are common nouns, whose referents are not
necessarily identified by the prenominal genitive und may need further elaboration in
the following context (see also 4.3.2 below).

It should be mentioned that a number of counterexamples to this argument can be
found in (35). Interestingly, these constructions are different in that they are frag-
ments, i.e. not part of a complete sentence. Moreover, in these examples the prosodic
accent lies on the prenominal genitive, since the accentuation of N2 is contextually
without meaning. This indicates that in these examples, the prenominal genitive has
the highest communicative value. The default situation is, however, that intonation
focus (prosodic weight) is placed on N2 (head noun or postnominal genitive) (cp. 4.2.2)
or it is equally divided over both N1 and N2.

(35) a. Er spürte eine Hand im Rücken – ↓Afa-s **Hand**   (Ks:324)
          He felt a hand in.the back – Afa-GEN hand
          'He felt a hand on his back – Afa's hand.'

      b. Und dann hörte er einen Wagen. Aber das war nicht Hendriks alte Karre,
          es war ein Jeep. Ein roter Jeep.
          ↓Patrick Lanson-s **Jeep** – tatsächlich.   (Ks:288)
          Patrick Lanson-GEN jeep – indeed
          'And then he heard a car. But it wasn't Henry's old car, it was a jeep. A red
          jeep. Patrick Lanson's jeep – indeed.'

Table 10. elaboration on N1 or N2 in the following sentence context

DW variation	N1 is elaborated on	N2 is elaborated on	No elaboration	(Total: 182)
PRE-	4 (5.26%)	41 (53.95%)	31 (40.79%)	(76)
POST-	10 (9.43%)	27 (25.47%)	69 (65.10%)	(106)

4.3.1.3   *Contrastive meaning.* The fact that in the combination [N1-N2], the second noun is focussed, be it the head noun (prenominal genitive) or the (postnominal) genitive itself, often implies a contrastive effect for N2 (Lauterbach 193: 67).[13] In other words: whereas die Schwimmer Frankreichs ('the swimmers of France') prototypically contrasts with die Schwimmer Deutschlands ('the swimmers of Germany'), Frankreichs Schwimmer ('France's swimmers') seems to contrast with Frankreichs Boxer ('France's boxers'). This difference in contrastiveness associated with difference in word order is clearly illustrated in examples in (36–37).

In (36a), the head (N2) is used contrastively. The governing party is opposed to the opposition parties. The prenominal genitive, by contrast, merely specifies the most important member of the governing party, president Mugabe. In (36b), the People's Party (N2, head) is contrasted with the Pakistani Muslim League. In (36c) the Senate is opposed to the Head of Government and his cabinet. In all three examples, the prenominal genitive (N1) could feasibly be omitted (cp. Section 4.3.1.1 above).

(36)   a.   <u>Mugabe-s</u>   **Regierungspartei**
             Mugabe-GEN government.party
             hat (...) die Parlamentsmehrheit eingebüßt. Die **Opposition** sieht sich darüber hinaus auch als Sieger der Präsidentenwahl.   (DW 02.04.08)
             'According to the national election commission Mugabe's government party has (...) lost its majority in parliament. In addition, the opposition parties see themselves as winners of the presidential election.'

       b.   Gilani wurde
             von <u>Bhutto-s</u>   **Volkspartei**
             by   Bhutto-GEN people's.party
             nominiert, er erhielt aber auch die Unterstützung der **Pakistanischen Muslimliga**.   (DW 25.03.08)
             'Gilani was nominated by Bhuttos People's Party, but also received the support of the Pakistani Muslim League.'

       c.   <u>Haiti-s</u>   **Senat**
             Haiti-GEN Senate
             hat **Regierungschef Jacques Edouard Alexis** und sein **Kabinett** entlassen.
                                                                  (DW 13.04.08)
             'Haiti's Senate has laid off Head of Government Jacques Edouard Alexis and his cabinet.'

In (37) on the other hand, it is the postnominal genitive (N2) that triggers a contrastive effect: Germany as opposed to France and Great-Britain (37a), Ireland as opposed to the European Union and Northern Ireland (37b), and Germany as opposed to Israel (37c).

(37)   a.   <u>Frankreich</u> und <u>Großbritannien</u> wollen auf ihrem Gipfel Pläne für eine engere Zusammenarbeit schmieden

      – auch auf **Kosten** <u>Deutschland-s.</u>   (DW 26.03.08)
      also at expense Germany-GEN
      'France and Great-Britain want to make plans for closer cooperation dur-
      ing their talks – also at the expense of Germany.'

  b. Ahern von der bürgerlichen Partei Fianna Fail ist seit 1997
      Ministerpräsident <u>Irland-s.</u>
      Prime.Minister   Ireland-GEN
      (...) Er ist einer der am längsten regierenden Ministerpräsidenten in der
      <u>EU</u> und hatte sich im Friedensprozess in der benachbarten Konfliktre-
      gion <u>Nordirland</u> international Anerkennung verdient.   (DW 02.04.08)
      'Ahern of the civil party Fianna Fail has been Prime Minister of Ireland
      since 1997 (...). He is one of the longest serving Prime Ministers in the EU
      and had earned international recognition in the peace process in the
      neighbouring region of Northern Ireland.'

  c. Merkel beteuerte angesichts der Drohungen der iranischen Führung ge-
      gen Israel, die historische Verantwortung für die Sicherheit <u>Israels</u> sei
      Teil **der**   **Staatsräson**   <u>Deutschland-s.</u>   (DW 19.03.08)
      part of.the reason.of.state Germany-GEN
      'With respect to the threats of the Iranian government against Israel,
      Merkel gave the assurance that the historical responsibility for the safety
      of Israel is part of the reason of state of Germany.'

The corpus counts in Table 11 show that in the prenominal genitive construction the head tends to have a contrastive value, whereas in the postnominal counterpart, a clear tendency towards contrastive value of the genitive can be observed.

    The following observation by Hartmann & Zimmermann (2003: 22–25) supports our line of argument, presented as a 'problem' in their analysis: the "problem concerns the fact that the postnominal genitive of a change of state noun, which should only allow the internal argument [Patient/object, PC.] interpretation, receives an additional modifier [Agent/subject, PC.] interpretation if it is contrastively focussed". Compare here the ungrammaticality judgement by Hartmann & Zimmermann of *die Explosion Hugos* when interpreted as 'explosion caused by Hugo' (cf. Section 4.1 above). Al-though we have claimed that the objective interpretation is prototypical, we mentioned the possibility of a peripheral agentive interpretation. Contrastive value can trigger this postnominal use of the agentive genitive (38).

Table 11. Contrastive meaning

DW variation	Contrast head	Contrast genitive	No contrast	(Total: 182)
PRE-	37 (**48.68%**)	22 (28.95%)	17 (22.37%)	(76 = 100%)
POST-	7 (6.60%)	56 (**52.83%**)	43 (40.57%)	(106 = 100%)

(38)   **Die Explosion** <u>Hugo-s</u>   erregte mehr Aufsehen als
     the explosion   Hugo-GEN caused more stir   than
     die   <u>Peter-s.</u>   (ibid.:[23])
     the.one   Peter-GEN
     'The explosion by Hugo caused more of a stir than the one by Peter.'

As Hartmann & Zimmermann (2003: 23) point out, contrastive focus can also license the co-occurrence of two postnominal genitives. Although a construction with two postnominal genitives accompanying the same head noun is prototypically excluded, the contrastive use of the second genitive can enhance the grammaticality of a double postnominal genitive construction (39). The second genitive is then always the one coding the extrinsic (agentive/possessive) relation. The intrinsic (Patient) relation should logically be adjacent to the head noun. The importance of prosodic accentuation and information focus discussed here can be related to the importance of prosodic weight discussed in Section 4.2.2 above.

(39)   **Die Bombardierung** <u>der</u>   Stadt <u>der</u>   Artillerie war
     the bombing   the.GEN city the.GEN.F artillery was
     stärker als **die**   <u>der</u>   LUFTwaffe.   (ibid.)
     heavier than the.one the.GEN.F air.force
     'The bombing of the city by the artillery was heavier than the one by the air force.'

4.3.2   *Participant identifiability and lookback*

Participant identifiability relates to the asymmetry in information and discourse flow traditionally known as referentially 'given' (known, identifiable) information versus 'new' information (e.g. Fox & Thompson 1990, Martin 1992).[14] What is of interest here is that the variation between pre- versus postnominal genitives is mainly restricted to proper names. Proper names usually relate to known, i.e. identifiable participants (e.g. Rosenbach 2003: 386–7), which can roughly be divided into five categories (from less to more identifiable) (e.g. Prince 1979, 1981; Fox & Thompson 1990; Payne 1992; Martin 1992; Givón 1993). The first two categories (i-ii) pertain to given participants which are not textually retrievable but relate to the real world knowledge of the reader/ hearer (40a–b), the others to textually retrievable participants (iii–v) (40c–e). An example illustrating a genitive providing new information is given in (40f).

i.   participant known to the narrator, but not necessarily to the reader/hearer (40a)
ii.   encyclopedically known participant (40b)
iii. implied participant ('Merkel' is known as the Chancellor of Germany: 40c)
iv. synonymously known participant ('Tibetans' also refers to 'Tibet': 40d)
v.   participant already evoked ('Wen' has been mentioned shortly before: 40e)

(40)   a.   **die Einmündung** <u>der</u>   Rue de Seine   (Pf: 51)
        the mouth   the.GEN.F Rue de Seine
        'the mouth of the Rue de Seine'

b. **die Ankündigung** <u>Frankreich-s</u>   (DW 23.03.08)
   the announcement France-GEN
   'the announcement of/by France'

c. Angela Merkel (...) **die Verantwortung** <u>Deutschland-s</u>   (DW 19.03.08)
   Angela Merkel   the responsibility   Germany-GEN
   'Angela Merkel (...) the responsibility of Germany'

d. Aufstand der   Tibeter (...) **Unabhängigkeit** <u>Tibet-s</u>
                                            (DW 13.03.08)
   Revolt   the.GEN.PL   Tibetans   independence   Tibet-GEN
   'revolt of the Tibetans'   'independence of Tibet'

e. Regierungschef   Wen Jiabao (...) <u>Wen-s</u>   **Stellvertreter**
                                              (DW 16.03.08)
   head.of.government Wen Jiabao   Wen-GEN substitute
   'head of government Wen Jiabao'   'Wen's substitute'

f. gegen   **Aushändigung** <u>einer</u>   <u>Quittung</u>   (Pf:10)
   against issue   a.GEN.F receipt
   'against the issue of a receipt'

In the light of our argument about information focus (Section 4.3.1), all pre- and post-nominal genitives in the corpus were analysed with respect to the parameters of participant identifiability *and* with respect to what is usually called 'textual lookback' (e.g. Brown 1983, Givón 1983, Taylor 1994, Stefanowitsch 2003: 439). Textual lookback pertains to how many sentences separate the genitive from its last mention in the text. Since the corpus examples were drawn from rather short newspaper reports, the values discerned were: 0/1/2/3/4/5+ lines. The hypothesis was that prenominal genitives generally have a higher textual identifiability and a smaller lookback than postnominal ones, which seems to be corroborated by the corpus data.

The number in bold in Table 12 illustrates that the referent of the prenominal genitive usually is identically evoked. This is not explicitly the case for the postnominal genitive (bearing in mind that all genitives involved are proper names, which are by definition identifiable in the sense of the 'real world knowledge' discussed above). The iconic principle, that the choice "is determined by the needs of speakers to place easily available information first in linear order" seems to be relevant here (Rosenbach 2003: 402). For these counts, the examples taken from headlines were omitted, as were those with participants that were only textually identifiable through the headline.

In Table 13, the numbers in bold show that a large majority of the referents of the prenominal genitive (71%) has already been mentioned in one of the preceding three sentences. This corresponds to Behaghel's claim (1923–32, VI: 192–3) that German tends to prepose anaphoric proper noun genitives (since anaphoric elements are usually preposed). 56% of the referents of the postnominal genitives (italic numbers) have already been mentioned in one of the preceding three sentences as well. However, the

Table 12. Participant identifiability

DW variation	Identically evoked (56)	Synonymously evoked (27)	Implied (7)	Encyclopedically known (25)	(Total: 115)
PRE-	23 (67.65%)	6 (17.65%)	1 (2.94%)	4 (11.76%)	(34) = 100%
POST-	33 (40.74%)	21 (25.925%)	6 (7.41%)	21 (25.925%)	(81) = 100%

referent of the postnominal genitive has more often been mentioned further away (more than 4 sentences), in the headline or not at all (underlined numbers: 43%), than its prenominal counterpart (28%). For these corpus counts, the examples taken from headlines were omitted.

Interestingly, newspaper headlines, at least in the Deutsche Welle reports, seem to contain more prenominal genitives than postnominal ones. In (41), for example, the headline and the first mention in the text show an opposite word order. One explanation might be that, since headlines are sentences without context, the informational organisation of the sentence works in a different way from that of context-embedded sentences. The first word may be used to draw the reader's attention. Another explanation might be that headlines are often written after the article, summarizing and reducing the article to its most important information, therefore often presupposing the content of the article. Rosenbach (2003: 399ff) mentions the economical tendency of prenominal genitives in this respect. The economical value of the 'shorter' prenominal genitive construction in headlines could be explained by the fact that the use of the prenominal genitive 'saves' on the number of words: in case of the postnominal genitive, an additional word (the definite article) is normally used (*der Tod Dianas*).[15]

Table 13. Lookback

DW Variation	same sentence	-1	-2	-3	-4	headline	none	(Total: 136)
PRE-	2 (5.13%)	13 (33.33%)	8 (20.51%)	5 (12.82%) = 71.79%	2 (5.13%)	5 (12.82%)	4 (10.26%) = 28.21%	(39) = 100%
POST-	5 (5.15%)	28 (28.86%)	15 (15.4%)	7 (7.22%) = 56.70%	5 (5.15%)	16 (16.50%)	21 (21.65%) = 43.30%	(97) = 100%

(41) Londoner Gericht:

Diana-s **Tod** war Unfall

Diana-GEN death was accident

LONDON: (...) stellte das Gericht fest, dass

der **Unfalltod** Diana-s (...)

the accidental.death Diana-GEN

auf Fahrlässigkeit ihres angetrunkenen Fahrers und der sie verfolgenden Fotografen zurückzuführen sei. (DW 08.04.08)

'London court: Diana's death was accident

London: (...) the court decided that the accidental death of Diana (...) is due to the carelessness of her drunken driver and of the photographers that pursued them.'

5. Conclusion

In this paper we have focussed on the variation between pre- and postnominal genitives in German. This topic has received little attention in grammars or recent linguistic literature, which is probably due to the restriction to unmodified proper names (Section 2.1). In contrast to what has previously been claimed (Section 2.3), there seems to be a relatively frequent alternation between pre- and postnominal genitives in certain German source texts, e.g. newspaper reports (Section 2.2). This does not, however, imply that the variation between the two constructions can be called 'free'. On the one hand, it is excluded by a number of constraints (Section 3) and the prenominal genitive has a specifying, determinative function that is absent from the postnominal genitive (Section 3.1.1). On the other hand, a variety of factors seems to play an important role when variation is possible. These factors are semantic (Section 4.1), syntactic (Section 4.2) or pragmatic (Section 4.3). The relative importance of these factors was not a topic of this paper and would be an interesting question for further research (see, for instance, Jäger & Rosenbach 2006 on probabilistic variation and hierarchy of variation factors, or Hinrichs & Szmrecsanyi 2007 on a multivariate analysis of the English genitive alternation).

Most of the factors described have been mentioned in the existing literature on genitive variation. However, they have never been discussed in combination, and the discussion has not been based on a systematic analysis of corpora. All factors were therefore listed together systematically and commented on in the light of our corpus data. The factors hampering genitive variation (Section 4), especially Agent/Patient-role and information focus, have not been analysed thoroughly and systematically before. The last factor in particular seems to support Rosenbach's general observation (2003: 383) that "even within (...) choice contexts there probably can never be complete synonymy between two alternating constructions", i.e. that "there appear to be further factors, which influence the likelihood of one construction or the other". In a large number of examples of potential variation, the two constructions are alternative ways of packaging the information, depending on the sentence context. A decomposition of the factor of pragmatic information revealed the importance of subfactors like minor relevance of N1 (4.3.1.1.), further elaboration of N2 (4.3.1.2), contrastive meaning (4.3.1.3), and higher participant identifiability of the genitive proper noun (4.3.2).

References

Primary Literature

DW: *Deutsche Welle/DW-World newsletter – Nachrichten* (2x daily)
        (http://www.dw.de/newsletter-registration/a-15718229-1)
Fr: Franck, Julia. 2003. *Lagerfeuer*. Köln: Dumont.
G&K: Geiger, Walter & Willi Kotte. 2008. *Handbuch Qualität*. Wiesbaden: Vieweg+Teubner Verlag.
Ks: Konsalik, Heinz. 1993. *Das Riff der roten Haie*. Bergisch Gladbach: Gustav Lübbe.
Nl: Noll, Ingrid. 1996. *Kalt ist der Abendhauch*. Zürich: Diogenes Verlag.
Pf: Süskind, Patrick. 1985. *Das Parfum. Die Geschichte eines Mörders*. Zürich: Diogenes Verlag.

Secondary Literature

Altenberg, Bengt. 1982. *The Genitive vs. the of-Construction. A Study of Syntactic Variation in 17th Century English*. Malmö: CWK Gleerup.
Ballweg, Joachim. 1998. Eine einheitliche Interpretation des attributiven Genitivs. In *Die Kasus im Deutschen. Form und Inhalt*, Marcel Vuillaume (ed.), 153–166. Tübingen: Stauffenburg Brigitte Narr.
Behaghel, Otto. 1923–32. *Deutsche Syntax: eine Geschichtliche Darstellung*. Heidelberg: Winter.
Bhatt, Christa. 1990. *Die Syntaktische Struktur der Nominalphrase im Deutschen*. Tübingen: Narr.
Brinkmann, Hennig. 1971. *Die deutsche Sprache. Gestalt und Leistung*. Düsseldorf: Schwann.
Brown, Cheryl. 1983. Topic continuity in written English narrative. In *Topic Continuity in Discourse: A Quantitative Cross-language Study*, Talmy Givón (ed.), 313–343. Amsterdam/ Philadelphia: John Benjamins.
Campe, Petra. 1997. Genitives and *von*-Datives in German: A Case of *free* Variation? In *Lexical and Syntactical Constructions and the Construction of Meaning*, Marjolijn Verspoor, Kee Dong Lee and Eve Sweetser (eds), 165–185. Amsterdam/Philadelphia: John Benjamins.
Campe, Petra. 1998. Paradigmatische Variation als linguistisches Instrument, oder wie sich der adnominale Genitiv im Deutschen gegen präpositionale Eindränger hält. *Leuvense Bijdragen* 87, 337–369.
Campe, Petra. 1999. Der adnominale Genitiv im heutigen Deutsch. Versuch einer kognitiv-linguistischen Analyse des reinen Kasus im Vergleich zu alternativen Konstruktionen. Unpublished PhD Dissertation, Katholieke Universiteit Leuven.
Campe, Petra. 2010. Syntactic variation in German adnominal constructions. An application to the alternatives 'genitive', 'apposition' and 'compound'. In *Grammar Between Norm and Variation*, Alexandra Lenz and Albrecht Plewnia (eds), 189–214. Frankfurt am Main: Peter Lang.

Deane, Paul. 1987. English possessives, topicality and the Silverstein hierarchy. *Berkeley Linguistics Society, Proceedings of the Thirteenth Annual Meeting.* 65–76.

De Wit, Petra and Schoorlemmer, Maaike. 1996. Prenominal arguments in Russian, German and Dutch. *ZAS Papers in Linguistics* 5, 184–202.

Demske, Ulrike. 2001. *Merkmale und Relationen. Diachrone Studien zur Nominalphrase des Deutschen.* Berlin/New York: Walter de Gruyter.

Duden. 2009. *Duden – Die Grammatik. Unentbehrlich für Richtiges Deutsch.* Mannheim: Dudenverlag.

Ebert, Robert Peter. 2003. Die Stellung des attributiven Genitivs in Luthers Schriften. *Sprachwissenschaft* 282, 195–229.

Ehrich, Veronika and Rapp, Irene. 2000. Sortale Bedeutung und Argumentstruktur: *ung*-Nominalisierungen im Deutschen. *Zeitschrift für Sprachwissenschaft* 19, 2, 245–303.

Eisenbeiss, Sonja. 2002. Merkmalsgesteuerter Grammatikerwerb. Eine Untersuchung zum Erwerb der Struktur und Flexion der Nominalphrase. PhD dissertation, University of Düsseldorf. (Consulted as: http://privatewww.essex.ac.uk/~seisen/my%20dissertation.htm).

Eisenberg, Peter. 1994. *Grundriss der deutschen Grammatik.* Stuttgart/Weimar: Metzler.

Engel, Ulrich. 1988. *Deutsche Grammatik.* Heidelberg: Groos.

Erben, Johannes. 1972. *Deutsche Grammatik. Ein Abriß.* München: Hueber.

Fox, Barbara and Thompson, Sandra. 1990. A discourse explanation of the grammar of relative clauses in English conversation. *Language* 66, 2, 297–316.

Givón, Talmy. 1983. Topic continuity in spoken English. In *Topic Continuity in Discourse: A Quantitative Cross-language Study*, Talmy Givón (ed.), 343–356. Amsterdam/Philadelphia: John Benjamins.

Givón, Talmy. 1993. *English Grammar. A Function-based Introduction.* Amsterdam/Philadelphia: John Benjamins.

Hartmann, Katharina and Zimmermann, Malte. 2003. Syntactic and semantic adnominal genitive. In *(A)Symmetrien – (A)Symmetries. Beiträge zu Ehren von Ewald Lang*, Claudia Maienborn (ed.), 171–202. Tübingen: Stauffenburg. (Consulted as: http://www.ling.uni-potsdam.de/~mzimmermann/papers/MZ2002-Genitive.pdf).

Harweg, Roland. 1967. Zur Wortstellung des artikellosen genitivischen Eigennamenattributs des Nhd. in Manifestationen von Nominalphrasen mit dem bestimmten Artikel. *Orbis* 16: 478–516.

Hentschel, Elke. 1994. Entwickeln sich im Deutschen Possessiv-Adjektive? Der -s-Genitiv bei Eigennamen. In *Satz – Text – Diskurs. Akten des 27. Linguistischen Kolloquiums Münster 1992, Band 1*, Susanne Beckmann et al. (eds), 17–25. Tübingen: Niemeyer.

Hinrichs, Lars and Szmrecsanyi, Benedikt. 2007. Recent changes in the function and frequency of Standard English genitive constructions: a multivariate analysis of tagged corpora. *English Language and Linguistics* 11, 3, 437–474.

Jäger, Gerhard and Rosenbach, Anette. 2006. The winner takes it all – almost: Cumulativity in grammatical variation. *Linguistics* 44, 5, 937–71.

Krause, Cornelia. 2000. Anmerkungen zum pränominalen Genitiv im Deutschen. In *Von der Philologie zur Grammatiktheorie. Peter Suchsland zum 65. Geburtstag*, Josef Bayer and Christine Römer (eds), 79–96. Niemeyer: Tübingen.

Langacker, Ronald W. 1991. *Foundations of Cognitive Grammar. Volume I: Theoretical Prerequisites.* Stanford: Stanford University Press.

Lanouette, Ruth. 1996. The attributive genitive in the history of German. In *Germanic Linguistics – Syntactic and Diachronic*, R.L. Lippi-Green and J.C. Salmons (eds), 85–102. Amsterdam/Philadelphia: John Benjamins.

Lattewitz, Karen. 1994. Eine Analyse des deutschen Genitivs. *Linguistische Berichte* 150, 118–146.

Lauterbach, Stefan. 1993. *Genitiv, Komposition und Präpositionalattribut. Zum System nominaler Relationen im Deutschen*. München: Iudicium.

Leys, Odo. 2007. Omtrent de pregenitief. *Verslagen en mededelingen van de Koninklijke Academie voor Nederlandse Taal- en Letterkunde*, 327–343.

Lindauer, T. 1995. *Genitivattribute. Eine morphosyntaktische Untersuchung zum deutschen DP/NP-System*. Tübingen: Niemeyer.

Marillier, Jean-François. 1992. Pränominaler und postnominaler Genitiv. In *Rechts von N. Untersuchungen zur Nominalgruppe im Deutschen*, Paul Valentin (ed.), 47–58. Tübingen: Narr.

Martin, J.R. 1992. *English Text: System and Structure*. Amsterdam/Philadelphia: John Benjamins.

Neef, Martin. 2006. Die Genitivflexion von artikellos verwendbaren Eigennamen als syntaktisch konditionierte Allomorphie. *Zeitschrift für Sprachwissenschaft* 25, 2, 273–299.

Olsen, Susan. 1991. Die deutsche Nominalphrase als 'Determinansphrase'. In *>det, comp und infl<*, Susan Olsen and Gisbert Fanselow (eds), 35–56. Tübingen: Niemeyer.

Payne, Doris. 1992. Nonidentifiable information and pragmatic order rules in O'odham. In *Pragmatics of Word Order Flexibility*, Doris Payne (ed.), 137–166. Amsterdam/Philadelphia: John Benjamins.

Prell, H.-P. 2000. Die Stellung des attributiven Genitivs im Mittelhochdeutschen. *Beiträge zur Geschichte der deutschen Sprache und Literatur* 122, 1, 23–39.

Prince, Ellen. 1979. On the given/new distinction. *Papers from the 15th Regional Meeting, Chicago Linguistic Society*, 267–278.

Prince, Ellen. 1981. Towards a taxonomy of given-new information. In *Radical pragmatics*, P. Cole (ed.), 223–255. New York: Academic Press.

Rosenbach, Anette. 2003. Aspects of iconicity and economy in the choice between the *s-genitive* and the *of-genitive* in English. In *Determinants of Grammatical Variation in English*, Günter Rohdenburg and Britta Mondorf (eds), 379–411. Berlin/New York: Mouton De Gruyter.

Rosenbach, Anette. 2005. Animacy versus weight as determinants of grammatical variation in English. *Language* 81, 3, 613–644.

Rozen, J. 1988. Les génitifs adnominaux pré- ou postposés: quelle difference? *Nouvaux Cahiers d' Allemand* 1988, 1, 23–37.

Sauter, R. 1983. *Le génitif allemand. Étude synchronique et diachronique*. Thèse de 3e cycle, Université de Lyon 2.

Speelman, Dirk. 1997. *Abundantia Verborum. A computer tool for carrying out corpus-based linguistic case studies*. PhD Dissertation, Katholieke Universiteit Leuven. (http://wwwling.arts.kuleuven.ac.be/genling/abundant/).

Spencer, Andrew. 2009. Realization-based morphosyntax. The German genitive. In *On inflection*, Patrick O. Steinkrüger and Manfred Krifka (eds), 173–218. Berlin/New York: Mouton De Gruyter.

Stefanowitsch, Anatol. 2003. Constructional semantics as a limit to grammatical alternation. In *Determinants of Grammatical Variation in English*, Günter Rohdenburg and Britta Mondorf (eds), 413–443. Berlin/New York: Mouton De Gruyter.

Taylor, John R. 1994. Possessives and topicality. *Functions of Language* 1, 1 67–94.

Ten Cate, Abraham P., Lodder, Hans G. and Koote, André. 2004. *Deutsche Grammatik*. Bussum: Coutinho.

Teuber, O. 2000. Gibt es zwei Genitive im Deutschen? In *Deutsche Grammatik in Theorie und Praxis*, R. Thieroff, M. Tamrat and N. Fuhrhop (eds), 171–183. Tübingen: Niemeyer.

Zifonun, Gisela, Hoffmann, Ludger and Strecker, Bruno (et al.). 1997. *Grammatik der deutschen Sprache*. Berlin/New York: Walter de Gruyter.

Endnotes

1. I would like to thank my colleagues T. Leuschner, M. Van de Velde and D. Chan, and the two anonymous reviewers for their most valuable comments and suggestions.

2. Occasionally the prenominal genitive is called 'saxon' genitive ('sächsischer Genitiv') (Zifonun et al. 1997: 2020; Demske 2001: 208). Morphological glossing provided for examples is minimal, except for the noun phrases containing genitives. The genitive *-s* for (masculine, female, neutral) proper names and (masculine, neutral) common nouns is marked explicitly as *-s* in the examples and is glossed according to the Leipzig Glossing Rules as '-GEN'. Other morphological genitive endings (e.g. in the definite article) are not marked explicitly in the examples and are glossed as '.GEN':

<blockquote>

die Röcke <u>Maria-s</u> (Neef 2006: 287) / **die Röcke** <u>der</u>   Maria (ibid.)

the skirts Maria-GEN   the skirts the.GEN.F Maria

'the skirts of Maria'   'the skirts of Maria'

</blockquote>

In all examples, the head noun of the relevant noun phrase is in bold, and the genitive (pre- or postnominal) is underlined.

3. 'DW' is the abbreviation of 'Deutsche Welle' and pertains to the daily electronic news reports of *Deutsche Welle* (http://www.dw-world.de/dw/0,,7561,00.html). 'Pf' and 'Ks' are the abbreviations of 'Parfum' and 'Konsalik', respectively, and pertain to the two novels used as corpus (see Section 2.2).

4. We will not go into the discussion whether genitives of proper names are really 'genitives' at all. This is the only construction in which female nouns – which normally do not have a morphological ending in German – take the masculine/neutral genitive *-s* ending (e.g. (1) 'Dianas'). For the topic of this paper, this discussion seems to be irrelevant. Compare e.g. Hentschel (1994), Neef (2006) or Spencer (2009). According to Demske (2001: 248) the prenominal genitive is no longer a morphological case but functions as a determiner, whereas the postnominal genitive is still a genuine representative of morphological case. Eisenbeiss (2002), moreover, shows that the postnominal genitive is acquired much later by German-speaking children than the prenominal genitive.

5. Occasionally kinterms are reinterpreted as proper names referring to humans and can then be used prenominally: e.g. <u>Großvater-s</u>   **Kuckucksuhr** (Nl 7–8: 5)

<blockquote>

grandfather-GEN   cuckoo.clock

'grandfather's   cuckoo clock'

</blockquote>

6. Cp. e.g. Olsen (1991: 48f.), Marillier (1992: 50), Lattewitz (1994: 120), Prell (2000: 37). See Neef (2006) and Spencer (2009) for a survey of which proper names must/can occur without the

article and which cannot, for the semantic differences and syntactic restrictions between the constructions with and without the article, and for a discussion under what conditions the genitive -*s* ending is realized or not. E.g.:

des	Pai-Ø Geschmack	≈ des	Pai-s Geschmack
the.GEN.M	Pai taste	the.GEN.M	Pai-GEN taste
'Pai's taste'		'Pai's taste'	

7.   Definite NPs are marked for the genitive with the genitive definite article, which only has an unambiguous genitive ending in the masculine/neutral singular form (*des*). The genitive feminine and plural definite article is *der*, which can however also be interpreted as a dative singular.

8.   Hartmann & Zimmermann (2003: 9) note that the indefinite pronouns *jedermann* ('everyone') and *niemand* ('no one') can be used prenominally as well: 'jedermann-s **Mutter**' ('someone's mother'), 'in niemand-es **Interesse**' ('in no one's interest') (ibid.). These genitives also occur postnominally, though rarely: '**die natürliche Verhaltensweise** jedermann-s' ('the natural behaviour of everyone') (G&K:173). Since our corpus contains no similar examples, we exclude this construction from our analysis.

9.   The Google searches were done on July 5th, 2011. Analogy with the general adjacency constraint for genitives may play a role here. This constraint says that genitives are usually not separated from their head noun by other constituents (Demske 2001: 268ff). In case of separation, *von* is used instead of the genitive. Although the title ('party leader', 'chancellor', ...) is not an individual constituent but a part of the genitive phrase, it does separate the genitive ('Kurt Beck', 'Angela Merkel') from its head noun ('Kurs', 'Rede').

10.   This was not the case in earlier stages of the German language (cp. Marillier 1992: 48, Prell 2000: 28–29): e.g.

bi	anderen dez	kunig-es dienerē	
			(Middle High German, Prell 2000: 28–29)
with other	the.GEN.M	king-GEN servants	
'with other servants of the king'			

For a semantico-syntactic explanation of (the historical evolution of) the prenominal genitive's defining function and of the incompatibility of prenominal genitives and (in)definite articles in Germanic languages, see Leys (2007).

11.   Resultative nominalizations profile "an entity that comes into existence as a consequence of the process, (...) the state resulting from an activity" (Taylor 1994: 215; e.g.: 'the decision of Carl'), as opposed to 'episodic' nominalizations that "nominalize a single instance, or episode, of the process expressed by the verb" (Langacker 1991: 24; e.g.: 'the deciding of legal questions').

12.   A Google search (June 22nd 2010) provided less than 25 hits for *Südamerikas Länder*, for instance, as opposed to more than 900 hits for *Länder Südamerikas* and 6 hits for *Kolumbiens Süden* as opposed to over 600 hits for *Süden Kolumbiens*.

13.   Marillier's observation that genitives introduced by a deictic element are prototypically used postnominally can be linked to this observation of the contrastive value of N2. Compare also Deane (1987: 66) for the relevance of contrastiveness for the English genitive alternation.

die Bedeutung *dieses*	Großvaters	(Marillier 1992: 52)
the importance this.GEN.M.DEM	grandfather-GEN	
'the importance of this grandfather'		

We focus on prototypical contrastiveness here. As has been mentioned above, accentuation and sentence context can predominate and thus change the contrast perspective.

14. Sometimes this opposition is also confusingly called 'topical' vs. 'non-topical information'. Compare e.g. Rosenbach (2003: 387): "With topicality I refer to the distinction between referentially given and new possessors".

15. One could argue that in a headline, the definite article could also be omitted in postnominal constructions. A Google search (June 23rd 2011) revealed, however, that *Tod Dianas* is definitely less frequent (8 < first 100 hits) than *der [den/dem/zum/am...] Tod Dianas* (22 < first 100 hits). The prenominal genitive *Dianas Tod* was, as was expected, far more frequent (79 < first 100 hits) than the postnominal genitives in headlines (30 < first 100 hits).

Tracing the origins of the Swedish group genitive

Muriel Norde
University of Groningen

The term "group genitive" refers to all constructions in Swedish where the invariable genitive morpheme is attached to the right edge of complex NPs, instead of to the head noun. This paper focuses on one particular type of group genitive, in which the genitive marker is enclitically attached to a postmodifying prepositional phrase. Drawing data from a selection of Middle and Early Modern Swedish texts, it discusses the emergence, in Late Middle Swedish, of a set of competing genitive constructions involving possessors with postmodifying prepositional phrases, of the type *The king of Denmark's son*. It will be examined whether these constructions, of which the group genitive was one, arose independently or out of each other, and how these developments relate to the shift of genitive -*s* from inflectional word marker to phrase marker.

1. Introduction[1]

1.1 On genitives and s-genitives

Rejected by normative grammarians but frequent in informal usage, the Modern Swedish group genitive construction is one of the most-discussed topics in Swedish grammar. The Modern Swedish genitive marker, or s-genitive, is the descendant of an Old Swedish inflectional genitive marker, but it differs from its ancestor in so many crucial ways that it is no longer appropriate to refer to it as a case marker. In this section, I will briefly explain why.

The inflectional genitive was found in all older Germanic languages as part of a four-case system. The genitive case was expressed by various endings depending on the number of the noun (singular or plural), and the declensional class to which it belonged. It was used primarily in genitival attributes denoting possession in the widest sense, but it could also be governed by prepositions, verbs, or adjectives. The former construction type is called "structural genitive", the latter, "lexical genitive" (Delsing 1991). Some Old Swedish examples (from Norde 1997: 148, 171, 173, 189, 192) are given below. Structural genitives could both precede (example (1a)) and follow (example (1b)) their head. In lexical genitive constructions, the genitive case could be governed by some prepositions (example (2a)), verbs (example (2b)), or adjectives (example (2c)):

(1) a. [...] hørþe han røst   fatøk-s   barn-s
         [...] heard he   voice poor-N.SG.GEN child-N.SG.GEN
         '[...] he heard the voice of a poor child' (Bur)[2]

     b. alle heþn-a   mann-a   guþa æru diæfla
         all pagan-M.PL.GEN man-M.PL.GEN gods are devils
         'All the gods of pagan men are devils.' (Bur)

(2) a. tha   han først til konunx   toks
         when he   first to king.M.SG.GEN was.elected
         'when he was first elected king' (MELL)

     b. at   han tørff engxsens   annar-s   widh
         that he   needs nobody.M.SG.GEN else-M.SG.GEN PART
         'that he does not need anybody else' (Mose)

     c. Fem hundradha ar-a   gamal war noe
         Five hundred   year-N.PL.GEN old   was Noah
         'Noah was five hundred years old.' (Mose)

The Modern Swedish s-genitive, by contrast, is exclusively structural and exclusively prepositive (except in predicative constructions like *bilen är min fars* 'the car is my father's'). All other genitive endings have been replaced by *s*, both in the singular and the plural. But perhaps the most crucial difference is morphosyntactic: where Old Swedish *-s* was obligatorily attached to all elements in a full NP (nouns, adjectives, pronouns etc.) the Modern Swedish s-genitive is a once-only marker which is attached to the rightmost edge of a full NP. Contrastive examples are given in (3):

(3) a. for hwar-s   en-s   cristin-s
         for each-M.SG.GEN one- M.SG.GEN Christian- M.SG.GEN
         man-s   helso
         man- M.SG.GEN salvation.F.SG.DAT
         'for the salvation of each and every Christian man' (Bir I)

     b. varje kristen   man=s   plikt
         [every Christian man]=GEN obligation
         'the obligation of every Christian man' (Modern Swedish)
         http://www.kentlundholm.com/recensioner.htm

The most salient examples of right-edge marking are so-called group genitives, where the s-genitive is attached to the right edge of a postmodifying prepositional phrase or relative clause, even if the final element belongs to a word class that cannot traditionally take a genitive marker. For instance, in (4a) the s-genitive is attached to an adverb, and in (4b) it is attached to a tensed verb (Teleman et al. 1999b: 130):

(4) a. familjen ovanpå=s   ungar
        [family upstairs]=GEN kids
        'the kids of the family (living) upstairs'

     b. det är dom som kommer=s   förtjänst
        it   is [those who come-PRES]=GEN merit
        'it is thanks to those who come'

The position of the s-genitive, its status as a once-only marker and the fact that it may attach to any word-class are three arguments to consider it a clitic rather than an in-flectional ending, which is why the s-genitive is glossed as <=GEN> in all Modern Swedish examples in this paper, except in those cases where it is overtly not enclitic (as in examples (9) and (10) in the next section).[3]

The outline of this paper is as follows: I will start with a review of the three main types of group genitive attested in present-day Swedish (Section 1.2), followed by a section on sources and method (Section 1.3). The second section provides background information on the Old Swedish case system and its demise (Section 2.1), as well as the three stages of development of the genitive from word-marking inflection to phrase-marking clitic (Section 2.2). In the third section, I will present the data of my case study, and Section 4 is the conclusion of this paper.

1.2   Group genitives

As we have seen in the examples in (4), the group genitive is a construction in which the s-genitive is attached to the right edge of a complex NP. There are several different types of complex NPs which may form part of a group genitive construction, the most important of which are illustrated in (5). In (5a) =GEN is attached to the second of two co-ordinated NPs, in (5b) it is attached to a postmodifying PP and in (5c) it is attached to a postmodifying relative clause:[4]

(5) a. farfar   och farmor=s   hem
        [grandpa and grandma]=GEN home
        'grandpa and grandma's home'[5]

     b. mann-en på gatan=s   smak
        [man-DEF on street-DEF]=GEN taste
        'the man in the street's taste'

     c. Fransmannen jag träffade igår='s[6]   musikvideo
        [Frenchman I   met   yesterday]=GEN music video
        'the Frenchman I met yesterday's music video'

In the following sections, I will discuss the different types of group genitive in some more detail.

1.2.1   Co-ordinated noun phrases

The group genitive with co-ordinated NPs is generally accepted (Wellander 1973: 96; Teleman et al. 1999b: 130), especially when the two NPs form a collective possessor, in which case group marking is preferred to individual marking. For instance, the group genitive *Victoria och Daniels bröllop* 'Victoria and Daniel's wedding' (example (6b); referring to the Swedish Crown princess's marriage to Daniel Westling in 2010) is much more frequent than the corresponding construction with individual marking (example (6a)). When the co-ordinated NPs are not the collective possessor however, group genitives are generally not possible. Thus, in example (6c) both possessors are marked with =GEN, since Victoria and Daniel may have their own friends, and they definitely have blood relatives they do not share. A structure like (6d), therefore, is questionable, if grammatical at all.

(6)   a.   Victoria=s   och Daniel=s   bröllop   [21,000 hits]
           Victoria=GEN and Daniel=GEN wedding
           'Victoria's and Daniel's wedding'

      b.   Victoria och Daniel=s   bröllop   [522,000 hits]
           [Victoria and Daniel]=GEN wedding
           'Victoria and Daniel's wedding'

      c.   Victoria=s   och Daniel=s   vänner och släktingar   [8 hits]
           Victoria=GEN and Daniel=GEN friends and family members
           'Victoria's and Daniel's friends and family members'

      d.   ?Victoria och Daniel=s   vänner och släktingar   [0 hits]
           [Victoria and Daniel]=GEN friends and family members
           'Victoria and Daniel's friends and family members'

1.2.2   Noun phrase + prepositional phrase

The type of group genitive exemplified in (5b) is accepted in most grammars of Swedish when the NP and the following PP form a lexicalized semantic unit, such as *mannen på gatan* 'the man in the street', or *kungen av Preussen* 'the king of Prussia' (Thorell 1977: 49; Teleman et al. 1999b: 131). In online documents, group genitives even appear to be the preferred construction type with such semantic units.[7] For instance, Google found 42 instances of the group genitive *drottningen av Englands* 'the queen of England's', as in (7a), and only 8 instances of *drottningens av England* 'the queen's of England', as in (7b):

(7)   a.   drottning-en av England=s   krona
           [queen-DEF of England]=GEN crown
           'the queen of England's crown'

b. drottning-en~s   av England vapen
   queen-DEF~GEN of England coat.of.arms
   'the queen of England's coat of arms'

But this pattern is by no means restricted to semantic units, as examples such as (8a–b) appear to be quite productive in spoken and informal written Swedish (Teleman et al. 1999b: 131) as well.

(8) a. i jonas med piercingen=s   rum
       in [Jonas with piercing-DEF]=GEN room
       'in the room of Jonas-with-the-piercing'

   b. den här killen   på cykeln=s   bror
      [this here guy-DEF on bike-DEF]=GEN brother
      'the brother of this guy with the bike'

Group genitive constructions such as (8a–b) are dispreferred by normative grammarians (cf. e.g. Wellander 1973, Sigurd 1995, SRB). Others have questioned the productivity of the construction, noting that alternative constructions have also been observed to occur. Thus, both Teleman et al. (1999b: 131) and Börjars (2003: 149) note that in formal written Swedish, the genitive marker is sometimes not attached to the right edge of the possessor NP, but to its head, as in (9).[8] This construction is, however, considered stiff, unnatural, or bookish in non-prescriptive works (e.g. Palmér 1945: 59; Thorell 1977: 49; Dahl 2003: 47; Hultman 2003: 212).

(9) institution-en~s   för slaviska språk   prefekt
    department-DEF~GEN for Slavonic languages head
    'the Head of the Department of Slavonic Languages'

A second alternative to group genitives was one in which the PP was extraposed, as in the following example (from the 1917 bible translation):

(10) kunskap-en~s   träd på gott och ont
     knowledge-DEF~GEN tree on good and evil
     'the tree of the knowledge of good and evil'

Genitive constructions such as (10) are no longer productive in Modern Swedish (see Section 4).

1.2.3 *Noun Phrase + Relative Clause*

In the third type of group genitives, =GEN is attached to a relative clause. The host of =GEN can be almost any part of speech, e.g. tensed verbs, as in (11a), or stranded prepositions, as in (11b).

(11) a. i de   som skrattar=s   ögon
        in [they who laugh]=GEN eyes
        'in the eyes of those who are laughing'

b. från dom sidor du surfar på's   perpektiv [sic]
from [the pages you surf   on]=GEN perspective
'from the perspective of the pages you are surfing'

There are three (regular) exceptions (Norde 2006: 216f.): (i) =GEN is incompatible with
the subject form of personal pronouns (e.g. *jags '*I's'), probably because possessive pronouns would be used instead (e.g. *min* 'my'); (ii) =GEN cannot be attached to plural
forms in *-s* (all of them English loans such as *happenings*); (iii) the s-genitive is not realized with nouns ending in *s*, which is optionally indicated by an apostrophe, as in *da-
gis(')* 'nursery's', but this is most probably a phonological rule, not a morphological one.

This type of group genitive is undoubtedly the most controversial type, which is
largely restricted to informal Swedish (both spoken and written). As an alternative to
the usage of a group genitive, the relative clause can be extraposed. Thus, in example
(12a) the head of the NP, a pronoun, ends up as a possessive pronoun (compare the
group genitive example in (4b)), and in (12b), =GEN is attached to the head noun
(Teleman et al. 1999b: 131, Börjars 2003: 150). Note that in other construction types,
too, it is common to extrapose the relative clause (example (12c)).

(12) a. det är **deras** förtjänst som kommer
it is their merit   who come
'It is thanks to those who come.'

b. fotbollsupportrarna=s   skrik   som just sett sitt   lag   förlora
football supporters=GEN shouts who just seen their.REFL team lose
med tre   mål
with three goals
'the shouts of the football supporters who had just seen their team lose by
three goals'

c. Här får ingen   komma som har kniv. (Teleman et al. 1999b: 557)
Here may nobody come   who has knife
'Nobody who has a knife can come in.'

Old Swedish had a construction similar to (12), with the relative clause extraposed
(example (13a)); alternatively, the entire complex possessor could follow the possessee,
as in (13b) (Norde 1997: 88):

(13) a. þerræ   mann-æ   þærwir sum rik-it   byggiæ
those.M.PL.GEN man- M.PL.GEN needs   who empire-DEF build up
'the needs of those men who build up the empire' (Vidh)

b. namn þerræ   mann-æ   ær   wæstrægötlanz
names those.M.PL.GEN man- M.PL.GEN who Västergötland.GEN
lagh görðþo
laws made
'the names of those men who made the laws of Västergötland' (Vidh)

This type of group genitive will not be further discussed in this paper.

1.3 Sources and method

The occurrence of the group genitives in (5) is the main motivation for the claim that the Modern Swedish s-genitive is not an affix, but a clitic, whereas the existence of constructions such as (9) and (12) has prompted some authors to argue that the Swedish s-genitive is not a full-fledged clitic but rather a phrasal affix. I will not repeat this discussion here (for the latter position see e.g. Börjars 2003, for the former see Norde 2006 and 2009: 162ff.). This paper will not be about the morphological status of the Modern Swedish s-genitive, but about the history of one particular type of group genitive, as I will explain in this section.

The construction under scrutiny is the equivalent of English constructions such as *the king of Denmark's son* or *King Christian of Denmark's son*, i.e. a complex NP consisting of a noun denoting some noble title (e.g. 'king'), optionally followed by a personal name, which forms a semantic unit with a PP consisting of a preposition plus a geographic name (e.g. 'of Denmark'). Irrespective of word order and position of the genitive marker(s), this construction will be abbreviated [[NP] [PP]]$_{gen}$. This particular construction has been selected for two reasons. Firstly, and most importantly, because it is generally considered the oldest type of group genitive (Delsing 1991: 28), predating the [[NP] [RelClause]]$_{gen}$ construction discussed in Section 1.2.3. The second reason for chosing this particular construction is that it is relatively easy to find in untagged corpora, as I will explain below.

This paper, then, presents a small corpus-based study of the relative frequency of [[NP] [PP]]$_{gen}$ constructions, concentrating on the Middle and Early Modern Swedish period. In examples (7a–b), repeated here as (14a–b), we have seen that there are two possessive constructions where [[NP] [PP]]$_{gen}$ precedes the possessee NP: the group genitive construction exemplified in (14a), and the construction in which the possessive marker is attached to the head noun of the possessor NP, as in (14b):

(14) a. drottning-en av England=s krona
      [queen-DEF of England]=GEN crown
      'the queen of England's crown

    b. drottning-en~s av England vapen
      queen-DEF~GEN of England coat.of.arms
      'the queen of England's coat of arms'

As we have seen above, both (14a) and (14b) have been rejected in Swedish grammars, for different reasons, the former as being illogical (because the genitive is not attached to the head of the possessor NP), the latter as being unnatural. Interestingly, the claim that (14b) is 'unswedish' dates back as long as 1753, when the Swedish linguist Sven Hof published a treatise on correct written Swedish that is considered the most reliable source of naturally occurring Swedish from that period (Thelander 1985:v). Hof notes that in a construction such as *kejsarens af Mogol rikedom* 'the emperor's of Mogol wealth', the genitive is placed in "the wrong position". He continues to write that "according to the spoken language, and disregarding Latin grammar, one should write *kejsaren af Mogols rikedom* ['the emperor of Mogol's wealth'] or *kejsarens rikedom i Mogol* ['the emperor's wealth in Mogol']" (Thelander 1985: 120; my translation). What makes this recommendation particularly interesting for the present purpose is that Hof allows both group genitives and the older construction in which the PP is extraposed, but not the construction in which *s* is attached to the head of the possessor NP, which he considers 'unswedish'. This is in line with Palmér's (1945: 59) assertion that this construction is "historically incorrect". Palmér's conclusion seemed plausible to me (2006: 227), but later I noted that I had given a Middle Swedish example of this "historically incorrect" construction myself (ibid.: 221), so apparently people *did* use it in the centuries preceding Hof's treatise.

To date, not much (diachronic) data about [[NP] [PP]]$_{gen}$ constructions is available. Early examples of group genitives are mentioned incidentally (e.g. in Delsing 1991: 28) but no systematic (corpus-based) studies have been carried out thus far. One reason for this may be that searching for group genitive constructions in historical sources is very time-consuming, not only because the construction is quite rare, but also because there are no tagged corpora of older Swedish texts, so that genitive constructions cannot be searched by means of POS queries. The only alternative, searching for all words ending in *s,* is obviously a needle in a haystack task. This is the reason why I decided to focus on [[NP] [PP]]$_{gen}$ construction, because for this particular type it would be possible to generate concordances of the preposition heading the PP. In older Swedish, two prepositions were used in [[NP] [PP]]$_{gen}$: *af* 'of', and *i* 'in'. Examples of NPs followed by a PP, both with and without personal names, are given in (15). All examples are from Brahe's chronicle (1585).

(15)　a.　konung-en　aff Danmarck
　　　　　　king-DEF　of Denmark

　　　b.　konung-en　i　Danmarck
　　　　　　king-DEF　in Denmark
　　　　　　'the king of/in Denmark'

　　　c.　konung Christian　aff Danmarck
　　　　　　king　　Christian　of Denmark

　　　d.　konung Christiern　i　Danmarck
　　　　　　king　　Christian　in Denmark
　　　　　　'king Christian of Denmark'

As regards sources, I have chosen to concentrate on late Middle Swedish and, especially, Early Modern Swedish texts, as it is assumed that it is in this period that group genitives started to emerge. The earliest examples were personal names such as *Swen i*

Kleffs tompt (1452) 'Swen of Kleff's property'. The construction where the head of the possessor NP is a noun is assumed to have emerged some 100 years later (Delsing 1991: 28). This is corroborated by my own investigation of the history of the Swedish genitive (Norde 1997) which was based primarily on Old and Middle Swedish texts, or parts of them: in that corpus I found no examples of [[NP] [PP]] group genitives at all. It may be considered a fortunate coincidence that many electronically available texts from this period are historical works, in which complex NPs of the type *king* (X) *of Denmark* are comparatively frequent. All in all, I have examined 10 Middle Swedish and 16 Early Modern Swedish texts. A chronological list of sources is given in Table 1.

I generated concordances for the two prepositions (the preposition *i* was spelled <i>, <j> or <ij>, the preposition *af* was spelled <af>, <aff> or <av>), and excerpted all relevant constructions manually. A full analysis of these [[NP] [PP]]$_{gen}$ constructions will be provided in Section 3.

1.4   A few notes on textual evidence

This study is based on a corpus of Middle and Early Modern Swedish texts. Although there is a fair amount of running text available from both periods, there are some problems with historical text research that are of relevance tot the study of Swedish group genitives. I will briefly discuss these in this section.

First of all, [[NP] [PP]]$_{gen}$ constructions are not particularly frequent in either period. Table 2 provides an overview of the number of words per text, the number of tokens of the prepositions *i* and *af*, as well as the number of group genitive constructions involving these two prepositions. These figures show that substantial amounts of texts have had to be searched to find just a handful of relevant constructions, and still a number of texts had no relevant examples at all. We may of course assume, with Lehmann (2004: 172), that the absence of a given form or construction does not necessarily imply that it did not exist at the time, a problem for which he coined the apt phrase "non-demonstrability of non-existence", but that will not help us decide which of the alternative genitive construction types is most frequent, or oldest.

A more serious problem raised by Janda & Joseph (2003: 17) concerns the over-representation of high-prestige sources: "there is little we can do to change the circumstance that the texts which most often tend to be written and preserved are those which least reflect everyday speech". In other words, the variation attested in older texts need not reflect variation in the spoken language. This is also true for the Middle and Early Modern Swedish corpus, which consists of genres written in formal or literary style (religious prose, sagas, chronicles).

In spite of these drawbacks, I think empirical data from historical texts can and should be used, provided they are treated with proper care. Nevertheless, the proviso needs be made that what is written here is true of genitive constructions in precisely these sources, and to which degree these reflect actual spoken Swedish at that time we are in no position to know.

Table 1. Sources

Abbr.	Source	(Approx.) Year	No. of words
Middle Swedish			
Bir	First book of Revelations of Saint Birgitta	end of 14th century	106,740
KM	*Karl Magnus Saga*; Swedish version of popular novella	end of 14th century	10,930
SVM	*Sju vise mästare*; Swedish version of popular novella	end of 14th century	16,240
Bild	*Codex Bildstenianus*. Compilation of legends, translated from Latin sources.	1st half 15th century	88,520
Barl	*Barlaam och Josaphat*; Swedish version of popular Christian legend	1440s	27,029
ProsKrön	Middle Swedish chronicle, based on older sources	1450s	4,730
ST	*Själens tröst I*. 'Comfort of the soul'; translation of the Low German devotional work *De seelen trost*.	1460	132,060
Did	*Didrikssagan*. Swedish version of the Saga of Theodoric of Bern.	>1480	48,855
Luc	Middle Swedish translation of *lucidarius*, a religious treatise	1487	28,187
PMB	*Peder Månssons Bondakonst*; Swedish adaptation of Columella's *De re rustica*	1510	41,517
Early Modern Swedish			
NT 1526	*New Testament*, Gospel of Mark	1526	14,187
Troj	*Historia Trojana*; Swedish translation of popular novella	1529	44,380
Petri	Chronicle written by Olavus Petri, covering the period from the beginning of time until the year 1520.	1530	108,000
Swart	Chronicle written by Peder Swart about the Swedish king Gustav Vasa (1496–1560).	1560	51,940
Brahe	Chronicle written by Per Brahe, covering the years 1532–1560.	1585	26,380
AV	Letters written by Anna Vasa	1591–1612	8,060
Gyll	Notes written by Carl Carlsson Gyllenhielm, covering the years 1597–1601.	1640	53,010
Horn	*Beskrifningh öfwer min wandringestidh*. Memoirs written by Agneta Horn.	1657	40,460
Hiärne	*Stratonice*. Autobiographical novel written by Urban Hiärne.	1665	11,030

Abbr.	Source	(Approx.) Year	No. of words
Columbus	*Måål-roo eller Roo-måål.* Anthology of anecdotes written by Samuel Columbus.	1675	20,260
Spegel	Diary written by Haqvin Spegel.	1680	32,720
Stål	Letters written by Jon Stålhammar.	1700–1708	44,780
Runius	Prose sketches written by Johan Runius.	1710	30,200
Argus	*Then Swänska Argus*, influential periodical written by Olof von Dalin	1732–1734	213,160
Högstr	*Beskrifning öfwer Sweriges Lapmarker*; description of Northern Swedish nature and Saami culture	1747	17,990
Qvirs	*Himmelska örtegårds-sällskap*; Swedish translation of a German collection of psalms	1758	6,783

2. Setting the scene

2.1 The Old Swedish case system

2.1.1 *Introduction*

Swedish forms part of the Scandinavian language family, a group of Germanic languages spoken in Denmark, Norway, Sweden, Iceland and the Faroe Islands. The Scandinavian languages can be subdivided into an insular branch (Icelandic, Faroese) and a continental branch (Danish, Swedish, Norwegian). The continental languages, unlike the insular languages, lost their case systems. As the loss of inflectional case played a major role in the rise of the s-genitive (Norde 1997), I will provide a very brief sketch of the demise of the case system in the history of Swedish. Detailed accounts of Scandinavian language history can be found in Haugen (1976), Venås (2002), or Torp (1982, 2002). A good introduction to deflexion in Scandinavian is Trosterud (2001).

As regards Swedish language history, the only evidence of the Swedish language before the introduction of writing (apart from names, words and glosses cited in foreign manuscripts) is found in runic inscriptions. The main motivation for distinguishing Runic Swedish from Old Swedish is the type of script: runes or the Latin alphabet, respectively (Wessén 1968: 28). Treating Runic Swedish and Old Swedish as separate periods is also valid on linguistic grounds, however. Traditionally (e.g. in Wessén 1968), the era from which texts written down in the Latin alphabet are available is subdivided into two main periods: *fornsvenska* ('early Swedish') and *nysvenska* ('new Swedish'). These periods, in turn, consist of two subdivisions, which produces the following chronology (note that the English terms are not literal translations, but terms which are more in line with periods in other languages, see Norde 1997: 15 for discussion):

Table 2. Tokens of prepositions and possessive constructions.

Text	No. of words	Tokens of *i*	POSS with *i*	Tokens of *af*	POSS with *af*	Total
Bir	106740	2243	0	634	0	0
KM	10930	191	0	121	1	1
SVM	16240	413	0	191	0	0
Bild	88520	1414	0	992	6	6
Barl	27029	549	0	375	0	0
ProsKrön	4730	189	0	56	3	3
ST	132060	2542	0	1627	4	4
Luc	28187	817	0	447	0	0
Did	48855	789	0	491	11	11
PMB	41517	1088	0	634	0	0
NT 1526	14187	284	0	60	0	0
Troj	44380	1456	0	656	2	2
Petri	108000	2450	4	1041	18	22
Swart	51940	879	0	463	1	1
Brahe	26380	366	7	137	2	9
AV	8060	231	0	25	0	0
Gyll	53010	668	5	426	3	8
Horn	40460	656	0	236	1	1
Hiärne	11030	157	1	79	0	1
Columbus	20260	437	1	146	0	1
Spegel	32720	353	1	272	5	6
Stål	44780	359	2	330	0	2
Runius	30200	550	1	311	2	3
Argus	213160	4845	0	1748	0	0
Högstr	17990	392	0	250	0	0
Qvirs	6783	170	0	49	0	0
Sum	1,228,148	24,488	22	11,797	59	81

runsvenska (Runic Swedish):	800–1225
klassisk fornsvenska (Old Swedish):	1225–1375
yngre fornsvenska (Middle Swedish):	1375–1526
äldre nysvenska (Early ModernSwedish):	1526–1732
yngre nysvenska (Late Modern Swedish):[9]	1732–

Old Swedish had a four-case system which was quite similar to the case systems in other older Germanic languages (see Table 3; for extensive surveys of Old Swedish morphology see Noreen 1904 or Wessén 1968. A brief overview is given in Delsing 2002).

Table 3. PGmc *dag-a-* 'day' in older Germanic languages.[18]

		Old Swedish	Old Icelandic	Gothic	Old High German	Old English
Sg.	N	dagher	dagr	dags	tag	dæg
	G	dags	dags	dagis	tages	dæges
	D	daghi	degi	daga	tage	dæge
	A	dagh	dag	dag	tag	dæg
Pl.	N	daghar	dagar	dagós	taga	dagas
	G	dagha	daga	dagê	tago	daga
	D	daghum	dǫgum	dagam	tagum	dagum
	A	dagha	daga	dagans	taga	dagas

Nouns, adjectives and the majority of pronouns were inflected for nominative, genitive, dative and accusative. An overview of all Old Swedish case endings on nouns is given in Table 4. For each declension, two forms are given – the forms in bold are the archaic forms, which are still attested, but increasingly give way to the reduced forms in the neighbouring column.

From this table it is evident that Old Swedish nominal paradigms were by no means maximally differentiated – singular dative and accusative forms, for example, had been levelled to a considerable extent, and many case forms had no ending at all. The Old Swedish case system has been simplified considerably when compared to reconstructed Proto-Germanic or Proto-Scandinavian (or even Old Norse) inflections (see further Noreen 1904: 280ff. or Wessén 1968: 94ff.). And in the centuries that followed, the Old Swedish case system disappeared entirely.

2.1.2   The loss of the Old Swedish case system

The loss of the four-case system was one of the most fundamental changes in the history of the Swedish language. It was a gradual process that lasted several centuries, covering the entire Old and Middle Swedish periods. In this section, I will briefly discuss the complex of factors, both language-internal and language-external, that triggered this process (for more details see Norde 1997: 27ff., Norde 2001, Trosterud 2001, for a brief survey see Mørck 2005).

As regards language-internal factors, phonological, morphological and syntactic changes are all of relevance. The shift, in Proto-Germanic, from pitch accent to stress accent on the first syllable of the word, probably resulted in phonological reduction or even loss of final syllables (typically inflectional endings). As Meillet (1922: 113) put it: "Cést la ruine phonétique qui a précipité la simplification de la flexion". This stress shift cannot have been the only factor, however, since other languages with stress accent on the first syllable (e.g. Finnish) do not have reduction or loss of final syllables (Haugen

Table 4. *Noun inflections in some Old Swedish declensions* (Norde 2001: 263)

	(j/i)a-stems		(j/i)ō-stems	i-stems		u-stems†		consonant stems			r-stems
	masc	neut	fem	masc	fem	masc	neut	masc	fem	neut	masc/fem
sg.nom	-er	-	-	-er	-	-er****	-	-er	-	-	-ir, -er
gen	-s	-s	-ar	-ar, -s	-ar, -s, -ar	-ar**, -s	-ar	-s	-ar	-ar	-ur(s), -or(s)
dat	-i	-i	[-u]‡	-i	[-u]‡	-i*	-	-i	-	-	-ur, -or, -r*
acc	-	-	-	-	-	****	-	-	-	-	-ur, -or
pl.nom	-ar	-	-ar	-ir	-ir	-ir*	-	-er*	-er*	-e	-er*
gen	-a	-a	-a	-a	-a	-a**	-	-a	-a	-æ	-ra*, -ræ*
dat	-um	-om	-um	-um	-um	-um***	-	-um	-um	-om	-rum*, -rom*
acc	-a	-	-a	-i	-ir	-i*	-	-er	-er	-e	-er*

‡: This ending is so rare that it is excluded from Noreen's (1904) tables, it is only mentioned as a characteristic of a handful of nouns (Noreen 1904: 301; 307).

†: U-stems are very rare in Old Swedish. Most masculine u-stems had already switched to a-stem inflection (Wessén 1968: 9) and there is probably only one neuter u-stem: *fæ* 'property, cattle', which is a singulare tantum (Norde 1997: 97).

*: with i-umlaut of the stem vowel
**: with a-breaking of the stem vowel
***: with u-breaking of the stem vowel
****: with u-umlaut or u-breaking of the stem vowel

(For a brief survey of umlaut (vowel mutation) and breaking (diphthongization) in the OSc languages see Haugen (1976: 152–153).

1976: 285). It therefore seems likely that the phonological changes coincided with morphological changes and that these two reinforced one another. The main morphological change, likewise dating back to Proto-Germanic, was the emergence of independent roots. While Proto-Indo-European nouns were inseparable units consisting of a root, a stem suffix and a (cumulative) inflectional ending, as in M.SG.ACC *dhogh^w-o-m 'day', nouns in early Germanic may lack either the stem suffix or the inflectional suffix, or both, as in Gothic and Old Norse M.SG.ACC dag-ø-ø 'day'. After the rise of such free roots the ending became, to quote Meillet (1922: 119) once more, "un accessoire". This is certainly true for Old Swedish – as can be seen in Table 4, many members of case paradigms were bare roots, especially in the singular. Such a system is evidently less vital than the Proto-Indo-European one.

A syntactic factor that is often mentioned as triggering the demise of the case system is the loss of syntactic freedom. For instance, it has been suggested by Marold (1984: 319ff.) that the establishment of a fixed position for the subject made the nominative case redundant. Jespersen (1922: 361) similarly argues that syntactic fixation must precede loss of inflections, because the opposite order of events would imply that there was "an intervening period in which the mutual relations of words were indicated in neither way; a period, in fact, in which speech was unintelligible and consequently practically useless." However, like the question in the preceding paragraph – whether phonology or morphology came first or morphology – the relation between syntactic fixation and loss of inflectional case is basically a chicken-or-egg problem, and again it seems most likely that both fed each other. A similar case can be made for the relation between deflexion and the rise of competing periphrastic expressions, primarily prepositional constructions (Norde 2001: 246ff.).

It seems likely that all of the above played a part in deflexion in Swedish, but they are not sufficient as an explanation, as the same changes occurred in languages which retained all four cases (Icelandic), or three of them (Faroese, in which the use of the genitive case is largely restricted to set expressions, Barnes 2005: 1581). To a large extent, the conservatism of Icelandic and, to a lesser extent, Faroese, is due to its geographical isolation. Because of their peripheral position, Icelandic and Faroese had little contact with other languages, whereas Danish, Swedish and Norwegian were profoundly influenced by other languages, primarily by Middle Low German in the Hanseatic period, and it is likely that this had an impact not only on the lexical level, but also on the morphological level (Norde 1997: 35ff., Norde 2000).

A detailed discussion of the intricate interplay between various internal and external factors falls outside of the scope of this paper – suffice it to say that without the demise of the case system it is unlikely that present-day Swedish would possess an s-genitive. In the following section, I will sketch the gradual development of s from word-marking inflection to phrase-marking inflection. The subsequent stage, at which group genitives emerged, will be discussed in Section 3.

2.2   Early history of the Swedish genitive

2.2.1   *Introduction: on morphological gradience*

From being an inflectional case marker that formed part of a restricted set of nominal declensions, the genitive has developed into a possessive marker that can be encliti-cally attached to complex noun phrases where its host need not even be a nominal element. In this development, several stages can be identified, but I wish to note in advance that I consider these stages gradient, so the notion of "gradience" needs to be defined. In his 2007 monograph on syntactic gradience, Aarts distinguishes two types: "subsective" and "intersective gradience". Subsective gradience is an intra-categorial notion, where a particular element x is more or less prototypical of a category α than is element y. In other words, category α contains core and peripheral members. Intersec-tive gradience, on the other hand, is an inter-categorial notion in which there are two distinct categories, α and β, plus a class of γ elements which has properties of both α and β. This distinction has been criticized (e.g. in Denison 2010) for not being strict. After all, if in the course of change an element x becomes a less prototypical member of category α (subsective gradience), it may acquire properties of another category (intersective gradience). I agree with Denison on this point.

As regards morphology, my view on gradience is similar. If we consider inflec-tional affixes and clitics as two morphological categories, α and β, then the develop-ment of possessive *s* can be recast as follows: originally, *s* was a prototypical member of the category of inflectional affixes, but as early as in Old Swedish it came to lose prop-erties typical of that category (e.g. the loss of case concord, see 2.2.2 below). Thus it gradually became a peripheral member of the category of inflections, while at the same time acquiring properties of clitics, such as decrease in selectivity with respect to the word it attaches to (see Norde 2006 for a detailed account of this development).[10]

2.2.2   *From word marker to phrase marker*

Originally, the genitive suffix -*s* was restricted to the declension of a-stems (including ja-stems and ia-stems) of masculine and neuter nouns, and it was only used in the singular (plural nouns had a genitive suffix -*a*). The suffix -*s* probably derives from the Proto-Scandinavian suffix -*as*, as in the masculine personal name *Gōdagas* (found in the runic inscription of Valsfjord, Norway, ca. 400), the vowel of which was syncopated in younger Proto-Scandinavian (see e.g. Boutkan 1995: 384ff.).

In Old Swedish, the genitive suffix -*s* was a word marker, that is, all members of a full NP were marked individually, as in the following example:

(16)   thin-s   brodhir-s   israel-s   budhskapir
       your-M.SG.GEN brother-M.SG.GEN Israel-M.SG.GEN message
       'your brother Israel's message' (Mose)

This was the common Indo-European type of case marking termed "concordial case", also found in NPs marked for other cases, such as M.SG.NOM in (17a), M.SG.DAT in (17b), and M.PL.DAT in (17c) (Norde 2001: 259).

(17) a. mykilhughæþ-ær maðþ-ær   oc girugh-ær
      proud-M.SG.NOM man- M.SG.NOM and avaricious- M.SG.NOM
      'a proud and avaricious man' (Vidh)

    b. innan en-om   gardh-e
      in   one-M.SG.DAT yard-M.SG.DAT
      'in one yard' (Mose)

    c. mz all-om   sin-om   son-um
      with all-M.PL.DAT his-M.PL.DAT son-M.PL.DAT
      'with all his sons' (Mose)

In definite nouns both the noun and the bound definite article[11] were inflected, as in *ærkibiscupsins swenæ* (Vidh) 'the archbishop's servants', where *s* is attached to both the noun and the definite article *-in-*.

In the Old and Middle Swedish periods, the suffix *-s* gradually spread to other declensions and to the plural, replacing other genitive suffixes (Norde 1997: 116ff.). The first nouns to adopt *-s* were other masculine nouns. This tendency dates back to Runic Swedish, when *-s* was frequently attached to the old genitive (oblique)[12] of masculine r-stems, e.g. **broþurs** on one of the runic inscriptions of Aspa (Sö 138). The first instances of the transfer of *-s* are best characterized as paradigm shifts (transfer of suffixes from one declension to another), not uncommon in Runic and Old Swedish. At a later stage, however, *-s* was attached to phrases rather than to stems, and these were not cases of paradigm shift, as I will argue in the remainder of this section.

In the Old and Middle Swedish periods, concordial case marking as in example (16) gradually disappeared to give way to single marking. In most cases, only the adjective was inflected, probably because adjectival endings were phonologically more salient than noun endings (Norde 2001: 259):

(18) a. een vng-er   konung
      a.ø young-M.SG.NOM king.ø
      'a young king' (ST)

    b. j syn-om   gardh
      in his-M.SG.DAT yard.ø
      'in his yard' (ST)

Interestingly, the only suffix that did not follow this pattern was *-s*, which was not attached to the adjective, but to the last element in an NP, irrespective of internal word order (Norde 2006: 206f.). If the suffix is attached to the right edge of an NP (without case concord in the rest of the NP), it will be glossed as <~GEN>:

(19) a. mangen riddari~s   blod
      many.ø knight~GEN blood
      'the blood of many a knight' (Did)

b. [...] kom iak heem til fadhir   min~s[13] hws
   [...] came I   home to father-ø my~GEN house
   '[...] I came home to my father's house' (Bir)

c. son ioachim   konung~x
   son Jehoiakim-ø king~GEN
   'king Jehoiakim's son' (Mose)

d. konung salmons   wisdom ST
   king-ø Solomon~GEN wisdom
   'king Solomon's wisdom'

With the exception of the NP in (19b), all NPs in the above example have a noun as their final element, and therefore it might seem as if -*s* was simply lost on adjectives and other modifiers but retained on nouns. That things were more complicated than that is evidenced by such forms as *domkirkyos* 'cathedral's', where ~*s* is attached to the old F.SG. OBL form, *gardzmestaras* 'gardener's', where ~*s* is attached to the old M.SG.OBL form, or *solennas* 'the sun's', where ~*s* is attached to the old F.SG.GEN.DEF form (Norde 1997: 125ff.). In these examples, the genitive marker did not simply replace an older ending, but was attached to forms already inflected, which suggests that it had developed into a marker on a morphological level different from affixes (see further Norde 2006).

The main reason why ~*s* is analysed as a suffix at this stage, not a clitic, is that it is still quite selective about the word it attaches to – it may be attached to nouns of all declensions and spreads to some pronouns (e.g. feminine *hennes* 'her' (Old Swedish *hænnar*), or plural *deras* (Old Swedish *þærra*) 'their'), but not to word classes that are not inflected for case. This sets affixal phrase-marking ~*s* apart from enclitic phrase-marking =*s* discussed in the next section.

The loss of concordial case marking, which in the case of *s* resulted in single, phrase-final marking, must have been a crucial stage in the history of the s-genitive. It seems plausible that when the genitive became a once-only marker, its scope could be expanded to include postmodifiers of the possessor noun phrase, such as prepositional phrases and relative clauses. The first occurrences of the [[NP] [PP]] group genitive construction such as *Swen i Kleffs tompt* (1452) 'Swen of Kleff's property' mark the acquisition of clitic properties.[14] Details about this development will be given in the next section.

3. Genitive NPs with prepositional attributes in the history of Swedish

3.1 Introduction

In this section, I will present the results of my corpus study. As I said in Section 1.3, [[NP] [PP]]$_{gen}$ patterns are quite rare, hence a corpus study only yields a modest amount of data. From the genitive forms I did find, a handful had to be excluded, for various reasons. First, I only looked at $[[NP] [PP]]_{gen}$ constructions in which the genitive marker was *s*. This means that constructions such as (20a), featuring the M.SG.GEN ending -*a*, or (20b) in which the Latin name retained its Latin M.SG.GEN ending, were not included.

(20) a. En-s   riddara   son af normandia.
A-M.SG.GEN knight.M.SG.GEN son of Normandy
'the son of a knight from Normandy/a knight's son from Normandy'
(Bild)

   b. Evdoxia theodosi-i   keysare   dotter   af Rom
Eudoxia Theodosius-M.SG.GEN emperor.ø daughter of Rome
'Eudoxia, daughter of emperor Theodosius of Rome' (Bild)

Secondly, NPs containing abbreviations, such as *kon. i Polandz läger* (Gyll) 'the king of Poland's encampment' were obviously not counted, because *kon.* can be either *konungens* or *konungen*. In the latter case, the construction would be a group genitive but as the word is not spelled out in full there is no way of knowing what the author had in mind, especially since many authors did not restrict themselves to one construction type (as I will show below).

Thirdly, I excluded elliptical constructions where there is no overt possessee, because in these cases, too, it is not possible to establish which construction type is being used.

Finally, NPs involving names ending in a sibilant such as *Fransis* (Brahe) have been excluded from the analysis, as it is not evident from the form whether or not this name is marked for genitive.

The remaining constructions were subdivided into four types, exemplified below in (21). In these constructions, [NP] is the noble title, optionally followed by a personal name; [PP] is the prepositional phrase that modifies [NP]; X is the possessee, the head to which $[[NP] [PP]]_{gen}$ is attributive; and subscript $_{gen}$ marks the position of the genitive marker(s). For reasons of clarity, English equivalents of the respective construction types are given.

(21) a. Type 1: $[[NP]_{gen} X [PP]]$ 'the king's son of Denmark'
   b. Type 2: $[[NP]_{gen} [PP] X]$ 'the king's of Denmark son'
   c. Type 3: $[[NP]_{gen} [PP]_{gen} X]$ 'the king's of Denmark's son'
   d. Type 4: $[[[NP] [PP]]_{gen}X]$ 'the king of Denmark's son' (group genitive)

Note that the numbers do not necessarily reflect chronological order – although type 1 is the only type found in Old Swedish (and hence the oldest),[15] it is difficult to establish the relative chronology of types 2, 3 and 4 on the basis of the data. I will return to this issue in Section 4.

A final note concerns glosses: as the changes from word-marking inflection to phrase-marking inflection to phrase-marking clitic were gradual (Norde 2006) it is not always possible to establish the morphological status of *s* in a specific construction. Yet each genitive had to be glossed in the examples. The notation -GEN (affixal word marker) is used when there is evidence for word marking in the text, e.g. *ens riks konunghs sons fæste mø* 'the fiancée of a rich king's son' in example (22a). The notation ~GEN (affixal phrase marker) was used when there was explicit evidence for *s* being a phrase marker, such as lack of concord (e.g. *themar-ø konung-s* instead of *themar-s konung-s* 'king Theodemir's' in (22d)) or the absence of internal inflection (e.g. *margreffuens* 'the margrave's' in (22b), for which the equivalent with internal inflection would have been *margreffuans*, or *konungens* in (22c), for which the equivalent with internal inflection would have been *konungsens*). Finally, I have chosen to only use the clitic notation =GEN in group genitive constructions.

3.2   PP's with *af* 'of'

As we have seen in Table 2, *af* is the most common preposition in the $[[NP] [PP]]_{gen}$ construction. The number of occurrences of the different construction types are given in Table 5. (Texts in which no relevant *af*-constructions were found have been excluded from this table).

The most archaic construction type $[[NP]_{gen} X [PP]]$ ('the king's son of Denmark') is clearly predominant, as 43 out of 59 *af*-constructions are of this type. Some examples are given in (22):

Table 5. Possessive constructions involving *av* PPs

Text	n	$[[NP]_{gen}X[PP]]$	$[[NP]_{gen}[PP]X]$	$[[NP]_{gen}[PP]_{gen}X]$	$[[[NP] [PP]]_{gen}X]$
KM	1	1	0	0	0
Bild	6	6	0	0	0
ProsKrön	3	1	1	1	0
ST	4	4	0	0	0
Did	11	10	1	0	0
Troj	2	2	0	0	0
Petri	18	14	4	0	0
Swart	1	0	1	0	0
Brahe	2	1	1	0	0
Gyll	3	0	1	1	1
Horn	1	0	0	0	1
Spegel	5	4	1	0	0
Runius	2	0	1	1	0
Sum	**59**	**43**	**11**	**3**	**2**

(22) a. Wm   then   thima   var   vrsula   konung-s   dottir   aff britania
          At   that   time   was   Ursula   king-M.SG.GEN   daughter   of Britain
          en-s   rik-s   konungh-s   son-s   fæste mø
          a-M.SG.GEN rich-M.SG.GEN king-M.SG.GEN   son-M.SG.GEN fiancée
          'At that time Ursula, the king of Britain's daughter, was betrothed to the
          son of a rich king.' (Bild)

      b. fick så   margreffue-n~s   dotter   aff Brandeborgh
          got   then margave-DEF~GEN   daughter   of Brandenburg
          '[he] then got the margrave of Brandenburg's daughter [for a wife].' (Petri)

      c. uti Konung-en~s   nampn af Danmark
          in   king-DEF~GEN   name   of Denmark
          'in the king of Denmark's name' (Spegel)

      d. iak är didrik   themar   konung~s sön aff bern
          I   am Theodoric [Theodemir king]~GEN   son of Bern
          'I am Theodoric, king Theodemir of Bern's son.' (Did)

The second most frequent type is [[NP]$_{gen}$ [PP] X] ('the king's of Denmark son'), exemplified in (23):

(23) a. ther stod   en kona   när [...]
          there stood a woman   near
          som sidan wart   konung tydrik~s   aff bern frilla
          that later became [king   Theodoric]~GEN of Bern concubine
          'A woman was standing close by, who was later to become king Theodoric
          of Bern's concubine.' (Did)

      b. [...] then Konung Erich~z   aff Pomeren   Foute   war på
          [...] who [king   Eric]~GEN of Pomerania guardian was on
          Westrårs
          Västerås
          '[...] who was King Eric of Pomerania's guardian in Västerås' (Swart)

Five texts (ProsKron, Did, Petri, Brahe and Spegel) feature this type besides [[NP]$_{gen}$ X
[PP]] (the king's son of Denmark). In one text (Petri) both types even occur within one
and the same sentence – Type I in *Greffue Henrics syster aff Holsten* 'Count Henry's
sister of Holstein', Type II in *hertogh Albrictz aff Mekelborgh frenko* 'Duke Albrecht of
Mecklenburg's kinswoman':

(24) at   konung Håkon skulle haffua hertogh Albrict~z   aff Mekelborgh
          that king   Håkon should have [duke   Albrecht]~GEN of Mecklenburg
          frenko,   jungfru Elizabeth Greffue Henric~s   syster aff Holsten
          kinswoman, Lady   Elizabeth [Count Henry]~GEN sister of Holstein
          '[...] that king Håkon should marry Lady Elizabeth, kinswoman of Duke
          Albrecht of Mecklenburg, sister of Count Henry of Holstein.' (Petri)

In the other three occurrences of the [[NP]$_{gen}$ X [PP]] construction in Petri, the preposition is not *af* but Low German *van*, as in (25). These do not strictly belong to the analysis of *af*-constructions, but I included them nevertheless. They are interesting because they evidently form a single unit (Swedish does not have a preposition *van*), yet they lack phrase-marking.

(25)   thet är alt vthdraget vthaff Tidhric~s   van bern fabele
       that is all taken   from Theodoric~GEN of Bern fable
       'That is all taken from the fable of Theodoric of Bern.' (Petri)

In my material I found three examples of the third construction type, [[NP]$_{gen}$ [PP]$_{gen}$ X] ('the king's of Denmark's son'), with the genitive expressed twice, both on the head of the possessor NP, and its right edge, as in the examples in (26). This construction possibly indicates that the author was uncertain about the position of the genitive marker, which certainly seems to be true of the authors of ProsKron and Gyllenhielm, who use three different construction types (see Table 5 and Table 6) with the genitive marker either on the head of the genitive NP (type 2), at the right edge (type 4, group genitive) and on both (type 3).

(26)   a.   en tysk   jungfru, Elisabeth Sijl,
            a German lady,   Elisabeth Sijl,
            uthur furstinna-n~s   aff Mechelnburg~s   fruentimmer
            from sovereign.F-DEF~GEN of Mecklenburg~GEN privy chamber
            'a German lady, Elisabeth Sijl, from the sovereign of Mecklenburg's privy chamber (i.e. who was lady in waiting to the sovereign of Mecklenburg's wife)' (Gyll)

       b.   [...] och dessutan   fruchtade för Marggrefwe-n~s
            [...] and furthermore feared   for margrave-DEF~GEN
            af Villa Mediana~s   anseende uti en Spansk   Province
            of Villa Mediana~GEN position in a Spanish province
            '[...] and [who] furthermore feared for the margrave of Villa Mediana's position in a Spanish province.' (Runius)

The fourth construction type, [[[NP] [PP]]$_{gen}$X] ('the king of Denmark's son'), is the group genitive construction still found in present-day Swedish. There are two examples of group genitives involving the preposition *af*, from the writings of Carl Carlsson Gyllenhielm (1640) and Agneta Horn (1657):

(27)   a.   efther herttig-en~s   befallning och greffve-n   af Nassou=s
            after duke-DEF~GEN command and [Count-DEF of Nassau]=GEN
            order
            orders
            'following the duke's command and the count of Nassau's orders' (Gyll)

b. och ginge forbi kurforsten af saxen=s lusthus
and went past [prince.elector-DEF of Saxony]=GEN pavilion
'and [we] went past the prince-elector of Saxony's pavilion.' (Horn)

3.3 PP's with *i* 'in'

[[NP] [PP]]$_{gen}$ constructions with the preposition *i* are of a later date than constructions with *af*. In the Middle Swedish texts *i* is not attested at all in this construction, and in later texts *af* and *i* alternate, with some authors preferring *af* in the [[NP] [PP]]$_{gen}$ construction, others, *i*, but *i* is on the whole less frequently attested than *af* (Cf. Table 2). Thus the usage of *i* in this construction appears to have been relatively short-lived, as *i* is no longer used in [[NP] [PP]]$_{gen}$ in Modern Swedish. The results are summarized in Table 6.

Genitive constructions involving *i* differ slightly from genitive constructions involving *af*. The number of examples is admittedly modest, but the available data show that types 1–3 occur with comparable frequency. The first type [[NP]$_{gen}$ X [PP]] ('the king's son of Denmark'), with six occurrences, is less dominant than equivalent constructions with *af*, but this is because *i*-constructions are not found in the oldest texts in this corpus. Some examples are given in (28):

(28) a. och han war biscop Bryniolff~z fadher i Skara
and he was [bishop Brynjolf]~GEN father in Skara
'and he was the father of bishop Brynjolf in Skara.' (Petri)

b. Samma dag kom Haxth[a]usen, konung-en~s stalmestare i
Same day came Haxthausen king-DEF~GEN equerry in
Danmark
Denmark
'On the same day Haxthausen came, the king of Denmark's equerry.'
(Spegel)

Table 6. Possessive constructions involving *i* PPs

Text	*n*	[[NP]$_{gen}$X[PP]]	[[NP]$_{gen}$[PP]X]	[[NP]$_{gen}$[PP]$_{gen}$X]	[[[NP] [PP]]$_{gen}$X]
Petri	4	4	0	0	0
Brahe	7	0	2	4	1
Gyll	5	0	2	1	2
Hiärne	1	0	0	1	0
Columbus	1	0	1	0	0
Spegel	1	1	0	0	0
Stål	2	1	0	1	0
Runius	1	0	1	0	0
Sum	**22**	**6**	**6**	**7**	**3**

Type 2, [[NP]$_{gen}$ [PP] X] ('the king's of Denmark son') is likewise attested in six constructions:

(29) a. En förtälde en gång i Brabant om
         One told   one time in Brabant about
         konung-en~s   i Swerje tapferhet
         king-DEF~GEN in Sweden courage
         'Somebody in Brabant once told [a story] about the king of Sweden's courage.' (Columbus)

    b. att giffva achtt   på konung-en~s   i Poland skipp
        to give attention on king-DEF~GEN in Poland ships
        'to keep an eye on the king of Poland's ships' (Gyll)

The third type, [[NP]$_{gen}$ [PP]$_{gen}$ X] ('the king's of Denmark's son') is the most frequent type of *i*-constructions, with seven occurrences. As we have seen in the previous section, authors may use this type besides type 2. Compare, for instance, (30b) with (29b)).

(30) a. och ginge så   strax wp til konung-en~s   i Danmarck~s
         and went then at.once up to king-DEF~GEN in Denmark~GEN
         paulun.
         pavilion
         'and then they went straight up to the king of Denmark's pavilion'(Brahe)

    b. [...] haffver konungen i Dannmark eftherlåtidt konung-en~s
        [...] has   king-DEF in Denmark let   king-DEF~GEN
        i Påland~z   skipp löpa igönom Öresundh
        in Poland~GEN ships pass through the Sound
        '[then] the king of Denmark let the king of Poland's ships pass through the Sound' (Gyll)

Finally, type 4, the group genitive, is attested three times:

(31) a. alle galier-ne   hade wendt alle-s   theras näbb thill sidland-et
         all galleys-DEF had turned all-GEN their bows to   coast-DEF
         emot   konung-en i Danmarck=s   krigzfolck
         against [king-DEF in Denmark]=GEN forces
         'All the galleys had turned their stems towards the coast, against the king of Denmark's armed forces.' (Brahe)

    b. att herr Jöran Boije, konungen i Sverige=s   felttherre [...]
        that Lord Jöran Boije, [king-DEF in Sweden]=GEN field.marshal
        måtte komma till hielp och bijståndh
        might come to   help and assistance
        'that Lord Jöran Boije, the king of Sweden's field marshal, might come to [their] assistance.' (Gyll)

3.4   Summary

Genitive constructions involving a possessor NP with a postmodifying PP are a rare phenomenon, yet a few patterns can be extracted from the material at hand.

Type 1, [[NP]$_{gen}$X[PP]] (the king's son of Denmark), is clearly the oldest pattern. Of all 25 occurrences in Middle Swedish (1375–1526) texts, 22 were of this type. The second construction to emerge in this corpus was [[NP]$_{gen}$[PP]X] (the king's of Denmark son). It occurs twice in Middle Swedish, and four times in one of the oldest Early Modern Swedish texts (Petri; 1530), although type 1 is still far more frequent in the latter text (with 18 attestations). Type 3, [[NP]$_{gen}$[PP]$_{gen}$X] (the king's of Denmark's son), is first found at the end of the 16th century (in Brahe; 1585). Interestingly, this construction occurs for the most part in texts where at least one other genitive construction is being used. I will discuss this issue further in Section 4. The group genitive, finally, makes its first appearance in Brahe's chronicle as well, and with 5 attestations it is the least frequent construction in this corpus.

One striking observation is that, even though the total number of occurrences per text rarely exceeds 10 (and in most cases is much smaller than that), most authors use more than one construction. The two oldest texts (Bild and ST; both mid-15th century) only have [[NP]$_{gen}$X[PP]], and texts with only one genitive [[NP] [PP]] construction obviously have no variation either, but all other authors use at least two patterns. This strongly suggests that several constructions were in competition to succeed the original [[NP]$_{gen}$X[PP]] pattern. It also backs up the case for a gradient view on the morphological status of the genitive marker made in Section 2.2.1. In type 2 constructions the genitive marker is a phrase-marker whereas in type 4 constructions it is a more clitic-like, since it is attached to a postmodifying PP (although in these examples it is still attached to nominal elements, i.e. place names such as *Danmark*). As authors may use both 2 and 4, the morphological status of the genitive is clearly not strictly demarcated.

The frequencies of all construction types are summarized in Figure 1, to show that most authors with more than one relevant example use two or more construction types. In Figure 1, *af*-constructions and *i*-constructions are taken together if authors use both.

Figure 1 also shows that type 1, [[NP]$_{gen}$X[PP]], is found in ten texts in the corpus; type 2, [[NP]$_{gen}$[PP]X], is also found in ten texts; type 3, [[NP]$_{gen}$[PP]$_{gen}$X], is found in six texts and type 4, the group genitive, is found in three. It furthermore shows that type 1 did not immediately disappear once competing constructions had emerged, as it is still in use in one of the youngest texts (Stålhammars letters from the beginning of the 18th century), whereas the group genitive appears relatively early in the corpus (at the end of the 16th century in Brahe's writings), but is not attested at all in some of the younger texts.

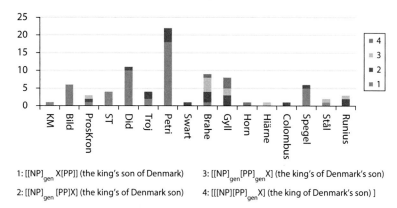

1: [[NP]_gen X[PP]] (the king's son of Denmark)   3: [[NP]_gen[PP]_gen X] (the king's of Denmark's son)

2: [[NP]_gen [PP]X] (the king's of Denmark son)   4: [[[NP][PP]_gen X] (the king of Denmark's son)]

Figure 1. Relative frequency of construction types

4. Discussion and suggestions for further research

From the data discussed in this paper, we may conclude the following: first, that the type 2 construction (*the king's of Denmark son*) did exist before Hof wrote his 1753 treatise saying that it had never been a feature of Swedish grammar. Second, that there are no distinct periods in which type 2, 3 and 4 were in use, rather, it seems that authors had various construction types at their disposal. And third, that apart from the oldest construction (*the king's son of Denmark*), all constructions are only found in texts where the genitive marker as a phrase marker clearly predominates, which is evidenced by lack of internal inflection or single, right-edge marking of full noun phrases.

As to the motivation for the rise of new [[NP] [PP]]_gen constructions, two possible scenarios present themselves. Both start with the observation that extraposition of the PP was no longer obligatory (below I will venture an explanation for this). According to the first scenario, the PP in the original type 1 construction was moved to the left of the possessee NP, yielding a type 2 construction (note that by "movement" I mean overt movement to another syntactic position, not "movement" in the generative sense). Once the possessor NP and its postmodifying PP had become adjacent, scope of the genitive marker was widened to include the PP, with a type 4 construction as its result. This course of events is illustrated by the (constructed) examples in (32):

(32) a. konung-en~s   son af Danmark [type 1]
          king-DEF~GEN son of Denmark
          'the king's son of Denmark'
          <<Movement of postmodifying PP>> →

    b. konung-en~s   af Danmark son
        king-DEF~GEN of Denmark son [type 2]
        'the king's of Denmark son'
        <<scope widening>> →

    c. konung-en af Danmark=s   son [type 4]
        [king-DEF   of Denmark]=GEN son
        'the king of Denmark's son'

In the second scenario, type 4 was not a subsequent stage to type 2, but arose simultaneously with it, or even before it. According to this scenario, the genitive marker, once
it could be attached once to full NPs instead of to every single word in them, widened
its scope to include postmodifying PPs, especially when these formed a semantic unit
with the possessor NP, such as *the king of Denmark*. It is even conceivable that type 4,
the group genitive, arose earlier than the type 2 construction. On this view, the rise of
type 2 may be seen as a type of hypercorrection of the group genitive construction:

(33) a. konung-en~s   son af Danmark [type 1]
          king-DEF~GEN son of Denmark
          'the king's son of Denmark'
          <<Scope widening enabling movement of postmodifying PP>> →

      b. konung-en af Danmark=s   son [type 4]
          [king-DEF   of Denmark]=GEN son
          'the king of Denmark's son'
          <<hypercorrection>> →

      c. *konung-en~s   af Danmark son*
          king-DEF~GEN of Denmark son [type 2]
          'the king's of Denmark son'

Before assessing the likelihood of these two scenarios I will discuss the role of type 3
(*the king's of Denmark's son*). In neither scenario does this type play an independent
role. In my view, the most plausible explanation for the occurrence of this construction
is that it is a contamination of types 2 and 4. Authors who use both 2 and 4 (ProsKron,
Brahe and Gyll) use type 3 as well. Thus the very existence of type 3 strongly suggests
that type 2 and 4 were contemporaneous.

   On the basis of the available data it is impossible to make a firm judgement. The
first scenario has the advantage of presenting a neat sequence of clearly distinguishable
steps, and type 2 does precede type 4 by some 100 years in the present corpus. However, it is not clear what the motivation for movement of the PP can have been if type
2 came first. It has been noted earlier (e.g. Kreyer 2003) that complex genitive constructions are difficult to process because they consist of a head (the possessee) and an
attributive NP (the possessor), which itself consists of a head followed by a postmodifying phrase or clause. For ease of processing, the postmodifier should be adjacent to

the head, as in the type 4 genitive construction in (34a). On the other hand, the head of the possessor NP and the possessee NP should likewise be in each other's vicinity, as in the type 1 genitive construction in (34b) (the – constructed – Old Swedish equivalent) . In the type 2 construction ((34c)), the postmodifying PP is adjacent to the possessor head, but the possessor head and the possessee head are separated by the postmodifying PP. A hearer confronted with (34c) may expect the possessee head to follow the genitive morpheme, but postponement of this head may make (34c) more difficult to process. In (34a) there is another problem because the possessor head is separated from the possessee head, but here the genitive marker is intermediate between the two noun phrases, which may make it easier to identify the two phrases. Thus, for processing reasons, the first scenario seems less likely than the second.

(34) a. [Kungen]$_{possessor\ head}$ av Danmark=s [son]$_{possessee\ head}$ [type 4]

b. [Konungsens]$_{possessor\ head}$ [son]$_{possessee\ head}$ av Danmark   [type 1]

c. [Kungens]$_{possessor\ head}$ av Danmark [son]$_{possessee\ head}$ [type 2]

'the king of Denmark's son'

Moreover, in languages closely related to Swedish that have an independent possessive morpheme, group genitives are clearly preferred with [[NP] [PP]] possessors as well. For example, in the so-called possessor doubling construction in languages like Dutch, group genitives like (35a) are perfectly possible in the spoken language, (35b) (the equivalent of [[NP]$_{gen}$X[PP]]) is awkward, if grammatical at all, and (35c) (the equivalent of [[NP]$_{gen}$[PP]X]) is definitely ungrammatical.

(35) a. de koning van Denemarken z'n zoon [type 4]
          the king   of   Denmark   his son

b. $^{??}$de koning z'n zoon van Denemarken [type 1]
          the king   his son of   Denmark

c. *de koning z'n van Denemarken zoon [type 2]
          the king his of   Denmark   son

As far as I know there is no psycholinguistic evidence corroborating a processing preference of type 4 possessive constructions over type 2 possessive constructions, and it would be interesting to see what the results of such an experiment (measuring processing time of (34c) as opposed to (34a)) would be.

A final argument in favour of the second scenario would be that [[NP] [PP]] constructions of *the king of Denmark* type are increasingly perceived as inseparable units, which may be derived from the fact that, in Modern Swedish, extraposition is impossible not only in constructions like (36a) (the Old Swedish [[NP]$_{gen}$X[PP]] construction), but in other constructions as well, e.g. (36b).[16] This must have something to do with the degree of semantic unity of the NP, because extraposition of the PP is still possible in construction types in which an NP and its postmodifying PP do not form a semantic unit. For example, in (36c) the PP *med Frankrike* is separated from its head *handeln* by the verb phrase *har ökat*:

(36) a. *kungens dotter av Sverige
'the king's daughter of Sweden'

     b. *kungen har anlänt av Sverige
the king has arrived of Sweden'

     c. Handel-n har ökat med Frankrike.   (Teleman et al. 1999b: 448)
Trade-DEF has risen with France
'Trade with France has risen.'

The inseparability of [NP] and [PP] was not a sufficient condition, however, since group genitives are only found in languages where case was lost as an inflectional category and the former M/N.SG.GEN inflection came to be attached to larger units. In languages where this did not happen, e.g. German or Icelandic, group genitives are impossible, even in the spoken language.[17]

Summing up thus far, the first scenario has the advantage of reflecting the chronology attested in the text corpus, whereas the second scenario seems more plausible because it is hard to see what the motivation for the emergence of [[NP]$_{gen}$[PP]] would have been. The awkwardness of the latter construction may, incidentally, have been the very reason why Hof (1753) felt so strongly about it.

But these are changes that occurred in a time long past. In order to assess whether the group genitive really did arise independently of the type 2 construction, yet more data could be analysed, but I am doubtful whether this would provide more explicit information than the present corpus. Given the gradient status of the genitive morpheme, types 2 and 4 may have arisen more or less simultaneously. Secondly, more insight into the development of the *king of Denmark* construction into an inseparable unit might help decide whether this development played a role in the rise of the group genitive, or whether it just happened to be a result of it.

Sources (other than the ones mentioned in Table 1)

Bir (1380s; approx. 105,960 words): *Heliga Birgittas uppenbarelser* I ed. by G.E. Klemming. (=*Svenska Fornskriftsällskapets Samlingar* 29). 1858. [Revelations of Saint Birgitta]

Bur (1350s; approx. 35,115 words): *Codex Bureanus*. In: *Ett forn-svenskt legendarium* ed. by George Stephens. (=*Svenska Fornskriftsällskapets Samlingar* 8, 9, 12, 17, 18, 28). 1847–1858. [Old Swedish book of legends]

MELL (ca. 1350; approx. 45,250 words) *Magnus Erikssons Landslag enligt Cod. Ups. B23* ed. by Per-Axel Wiktorsson. (=*Svenska Fornskriftsällskapets Samlingar* 258). 1989. [Magnus Erikssons National Law]

Mose (1330s; approx. 139,070 words): *Fem moseböcker på fornsvenska enligt Cod. Holm. A1* ed. by Olof Thorell. (= *Skrifter utgivna av Svenska Fornskriftsällskapets samlingar* 212, 218, 223) 1959. [Old Swedish adaptation of the Pentateuch]

Vidh (1325; approx. 6,070 words): *Vidhemsprästens anteckningar.* In: *Corpus iuris Sueo-Gotorum antiqui I* ed. by H.S. Collin & C.J. Schlyter. 1827. [Notes of a priest in Vedum]

Electronic versions of all texts used for this paper can be found at http://www.nordlund.lu.se/Fornsvenska/Fsv%20Folder/index.html

References

Aarts, Bas. 2007. *Syntactic Gradience. The Nature of Grammatical Indeterminacy.* Oxford: Oxford University Press.

Allen, Cynthia L. 2008. *Genitives in Early English.* Oxford: Oxford University Press.

Barnes, Michael P. 2005. The standard languages and their systems in the 20th century II: Faroese. In *The Nordic Languages. An International Handbook of the History of the North Germanic Languages, Vol.II*, Oskar Bandle et al. (eds) 1574–1584. Berlin/New York: Walter de Gruyter.

Börjars, Kersti. 2003. Morphological status and (de)grammaticalisation: the Swedish possessive. *Nordic journal of linguistics* 26, 2, 133–163.

Börjars, Kersti and Harries, Pauline. 2008. The clitic-affix distinction, historical change, and Scandinavian bound definiteness marking. *Journal of Germanic Linguistics* 20, 4, 289–350.

Boutkan, Dirk. 1995. *The Germanic 'Auslautgesetze'.* Amsterdam/Atlanta: Rodopi.

Braune, Wilhelm. 1981 [1880]. *Gotische Grammatik. 19. Auflage neu bearbeitet von Ernst A. Ebbinghaus.* Tübingen: Max Niemeyer Verlag.

Braune, Wilhelm. 1987 [1886]. *Althochdeutsche Grammatik. 14. Auflage bearbeitet von Hans Eggers.* Tübingen: Max Niemeyer Verlag.

Campbell, A. 1959. *Old English Grammar.* Oxford: Oxford University Press.

Dahl, Östen. 2003. *Grammatik.* Lund: Studentlitteratur.

Delsing, Lars-Olof. 1991. Om genitivens utveckling i fornsvenskan. In *Studier i svensk språkhistoria 2*, Sven Göran Malmgren and Bo Ralph (eds), 12–30. Göteborg: Institutionen för Nordiska Språk.

Delsing, Lars-Olof. 1993. *The Internal Structure of Noun Phrases in the Scandinavian Languages. A Comparative Study.* Lund: Department of Scandinavian Languages.

Delsing, Lars-Olof. 1999. Review of Norde 1997. *Nordic Journal of Linguistics* 22, 77–90.

Delsing, Lars-Olof. 2002. The morphology of Old Nordic II: Old Swedish and Old Danish. In *The Nordic Languages. An International Handbook of the History of the North Germanic Languages, Vol. I*, Oskar Bandle et al. (eds), 925–939. Berlin/New York: Walter de Gruyter.

Denison, David. 2010. Category change in English with and without structural change. In *Gradience, Gradualness and Grammaticalization*, Elizabeth Closs Traugott and Graeme Trousdale (eds), 105–128. Amsterdam/Philadelphia: John Benjamins.

Faarlund, Jan Terje. 2007. From clitic to affix: the Norwegian definite article. *Working papers in Scandinavian syntax* 79, 21–46.

Haugen, Einar. 1976. *The Scandinavian Languages.* London: Faber and Faber.

Hof, Sven. 1753. See Thelander, 1985.

Hultman, Tor G. 2003. *Svenska Akademiens Språklära.* Stockholm: Norstedts.

Janda, Richard D. and Joseph Brian D. 2003. On language, change, and language change – Or, of history, linguistics, and historical linguistics. In *The Handbook of Historical Linguistics*, Brian D. Joseph and Richard D. Janda (eds), 3–180. Oxford: Blackwell.

Jespersen, Otto. 1894. *Progress in Language. With Special Reference to English*. London: Swan Sonnenschein & Co.

Jespersen, Otto. 1922. *Language. Its Nature, Development and Origin*. London: George Allen & Unwin.

Kreyer, Rolf. 2003. Genitive and *of*-construction in modern written English. Processability and human involvement. *International Journal of Corpus Linguistics* 8, 2, 169–207.

Larm, Karl. 1933. Morfologiska faktorers inverkan på utbredningen av suffigerad artikel i lagsvenskan. *Arkiv för Nordisk Filologi* 49, 374–385.

Larm, Karl. 1936. *Den bestämda artikeln i äldre fornsvenska. En historisk-syntaktisk studie*. Stockholm: Albert Bonniers Boktryckeri.

Lehmann, Christian. 2004. Theory and method in grammaticalization. *Zeitschrift für Germanistische Linguistik* 32, 2, 152–187.

Marold, Edith. 1984. Überlegungen zur Entwicklung der Substantiv-flexion in den skandinavischen Sprachen. In *Linguistica et philologica. Gedenkschrift für Björn Collinder*, Otto Gschwantler et al. (eds), 307–330. Wien: Wilhelm Braumüller Universitäts-Verlagsbuchhandlung.

Meillet, Antoine. 1922 [1917]. *Caractères généraux des langues germaniques*. Deuxième édition. Paris: Librairie Hachette et Cie.

Mørck, Endre. 2005. Morphological developments from Old Nordic to Early Modern Nordic: inflexion and word formation. In *The Nordic Languages. An International Handbook of the History of the North Germanic Languages, Vol.II*, Oskar Bandle et al. (eds), 1128–1148. Berlin/New York: Walter de Gruyter.

Norde, Muriel. 1997. The history of the genitive in Swedish. A case study in degrammaticalization. PhD Dissertation, University of Amsterdam.

Norde, Muriel. 2000. Nya perspektiv på de medellågtyska lånordens böjning i fornsvenskan. In *Språkkontakt – Innverknaden frå nedertysk på andre nordeuropeiske språk*, Ernst Håkon Jahr (ed.), 217–234. København: Nordisk Ministerråd.

Norde, Muriel. 2001. The loss of lexical case in Swedish. In *Grammatical Relations in Change*, Jan Terje Faarlund (ed.), 241–272. Amsterdam/Philadelphia: John Benjamins.

Norde, Muriel. 2006. Demarcating degrammaticalization: the Swedish s-genitive revisited. *Nordic Journal of Linguistics* 29, 2, 201–238.

Norde, Muriel. 2009. *Degrammaticalization*. Oxford: Oxford University Press.

Noreen, Adolf. 1904. *Altschwedische Grammatik mit Einschluss des altgutnischen*. Halle: Max Niemeyer.

Noreen, Adolf. 1923 [1884]. *Altisländische und altnorwegische Grammatik. 4. Vollständig umgearbeitete Auflage*. Halle: Verlag von Max Niemeyer.

Palmér, Johan. 1945. *Språkutveckling och språkvård*. Lund: C.W.K. Gleerups Förlag.

Perridon, Harry. 1989. Reference, definiteness and the noun phrase in Swedish. PhD Dissertation, University of Amsterdam.

Teleman, Ulf, Hellberg, Staffan andAndersson, Erik. 1999a. *Svenska Akademiens Grammatik II: Ord*. Stockholm: Norstedts.

Teleman, Ulf, Hellberg, Staffan andAndersson, Erik. 1999b. *Svenska Akademiens Grammatik III: Fraser*. Stockholm: Norstedts.

Sigurd, Bengt. 1995. Konungens av Danmark bröstkarameller och genitivreglerna. *Språkvard* 1995: 1, 9–15.

SRB = 2005. *Språkriktighetsboken. Utarbetad av Svenska Språknämnden.* Stockholm: Norstedts Akademiska Förlag.

Stoett, F.A. 1923 [1889]. *Middelnederlandse Spraakkunst. Syntaxis. 3ᵉ herziene druk.* 's Gravenhage: Martinus Nijhoff.

Stroh-Wollin, Ulla. 2009. On the development of definite markers in Scandinavian. *Working papers in Scandinavian syntax* 83, 1–25.

Thelander, Mats. 1985. *Sven Hof: Swänska språkets rätta skrifsätt* (1753). *Med ordstatistik och flera register i ny utgåva.* Uppsala: Institutionen för nordiska språk.

Thorell, Olof. 1977. *Svensk grammatik. Andra upplagan.* Stockholm: Esselte Studium.

Torp, Arne. 1982. *Norsk og nordisk før og nå.* Oslo: Universitetsforlaget.

Torp, Arne. 2002. The Nordic languages in a Germanic perspective. In *The Nordic Languages. An International Handbook of the History of the North Germanic Languages, Vol. I,* Oskar Bandle et al. (eds), 13–24. Berlin/New York: Walter de Gruyter.

Trosterud, Trond. 2001. The changes in Scandinavian morphology from 1100 to 1500. *Arkiv för Nordisk Filologi* 116, 153–191.

Venås, Kjell. 2002. Previous attempts at establishing periods in Nordic language history. In *The Nordic Languages. An International Handbook of the History of the North Germanic Languages, Vol. I,* Oskar Bandle et al. (eds), 31–38. Berlin/New York: Walter de Gruyter.

Wellander, Erik. 1973 [1939] *Riktig svenska. Fjärde, omarbetade upplagan.* Stockholm: Esselte Studium.

Wessén, Elias. 1965. *Svensk språkhistoria III: Grundlinjer till en historisk syntax.* Reprinted. Edsbruk: Akademitryck 1992.

Wessén, Elias. 1968. *Svensk språkhistoria I: Ljudlära och ordböjningslära.* (Reprinted. Edsbruk: Akademitryck 1992)

Endnotes

1.   Thanks are due to Therese Lindström Tiedemann, two anonymous referees and the editors of this volume for valuable comments and suggestions.

2.   As all sources used in this paper are electronically available (see references), I have refrained from giving page numbers in the printed editions. In the glosses, I use the standard abbreviations of the Leipzig Glossing Rules, with the addition of PART for verbal particle, and ø for the absence of an (expected) inflectional suffix. For the genitive I distinguish between -GEN for word-marking inflectional genitive, ~GEN for phrase-marking inflectional genitive and -GEN enclitic s-genitive. For reasons of space and clarity, the morpheme-by-morpheme glosses only contain grammatical information that is exemplified in that example, or is required for a correct understanding.

3.   As I will be arguing further on in this paper, the genitive marker could be either an enclitic word marker (denoted by -s or glossed as -GEN), an inflectional phrase marker (denoted by ~s or glossed as ~GEN), or an enclitic phrase marker (denoted by =s or glossed as -GEN). When no specific morphological realization of the genitive marker is referred to, I will simply use s.

4. When no other source is given, the examples in this section were found in a Google search on December 20th, 2009. Any figures used in this section also refer to this Google search.

5. English, like Swedish, has an invariant possessive morpheme that can be attached to complex noun phrases, hence the examples of Swedish group genitives can be readily translated into English. However, there are crucial distributional differences between the English and the Swedish genitive (notably the fact that English group genitives with NPs with plural heads are highly marked, if not ungrammatical). Since this paper is exclusively about the Swedish group genitive, its findings and conclusions do not necessarily apply to English as well (see further Norde 2009: 160ff.).

6. Unlike English, Swedish does not use an apostrophe in s-genitive constructions (except, optionally, when the possessor noun ends in a sibilant; Teleman et al. 1999a:112). Nevertheless, apostrophes are used in informal writing, possibly the result of English influence, but this usage is not accepted by the Swedish Language Council (http://www.sprakradet.se/GetDoc?meta_id=1950).

7. It is difficult to obtain statistics regarding this construction, as s-genitives are eagerly discussed on internet fora and blogs. As a consequence, if one searches for structures like *kungens av Danmark* or *kungen av Danmarks* 'the king's of Denmark/the king of Denmark's' many of the hits are from pages where this very construction is being discussed, hence they do not contain examples of spontaneous usage.

8. There is a third alternative, which is usually recommended in normative sources, e.g. by The Swedish language Council (*Språkrådet*), which is to avoid the genitive altogether and use a periphrastic construction instead. For instance, instead of *skolorna i Stockholms elevantal* ([schools-DEF in Stockholm]=GEN student number) one should write *elevantalet i skolorna i Stockholm* 'the number of students in the schools in Stockholm' (http://www.sprakradet.se/GetDoc?meta_id=1950). This construction will not be further discussed in this paper.

9. In addition, the term *nusvenska* is used to refer to contemporary Swedish.

10 In their criticism of Norde (1997), Delsing (1999), Börjars (2003) and Allen (2008: 155ff.) appear to miss this point. The purpose of my 1997 thesis was to show that, when the Old Swedish case system started to collapse, genitive *s* developed in a direction different from the other (former) case suffixes, and thus became more clitic-like and less affix-like. From the point of view of gradience, the observation that Modern Swedish still allows for head-marking possessive constructions (comparable to English *the king's sword of England*) besides group genitives (Börjars 2003) is irrelevant. The interesting question is not whether the Swedish s-genitive is a full fledged clitic with not a single trace of a less clitic-like status (which it is not), but whether it has acquired properties of clitics (which nobody will deny it has).

11. This bound article derives from a demonstrative pronoun (*h*)*inn* which followed the noun in Proto-Scandinavian and was subsequently cliticized to the noun. Its exact history is very complex and cannot be discussed here (see e.g. Larm 1933, 1936; Perridon 1989: 129ff.; Faarlund 2007; Börjars & Harries 2008; Stroh-Wollin 2009: 8f.).

12. Old Swedish n-stems and r-stems did not have separate forms for the genitive, dative and accusative in the singular; for this common case form, the term "oblique" is used.

13. Wessén (1965: 115) regards postpositive possessive pronouns as enclitic, but that would still make ~*s* a phrase-marker, as word-marking inflections cannot be attached to material containing clitics (Norde 2006: 22).

14. A second development in the noun phrase that played a crucial role in the rise of the group genitive was the emergence of a fixed position for determiners, which allowed for the genitive marker to be reanalysed as a determiner. See Delsing (1991, 1993) for a generative account of this development, or Norde (2009: 165f.) for a summary of it.

15. This construction type was found in other older Germanic languages as well, compare e.g. Old English *I am the lordes doughter of this castel* (Jespersen 1894: 293) or Middle Dutch *des hertoghen dochter van Bruynswijck* (the-GEN duke-GEN daughter of Bruynswijck) 'the duke of Bruynswijck's daughter' (Stoett 1923: 105).

16. Thanks to Therese Lindström Tiedemann for confirming this.

17. Thanks to Alexandra Lenz and Jóhanna Barðdal for confirming this.

18. Only the cases that are found in all languages are given in this table, thus excluding the Gothic vocative and the Old High German instrumental. Also, only one form is given for each case; for a full account of the case endings and their allomorphs the reader is referred to reference grammars such as Noreen 1904 (Old Swedish), Noreen 1923 (Old Icelandic), Braune/Ebbinghaus 1981 (Gothic), Braune/Eggers 1987 (Old High German), or Campbell 1959 (Old English).

Floating genitives and possessive framing in Northern Akhvakh

Denis Creissels
Université Lumière (Lyon2)

This paper analyzes a construction involving genitives in Northern Akhvakh, the *floating genitive construction*. In this construction, a genitive NP is related to a noun in S or P role but is not included in the NP headed by this noun. The floating genitive identifies the personal sphere of its referent as the frame within which the predication expressed by the clause holds. Functionally, this construction combines the pragmatic motivations of framing constructions with the semantic effects common to other types of external possession constructions. Parallels are proposed between the floating genitives of Northern Akhvakh and functionally comparable constructions found in other languages. This construction illustrates the development of an uncommon type of external possessors in a language family in which external possession has so far been considered relatively marginal.

1. Introduction[1]

This paper establishes the specificity of a particular type of construction involving the genitives of Northern Akhvakh and analyzes it from a typological perspective. In this construction, designated here as *floating genitive construction*, a possessor and a possessee are encoded as a genitive NP and a nominative NP in S or P role respectively, but the genitive NP is not included in the nominative NP headed by the noun with which it stands in a possessive relationship. This construction has a *possessive framing* function, in the sense that the floating genitive identifies the personal sphere of its referent as the frame within which the predication expressed by the clause holds.

Akhvakh (*ašʷaᴸi mič̄’i*, Russian *axvaxskij jazyk*) belongs to the Andic (sub-)branch of the Northeast Caucasian (or Nakh-Daghestanian) family.[2] According to Magomedova and Abdulaeva (2007), Akhvakh has approximately 20 000 speakers. Four dialects are traditionally recognized. One of them is designated as Northern Akhvakh, whereas the other three are grouped under the label of Southern Akhvakh.

Northern Akhvakh is spoken in four villages of the Axvaxskij Rajon in the western part of Daghestan (Tadmagitl', Lologonitl', Kudijab-Roso, and Izani), in recent settlements in the lowlands of Daghestan (Kamyškutan, Sovetskoe), and in Axaxdərə near Zaqatala (Azerbaijan). The Southern Akhvakh dialects are spoken in one village each (Cegob, Tljanub and Ratlub), all situated in the Šamil'skij Rajon of Daghestan.

Magomedbekova (1967) and Magomedova & Abdulaeva (2007) are the main references on Akhvakh. The analysis proposed in this paper is based on field work carried out in Axaxdərə, Tadmagitl', Lologonitl' and Sovetskoe.

Like the other Andic languages, Akhvakh has no writing tradition. The Akhvakh-Russian dictionary (Magomedova & Abdulaeva 2007) uses an adaptation of the Avar version of the cyrillic alphabet. The transcription used in this paper departs from the IPA conventions on the following points: alveolar voiceless affricate *c*; palato-alveolar fricatives *š* (voiceless) and *ž* (voiced); palato-alveolar affricates *č* (voiceless) and *ǯ* (voiced); lateral voiceless affricate *ʟ*; the macron is used for long vowels and strong consonants.

The paper is organized as follows. Section 2 presents the basics of Northern Akhvakh morphosyntax. Section 3 describes the formation and morphological properties of Northern Akhvakh genitives. Section 4 reviews the functions fulfilled by genitives in Northern Akhvakh syntax. Section 5 deals with the floating genitives of Northern Akhvakh, which constitute the main topic of this paper. In Section 6, some parallels are proposed between the floating genitives of Northern Akhvakh and functionally comparable constructions found in other languages.

2.   General remarks on Akhvakh morphosyntax

2.1   Clause structure

Akhvakh clause structure is characterized by flexible constituent order. Case marking and gender-number agreement between the verb and its core arguments are consistently ergative.

Arguments whose identity is recoverable from the context can freely be omitted, and unexpressed arguments receiving an arbitrary or unspecified interpretation are common too.

Causative is the only valency-changing mechanism systematically expressed via verb morphology or grammaticalized periphrases.

2.2   Nouns and noun phrases

Three semantically transparent agreement classes of nouns are distinguished in the singular: human masculine (M), human feminine (F), and non-human (N). In the plural, the distinction *masculine* vs. *feminine* is neutralized, resulting in a binary opposition *human plural* (HPL) vs. *non-human plural* (NPL). The only exceptions to the semantic rule of gender assignment are *āde* 'person' and *mik'e* 'child', which in the singular trigger N agreement, whereas the corresponding plural forms *ādo* and *mik'eli* trigger regular HPL agreement.

In canonical NPs, the head noun is in final position and is inflected for number and case. Number inflection of nouns is irregular and involves a considerable amount of free variation. In headless NPs (i.e. complex NPs whose head noun has been elided), gender-number and case markers attach to the noun dependent that, in the absence of an overt head noun, constitutes the last word of the NP.

Most noun dependents in canonical NPs optionally include gender-number suffixes agreeing with the head noun. In addition, some adjectives have obligatory gender-number agreement prefixes. However, not all adjectives have gender-number agreement prefixes, noun dependents other than adjectives very rarely occur with agreement suffixes in canonical NPs, and suffixal agreement of adjectives is common only in the HPL class. Akhvakh does not have case agreement.

The 1st and 2nd person pronouns show irregularities in their case inflection, but distinguish the same cases as nouns. Akhvakh has an inclusive pronoun distinct from the 1st person plural pronoun, but no 3rd person pronoun proper; demonstratives are used in the discursive function fulfilled by dedicated 3rd person pronouns in other languages.

The nominative (alias absolute), used in the extra-syntactic function of quotation or designation, in S or P roles, and in predicate function, has no overt mark. Case suffixes may attach to a stem identical with the nominative, or to a special *oblique stem* (signaled in the glosses as $..._o$). In the singular, the formation of the oblique stem is very irregular and involves a considerable amount of free variation. The standard 'oblique stem markers' added to the nominative form of nouns and expressing gender-number distinctions (M_o -*šu*-, F_o/N_o -*ĭi*-) are found only with some nouns, and are often in free variation with other types of oblique stem formation. In the plural, the use of the oblique stem markers HPL_o -*lo*- and NPL_o -*li*- or -*le*- is more regular. In headless NPs, the use of the standard oblique stem markers is systematic.

Case inflection includes the following cases:

- three 'syntactic cases': ERG (ergative) -*de*, DAT (dative) -*la*, and GEN (genitive) $Ø(-AGR)$ or -*ĭi*;[3]
- three spatial cases: LOC (locative) -*i* or -*e*, ALL (allative) -*a*, and ABL (ablative) -*u(ne)*;
- three peripheral cases or case-like forms: COM (comitative) -*k'ena*, ESS (essive) -*ĭe* or -*ĭ-AGR* and MDT (mediative) -*guĭe* or or -*guĭ-AGR*.[4]
- two postpositional clitics, CAUSAL -*вana* attached to the 'dallative' form of nouns (see further in this section), and VERS (versative) -*ša* attached to the allative.

The spatial case markers are shared by nouns and spatial adverbs. In noun inflection, they are normally preceded by *orientation markers* (OR) expressing types of spatial configurations (in, under, etc.), which can be dropped only in particular conditions. Northern Akhvakh has five productive orientation markers (-g-, -χar- ~ -ɫir-, -q̄-, -ɫ'i-, and -ɫi-) and vestiges of a sixth orientation marker -r-. A straightforward semantic characterization is possible for only two of them (-χar- ~ -ɫir- 'beside' and -ɫ'i- 'under'). The other three are polysemous in such a way that no simple semantic characterization is possible, and the use of semantically motivated labels could only give a distorted image of their meanings; this is the reason why I prefer to simply number them in the order in which they are listed above. For more details on the meanings carried by the orientation markers of Akhvakh, see Creissels (2009b). Given the topic of this paper, it is sufficient to mention here that OR_1 -g- can be viewed as a default orientation marker that does not specify a particular spatial configuration by itself.

The encoding of spatial relationships may involve a construction in which a noun phrase referring to the orienter combines with a spatial adverb or locational noun. This construction is functionally similar to adposition phrases found in other languages (in the sense that the spatial configuration is encoded by the spatial adverb or locational noun), but formally different in that the NP referring to the orienter and the spatial adverb or locational noun exhibit parallel spatial case inflection:

qẽɫeno-g-e geɫ̄-i |bag-OR_1-LOC inside-LOC| 'in the bag' (static location)
qẽɫeno-g-a geɫ̄-a |bag- OR_1-ALL inside-ALL| 'into the bag'
qẽɫeno-g-u geɫ̄-u |bag- OR_1-ABL inside-ABL| 'out of the bag'

A problematic aspect of the Akhvakh case system is the existence of a syncretic noun ending -a neutralizing the distinction between dative -ʟa and allative$_1$ -g-a. This ending is found in contexts where it can be substituted by forms unambiguously identifiable as dative or allative$_1$, and is therefore analyzable as an allomorph either of the dative or of the allative$_1$, but it also occurs in contexts where it seems impossible to decide whether it constitutes an allomorph of the dative or of the allative$_1$. The existence of such contexts suggests the need to recognize an additional case, called *dallative* here, whose distribution overlaps with that of the dative and allative$_1$.

There are two possible constructions for NP co-ordination: either "NP$_1$-kena NP$_2$", where -kena is the suffix of the comitative case (also used for comitative adjuncts), or "NP$_1$-la NP$_2$-la", where -la is an additive particle (glossed ADD) also found in contexts corresponding to English 'also', 'in turn', or 'even'.

2.3   Verb inflection

Akhvakh verbs always exhibit an overt inflectional suffix, but with respect to prefixal inflection, they are divided into two morphological classes: those including a prefixal slot that cannot be left empty, and those that cannot take prefixes. The prefixal inflection of the verbs that take inflectional prefixes is limited to the expression of gender-number agreement with the nominative argument (S or P).

Suffixal inflection is identical for all verbs and expresses TAM, evidentiality/mira-tivity, polarity, finiteness, and gender-number agreement with the nominative argu-ment. Person distinctions are involved in the contrast between the forms labeled here perfective$_1$ and perfective$_2$, but they follow a typologically rare pattern called "con-junct/disjunct system" in the literature. For a detailed presentation of this aspect of the verbal system of Akhvakh, which can be analyzed as a particular type of evidentiality marking rather than person marking proper, see Creissels (2008a and 2008b).[5]

The synthetic verb forms that can head independent clauses are characterized by the following paradigm of suffixes (or combinations of suffixes): [6]

- perfective$_1$: HPL -*iri*, other classes -*ari* or -*eri*
- perfective$_2$: HPL -*idi*, other classes -*ada* or -*ad(a)*-AGR
- 'short' perfective:[7] HPL -*i*, other classes -*a*
- perfective negative: -*iʟ-a*, *iʟ-a*-AGR or *iʟ*-AGR
- perfective$_3$:[8] -AGR-*wudi*
- perfective$_3$ negative: -*iʟ*-AGR-*wudi*
- perfective$_4$: -AGR-*wa*
- perfective$_4$ negative: -*uš*-AGR-*wa*
- imperfective$_1$: -*iri*
- imperfective$_2$: -*ida* or -*id(a)*-AGR
- imperfective$_1$ negative: -*iki*
- imperfective$_2$ negative: -*ika* or -*ik(a)*-AGR
- potential:[9] HPL -*oji*, other classes -AGR-*wa*
- imperative: -*a*
- prohibitive: -*uba*
- optative$_1$ (general optative): -*ƛ'a* added to the imperative (-*a*)
- optative$_1$ negative: -*ƛ'a* added to the prohibitive (-*uba*)
- optative$_2$ (restricted to wishes that specifically involve the addressee): -*ada* fol-lowed by a gender-number suffix agreeing with the addressee irrespective of the syntactic role of the 2nd person pronoun in the clause
- apprehensive: -*gole* added to the conditional converb (-*ala*)[10]

The two imperfectives are used interchangeably in assertive or interrogative clauses referring to habitual or permanent events, and the imperfective$_2$ tends to be more fre-quent in this use, but the imperfective$_1$ also has modal uses in which it cannot be re-placed by the imperfective$_2$.

The four perfectives do not differ in their TAM value, but only in their evidential-ity/mirativity implications. The perfective$_1$ and the perfective$_2$ share the implication that the speaker has a direct knowledge of the event (s)he is relating. The perfective$_2$ adds the implication that the assertor (1st person in declarative clauses, 2nd person in questions) was actively involved in the event. The perfective$_3$ implies indirect knowl-edge (inference or hearsay), and the perfective$_4$ may encode either surprise, or a par-ticular attitude of the speaker imposing him/herself as an epistemic authority.

Additional TAM or evidentiality/mirativity values are expressed by analytic verb forms with the copula *godi*, the verb *bik'uruLa* 'be', or the verb *mičunuLa* 'be found' in auxiliary function.

Akhvakh has no form specialized in participial function, but four of the independent verb forms listed above are also used as participles: perfective$_2$, perfective negative, imperfective$_2$, and imperfective negative$_2$. On the participles of Northern Akhvakh, see Creissels (2009a).

Strictly dependent verb forms include a verbal noun or "masdar" (*-e*), an infinitive (*-uruLa*), a spatial form (*-iɫ-i/a/u(ne)* 'at/to/from the place where ...'), a general converb, a progressive converb (*-ere*), and several specialized converbs expressing various semantic types of adverbial subordination. On the general converb of Northern Akhvakh, see Creissels (2012). On the other converbs of Northern Akhvakh, see Creissels (2010).

3.   Genitive formation in Northern Akhvakh

3.1   Genitives with and without the genitive suffix *-ɫi*

Morphologically, Northern Akhvakh has two variants of the genitive case: a variant in which no specific marker of the genitive case is added to the oblique stem of the noun, and a variant marked by the suffix *-ɫi*. The genitive marker *-ɫi* is homonymous with the spatial suffix *-ɫ-i*, where *-i* marks locative case, and *-ɫ-*, conventionally labeled OR$_5$, is an orientation marker conflating the spatial configurations 'in a filled, dense space, among the elements of a set' and 'adhering to a non-horizontal surface'.

The use of the two morphological variants of the genitive does not involve any semantic distinction in the relation between the genitive and its head. Their distribution is automatically conditioned by the gender-number of the noun in genitive function, with some amount of free variation which will be commented on below.

3.2   Zero-marked genitives

The variant of the genitive case including no specific marker is used in principle with M and HPL nouns. It corresponds to the formation of the genitive traditionally described in other Andic languages as a formation in which a gender-number suffix expressing gender-number agreement with the head of the genitive serves to mark the genitive, as in the following example from Andi (Cercvadze 1965: 331):

(1)   *Gender-number suffixes in the formation of the genitive in Andi*
  a.   *ima* 'father', oblique stem *imu-*

  b.   *imu-w   woči*   'the father's brother'
       imu-j   joči   'the father's sister'
       imu-b   k'otu 'the father's horse'
       imu-r   haq'u 'the father's house'

The traditional characterization of this type of genitive formation in the Andic languages is theoretically questionable. It is a common property of agreement markers to contribute to the identification of the syntactic status of the word to which they are attached, but this does not imply that they should be analyzed as markers of the syntactic role they help to identify. In the type of genitive formation illustrated in (1), the agreement marker attaches to the oblique stem of the noun, normally followed by an overt case marker. Consequently, it can be argued that the genitive marker proper is not the agreement marker, but the absence of any overt element in the morphological slot reserved for case markers. In other words, the form presented as *imu-w* above is in fact *imu-Ø-w* |father$_o$-GEN-M|.[11]

The need to revise the traditional analysis of this type of genitive formation is particularly obvious in the case of Akhvakh, due to a general tendency to eliminate gender-number agreement between the noun and its dependents, including attributive genitives, as shown in (2).

(2) *Optional gender-number suffixes attached to Northern Akhvakh genitives in the absence of the genitive suffix -Łi*

    a.   *ima* 'father', oblique stem *imo-*

    b.   *imo(-we) wāči*   'the father's brother (M)'
        imo(-je) jāči   'the father's sister (F)'
        imo(-be) x̌ʷani   'the father's horse (N)'

In the case of the genitive, the result of this tendency is that forms consisting of the oblique stem devoid of any overt mark can fulfill the function considered most typical for genitives (the attributive function), and are in fact much more common in this function than forms including a gender-number suffix. Consequently, the notion of zero-marked genitives coinciding with the oblique stem and to which agreement markers may be added, quite obviously provides a better account of this type of formation of Akhvakh genitives than the traditional notion of agreement marker used in the function of genitive marker.

The tendency to eliminate gender-number markers that initially characterized the first variant of the genitive in Akhvakh has an interesting consequence for the analysis of the genitive, since it facilitates the recognition of an important functional distinction. The point is that the elimination of the gender-number markers characteristic of the first variant of the genitive depends on the syntactic function of the genitive: as will be developed in § 5.2, floating genitives (i.e., genitives in possessive framing function) show a very strong tendency to retain their gender-number suffix if they are not formed by means of the genitive marker -*Łi*, even for speakers who never use gender-number suffixes with attributive genitives.

In the examples, genitive forms coinciding with the oblique stem are glossed as '... [GEN]', irrespective of the presence or absence of a gender-number suffix.

3.3   Genitives marked by the suffix *-ɫi*

The genitive suffix *-ɫi* is used in principle with F, N or NPL nouns. Its homonymy with a spatial ending is not peculiar to Northern Akhvakh: in the other Andic languages too, the formation of the genitive by means of gender-number suffixes is in competition with genitive markers either identical or at least very similar to a spatial ending close to Akhvakh *-ɫ-i* both in form and meaning. A plausible scenario is that the original function of *-ɫi* was spatial, and that it started being reanalyzed as a genitive marker with inanimate nouns, which typically occur in genitival constructions expressing whole-part relationships – see Alekseev (2003: 100–110).

3.4   Variations in the distribution of the two variants of the genitive

As already mentioned above, the distribution of the two variants of the genitive is not strict, and speakers may be more or less liberal in their judgments about genitive forms that do not respect the traditional norm. In principle, the zero-marked genitive with optional gender-number markers must be used for M or HPL possessors, whereas the suffix *-ɫi* is used with F, N or NPL possessors, but this rule is not always respected. Some F nouns with an oblique stem of a non-standard type may occur in the zero-marked genitive. For example, the regular genitive form of *ak'i* 'wife' is *ak'o-ɫi*, but in ex. (5) in § 4.2 below, this noun occurs in a zero-marked genitive form. But it is much more common to find M or HPL nouns with the genitive suffix *-ɫi*, in particular in the case of nouns whose oblique stem coincides with the nominative. The tendency to generalize the *ɫi*-marked genitive even with nouns whose oblique stem is different from the nominative seems to be characteristic of children's speech, especially in Axaxdərə.

1st and 2nd person pronouns are the only nominals that never occur with the genitive marker *-ɫi*, and for which the only possible genitive form is the zero-marked genitive with an optional agreement marker, even in the speech of children that otherwise tend to generalize the use of *-ɫi* to M and HPL nouns:

dene	1st pers. sing.	→	oblique stem	*di-*	genitive	*di(-AGR)*
mene	2nd pers. sing.	→	oblique stem	*du-*	genitive	*du(-AGR)*
iši	1st pers. pl.	→	oblique stem	*eše-*	genitive	*eše(-AGR)*
iɫi	incl.	→	oblique stem	*eɫe-*	genitive	*eɫe(-AGR)*
ušti	2nd pers. pl.	→	oblique stem	*ošte-*	genitive	*ošte(-AGR)*

4.   Attributive genitives and other syntactic uses of genitives in Northern Akhvakh

4.1   Attributive genitives

By definition, the use of the genitive form of canonical NPs in noun dependent function is crucial in the notion of genitive: the recognition of noun forms as genitives

implies minimally that the forms in question can be used as noun dependents referring to an individual whose personal sphere includes the referent of the head noun
(Creissels 1979: 127–176, Creissels 2006a: 141–160).[12]

Akhvakh genitives fulfill this prototypical function of genitives without any particular complication. They are not sensitive to alienability distinctions, and the same
construction *genitive + noun* is used with reference to the following three types of relationships, considered central in the notion of personal sphere:

- person-bodyparts (*jašo-ɬi ʁoso* 'the girl's hair'),
- person-relatives (*jašo-ɬi ima* 'the girl's father'),
- person-objects (*jašo-ɬi šišaʟ'e* 'the girl's dress').

Attributive genitives are also productively used with reference to the following types of
relationships:

- whole-part relationships (*mašina-ɬi īc'o* 'the door of the car'),
- members-group relationships (*x̄ʷanale-ɬi rex̌et'i* 'a herd of horses'),
- material-object relationships (*īče-ɬi q̇ĕda* 'stone wall'),
- object/person-quality relationships (*ɬē-ɬi t'āʃa* 'the taste of the water', *jašo-ɬi ʃama* 'the girl's personality'),
- quality-object/person relationships (*koša t'āʃa-ɬi ɬē* 'bad-tasting water', lit. 'water of bad taste'),
- time-event relationships (*čibero-ɬi žaho* 'winter cold'),
- place-object relationships (*beča-ɬi čīči* 'moutain flower'),
- destination-object relationships (*jašo-ɬi šišaʟ'e* quoted above with the meaning 'the girl's dress' is in fact ambiguous between this meaning and 'a dress for girls'),
- author-creation or origin-phenomenon relationships (*jašo-ɬi kaʁa* 'the letter writ-ten by the girl', *čīči-ɬi šʷani* 'the smell of the flower'),
- product-origin relationships (*ʃeče-ɬi ruša* 'apple-tree') etc.

The genitive may also be used with reference to substance-measure relationships, as
in *k'eda mina raži-ɬi* 'two cloves (lit. heads) of garlic', but in this construction, the
genitive *raži-ɬi* follows *mina* 'head' which might be analyzed as its head (in uncontroversial cases of attributive genitives, the only possible order is *genitive – head noun*).
Moreover, in this construction, the noun referring to the substance measured is not
necessarily in the genitive: *k'eda mina raži*, lit. 'two head garlic' is possible with the
same meaning.

4.2   Other syntactic uses of genitives in Northern Akhvakh

In Northern Akhvakh, the use of genitives in a function similar to the canonical function of other cases, i.e. as verb dependents denoting participants in the event encoded
by the verb, is very marginal. Genitive NPs in verb modifier function are not attested

at all, and the only verbs with argumental genitives I am aware of are *mačunuLa* 'speak about', *bečuruLa* 'be full of', *bečōruLa* 'fill with', *boɫuruLa* 'form from', *boɫōruLa* 'create from', and *gūruLa* 'make' in the sense of 'create from'.

Like other noun dependents (adjectives or determiners), genitives can nominalize, i.e. they can constitute headless NPs by themselves. If a nominalized zero-marked genitive occupies a role requiring the nominative case, the gender-number suffix, optional in noun dependent function, is obligatory. Nominalized *ɫi*-marked genitives in roles requiring the nominative case may take a gender-number suffix too, but this is not obligatory. In syntactic roles requiring a case other than the nominative, the oblique stem of nominalized genitives, like that of other nominalized noun dependents, is formed by adding an oblique stem marker:

waša	'boy' →	*wašo(-be) ťale*	'the boy's hat'
		wašo-be, obl. stem *wašo-ɫi-*	'that (N) of the boy'
mašina	'car' →	*mašina-ɫi īč'o*	'the door of the car'
		mašina-ɫi(-be), obl. stem *mašina-ɫi-ɫi-*	'that (N) of the car'

In ex. (3), the nominalized genitives *ēse-be* 'ours (N)' and *ēse-re* 'ours (NPL)' are interpreted as the reduced form of the full NPs *ēse(-be) boč'o* 'our moon' and *ēse(-re) č'ʷariba* 'our stars', respectively.

(3)   ošte   boč'o-la   ese-be-gula   godi,
AXD[13]   2PL$_0$[GEN] moon-ADD 1PL$_0$-N-like   COP.N
'Your moon is like ours,

ošte   č'ʷari-ba-la ese-re-gula   gedi.
2PL$_0$[GEN] star-PL-ADD 1PL$_0$-NPL-like COP.NPL
and your stars are like ours.'[14]

In example (4), taken from an anecdote in which the miller sees Molla taking wheat from other people's bags to put it into his own bag, *du-ɫi-g-une* 'from yours' and *ek'o-ɫi-g-a* 'into other people's' are nominalized genitives, interpreted in this context as the reduced form of the full NPs *du(-be) qĕLeno-g-une* 'from your bag' and *ek'o(-be) qĕLeno-g-a* 'into other people's bag', respectively.

(4)   mene hu-šte   ʃadada w-ūč-ala,
AXD   2SG   DIST-thus mad   M-be.found-COND
'If you are as mad [as you pretend to be],

du-ɫi-g-une   ek'o-ɫi-g-a
2SG$_0$[GEN]-N$_0$-OR$_1$-ABL other.people[GEN]-N-OR$_1$-ALL

čugu   ť.ōš-a-wa?
why   put.NEG-N-PF$_4$[15]
why didn't you put [wheat] from your [bag] into [the bag] of other people?'

As illustrated by ex. (5) & (6), genitives can take a predicate function in a construction in which they immediately precede the non-verbal copula *godi* or the copulative verb *bik'uruʟa* 'be'. This can be viewed as a particular use of nominalized genitives, since nouns in the nominative case take a predicate function exactly in the same way.

(5) di-be   goʟe,   aⱪ'o-be   gʷede.
AXD 1SG$_0$[GEN]-N COP.NEG.N wife$_0$[GEN]-N COP.N
'It is not mine, it belongs to my wife.' (lit. 'it is my wife's')

(6) eše   č'eko-ʟ̄'-i-še   ūši eše-be   gʷede.
TDM 1PL$_0$[GEN] foot$_0$-OR$_4$-LOC-ADJZ soil 1PL$_0$[GEN]-N COP.N
'The soil under our feet is ours.'

The uses of Northern Akhvakh genitives examined so far are cross-linguistically common. Floating genitives, which will be described in the following section, are less common. An interesting peculiarity of Northern Akhvakh is that variations in the use of gender-number suffixes in the different possible functions fulfilled by genitives contribute to make the distinction between floating genitives and other uses of genitives relatively easy to recognize.

5. Floating genitives

5.1 The notion of floating genitive

Examples (7) to (10) provide a first illustration of what I call floating genitives. This term is motivated by the fact that, semantically speaking, there is clearly a possessive relationship between the genitive and another word in the same sentence, but this possessive relationship is not encoded as a head-dependent relation in the construction of a noun phrase.

(7) īc'o   č'or-ere   b-ik'ʷ-a-wi če ek'ʷa-š̄ʷ-e   **moʟa rasadi-be.**
AXD door knock-PROG N-be-N-PF$_3$ one man-M$_0$-ERG Molla Rasadi[GEN]-N
'A man knocked at Molla Rasadi's door.'
lit. 'The door was hit by a man, of Molla Rasadi.'

(8) čaka k'eha b-oʟ'-ere   godi **di-be.**
AXD much eye   N-ache-PROG COP.N 1SG$_0$[GEN]-N
'My eye is giving me much pain.'
lit. 'The eye is giving much pain, of me.'

(9) č'ek'-i ʁad-e   q'ʷ.ēne   r-ik'ʷ-a-wi **hu-šu-re.**
AXD leg-PL on.the.ground-LOC reach-PROG NPL-be-N-PF$_3$ DIST-M$_0$[GEN]-NPL
'His legs reached the ground.'
lit. 'The legs reached the ground, of him.'

(10) ʁe-ɫi   jaše-ɫi-q̄-e   kʼeha b-ux̄-ari ha-šu-be.
AXD   neighborhood-GEN girl-F_0-OR_3-LOC eye N-fall-PF_1 PROX-M[GEN]-N
      'He noticed a young girl from the neighborhood.'
      lit. 'The eye fell on a girl, of him'

The fact that such genitives can freely occur at the beginning or at the end of the sentence, irrespective of the position of the noun to which they are semantically related, is particularly significant in a language like Akhvakh, in which the extreme flexibility of constituent order at clause level sharply contrasts with the rigidity of noun phrase structure.

5.2   Agreement properties and syntactic status of floating genitives

In Northern Akhvakh, gender-number agreement of zero-marked genitives supports the recognition of floating genitives as involving a specific construction.

As already explained, Akhvakh has two morphological types of genitives: zero-marked genitives and ɫi-marked genitives. In attributive function, zero-marked genitives may express agreement with their head, but I have no unambiguous example of attributive genitives with gender-number suffixes in the texts I collected in Axaxdərə, and very few examples in my texts from Tadmagitl'. By contrast, zero-marked genitives in the construction illustrated by ex. (7) to (10) above invariably show gender-number suffixes.[16]

Additional evidence that floating genitives involve a specific type of construction comes from the fact that they are found only in clauses where the possessee is the nominative argument, i.e. the NP in the nominative case (P in transitive constructions and S in intransitive constructions) governing the gender-number agreement of the verb.[17]

An extraction analysis of floating genitives remains of course possible from a formal point of view, at least from the perspective of theories that allow syntactic movement operations, but it requires positing conditions on extraction that can be viewed as equivalent to the recognition of a separate construction:

– the extraction of genitives is extremely productive, whereas the extraction of other types of noun dependents is exceptional, or not attested at all;
– the extraction of zero-marked genitives implies overt gender-number agreement;
– genitives can be extracted from NPs in S/P role only.

At this point, it is important to mention that Northern Akhvakh has several cases of 'adverbial concord', i.e. of adjunct phrases agreeing with the nominative argument of the clause. This is the case, for example, for many manner adverbs, such as *īhahime* (M *īhahimo*, HPL *īhahimi*) 'slowly', *hušte* (M *hušto*, HPL *hušti*) 'thus', *čʷige* (M *čʷigo*, HPL *čʷigi*) 'how?', etc.

(11) a. čʷig-o   me-de **hu-du ekʷ'a** t'ubal-o   w-uk'-ada?

TDM   how-M[ADV] 2SG-ERG DIST-SL man bury-M[ADV] M-be-PF$_2$

'How(M) did you bury that man?'

   b. **čʷig-i**   me-de **hu-du ãd-o**

ELIC   how-HPL[ADV] 2SG-ERG DIST-SL person-PL

t'ubal-i   b-ak'-idi?

bury-HPL[ADV] HPL-be-PF$_2$.HPL

'How(HPL) did you bury those people?'

Consequently, the fact that floating genitives agree with the nominative argument cannot be viewed as evidence supporting the extraction analysis, since Akhvakh has uncontroversial cases of agreement between the nominative argument and another term of the clause that cannot be analyzed as extracted from the NP in S or P role.

5.3   Semantic properties of floating genitives

In addition to the morphosyntactic evidence presented above, an analysis of floating genitives that does not recognize them as a specific construction would be problematic from the point of view of the syntax-semantics interface. Floating genitives do not differ from attributive genitives in their contribution to denotative meaning, but they carry different implications with respect to information structure and/or the way they emphasize particular aspects of the denotative meaning.

Unlike attributive genitives, which have a much broader range of values (see Section 4.1 above), floating genitives are overwhelmingly found with animate possessors involved in one of the varieties of possessive relationships commonly considered prototypical (person-bodyparts, person-relatives and person-objects relationships). Floating genitives referring to whole-part relationships and object/person-quality relationships are attested too, though much less frequently, and the other types of relationships to which attributive genitives can refer are not attested in the floating genitive construction.

In addition, Akhvakh has no systematic expression of definiteness contrasts at NP level, but floating genitives may contrast with attributive genitives from this point of view. As illustrated by ex. (12), NPs including an attributive genitive that clearly refers to a specific individual tend to be interpreted as definite descriptions, whereas no such implication is carried by the floating genitive construction.

(12) a. di   ištuda lãgi   b-uq-ari.

AXD   1SG$_0$[GEN] five   sheep N-get.lost-PF$_1$

'My five sheep got lost' (attributive genitive)

   b. ištuda lãgi b-uq-ari   di-be.

five   sheep N-get.lost-PF$_1$ 1SG$_0$[GEN]-N

'Five of my sheep got lost'

lit. 'Five sheep got lost, of me.' (floating genitive)

The obvious function of attributive genitives is to restrict the denotation of their head, and the explanation of the definiteness effects often observed cross-linguistically for attributive genitives is that, in terms of discourse strategy, the optimal situation is one in which the presence of a restrictive modifier uniquely determines the referent of its head. Consequently, the fact that floating genitives trigger no definiteness effect can be accounted for by positing that, in terms of discourse strategy, they do not operate directly on the denotation of an NP, but rather on the scope of the predication.

This hypothesis is consistent with the empathy effects triggered by floating genitives. Let us consider the following minimal pair:

(13) a.   ēśe-je   ila   j-iʟ'-e   gida.
AXD   1PL$_0$[GEN]-F grandmother F-die-F[ADV] COP.F
           lit. 'Of us, a/the grandmother has died.' (floating genitive)

      b.   ēśe   ila   j-iʟ'-e   gida.
           1PL$_0$[GEN] grandmother F-die-F[ADV] COP.F
           'Our grandmother has died.'

At least for speakers that never use gender-number suffixes with attributive genitives (which was in particular the case for my main informant in Axaxdərə), this is unambiguously an instance of the contrast between floating and attributive genitive (For speakers who sometimes use gender-number suffixes with attributive genitives, a variant of sentence (a) with the genitive in final position would unambiguously involve a floating genitive: *ila jiʟ'e gida ēśeje*).

In English, it is difficult to find a satisfactory translational equivalent of sentence (13a). By contrast, equivalents of this sentence can be proposed for French (*Nous avons notre grand-mère qui est morte* vs. *Notre grand-mère est morte*), Spanish (*Se nos ha muerto la abuela* vs. *Nuestra abuela se ha muerto*), Basque (*Hil zaigu amona* vs. *Gure amona hil da*) or Russian (*У нас бабушка умерла* vs. *Наша бабушка умерла*). We will return to this point in Section 6, but note that such translations correctly reflect the fact that, in Akhvakh, an empathy effect follows from the fact that sentence (a) considers the situation from the point of view of the possessor, whereas sentence (b) can be viewed as a matter-of-fact way to inform about the grandmother's death.

To summarize, floating genitives have in common with attributive genitives that they encode possessors related to a possessee overtly expressed in the same clause. They differ from them in that attributive genitives restrict the denotation of their head without any particular implication for information structure, whereas floating genitives express that the situation to which the clause refers is the personal sphere of their referent.

5.4 Possessive predication, a particular case of the floating genitive construction

Possessive predications are constructions that, if no particular discourse device is applied, are interpreted as attributing to an individual (the possessor) the presence of an entity (the possessee) in their personal sphere.

As illustrated by ex. (14) to (18), Northern Akhvakh has a predicative construction expressing possession in which the NP representing the possessor shows genitive marking (a type of possessive predication also found for example in Turkic languages).[18]

(14) če x̄ʷani-ɫunu di-be   b-ik'-iL-a.
SOV   one horse-RESTR 1SG$_0$[GEN]-N N-be-NEG-PF
      'I had only a horse.'

(15) di-be   b-ik'-iL-a ači.
SOV   1SG$_0$[GEN]-N N-be-NEG-PF money
      'I had no money.'

(16) hu muħamadibi-šu-be   b-ik'ʷ-a-wi boq'oda mik'e.
TDM   DIST Muhamadibi-M$_0$[GEN]-N N-be-N-PF$_3$ four   child
      'That Muhamadibi had four children.'

(17) čami   reše gʷeda du-be?
AXD   how.much year COP.N 2SG$_0$[GEN]-N
      'How old are you?'
      lit. 'Of you, how many years exist?'

(18) ha-de-štada-be taχa di-be-la   gʷede.
DIC   PROX-SL-such-N bag 1SG$_0$[GEN]-N-ADD COP.N
      'I too have such a bag.'

There has been a lot of debate among scholars about the analysis of possessive predications of this type, either as constructions involving two distinct core NPs, or as constructions in which a single core NP representing the possessee includes a genitival dependent representing the possessor (something like 'X's Y exists'). However, whatever the arguments invoked in the analysis of similar constructions in other languages, what is crucial for Northern Akhvakh is that here, possessive predication is very clearly a particular case of the floating genitive construction, in which the floating genitive behaves exactly in the way described in the preceding sections, and consequently can be analyzed syntactically as an adjunct having a particular relationship (concretized by an agreement mechanism) with the S argument of the clause.

5.5   Conclusion

Before turning to typological considerations, let me briefly summarize the main conclusions of the analysis of the floating genitives of Akhvakh. I have presented evidence, both morphological and syntactic, that floating genitives are involved in a specific type of construction, not amenable to the other constructions in which genitives can be found. In this construction, the floating genitive is syntactically in adjunct function. In addition, the recognition of a specific floating genitive construction straightforwardly accounts for semantic properties of floating genitives that would not be expected if they were simply attributive genitives in non-canonical position. The observations on the meaning of the floating genitive construction can be summarized by saying that floating genitives have a framing function: they restrict the scope of the predication to the personal sphere of their referent, implying that an element of the personal sphere of their referent is involved in the predication in S or P role.

In other words, the floating genitives of Akhvakh are a particular subtype of the general category of frame adjuncts. In the literature, the notion of frame adjunct has mainly been applied to spatial or temporal expressions,[19] but Akhvakh supports the recognition of other subtypes of frame adjuncts, in particular, of genitival adjuncts fulfilling a function of possessive framing.

6.   The floating genitives of Akhvakh in typological perspective

From a functional and typological point of view, floating genitives constitute a particular variety of external possession, since the floating genitive construction implies that the referent of the genitive in frame adjunct function is a possessor whose personal sphere includes the referent of the nominative argument of the clause.

Constructions in which a possessor is encoded by a dative NP in the same way as participants assuming a role of recipient/beneficiary in the event are the most common type of external possession constructions.[20] Their functional motivation is essentially semantic. As argued by Creissels (1979: 535-551),[21] the explanation of the cross-linguistic variation between attributive genitives and dative NPs in external possession constructions is that a possessor is always at least to some extent concerned by events involving entities belonging to his/her personal sphere, and consequently can be conceptualized as a participant in beneficiary/maleficiary role.

Possessive framing, like other types of framing, has a pragmatic motivation. A separate statement of restrictions on the scope of the predication contributes to limit the complexity of the information that must be encoded within the predicative construction proper, and allows one to make more explicit the way the utterance relates to the preceding discourse. In addition, by identifying the scope of the predication to the personal sphere of an individual, possessive framing highlights the involvement of this person in an event in which (s)he does not fulfill a core participant role, resulting in effects similar to those produced by other types of external possession, as already suggested by the parallelism proposed in Section 5.4 between the floating genitive construction of Akhvakh and the dative constructions of Spanish and Basque.

There do not seem to be very many languages that widely use a possessive framing construction similar to the floating genitive construction of Akhvakh. However, interesting parallels can be proposed with other languages that have possessive framing constructions in which the person whose personal sphere delimits the domain of predication is encoded like the possessor in possessive predication. Russian and French are two cases in point.

In Russian, *u* is a spatial preposition expressing location of the figure in the vicinity of the ground, as in ex. (19). Interestingly, this preposition is mainly used with human nouns, expressing 'at N's place', as in ex. (20). Preposition phrases headed by this preposition are also used to encode the possessor in possessive predication, as in ex. (21). Russian also has a widely used framing construction in which a preposition phrase headed by *u* shows all properties typical of preposition phrases in frame adjunct function, as in (22), to be compared with (23), which conveys the same denotative meaning with the possessor encoded as an attributive genitive NP.

(19) Dom   stoit   u reki.
      house.SG stand.PRS.3SG by river.SG.GEN
      'The house stands by the river.'

(20) On   ostalsja   u nas.
      3SGM remain.PFV.PST.SGM by 1PL.GEN
      'He stayed at our place.'

(21) U nego   est'   mašina.
      by 3SGM.GEN there.is car.SG
      'He has a car.'

(22) U nego   zagorelis'   glaza.
      by 3SGM.GEN light.up.PFV.PST.PL eye.PL
      'His eyes lit up.', lit. 'By him lit up the eyes.'

(23) Ego   glaza zagorelis'.
      3SGM.GEN eye.PL light.up.PFV.PST.PL
      'His eyes lit up.'

The possessive predication of Russian can be analyzed as a variety of existential predication, whose domain is the personal sphere of the referent of the *u*-phrase, and where the notion of possessive framing provides a more general characterization of *u*-phrases in frame adjunct function.

The other case in point is a French construction in which the transitive verb of possession *avoir* 'have' combines with another verb in the way illustrated by ex. (24), to be compared with the possessive predication (25) and the encoding of the same event without possessive framing (26).

(24) Jean a   son   fils
      Jean have.PRS.3SG POSS3SG.3SGM son.SG

      qui   se   marie   demain.
      COMP[22] REFL marry.PRS.3SG tomorrow
      'Jean's son is marrying tomorrow.'
      lit. 'Jean has his son that is marrying tomorrow.'

(25) Jean a   un fils.
      Jean have.PRS.3SG one son.SG
      'Jean has a son.'

(26) Le   fils   de Jean se   marie   demain.
     DEF.SGM son.SG of Jean REFL marry.PRS.3SG tomorrow
     'Jean's son is marrying tomorrow.'

The French construction illustrated by ex. (24) has exactly the same function as the Russian construction with an *u*-phrase in frame adjunct function. Syntactically, however, the French construction involves an operation that is more complex than the mere fronting of a frame adjunct. A possible analysis consists in positing a parallelism with a construction in which the object NP in the construction of *avoir* 'have' is followed by an adjective in secondary predicate function (in the terminology of traditional French grammar: 'attribut de l'objet'), as in (27).

(27) Jean a   son   fils   malade.
     Jean have.PRS.3SG POSS3SG.3SGM son.SG sick
     'Jean's son is sick.', lit. 'Jean has his son sick.'

It has long been observed by French grammarians that this construction belongs to a subclass of 'attribut de l'objet' constructions in which the suppression of the 'attribut de l'objet' is not possible, or implies important changes in the meaning of the construction. Using the notions of modern linguistics, this can be accounted for by a raising-to-object analysis: in the 'attribut de l'objet' construction illustrated by ex. (27), the object of *avoir* does not receive the role of possessee it would be assigned in the absence of the adjective in 'attribut de l'objet' function. The morphosyntactic slot of the object NP does not receive any role from *avoir*, and the only semantic role assigned to the NP occupying this slot comes from the adjective.

Similarly, the possessive framing construction illustrated by ex. (24) can be accounted for by positing a raising-to-object construction in which:

- *avoir* has two complements,
- *avoir* assigns the role of frame (historically derived from the role of possessor) to its subject, but has no role to assign to an object NP,
- the second complement of *avoir* is a subjectless complement clause,
- the first complement of *avoir* is an NP to which the embedded verb assigns the role that cannot be assigned to the missing subject.

There is also an interesting parallelism between the floating genitive construction of Akhvakh analyzed in this paper and the external possessors of Greek analyzed in König & Haspelmath (1997: 554–5 & 584–6). Akhvakh and Greek share the use of the same case for internal and external possessors. In the case of Greek it may be argued that this situation is in some way or other the result of the loss of the distinction between the genitive and the dative in a language from a family in which dative-marked external possessors are common. Such an explanation is excluded in the case of Akhvakh, since dative-marked external possessors do not seem to exist in Andic languages, and there is no evidence of a possible historical connection between genitive and dative in the history of Andic languages either.

7. Conclusion

In this paper, I have tried to show that Akhvakh has a possessive framing construction that functionally combines the pragmatic motivations of framing constructions with the semantic effects common to other types of external possession constructions. In comparison with other languages that use a possessive framing construction widely, like French or Russian, the originality of Akhvakh is that it straightforwardly uses genitives in frame adjunct function, with a morphosyntactic device to prevent possible ambiguities between attributive genitives and floating genitives, since these two syntactic varieties of genitive NPs do not put into play the same rules of gender-number agreement. The floating genitives of Akhvakh, therefore, make an interesting contribution to the general typology of external possession by illustrating the development of an uncommon type of external possessors in a language family in which external possession has been so far considered relatively marginal.

References

Alekseev, Mixail E. 2003. *Sravnitel'no-istoričeskaja morfologija naxsko-dagestanskix jazykov. Kategorii imeni* [Comparative-historical Morphology of Nakh-Daghestanian Languages. Nominal Categories – in Russian]. Moscow: Academia.

Cercvadze, Il'ja I. 1965. *Andiuri ena* [The Andi Language – in Georgian]. Tbilisi: Mecniereba.

Charolles, Michel and Péry-Woodley, Marie-Paule (eds). 2005. *Les adverbiaux cadratifs* (= *Langue Française* 148). Paris: Armand Colin.

Charolles, Michel and Prévost, Sophie (eds). 2003. *Adverbiaux et topiques* (= *Travaux de Linguistique* 47). Bruxelles: De Boeck.

Creissels, Denis, 1979. Les constructions dites "possessives", étude de linguistique générale et de typologie linguistique. Thèse de doctorat d'état, Université Paris 4.

Creissels, Denis, 2006a. *Syntaxe générale, une introduction typologique 1. Catégories et constructions.* Paris: Hermès.

Creissels, Denis, 2006b. *Syntaxe générale, une introduction typologique 2. La phrase.* Paris: Hermès.

Creissels, Denis, 2008a. Person variations in Akhvakh verb morphology: functional motivation and origin of an uncommon pattern. *Sprachtypologie und Universalienforschung* 61, 4, 309–325.

Creissels, Denis, 2008b. Remarks on so-called "conjunct/disjunct" systems. Paper presented at the conference *Syntax of the world's languages III*, Berlin.

Creissels, Denis, 2009a. Participles and finiteness: The case of Akhvakh. *Linguistic Discovery.*

Creissels, Denis, 2009b. Non-spatial functions of spatial forms in Northern Akhvakh. Paper presented at the workshop *Non-spatial functions of spatial forms in East Caucasian*, Helsinki.

Creissels, Denis. 2010. Specialized converbs and adverbial subordination in Axaxdərə Akhvakh. In *Clause-Hierarchy and Clause-Linking: Syntax and Pragmatics,* Isabelle Bril (ed.), 105–142. Amsterdam: John Benjamins.

Creissels, Denis. 2012. External agreement in the converbal construction of Northern Akhvakh. In *Clause Linkage in Cross-linguistic Perspective*, Holger Diessel and Volker Gast (eds), 127–156. Berlin: Mouton de Gruyter.

König, Ekkehard & Haspelmath, Martin 1997. Les constructions à possesseur externe dans les langues d'Europe. In *Actance et Valence dans les Langues d'Europe*, J. Feuillet (ed.), 525–606. Berlin: Mouton de Gruyter.

Lang, Ewald, Maienborn, Claudia and Fabricius-Hansen Cathrine (eds). 2003. *Modifying Adjuncts*. Berlin: Mouton de Gruyter.

Magomedbekova, Zagidat Magomedovna. 1967. *Axvaxskij jazyk (grammatičeskij analiz, teksty, slovar')* [The Akhvakh Language (Grammatical Analysis, Texts, Lexicon) – in Russian]. Tbilisi: Mecniereba.

Magomedova, Patimat and Abdullaeva, Indira. 2007. *Axvaxsko-russkij slovar'* [Akhvakh-Russian Dictionary]. Maxačkala: Dagestanskij Naučnyj Centr Rossiskoj Akademii Nauk.

Payne, Doris and Barshi, Immanuel (eds). 1999. *External Possession*. Amsterdam: John Benjamins.

Endnotes

1.   This paper has benefited from comments by Michael Daniel, Martin Haspelmath, Andrej Malchukov, Wolfgang Schulze, and also by two anonymous readers and the editors of the volume.

2.   The other Andic languages are Andi, Bagvalal, Botlikh, Chamalal, Godoberi, Karata, and Tindi. None of them has a particularly close relationship to Akhvakh. Andic languages are traditionally grouped with Avar and Tsezic languages into a single branch of the Northeast Caucasian family. The other branches of the Northeast Caucasian family are Lak, Dargi (or Dargwa), Lezgi, Khinalug (sometimes considered a marginal member of the Lezgi branch), and Nakh.

3.   The distribution of the two variants of the genitive is discussed in Section 3.

4.   Although this is not absolutely obligatory, the essive and mediative suffixes are typically followed by a suffix marking gender-number agreement with the S/P argument. The same set of agreement markers is found in several types of forms (including the general converb) fulfilling adverbial functions. Note that the mediative suffix can be decomposed as 'OR$_1$ (*g*) + ABL (*u*) + ESS'.

5.   Morphologically, the suffixal inflection of verbs is predominantly agglutinative, with endings beginning with a vowel added to stems ending with a consonant, but there is a class of verb stems ending with an 'unstable consonant' whose deletion triggers fusion of the preceding vowel with the first vowel of the ending.

6.   In cases of allomorphic variation, whenever possible I have selected a single quotation form that can be analyzed as a relatively direct representation of the underlying form. Variants are listed only in cases of allomorphic variations that do not lend themselves straightforwardly to such an analysis. AGR stands for 'gender-number agreement marker'. The inflectional forms of

the verb do not behave in a uniform way with respect to gender-number agreement, but these variations have no obvious relationship with finiteness. Note also that there are several sets of agreement markers whose distribution lends itself to no generalization.

7. This form occurs, sometimes obligatorily and sometimes optionally, in contexts in which it can be analyzed as a variant, either of Perfective$_1$ or Perfective$_2$.

8. Perfective$_3$ has no form expressing HPL agreement. In contexts in which Perfective$_3$ would be expected, the presence of a HPL nominative argument triggers the use of the perfect (an analytic tense combining the general converb of the auxiliated verb with the copula in auxiliary function).

9. The potential and perfective$_4$ markers are both -*wa*, but they do not have the same accentual properties, and they combine with different sets of gender-number agreement markers.

10. The conditional converb is a strictly dependent verb form, but the apprehensive derived from it by means of the addition of -*gole* may head independent as well as subordinate clauses.

11. Attributive genitives agreeing with their head are attested in other language families, for example in Bantu languages. However, the agreeing genitives of Bantu languages are easier to analyze, since the class agreement marker included in Bantu genitives can be isolated from a segment -*a*- that remains constant, and therefore constitutes the genitive marker proper. In Andic genitives of the type illustrated in (1), no overt genitive marker can be isolated from the agreement marker, which explains the traditional view according to which the agreement marker itself fulfills the function of genitive marker. Note that the analysis proposed here is consistent with the fact that case forms of nouns including an obligatory agreement marker in addition to an overt case marker are not uncommon in East Caucasian languages. For example, Andi has an "affective" case used to mark the experiencer in the construction of verbs such as 'see' or 'hear', and the marker of the affective case -*o* obligatorily combines with a suffix expressing gender-number agreement with the nominative argument of the verb, as illustrated by *imu-w-o wōci haq'ido* |father$_o$-M-AFF|brother|see.IPF| 'The father sees [his] brother' vs. *imu-j-o jōci haq'ido* |father$_o$-F-AFF|sister|see.IPF| 'The father sees [his] sister' (Cercvadze 1965: 332).

12. Note that this formulation takes into account the fact that, in many languages, pronouns cannot straightforwardly take the place of NPs in noun dependent function, and the semantic types of noun modification expressed by genitive NPs are encoded by means of special 'possessive' determiners or adjectives if the possessor is a speech act participant or a discursively salient entity that, in other syntactic contexts, would be represented by a 3rd person pronoun.

13. The origin of the examples is indicated as follows: AXD = texts collected in Axaxdərə, TDM = texts collected in Tadmagitl', SOV = texts collected in Sovetskoe, DIC = taken from the Akhvakh-Russian dictionary, ELIC = elicited.

14. Among the abbreviations used in glossing examples, the following ones are not found in the Leipzig Glossing Rules, or are used with a different meaning: ADD = additive particle, ADJZ = adjectivizer, ADV = second formative of endings expressing adverbial agreement, HPL = human plural, IPF = imperfective (inflectional), LL = lower level (spatial deixis), N = non-human, NPL = non-human plural, ...$_o$ = oblique stem, OR = spatial orientation marker (first formative of spatial case endings), PF = perfective (inflectional), PFV = perfective (derivational), RESTR = restrictive, SL = same level (spatial deixis), UL = upper level (spatial deixis).

15. The symbol '.' signals that a morpheme boundary has been blurred by the fusion of two underlying vowels into a long vowel, as in |t'ă-uš-a-wa| → *t'ŏšawa*. In the segmentation of

Akhvakh words, '.' is conventionally written before the long vowel resulting from this process (t'.õš-a-wa).

16. Interestingly, judging from the available texts, floating genitives are extremely frequent in other Andic languages too, and the lack of acknowledgement of their existence in the literature is certainly due to the fact that Akhvakh is apparently the only Andic language in which the agreement properties of floating genitives differ from those of ordinary attributive genitives.

17. This observation calls for two comments. First, in Akhvakh texts, floating genitives related to a possessee in S or P role are equally well attested. Second, I am not claiming here that the fact that S patterns with P in the floating genitive construction has anything to do with the ergative alignment observed in the encoding of core syntactic roles. It is well-known that some syntactic mechanisms favor ergative or accusative alignment irrespective of the type of alignment manifested in the encoding of core syntactic roles, and observations on a single language are not sufficient to propose a hypothesis about the status of floating genitives in this respect.

18. This construction expresses relatively permanent possession. For temporary possession ('have something momentarily at one's disposal'), Northern Akhvakh uses a construction in which the NP representing the possessor is in a spatial form (locative$_2$) whose basic meaning is proximity, as in *boqòda teki g^{w}ede di-χar-i* |four|ace|COP.N|1SG$_o$-OR$_2$-LOC| 'I have four aces'.

19. On frame adjuncts, see Charolles & Péry-Woodley (eds., 2005), Charolles & Prevost (eds., 2003), Lang & al. (eds., 2003).

20. On external possession, see Payne & Barshi (1999), König & Haspelmath (1997).

21. A summary of the discussion can be found in Creissels (2006b: 104-107).

22. Traditional French grammar would identify *qui* as a relative pronoun. However, it can be shown that, in modern French, *qui* as a relative pronoun subsists only in free (or antecedentless) relatives, whereas *qui* introducing postnominal relatives has been reanalyzed as a contextual variant of the complementizer *que*. For a summary of the discussion about the status of *qui*, see (Creissels 2006b: 233–235)

Index